Gustave Doré, Henry Francis Cary

The Vision of Purgatory and Paradise

Gustave Doré, Henry Francis Cary
The Vision of Purgatory and Paradise
ISBN/EAN: 9783744790550
Printed in Europe, USA, Canada, Australia, Japan
Cover: Foto ©Lupo / pixelio.de

More available books at **www.hansebooks.com**

PURGATORY AND PARADISE

Hearing the air cut by their verdant plumes,
The serpent fled; and, to their stations, back
The angels up return'd with equal flight.
Canto VIII., lines 105—107.

THE VISION

OF

PURGATORY AND PARADISE

BY

DANTE ALIGHIERI

TRANSLATED BY

THE REV. HENRY FRANCIS CARY M.A.

AND ILLUSTRATED WITH THE SIXTY DESIGNS OF

GUSTAVE DORÉ

Popular Edition

With Critical and Explanatory Notes

CASSELL AND COMPANY LIMITED

LONDON PARIS & MELBOURNE

1893

CONTENTS.

PURGATORY.

CANTO I.

The Poet describes the delight he experienced at issuing a little before dawn from the infernal regions, into the pure air that surrounds the isle of Purgatory; and then relates how, turning to the right, he beheld four stars never seen before but by our first parents, and met on his left the shade of Cato of Utica, who, having warned him and Virgil what is needful to be done before they proceed on their way through Purgatory, disappears; and the two Poets go towards the shore, where Virgil cleanses Dante's face with the dew, and girds him with a reed as Cato had commanded 1

CANTO II.

They behold a vessel under conduct of an angel, coming over the waves with spirits to Purgatory, among whom, when the passengers have landed, Dante recognises his friend Casella; but, while they are entertained by him with a song, they hear Cato exclaiming against their negligent loitering, and at that rebuke hasten forwards to the mountain 10

CANTO III.

Our Poet, perceiving no shadow except that cast by his own body, is fearful that Virgil has deserted him; but he is freed from that error, and both arrive together at the foot of the mountain. On finding it too steep to climb, they inquire the way from a troop of spirits that are coming towards them, and are by them shown which is the easiest ascent. Manfredi, King of Naples, who is one of these spirits, bids Dante inform his daughter, Costanza, Queen of Arragon, of the manner in which he had died 19

CANTO IV.

Dante and Virgil ascend the mountain of Purgatory, by a steep and narrow path pent in on each side by rock, till they reach a part of it that opens into a ledge or cornice. There seating themselves, and turning to the east, Dante wonders at seeing the sun on their left, the cause of which is explained to him by Virgil; and while they continue their discourse, a voice addresses them, at which they turn, and find several spirits behind the rock, and amongst the rest one named Belacqua, who had been known to our Poet on earth, and who tells that he is doomed to linger there on account of his having delayed his repentance to the last 26

CANTO V.

They meet with others, who had deferred their repentance till they were overtaken by a violent death, when sufficient space being allowed them, they were then saved; and amongst these Giacopo del Cassero, Buonconte da Montefeltro, and Pia, a lady of Sienna 35

CANTO VI.

Many besides, who are in like case with those spoken of in the last Canto, beseech our Poet to obtain for them the prayers of their friends, when he shall be returned to this world. This moves him to express a doubt to his guide, how the dead can be profited by the prayers of the living; for the solution of which doubt he is referred to Beatrice. Afterwards he meets with Sordello, the Mantuan, whose affection, shown to Virgil, his countryman, leads Dante to break forth into an invective against the unnatural divisions with which Italy, and more especially Florence, was distracted 44

CANTO VII.

The approach of night hindering further ascent, Sordello conducts our Poet apart to an eminence, from whence they behold a pleasant recess, in form of a flowery valley, scooped out of the mountain; where are many famous spirits, and among them the Emperor Rodolph, Ottocar, King of Bohemia, Philip III. of France, Henry of Navarre, Peter III. of Arragon, Charles I. of Naples, Henry III. of England, and William, Marquis of Montferrat 52

CONTENTS.

CANTO VIII.

Two angels, with flaming swords broken at the points, descend to keep watch over the valley, into which Virgil and Dante entering by desire of Sordello, our Poet meets with joy the spirit of Nino, the judge of Gallura, one who was well known to him. Meantime three exceedingly bright stars appear near the pole, and a serpent creeps subtly into the valley, but flees at hearing the approach of those angelic guards. Lastly, Conrad Malaspina predicts to our Poet his future banishment 61

CANTO IX.

Dante is carried up the mountain, asleep and dreaming, by Lucia; and, on wakening, finds himself, two hours after sunrise, with Virgil, near the gate of Purgatory, through which they are admitted by the angel deputed by St. Peter to keep it 66

CANTO X.

Being admitted at the gate of Purgatory, our Poets ascend a winding path up the rock till they reach an open and level space that extends each way round the mountain. On the side that rises, and which is of white marble, are seen artfully engraven many stories of humility, which whilst they are contemplating, there approach the souls of those who expiate the sin of pride, and who are bent down beneath the weight of heavy stones . . . 77

CANTO XI.

After a prayer uttered by the spirits who were spoken of in the last Canto, Virgil inquires the way upwards, and is answered by one, who declares himself to have been Omberto, son of the Count of Santafiore. Next our Poet distinguishes Oderigi, the illuminator, who discourses on the vanity of worldly fame, and points out to him the soul of Provenzano Salvani 84

CANTO XII.

Dante being desired by Virgil to look down on the ground which they are treading, observes that it is wrought over with imagery exhibiting various instances of pride recorded in history and fable. They leave the first cornice, and are ushered to the next by an angel who points out the way 90

CANTO XIII.

They gain the second cornice, where the sin of envy is purged; and having proceeded a little to the right, they hear voices uttered by invisible spirits recounting famous examples of charity, and next behold the shades, or souls, of the envious clad in sackcloth, and having their eyes sewed up with an iron thread. Amongst these Dante finds Sapia, a Siennese lady, from whom he learns the cause of her being there 98

CANTO XIV.

Our Poet on this second cornice finds also the souls of Guido del Duca of Brettinoro, and Rinieri da Calboli of Romagna; the latter of whom, hearing that he comes from the banks of the Arno, inveighs against the degeneracy of all those who dwell in the cities visited by that stream; and the former, in like manner, against the inhabitants of Romagna. On leaving these, our Poets hear voices recording noted instances of envy . . 107

CANTO XV.

An angel invites them to ascend the next steep. On their way Dante suggests certain doubts, which are resolved by Virgil; and, when they reach the third cornice, where the sin of anger is purged, our Poet, in a kind of waking dream, beholds remarkable instances of patience; and soon after they are enveloped in a dense fog . . . 113

CANTO XVI.

As they proceed through the mist, they hear the voices of spirits praying. Marco Lombardo, one of these, points out to Dante the error of such as impute our actions to necessity; explains to him that man is endued with free will; and shows that much of human depravity results from the undue mixture of spiritual and temporal authority in rulers 120

CANTO XVII.

The Poet issues from that thick vapour; and soon after his fancy represents to him in lively portraiture some noted examples of anger. This imagination is dissipated by the appearance of an angel, who marshals them onward to the fourth cornice, on which the sin of gloominess or indifference is purged; and here Virgil shows him that this vice proceeds from a defect of love, and that all love can be only of two sorts, either natural, or of the soul; of which sorts the former is always right, but the latter may err either in respect of object or of degree . . 129

CANTO XVIII.

Virgil discourses further concerning the nature of love. Then a multitude of spirits rush by; two of whom, in van of the rest, record instances of zeal and fervent affection, and another, who was abbot of San Zeno in Verona, declares himself to Virgil and Dante; and lastly follow other spirits, shouting forth memorable examples of the sin for which they suffer. The Poet, pursuing his meditations, falls into a dreamy slumber 134

CONTENTS.

CANTO XIX.

The Poet, after describing his dream, relates how, at the summoning of an angel, he ascends with Virgil to the fifth cornice, where the sin of avarice is cleansed, and where he finds Pope Adrian V. 141

CANTO XX.

Among those on the fifth cornice, Hugh Capet records illustrious examples of voluntary poverty and of bounty; then tells who himself is, and speaks of his descendants on the French throne; and, lastly, adds some noted instances of avarice. When he has ended, the mountain shakes, and all the spirits sing "Glory to God" . . . 150

CANTO XXI.

The two Poets are overtaken by the spirit of Statius, who, being cleansed, is on his way to Paradise, and who explains the cause of the mountain shaking, and of the hymn; his joy at beholding Virgil 158

CANTO XXII.

Dante, Virgil, and Statius mount to the sixth cornice, where the sin of gluttony is cleansed, the two Latin Poets discoursing by the way. Turning to the right, they find a tree hung with sweet-smelling fruit, and watered by a shower that issues from the rock. Voices are heard to proceed from among the leaves, recording examples of temperance 163

CANTO XXIII.

They are overtaken by the spirit of Forese, who had been a friend of our Poet's on earth, and who now inveighs bitterly against the immodest dress of their countrywomen at Florence. 169

CANTO XXIV.

Forese points out several others by name who are here, like himself, purifying themselves from the vice of gluttony; and amongst the rest, Buonaggiunta of Lucca, with whom our Poet converses. Forese then predicts the violent end of Dante's political enemy, Corso Donati; and when he has quitted them, the Poet, in company with Statius and Virgil, arrives at another tree, from whence issue voices that record ancient examples of gluttony; and proceeding forwards, they are directed by an angel which way to ascend to the next cornice of the mountain 177

CANTO XXV.

Virgil and Statius resolve some doubts that have arisen in the mind of Dante from what he had just seen. They all arrive on the seventh and last cornice, where the sin of incontinence is purged in fire; and the spirits of those suffering therein are heard to record illustrious instances of chastity 185

CANTO XXVI.

The spirits wonder at seeing the shadow cast by the body of Dante on the flame as he passes it. This moves one of them to address him. It proves to be Guido Guinicelli, the Italian poet, who points out to him the spirit of Arnault Daniel, the Provençal, with whom he also speaks 194

CANTO XXVII.

An angel sends them forward through the fire to the last ascent, which leads to the terrestrial Paradise, situated on the summit of the mountain. They have not proceeded many steps on their way upward, when the fall of night hinders them from going further; and our Poet, who has lain down with Virgil and Statius to rest, beholds in a dream two females, figuring the active and contemplative life. With the return of morning, they reach the height; and here Virgil gives Dante full liberty to use his own pleasure and judgment in the choice of his way, till he shall meet with Beatrice 202

CANTO XXVIII.

Dante wanders through the forest of the terrestrial Paradise, till he is stopped by a stream, on the other side of which he beholds a fair lady, culling flowers. He speaks to her; and she, in reply, explains to him certain things touching the nature of that place, and tells that the water, which flows between them, is here called Lethe, and in another place has the name of Eunoe 209

CANTO XXIX.

The lady, who in a following Canto is called Matilda, moves along the side of the stream in a contrary direction to the current, and Dante keeps equal pace with her on the opposite bank. A marvellous sight, preceded by music, appears in view 216

CANTO XXX.

Beatrice descends from heaven, and rebukes the Poet 225

CONTENTS.

CANTO XXXI.

Beatrice continues her reprehension of Dante, who confesses his error, and falls to the ground. Coming to himself again, he is by Matilda drawn through the waters of Lethe, and presented first to the four virgins who figure the cardinal virtues; these in their turn lead him to the Gryphon, a symbol of our Saviour; and the three virgins representing the evangelical virtues intercede for him with Beatrice, that she would display to him her second beauty 232

CANTO XXXII.

Dante is warned not to gaze too fixedly on Beatrice. The procession moves on, accompanied by Matilda, Statius, and Dante, till they reach an exceeding lofty tree, where divers strange chances befall 239

CANTO XXXIII.

After a hymn sung, Beatrice leaves the tree, and takes with her the seven virgins, Matilda, Statius, and Dante. She then darkly predicts to our Poets some future events. Lastly, the whole band arrive at the fountain, from whence the two streams, Lethe and Eunoe, separating, flow different ways; and Matilda, at the desire of Beatrice, causes our Poet to drink of the latter stream 246

PARADISE.

CANTO I.

The Poet ascends with Beatrice towards the first heaven, and is by her resolved of certain doubts which arise in his mind 255

CANTO II.

Dante and his celestial guide enter the moon. The cause of the spots or shadows which appear in that body is explained to him 260

CANTO III.

In the moon Dante meets with Piccarda, the sister of Forese, who tells him that this planet is allotted to those who, after having made profession of chastity and a religious life, had been compelled to violate their vows; and she then points out to him the spirit of the Empress Costanza 267

CANTO IV.

While they still continue in the moon, Beatrice removes certain doubts which Dante had conceived respecting the place assigned to the blessed, and respecting the will absolute or conditional. He inquires whether it is possible to make satisfaction for a vow broken 271

CANTO V.

The question proposed in the last Canto is answered. Dante ascends with Beatrice to the planet Mercury, which is the second heaven; and here he finds a multitude of spirits, one of whom offers to satisfy him of anything he may desire to know from them 276

CANTO VI.

The spirit, who had offered to satisfy the inquiries of Dante, declares himself to be the Emperor Justinian; and after speaking of his own actions, recounts the victories, before him, obtained under the Roman Eagle. He then informs our Poet that the soul of Romeo the pilgrim is in the same star 282

CANTO VII.

In consequence of what had been said by Justinian, who together with the other spirits have now disappeared, some doubts arise in the mind of Dante respecting the human redemption. These difficulties are fully explained by Beatrice 288

CANTO VIII.

The Poet ascends with Beatrice to the third heaven, which is the planet Venus; and here finds the soul of Charles Martel, King of Hungary, who had been Dante's friend on earth, and who now, after speaking of the realms to which he was heir, unfolds the cause why children differ in disposition from their parents 294

CONTENTS.

CANTO IX.

The next spirit, who converses with our Poet in the planet Venus, is the amorous Cunizza. To her succeeds Folco, or Folques, the Provençal bard, who declares that the soul of Rahab the harlot is there also; and then, blaming the Pope for his neglect of the Holy Land, prognosticates some reverse to the Papal power. . . . 301

CANTO X.

Their next ascent carries them into the sun, which is the fourth heaven. Here they are encompassed with a wreath of blessed spirits, twelve in number. Thomas Aquinas, who is one of these, declares the names and endowments of the rest 307

CANTO XI.

Thomas Aquinas enters at large into the life and character of St. Francis; and then solves one of two difficulties which he perceives to have risen in Dante's mind from what he had heard in the last Canto 312

CANTO XII.

A second circle of glorified souls encompasses the first. Buonaventura, who is one of them, celebrates the praises of Saint Dominic, and informs Dante who the other eleven are that are in this second circle or garland . . 317

CANTO XIII.

Thomas Aquinas resumes his speech. He solves the other of those doubts which he discerned in the mind of Dante, and warns him earnestly against assenting to any proposition without having duly examined it . . 325

CANTO XIV.

Solomon, who is one of the spirits in the inner circle, declares what the appearance of the blest will be after the resurrection of the body. Beatrice and Dante are translated into the fifth heaven, which is that of Mars, and here behold the souls of those who had died fighting for the true faith, ranged in the sign of a cross, athwart which the spirits move to the sound of a melodious hymn 330

CANTO XV.

The spirit of Cacciaguida, our Poet's ancestor, glides rapidly to the foot of the cross, tells who he is, and speaks of the simplicity of the Florentines in his days, since then much corrupted 338

CANTO XVI.

Cacciaguida relates the time of his birth, and, describing the extent of Florence when he lived there, recounts the names of the chief families who then inhabited it. Its degeneracy, and subsequent disgrace, he attributes to the introduction of families from the neighbouring country and villages, and to their mixture with the primitive citizens 343

CANTO XVII.

Cacciaguida predicts to our Poet his exile and the calamities he had to suffer; and, lastly, exhorts him to write the present poem 351

CANTO XVIII.

Dante sees the souls of many renowned warriors and crusaders in the planet Mars, and then ascends with Beatrice to Jupiter, the sixth heaven, in which he finds the souls of those who had administered justice rightly in the world, so disposed as to form the figure of an eagle. The Canto concludes with an invective against the avarice of the clergy, and especially of the Pope 356

CANTO XIX.

The eagle speaks as with one voice proceeding from a multitude of spirits that compose it, and declares the cause for which it is exalted to that state of glory. It then solves a doubt which our Poet had entertained respecting the possibility of salvation without belief in Christ; exposes the inefficacy of a mere profession of such belief; and prophesies the evil appearance that many Christian potentates will make at the day of judgment . . 365

CANTO XX.

The eagle celebrates the praise of certain kings, whose glorified spirits form the eye of the bird. In the pupil is David, and in the circle round it, Trajan, Hezekiah, Constantine, William II. of Sicily, and Ripheus. It explains to our Poet how the souls of those whom he supposed to have had no means of believing in Christ, came to be in heaven; and concludes with an admonition against presuming to fathom the counsels of God . 372

CANTO XXI.

Dante ascends with Beatrice to the seventh heaven, which is the planet Saturn; wherein is placed a ladder so lofty, that the top of it is out of his sight. Here are the souls of those who had passed their life in holy retirement and contemplation. Piero Damiano comes near them, and answers questions put to him by Dante; then declares who he was on earth, and ends by declaiming against the luxury of pastors and prelates in those times 381

CONTENTS.

PAGE

CANTO XXII.

He beholds many other spirits of the devout and contemplative ; and amongst these is addressed by St. Benedict, who, after disclosing his own name and the names of certain of his companions in bliss, replies to the request made by our Poet that he might look on the form of the saint without that covering of splendour which then invested it ; and then proceeds, lastly, to inveigh against the corruption of the monks. Next Dante mounts with his heavenly conductress to the eighth heaven, or that of the fixed stars, which he enters at the constellation of the Twins ; and thence looking back, reviews all the space he has passed between his present station and the earth 388

CANTO XXIII.

He sees Christ triumphing with His church. The Saviour ascends, followed by His virgin Mother. The others remain with St. Peter 393

CANTO XXIV.

St. Peter examines Dante touching Faith, and is contented with his answers. 397

CANTO XXV.

St. James questions our Poet concerning Hope. Next St. John appears ; and, on perceiving that Dante looks intently on him, informs him that he (St. John) had left his body resolved into earth, upon the earth ; and that Christ and the Virgin alone had come with their bodies into heaven 403

CANTO XXVI.

St. James examines our Poet touching Charity. Afterwards Adam tells when he was created, and placed in the terrestrial Paradise ; how long he remained in that state ; what was the occasion of his fall ; when he was admitted into heaven ; and what language he spake 408

CANTO XXVII.

St. Peter bitterly rebukes the covetousness of his successors in the apostolic see, while all the heavenly host sympathise in his indignation : they then vanish upwards. Beatrice bids Dante again cast his view below. Afterwards they are borne into the ninth heaven, of which she shows him the nature and properties ; blaming the perverseness of man, who places his will on low and perishable things 415

CANTO XXVIII.

Still in the ninth heaven, our Poet is permitted to behold the divine essence ; and then sees, in three hierarchies, the nine choirs of angels. Beatrice clears some difficulties which occur to him on this occasion 422

CANTO XXIX.

Beatrice beholds, in the mirror of divine truth, some doubts which had entered the mind of Dante. These she resolves ; and then digresses into a vehement reprehension of certain theologians and preachers in those days, whose ignorance or avarice induced them to substitute their own inventions for the pure word of the Gospel . . 428

CANTO XXX.

Dante is taken up with Beatrice into the empyrean ; and there having his sight strengthened by her aid, and by the virtue derived from looking on the river of light, he sees the triumph of the angels and of the souls of the blessed 433

CANTO XXXI.

The Poet expatiates further on the glorious vision described in the last Canto. On looking round for Beatrice, he finds that she has left him, and that an old man is at his side. This proves to be St. Bernard, who shows him that Beatrice has returned to her throne, and then points out to him the blessedness of the Virgin Mother . 438

CANTO XXXII.

St. Bernard shows him, on their several thrones, the other blessed souls, both of the Old and New Testament ; explains to him that their places are assigned them by grace, and not according to merit ; and lastly, tells him that if he would obtain power to descry what remained of the heavenly vision, he must unite with him in supplication to Mary 447

CANTO XXXIII.

St. Bernard supplicates the Virgin Mary that Dante may have grace given him to contemplate the brightness of the Divine Majesty, which is accordingly granted ; and Dante then himself prays to God for ability to show forth some part of the celestial glory in his writings. Lastly, he is admitted to a glimpse of the great mystery ; the Trinity, and the union of man with God 451

LIST OF ILLUSTRATIONS.

PURGATORY.

	CANTO	LINE	PAGE
The radiant planet, that to love invites	I.	19	3
My guide, then laying hold on me, by words	I.	49	7
Then when he knew the pilot	II.	27	11
The heavenly steersman at the prow was seen	II.	42	15
And while, with looks directed to the ground	III.	54	21
While underneath, the ground	IV.	31	27
And there were some, who in the shady place	IV.	100	33
"Many," exclaim'd the bard, "are these, who throng around us"	V.	42	37
From my breast loosening the cross	V.	123	41
"Then remember me. I once was Pia"	V.	130	45
"Through every orb of that sad region"	VII.	21	53
"Salve Regina," on the grass and flowers, here chanting	VII.	82	... 57
Hearing the air cut by their verdant plumes	VIII.	105	(*Frontispiece*)
Now the fair consort of Tithonus old	IX.	1	67
There both, I thought, the eagle and myself did burn	IX.	29	71
In visage such, as past my power to bear	IX.	74	75
The wretch appear'd amid all these to say	X.	74	79
With equal pace, as oxen in the yoke	XII.	1	91
O fond Arachne! thee I also saw	XII.	39	95
E'en thus the blind and poor	XIII.	55	99
"Who then, amongst us here aloft, hath brought thee?"	XIII.	129	103
After that I saw a multitude	XV.	103	117
"Now who art thou, that through our smoke dost cleave?"	XVI.	23	121
"Long as 'tis lawful for me, shall my steps follow on thine"	XVI.	32	125
But not long slumber'd	XVIII.	87	137
"What aileth thee, that still thou look'st to earth?"	XIX.	51	143
"Up," he exclaim'd, "brother! upon thy feet arise"	XIX.	131	147
With wary steps and slow we pass'd	XX.	17	151
"And who are those twain spirits?"	XXIII.	47	171
The shadowy forms	XXIV.	4	175
At length, as undeceived, they went their way	XXIV.	112	181
Here the rocky precipice	XXV.	107	187
Then from the bosom of the burning mass	XXV.	117	191
And when I saw spirits along the flame proceeding	XXV.	119	195
A lady young and beautiful, I dream'd, was passing o'er a lea	XXVII.	97	205

	CANTO	LINE	PAGE
Already had my steps	XXVIII.	22	211
Beneath a sky so beautiful	XXIX.	80	217
Three nymphs, at the right wheel	XXIX.	116	221
Thus, in a cloud of flowers	XXX.	28	227
The beauteous dame, her arms expanding, clasp'd my temples	XXXI.	100	235
At her side, as 'twere that none might bear her off	XXXII.	148	243
Were further space allow'd	XXXIII.	134	251

PARADISE.

	CANTO	LINE	PAGE
Such saw I many a face	III.	14	265
So drew full more than thousand splendours towards us	V.	99	279
The left bank	VIII.	60	295
About us thus	XII.	16	319
And I beheld myself	XIV.	77	331
Christ beam'd on that cross	XIV.	96	335
But so was doom'd	XVI.	143	349
So, within the lights, the saintly creatures flying, sang	XVIII.	70	359
Ye host of heaven, whose glory I survey!	XVIII.	120	363
Before my sight appear'd, with open wings, the beauteous image	XIX.	1	367
For that all those living lights	XX.	10	373
Again mine eyes were fix'd on Beatrice	XXI.	1	379
Down whose steps	XXI.	28	383
Say then, beginning, to what point thy soul aspires	XXVI.	7	409
Then "Glory to the Father, to the Son"	XXVII.	1	417
Not unlike to iron in the furnace	XXVIII.	80	423
In fashion, as a snow white rose	XXXI.	1	439
Answering not, mine eyes I raised	XXXI.	64	443

PURGATORY

THE VISION OF DANTE.

Purgatory.

CANTO I.

ARGUMENT.

The Poet describes the delight he experienced at issuing a little before dawn from the infernal regions, into the pure air that surrounds the isle of Purgatory; and then relates how, turning to the right, he beheld four stars never seen before but by our first parents, and met on his left the shade of Cato of Utica, who, having warned him and Virgil what is needful to be done before they proceed on their way through Purgatory, disappears; and the two poets go towards the shore, where Virgil cleanses Dante's face with the dew, and girds him with a reed, as Cato had commanded.

O'ER better waves[1] to speed her rapid course
    The light bark of my genius lifts the sail,
Well pleased to leave so cruel sea behind;
And of that second region will I sing,
In which the human spirit from sinful blot
Is purged, and for ascent to Heaven prepares.
    Here, O ye hallow'd Nine! for in your train
I follow, here the deaden'd strain revive;
Nor let Calliope refuse to sound
A somewhat higher song, of that loud tone
Which when the wretched birds of chattering note[2]
Had heard, they of forgiveness lost all hope.
    Sweet hue of eastern sapphire, that was spread
O'er the serene aspect of the pure air,
High up as the first circle,[3] to mine eyes
Unwonted joy renew'd, soon as I 'scaped
Forth from the atmosphere of deadly gloom,

---

[1] *O'er better waves.*—So Berni, "Orlando Innamorato," lib. ii., c. i. :
"Per correr maggior acqua alza le vele,
O debil navicella del mio ingegno."

[2] *Birds of chattering note.*—For the fable of the daughters of Pierus, who challenged the muses to sing, and were by them changed into magpies, see Ovid, "Metamorphoses," lib. v., fab. 5.

[3] *The first circle.*—Either, as some suppose, the moon; or as Lombardi (who likes to be as far off the rest of the commentators as possible), will have it, the highest circle of the stars.

That had mine eyes and bosom fill'd with grief.
The radiant planet,[1] that to love invites,
Made all the orient laugh,[2] and veil'd beneath
The Pisces' light,[3] that in his escort came.

To the right hand I turn'd, and fix'd my mind
On the other pole attentive, where I saw
Four stars[4] ne'er seen before save by the ken
Of our first parents.[5] Heaven of their rays
Seem'd joyous. O thou northern site! bereft
Indeed, and widow'd, since of these deprived.

As from this view I had desisted, straight
Turning a little towards the other pole,
There from whence now the wain[6] had disappear'd,
I saw an old man[7] standing by my side
Alone, so worthy of reverence in his look,
That ne'er from son to father more was owed.
Low down his beard, and mix'd with hoary white,
Descended, like his locks, which, parting, fell
Upon his breast in double fold. The beams
Of those four luminaries on his face
So brightly shone, and with such radiance clear
Deck'd it, that I beheld him as the sun.

"Say who are ye, that stemming the blind stream,
Forth from the eternal prison-house have fled?"
He spoke and moved those venerable plumes.[8]

---

[1] *Planet.*—Venus.
[2] *Made all the orient laugh.*—Hence Chaucer, "Knight's Tale:"
"And all the orisont laugheth of the sight."
It is sometimes read "orient."
[3] *The Pisces' light.*—The constellation of the Fish veiled by the more luminous body of Venus, then a morning star.
[4] *Four stars.*—Venturi observes that "Dante here speaks as a poet, and almost in the spirit of prophecy; or, what is more likely, describes the heaven about that pole according to his own invention. In our days," he adds, "the cross, composed of four stars, three of the second and one of the third magnitude, serves as a guide to those who sail from Europe to the south; but in the age of Dante these discoveries had not been made:" yet it appears probable, that either from long tradition, or from the relation of later voyagers, the real truth might not have been unknown to our poet. Seneca's prediction of the discovery of America may be accounted for in a similar manner. But whatever may be thought of this, it is certain that the four stars are here symbolical of the four cardinal virtues, Prudence, Justice, Fortitude, and Temperance. See canto xxxi., v. 105. M. Artaud mentions a globe constructed by an Arabian in Egypt, with the date of the year 622 of the Hegira, corresponding to 1225 of our era, in which the southern cross is positively marked. See his "Histoire de Dante," chap. xxxi. and xl., 8º., Par., 1841.
[5] *Our first parents.*—In the terrestrial paradise, placed, as we shall see, by our poet, on the summit of Purgatory.
[6] *The wain.*—Charles's Wain, or Boötes.
[7] *An old man.*—Cato.
"Secretosque pios; his dantem jura Catonem."
Virgil, Æneid, viii. 670.
The commentators, and Lombardi amongst the rest, might have saved themselves and their readers much needless trouble if they would have consulted the prose writings of Dante with more diligence. In the "Convito," p. 211, he has himself declared his opinion of the illustrious Roman:—"Quale uomo," &c., "What earthly man was more worthy to follow God than Cato? Certainly none." And again, p. 212:—"Nel nome di cui," &c., "In whose name, whatever needs be said concerning the signs of nobility may be concluded; for in him that nobility displays them all throughout the ages."
[8] *Venerable plumes.*—
"Insperata tuæ quum veniet pluma superbiæ."
Horace, Carm., lib. iv., ode 10.
The same metaphor has occurred in "Hell," canto x., v. 41:

The radiant planet, that to love invites,
Made all the orient laugh, and veil'd beneath
The Pisces' light, that in his escort came.
                                    Canto I., lines 19—21.

"Who hath conducted, or with lantern sure
Lights you emerging from the depth of night,
That makes the infernal valley ever black?
Are the firm statutes of the dread abyss
Broken, or in high heaven new laws ordain'd,
That thus, condemn'd, ye to my caves approach?

My guide, then laying hold on me, by words
And intimations given with hand and head,
Made my bent knees and eye submissive pay
Due reverence; then thus to him replied:

"Not of myself I come; a Dame from heaven[1]
Descending, him besought me in my charge
To bring. But since thy will implies, that more
Our true condition I unfold at large,
Mine is not to deny thee thy request.
This mortal ne'er hath seen the furthest gloom;[2]
But erring by his folly had approach'd
So near, that little space was left to turn.
Then, as before I told, I was dispatch'd
To work his rescue; and no way remain'd
Save this which I have ta'en. I have display'd
Before him all the regions of the bad;
And purpose now those spirits to display,
That under thy command are purged from sin.
How I have brought him would be long to say.
From high descends the virtue, by whose aid
I to thy sight and hearing him have led.
Now may our coming please thee. In the search
Of liberty he journeys; that how dear,
They know who for her sake have life refused.
Thou knowest, to whom death for her was sweet
In Utica, where thou didst leave those weeds,
That in the last great day will shine so bright.
For us the eternal edicts are unmoved:
He breathes, and I of Minos am not bound,[3]

"The plumes,
That mark'd the better sex."
It is used by Ford in the "Lady's Trial," act iv., sc. 2:
"Now the down
Of softness is exchanged for plumes of age."
[1] *A Dame from heaven.*—Beatrice. See "Hell,"ii.54.
[2] *The furthest gloom.*—" L'ultima sera." So Ariosto, "Orlando Furioso," canto xxxiv., st. 59:

"Che non han visto ancor l'ultima sera."
And "Filicaja," canto ix.:
"Al Sonno. L'ultima sera."
And Mr. Mathias, "Canzone a Guglielmo Roscoe premessa alla Storia della Poesia Italiana," p. 13:
"Di morte non vedrà l'ultima sera."
[3] *Of Minos am not bound.*—See "Hell," v. 4.

Abiding in that circle, where the eyes
Of thy chaste Marcia[1] beam, who still in look
Prays thee, O hallow'd spirit! to own her thine.
Then by her love we implore thee, let us pass
Through thy seven regions;[2] for which, best thanks
I for thy favour will to her return,
If mention there below thou not disdain."

"Marcia so pleasing in my sight was found,"
He then to him rejoin'd, "while I was there,
That all she ask'd me I was fain to grant.
Now that beyond the accursed stream she dwells,
She may no longer move me, by that law,[3]
Which was ordain'd me, when I issued thence.
Not so, if Dame from heaven, as thou sayst,
Moves and directs thee; then no flattery needs.
Enough for me that in her name thou ask.
Go therefore now; and with a slender reed[4]
See that thou duly gird him, and his face
Lave, till all sordid stain thou wipe from thence.
For not with eye, by any cloud obscured,
Would it be seemly before him to come,
Who stands the foremost minister in heaven.
This islet all around, there far beneath,
Where the wave beats it, on the oozy bed
Produces store of reeds. No other plant,
Cover'd with leaves, or harden'd in its stalk,
There lives, not bending to the water's sway.
After, this way return not; but the sun
Will show you, that now rises, where to take[5]
The mountain in its easiest ascent."

---

[1] *Marcia.*—
"Da fœdera prisci
Illibata tori: da tantum nomen inane
Connubii: liceat tumulo scripsisse Catonis
Martia." *Lucan, Pharsalia,* lib. ii. 344.

Our author's habit of putting an allegorical interpretation on everything—a habit which appears to have descended to that age from certain fathers of the church—is nowhere more apparent than in his explanation of this passage. See "Convito," p. 211: "Marzia fu vergine," &c., "Marcia was a virgin, and in that state she signifies childhood; then she came to Cato, and in that state she represents youth; she then bare children, by whom are represented the virtues that we have said belong to that age." Dante would surely have done well to remember his own rule laid down in the "De Monarchiâ," lib. iii.: "Advertendum," &c., "Concerning the mystical sense, it must be observed that we may err in two ways, either by seeing it where it is not, or by taking it otherwise than it ought to be taken."

[2] *Through thy seven regions.*—The seven rounds of Purgatory, in which the seven capital sins are punished.

[3] *By that law.*—When he was delivered by Christ from limbo, a change of affections accompanied his change of place.

[4] *A slender reed.*—The reed is here supposed, with sufficient probability, to be meant for a type of simplicity and patience.

[5] *Where to take.*—"Prendere il monte," a reading which Lombardi claims for his favourite Nidobeatina edition, is also found in Landino's of 1484.

My guide, then laying hold on me, by words
And intimations given with hand and head,
Made my bent knees and eye submissive pay
Due reverence.   *Canto I., lines 49—52.*

He disappear'd; and I myself upraised
Speechless, and to my guide retiring close,
Toward him turn'd mine eyes. He thus began:
"My son! observant thou my steps pursue.
We must retreat to rereward; for that way
The champain to its low extreme declines."

 The dawn had chased the matin hour of prime,
Which fled before it, so that from afar
I spied the trembling of the ocean stream.[1]

 We traversed the deserted plain, as one
Who, wander'd from his track, thinks every step
Trodden in vain till he regain the path.

 When we had come, where yet the tender dew
Strove with the sun, and in a place where fresh
The wind breathed o'er it, while it slowly dried;
Both hands extended on the watery grass
My master placed, in graceful act and kind.
Whence I of his intent before apprised,
Stretch'd out to him my cheeks suffused with tears,
There to my visage he anew restored
That hue which the dun shades of hell conceal'd.

 Then on the solitary shore arrived,
That never sailing on its waters saw
Man that could after measure back his course,
He girt me in such manner as had pleased
Him who instructed; and, O strange to tell!
As he selected every humble plant,
Wherever one was pluck'd another[2] there
Resembling, straightway in its place arose.

---

[1] *I spied the trembling of the ocean stream.—*
"Conobbi il tremolar della marina."
So Tressino, in the "Sofonisba:"
"E resta in tremolar l'onda marina."
And Fortiguerra, "Ricciardetto," canto ix., st. 17:
"Visto il tremolar della marina."

[2] *Another.—*From Virgil, "Æneid," lib. vi. 143:
"Primo avulso non deficit alter."

CANTO II.

ARGUMENT.

They behold a vessel under conduct of an angel, coming over the waves with spirits to Purgatory, among whom, when the passengers have landed, Dante recognises his friend Casella; but, while they are entertained by him with a song, they hear Cato exclaiming against their negligent loitering, and at that rebuke hasten forwards to the mountain.

NOW had the sun[1] to that horizon reach'd,
That covers, with the most exalted point
Of its meridian circle, Salem's walls;
And night, that opposite to him her orb
Rounds, from the stream of Ganges issued forth,
Holding the scales,[2] that from her hands are dropt
When she reigns highest:[3] so that where I was,
Aurora's white and vermeil-tinctured cheek
To orange turn'd[4] as she in age increased.

Meanwhile we linger'd by the water's brink,
Like men,[5] who, musing on their road, in thought
Journey, while motionless the body rests.
When lo! as, near upon the hour of dawn,
Through the thick vapours[6] Mars with fiery beam
Glares down in west, over the ocean floor;
So seem'd, what once again I hope to view,
A light, so swiftly coming through the sea,
No winged course might equal its career.
From which when for a space I had withdrawn
Mine eyes, to make inquiry of my guide,

---

[1] *Now had the sun.*—Dante was now antipodal to Jerusalem; so that while the sun was setting with respect to that place, which he supposes to be the middle of the inhabited earth, to him it was rising. See Routh's " Reliquiæ Sacræ," tom. iii., p. 256. So Fazio degli Uberti, " Dittamondo," lib. vi., cap. vi. :
" Questo monte è quello
Ch' in mezzo il mondo apunto si divisa."

[2] *The scales.*—The constellation Libra.

[3] *When she reigns highest.*—" Quando soverchia " is (according to Venturi, whom I have followed), " when the autumnal equinox is passed." Lombardi supposes it to mean " when the nights begin to increase; that is, after the summer solstice."

[4] *To orange turn'd.*—" L'aurora già di vermiglia cominciava appressandosi il sole a divenir rancia." Boccaccio, " Decameron," Giorn. iii., at the beginning. See notes to " Hell," xxiii. 101.

[5] *Like men.—*
" Che va col cuore e col corpo dimora."
So Frezzi:
" E mentre il corpo posa, col cor varca."
Il Quadriregio, lib. iv., cap. 8.

[6] *Through the thick vapours.*—So in the " Convito," p. 72 : " Esso pare," &c., " He (Mars) appears more or less inflamed with heat, according to the thickness or rarity of the vapours that follow him."

Then when he knew
The pilot, cried aloud, "Down, down; bend low
Thy knees; behold God's angel; fold thy hands:
Now shalt thou see true ministers indeed."
Canto II., lines 27—30.

Again I look'd, and saw it grown in size
And brightness: then on either side appear'd
Something, but what I knew not, of bright hue,
And by degrees from underneath it came
Another. My preceptor silent yet
Stood, while the brightness, that we first discern'd,
Open'd the form of wings: then when he knew
The pilot, cried aloud, "Down, down; bend low
Thy knees; behold God's angel: fold thy hands:
Now shalt thou see true ministers indeed.
Lo! how all human means he sets at nought;
So that nor oar he needs, nor other sail
Except his wings,[1] between such distant shores.
Lo! how straight up to heaven he holds them rear'd,
Winnowing the air[2] with those eternal plumes,
That not like mortal hairs fall off or change."

As more and more towards us came, more bright
Appear'd the bird of God, nor could the eye
Endure his splendour near: I mine bent down.
He drove ashore in a small bark so swift
And light, that in its course no wave it drank
The heavenly steersman at the prow was seen,
Visibly written Blessed in his looks.
Within, a hundred spirits and more there sat.

"In Exitu[3] Israel de Egypto,"
All with one voice together sang, with what
In the remainder of that hymn is writ.
Then soon as with the sign of holy cross
He bless'd them, they at once leap'd out on land:
He, swiftly as he came, return'd. The crew,
There left, appear'd astounded with the place,
Gazing around, as one who sees new sights.

From every side the sun darted his beams,
And with his arrowy radiance[4] from mid heaven

---

[1] *Except his wings.*—Hence Milton:
"Who after came from earth, sailing arrived
Wafted by angels."
Paradise Lost, b. iii., ver. 521.

[2] *Winnowing the air.*—
"Trattando l'aere con l'eterne penne."
So "Filicaja," canz. viii., st. 11:
"Ma trattar l'aere coll' eterne piume."

[3] *In Exitu.*—"When Israel came out of Egypt."
Ps. cxiv.

[4] *With his arrowy radiance.*—So Milton:
"And now when forth the morn:
. . . from before her vanish'd night,
Shot through with orient beams."
Paradise Lost, b. vi., ver. 15.
This has been regarded by some critics as a conceit,
into which Milton was betrayed by the Italian poets;

Had chased the Capricorn, when that strange tribe,
Lifting their eyes toward us: "If ye know,
Declare what path will lead us to the mount."

  Then Virgil answer'd: "Ye suppose, perchance,
Us well acquainted with this place: but here,
We, as yourselves, are strangers. Not long erst
We came, before you but a little space,
By other road so rough and hard, that now
The ascent will seem to us as play." The spirits,
Who from my breathing had perceived I lived,
Grew pale with wonder. As the multitude
Flock round a herald sent with olive branch,
To hear what news he brings, and in their haste
Tread one another down; e'en so at sight
Of me those happy spirits were fix'd, each one
Forgetful of its errand to depart
Where, cleansed from sin, it might be made all fair.

  Then one I saw darting before the rest
With such fond ardour to embrace me, I
To do the like was moved. O shadows vain!
Except in outward semblance: thrice my hands[1]
I clasp'd behind it, they as oft return'd
Empty into my breast again. Surprise
I need must think was painted in my looks,
For that the shadow smiled and backward drew.
To follow it I hasten'd, but with voice
Of sweetness it enjoin'd me to desist.
Then who it was I knew, and pray'd of it,
To talk with me it would a little pause.
It answer'd: "Thee as in my mortal frame
I loved, so loosed from it I love thee still,
And therefore pause: but why walkest thou here?"

  "Not without purpose once more to return,

---

but it is, in truth, authorised by one of the correctest of the Grecians:

  Ὃν αἰόλα νὺξ ἐναριζομένα
  τίκτει, κατευνάζει τε, φλογιζόμενον
  Ἅλιον. *Sophocles, Trachin.*, 96.

"Ecco dinanzi a te fugge repente
 Saettata la notte."
 Marini, Son. al Sig. Cinthio Aldobrandino.

[1] *Thrice my hands.*—
"Ter conatus ibi collo dare brachia circum,
Ter frustra comprensa manus effugit imago,

Par levibus ventis volucrique simillima somno."
    Virgil, Æneid, ii. 794.

Compare Homer, "Odyssey," xi. 205. The incident in the text is pleasantly alluded to in that delightful book the "Capricci del Botaio" of Gelli (Opere, Milan, 1805, v. ii., p. 26), of which there is an English translation entitled "The Fearfull Fancies of the Florentine Cooper. Written in Toscane, by John Baptist Gelli, one of the Free Studie of Florence; and for recreation translated into English by W. Barker." 8vo, London, 1599.

The heavenly steersman at the prow was seen,
Visibly written Blessed in his looks.
Canto II., lines 42, 43.

Thou find'st me, my Casella,[1] where I am,[2]
Journeying this way," I said. "But how of thee
Hath so much time been lost?"[3] He answer'd straight:
"No outrage hath been done to me, if he,[4]
Who when and whom he chooses takes, hath oft
Denied me passage here; since of just will
His will he makes. These three months past[5] indeed,
He, whoso chose to enter, with free leave
Hath taken; whence I wandering by the shore[6]
Where Tiber's wave grows salt, of him gain'd kind
Admittance, at that river's mouth, toward which
His wings are pointed; for there always throng
All such as not to Acheron descend."
Then I: "If new law taketh not from thee
Memory or custom of love-tuned song,
That whilom all my cares had power to 'swage;
Please thee therewith a little to console
My spirit, that encumber'd with its frame,
Travelling so far, of pain is overcome."
"Love, that discourses in my thoughts,"[7] he then
Began in such soft accents, that within
The sweetness thrills me yet. My gentle guide,
And all who came with him, so well were pleased,
That seem'd nought else might in their thoughts have room.
Fast fix'd in mute attention to his notes
We stood, when lo! that old man venerable
Exclaiming, "How is this, ye tardy spirits?

---

[1] *My Casella.*—A Florentine, celebrated for his skill in music, "in whose company," says Landino, "Dante often recreated his spirits, wearied by severer studies." See Dr. Burney's "History of Music," vol. ii., cap. iv., p. 322. Milton has a fine allusion to this meeting in his sonnet to Henry Lawes:

"Dante shall give fame leave to set thee higher
  Than his Casella, whom he wooed to sing,
  Met in the milder shades of Purgatory."

[2] *Where I am.*—"La dove io son." Lombardi understands this differently: "Not without purpose to return again to the earth, where I am; that is, where I usually dwell."

[3] *Hath so much time been lost.*—There is some uncertainty in this passage. If we read—

"Ma a te com' era tanta terra tolta?"

with the Nidobeatina and Aldine editions, and many MSS., it signifies, "why art thou deprived of so desirable a region as that of Purgatory? why dost thou not hasten to be cleansed of thy sins?" If, with the Academicians della Crusca, we read—

"Diss 'io, ma a te come tant' ora è tolta?"

which is not destitute of authority to support it, and which has the advantage over the other, as it marks Dante's speech from Casella's, then it must mean, as I have translated it, "why hast thou lost so much time in arriving here?" Lombardi, who is for the former reading, supposes Casella to be just dead; those who prefer the latter, suppose him to have been dead some years, but now only just arrived.

[4] *He.*—The conducting angel.

[5] *These three months past.*—Since the time of the Jubilee, during which all spirits not condemned to eternal punishment were supposed to pass over to Purgatory as soon as they pleased.

[6] *The shore.*—Ostia.

[7] *Love, that discourses in my thoughts.*—

"Amor che nella mente mi ragiona,"

the first verse of a canzone in the "Convito" of Dante, which he again cites in his treatise "De Vulgari Eloquentia," lib. ii., cap. 6.

What negligence detains you loitering here?
Run to the mountain to cast off those scales,
That from your eyes the sight of God conceal."

   As a wild flock of pigeons, to their food
Collected, blade or tares, without their pride
Accustom'd, and in still and quiet sort,
If aught alarm them, suddenly desert
Their meal, assail'd by more important care;
So I that new-come troop beheld, the song
Deserting, hasten to the mountain's side,
As one who goes, yet, where he tends, knows not.[1]
   Nor with less hurried step did we depart.

---

[1] *As one who goes, yet, where he tends, knows not.*—
"Com' uom, che va, nè sa dove riesca."

So Frezzi:
"Come chi va, nè sa dove camina."
Il Quadriregio, lib. i., cap. 3.

CANTO III.

ARGUMENT.

Our Poet, perceiving no shadow except that cast by his own body, is fearful that Virgil has deserted him; but he is freed from that error, and both arrive together at the foot of the mountain. On finding it too steep to climb, they inquire the way from a troop of spirits that are coming towards them, and are by them shown which is the easiest ascent. Manfredi, King of Naples, who is one of these spirits, bids Dante inform his daughter Costanza, Queen of Arragon, of the manner in which he had died.

THEM sudden flight had scatter'd o'er the plain,
Turn'd towards the mountain, whither reason's voice
Drives us: I, to my faithful company
Adhering, left it not. For how, of him
Deprived, might I have sped? or who, beside,
Would o'er the mountainous tract have led my steps?
He, with the bitter pang of self-remorse,
Seem'd smitten. O clear conscience, and upright!
How doth a little failing wound thee sore.[1]

Soon as his feet desisted (slackening pace)
From haste, that mars all decency of act,[2]
My mind, that in itself before was wrapt,
Its thought expanded, as with joy restored;
And full against the steep ascent I set
My face, where highest[3] to heaven its top o'erflows.

The sun, that flared behind, with ruddy beam
Before my form was broken; for in me
His rays resistance met. I turn'd aside
With fear of being left, when I beheld
Only before myself the ground obscured.

---

[1]   *O clear conscience, and upright!*
   How doth a little failing wound thee sore.—
"Ch' era al cor picciol fallo amaro morso."
            Tasso, Gierusalemme Liberata
            c. x., st. 59.

[2] *Haste, that mars all decency of act.*—Aristotle, in his "Physiog.," c. iii., reckons it among the ἀναιδοῦς σημεῖα ("the signs of an impudent man"), that he is ἐν ταῖς κινήσεσιν ὀξύς ("quick in his motions"). Compare Sophocles, "Electra," 878:
      Τὸ κόσμιον μεθεῖσα.

"Joy, my dear sister, wings my quick return,
And with more speed than decency allows."
                      Potter.

[3] *Where highest.*—Lombardi proposes, with some hesitation, a different meaning from that which has hitherto been affixed to the words—
"Che 'nverso 'l ciel più alto si dislaga;"
and would construe them, "that raises itself higher than every other mountain above the sea" ("sopra l'allagamento delle acque del mare"). The conjecture is at least ingenious, and has obtained new force by the arguments of Monti in his "Proposta."

When thus my solace, turning him around,
Bespake me kindly: "Why distrustest thou?
Believest not I am with thee, thy sure guide?
It now is evening there, where buried lies
The body in which I cast a shade, removed
To Naples[1] from Brundusium's wall. Nor thou
Marvel, if before me no shadow fall,
More than that in the skyey element
One ray obstructs not other. To endure
Torments of heat and cold extreme, like frames
That virtue hath disposed, which, how it works,
Wills not to us should be reveal'd. Insane,
Who hopes our reason may that space explore,
Which holds three persons in one substance knit.
Seek not the wherefore, race of human kind;
Could ye have seen the whole, no need had been
For Mary to bring forth. Moreover, ye
Have seen such men desiring fruitlessly;[2]
To whose desires, repose would have been given,
That now but serve them for eternal grief.
I speak of Plato, and the Stagirite,
And others many more." And then he bent
Downwards his forehead, and in troubled mood[3]
Broke off his speech. Meanwhile we had arrived
Far as the mountain's foot, and there the rock
Found of so steep ascent, that nimblest steps
To climb it had been vain. The most remote,
Most wild, untrodden path, in all the tract
'Twixt Lerice and Turbia,[4] were to this
A ladder easy and open of access.

"Who knows on which hand now the steep declines?"
My master said, and paused; "so that he may
Ascend, who journeys without aid of wing?"
And while, with looks directed to the ground,

---

[1] *To Naples.*—Virgil died at Brundusium, from whence his body is said to have been removed to Naples.
[2] *Desiring fruitlessly.*—See "Hell," canto iv. 39.
[3] *In troubled mood.*—Because he himself (Virgil) was amongst the number of spirits who thus desired without hope.
[4] *'Twixt Lerice and Turbia.*—At that time the two extremities of the Genoese republic; the former on the east, the latter on the west. A very ingenious writer has had occasion, for a different purpose, to mention one of these places as remarkably secluded by its mountainous situation. "On an eminence among the mountains, between the two little cities, Nice and Monaco, is the village of Torbia, a name formed from the Greek τρόπαια."—*Mitford on the Harmony of Language*, sect. xv., p. 351, 2nd edit.

And while, with looks directed to the ground,
The meaning of the pathway he explored,
And I gazed upward round the stony height;
On the left hand appear'd to us a troop
Of spirits, that toward us moved their steps;
Yet moving seem'd not, they so slow approach'd.
Canto III., lines 54—59.

The meaning of the pathway he explored,[1]
And I gazed upward round the stony height;
On the left hand appear'd to us a troop
Of spirits, that toward us moved their steps;
Yet moving seem'd not, they so slow approach'd.
 I thus my guide address'd: "Upraise thine eyes:
Lo! that way some, of whom thou mayst obtain
Counsel, if of thyself thou find'st it not."
 Straightway he look'd, and with free speech replied:
"Let us tend thither: they but softly come.
And thou be firm in hope, my son beloved."
 Now was that crowd from us distant as far,
(When we some thousand steps,[2] I say, had past,)
As at a throw the nervous arm could fling;
When all drew backward on the massy crags
Of the steep bank, and firmly stood unmoved,
As one, who walks in doubt, might stand to look.
 "O spirits perfect! O already chosen!"
Virgil to them began: "by that blest peace,
Which, as I deem, is for you all prepared,
Instruct us where the mountain low declines,
So that attempt to mount it be not vain.
For who knows most, him loss of time most grieves."
 As sheep,[3] that step from forth their fold, by one,
Or pairs, or three at once; meanwhile the rest
Stand fearfully, bending the eye and nose
To ground, and what the foremost does, that do
The others, gathering round her if she stops,
Simple and quiet, nor the cause discern;
So saw I moving to advance the first,
Who of that fortunate crew were at the head,
Of modest mien, and graceful in their gait.
When they before me had beheld the light

---

[1] *The meaning of the pathway he explored.—* Lombardi reads—

"Tenea 'l viso basso,
Esaminando del cammin la mente,"

and explains it, "he bent down his face, his mind being occupied with considering their way to ascend the mountain." I doubt much whether the words can bear that construction.

[2] *When we some thousand steps.—*Mr. Carlyle puts a query to my former translation of this passage. It was certainly erroneous.

[3] *As sheep.—*The imitative nature of these animals supplies our poet with another comparison in his "Convito," p. 34: "Questi sono da chiamare pecore," &c., "These may be called flocks of sheep and not men; for if one sheep should throw himself down a precipice of a thousand feet, all the rest would follow; and if one for any cause in passing a road should leap, all the rest would do the same, though they saw nothing to leap over."

From my right side fall broken on the ground,
So that the shadow reach'd the cave; they stopp'd,
And somewhat back retired: the same did all
Who follow'd, though unweeting of the cause.
  "Unask'd of you, yet freely I confess,
This is a human body which ye see.
That the sun's light is broken on the ground,
Marvel not: but believe, that not without
Virtue derived from Heaven, we to climb
Over this wall aspire." So them bespake
My master; and that virtuous tribe rejoin'd:
"Turn, and before you there the entrance lies;"
Making a signal to us with bent hands.
  Then of them one began. "Whoe'er thou art,
Who journey'st thus this way, thy visage turn;
Think if me elsewhere thou hast ever seen."
  I towards him turn'd, and with fix'd eye beheld.
Comely and fair, and gentle of aspect
He seem'd, but on one brow a gash was mark'd.
  When humbly I disclaim'd to have beheld
Him ever: "Now behold!" he said, and show'd
High on his breast a wound: then smiling spake.
  "I am Manfredi,[1] grandson to the Queen
Costanza:[2] whence I pray thee, when return'd,
To my fair daughter[3] go, the parent glad

---

[1] *Manfredi.*—King of Naples and Sicily, and the natural son of Frederick II. He was lively and agreeable in his manners, and delighted in poetry, music, and dancing. But he was luxurious and ambitious, void of religion, and in his philosophy an Epicurean. See G. Villani, lib. vi., cap. xlvii., and Mr. Mathias's "Tiraboschi," vol. i., p. 99. He fell in the battle with Charles of Anjou in 1265, alluded to in canto xxviii. of "Hell," v. 13, or rather in that which ensued in the course of a few days at Benevento. But the successes of Charles were so rapidly followed up, that our author, exact as he generally is, might not have thought it necessary to distinguish them in point of time; for this seems the best method of reconciling some little apparent inconsistency between him and the annalist. "Dying excommunicated, King Charles did not allow of his being buried in sacred ground, but he was interred near the bridge of Benevento; and on his grave there was cast a stone by every one of the army, whence there was formed a great mound of stones. But some have said that afterwards, by command of the Pope, the Bishop of Cosenza took up his body and sent it out of the kingdom, because it was the land of the church; and that it was buried by the river Verde, on the borders of the kingdom and of Campagna. This, however, we do not affirm."—G. Villani, "Hist.," lib. vii., cap. ix. Manfredi and his father are spoken of by our poet in his "De Vulgari Eloquentia," lib. i., cap. 12, with singular commendation: "Siquidem illustres," &c., "Those illustrious worthies, Frederick the Emperor, and his well-born son Manfredi, manifested their nobility and uprightness of form, as long as fortune remained, by following pursuits worthy of men, and disdained those which are suited only to brutes. Such, therefore, as were of a lofty spirit, and graced with natural endowments, endeavoured to walk in the track which the majesty of such great princes had marked out for them: so that whatever was in their time attempted by eminent Italians, first made its appearance in the court of crowned sovereigns; and because Sicily was a royal throne, it came to pass that whatever was produced in the vernacular tongue by our predecessors was called Sicilian; which neither we nor our posterity shall be able to change."

[2] *Costanza.*—See "Paradise," canto iii. 121.

[3] *My fair daughter.*—Costanza, the daughter of Manfredi, and wife of Peter III., King of Arragon, by whom she was mother to Frederick, King of Sicily, and James, King of Arragon. With the latter of these she was at Rome 1296. See G. Villani, lib. viii., cap. xviii., and notes to canto vii.

Of Aragonia and Sicilia's pride;
And of the truth inform her, if of me
Aught else be told. When by two mortal blows
My frame was shatter'd, I betook myself
Weeping to him, who of free will forgives.
My sins were horrible: but so wide arms
Hath goodness infinite, that it receives
All who turn to it. Had this text divine
Been of Cosenza's shepherd better scann'd,
Who then by Clement on my hunt was set,[1]
Yet at the bridge's head my bones had lain,
Near Benevento, by the heavy mole
Protected; but the rain now drenches them,
And the wind drives, out of the kingdom's bounds,
Far as the stream of Verde,[2] where, with lights
Extinguish'd, he removed them from their bed.
Yet by their curse we are not so destroy'd,
But that the eternal love may turn, while hope[3]
Retains her verdant blossom. True it is,
That such one as in contumacy dies
Against the holy church, though he repent,
Must wander thirty-fold for all the time
In his presumption past; if such decree
Be not by prayers of good men shorter made.
Look therefore if thou canst advance my bliss;
Revealing to my good Costanza how
Thou hast beheld me, and beside, the terms
Laid on me of that interdict; for here
By means of those below much profit comes."

---

[1] *Who then by Clement on my hunt was set.*—Pope Clement IV.

[2] *The stream of Verde.*—A river near Ascoli, that falls into the Tronto. The "extinguished lights" formed part of the ceremony at the interment of one excommunicated:

"Passa la mora di Manfrè, cui lava
Il Verde." *Uberti, Dittamondo*, lib. iii., cap. i., as corrected by Perticari.

[3] *Hope.*—"Mentre che la speranza ha fior del verde." So Tasso, "Gierusalemme Liberata," canto xix., st. 53:
"Infin che verde è fior di speme."

CANTO IV.

ARGUMENT.

Dante and Virgil ascend the mountain of Purgatory, by a steep and narrow path pent in on each side by rock, till they reach a part of it that opens into a ledge or cornice. There seating themselves, and turning to the east, Dante wonders at seeing the sun on their left, the cause of which is explained to him by Virgil; and while they continue their discourse, a voice addresses them, at which they turn, and find several spirits behind the rock, and amongst the rest one named Belacqua, who had been known to our Poet on earth, and who tells that he is doomed to linger there on account of his having delayed his repentance to the last.

WHEN[1] by sensations of delight or pain,
    That any of our faculties hath seized,
Entire the soul collects herself, it seems
She is intent upon that power alone;
And thus the error is disproved, which holds
The soul not singly lighted in the breast.
And therefore whenas aught is heard or seen,
That firmly keeps the soul toward it turn'd,
Time passes, and a man perceives it not.
For that, whereby we hearken, is one power;
Another that, which the whole spirit hath:
This is as it were bound, while that is free.
    This found I true by proof, hearing that spirit,
And wondering; for full fifty steps[2] aloft
The sun had measured, unobserved of me,
When we arrived where all with one accord
The spirits shouted, "Here is what ye ask."

---

[1] *When.*—It must be owned the beginning of this canto is somewhat obscure. Vellutello refers, for an elucidation of it, to the reasoning of Statius in the twenty-fifth canto. Perhaps some illustration may be derived from the following passage in the "Summa Theologiæ" of Thomas Aquinas: "Some say that in addition to the vegetable soul, which was present from the first, there supervenes another soul, which is the sensitive; and again, in addition to that, another, which is the intellective. And so there are in man three souls, one of which exists potentially with regard to another: but this has been already disproved. And accordingly others say that that same soul, which at first was merely vegetative, is, through action of the seminal virtue, carried forward till it reaches to that point in which, being still the same, it nevertheless becomes sensitive; and at length the same, by an ulterior progression, is led on till it becomes intellective; not, indeed, through the seminal virtue acting in it, but by virtue of a superior agent, that is, God, enlightening it from without." This opinion he next proceeds to confute. "Dicunt ergo quidam quòd supra animam vegetabilem, quæ primo inerat, supervenit alia anima, quæ est sensitiva, supra illam iterum alia quæ est intellectiva. Et sic sunt in homine tres animæ, quarum una est in potentia ad aliam, quod supra improbatum est. Et ideo alii dicunt, quòd illa eadem anima, quæ primo fuit vegetativa tantum, postmodum per actionem virtutis, quæ est in semine, perducitur ad hoc, ut ipsa eadem fiat sensitiva; et tandem ipsa eadem perducitur ad hoc, ut ipsa eadem fiat intellectiva, non quidem per virtutem activam seminis, sed per virtutem superioris agentis, scilicet Dei deforis illustrantis."—*Thom. Aquin. Opera* Edit. Venet., 1595, tom. x., *Summa Theolog.*, Ima Pars., Quæstio cxviii., Art ii. See also "Lettere di Fra Guittone," 4to, Roma, 1745, p. 15; and Routh's note on the "Gorgias" of Plato, p. 451.

[2] *Full fifty steps.*—Three hours and twenty minutes, fifteen degrees being reckoned to an hour.

While underneath, the ground
Ask'd help of hands and feet.
Canto IV., lines 31, 32.

A larger aperture oft-times is stopt,
With forked stake of thorn by villager,
When the ripe grape imbrowns, than was the path
By which my guide, and I behind him close,
Ascended solitary, when that troop
Departing left us. On Sanleo's[1] road
Who journeys, or to Noli[2] low descends,
Or mounts Bismantua's[3] height, must use his feet;
But here a man had need to fly, I mean
With the swift wing[4] and plumes of high desire,
Conducted by his aid, who gave me hope,
And with light furnish'd to direct my way.

We through the broken rock ascended, close
Pent on each side, while underneath, the ground
Ask'd help of hands and feet. When we arrived
Near on the highest ridge of the steep bank,
Where the plain level open'd, I exclaim'd,
"O Master! say, which way can we proceed."

He answer'd, "Let no step of thine recede.
Behind me gain the mountain, till to us
Some practised guide appear." That eminence
Was lofty, that no eye might reach its point;
And the side proudly rising, more than line[5]
From the mid quadrant to the centre drawn.
I, wearied, thus began : "Parent beloved!
Turn and behold how I remain alone,
If thou stay not." "My son!" he straight replied,
"Thus far put forth thy strength;" and to a track
Pointed, that, on this side projecting, round
Circles the hill. His words so spurr'd me on,
That I, behind him, clambering, forced myself,
Till my feet press'd the circuit plain beneath.
There both together seated, turn'd we round
To eastward, whence was our ascent: and oft
Many beside have with delight look'd back.

---

[1] *Sanleo.*—A fortress on the summit of Montefeltro. The situation is described by Troya, "Veltro Allegorico," p. 11. It is a conspicuous object to travellers along the cornice on the Riviera di Genova.

[2] *Noli.*—In the Genoese territory, between Finale and Savona.

[3] *Bismantua.*—A steep mountain in the territory of Reggio.

[4] *With the swift wing.*—Compare "Paradise," canto xxxiii. 17.

[5] *More than line.*—It was much nearer to being perpendicular than horizontal.

First on the nether shores I turn'd mine eyes,
Then raised them to the sun, and wondering mark'd
That from the left[1] it smote us. Soon perceived
That poet sage, how at the car of light
Amazed[2] I stood, where 'twixt us and the north
Its course it enter'd. Whence he thus to me:
"Were Leda's offspring[3] now in company
Of that broad mirror, that high up and low
Imparts his light beneath, thou mightst behold
The ruddy Zodiac nearer to the Bears
Wheel, if its ancient course it not forsook.
How that may be, if thou wouldst think; within
Pondering, imagine Sion with this mount
Placed on the earth, so that to both be one
Horizon, and two hemispheres apart,
Where lies the path[4] that Phaëton ill knew
To guide his erring chariot: thou wilt see[5]
How of necessity by this, on one,
He passes, while by that on the other side;
If with that clear view thine intellect attend."

"Of truth, kind teacher!" I exclaim'd, "so clear
Aught saw I never, as I now discern,
Where seem'd my ken to fail, that the mid orb[6]
Of the supernal motion (which in terms
Of art is call'd the Equator, and remains
Still 'twixt the sun and winter) for the cause
Thou hast assign'd, from hence toward the north
Departs, when those, who in the Hebrew land
Were dwellers, saw it towards the warmer part.
But if it please thee, I would gladly know,

---

[1] *From the left.*—Vellutello observes an imitation of Lucan in this passage:
"Ignotum vobis, Arabes, venistis in orbem,
Umbras mirati nemorum non ire sinistras."
Pharsalia, lib. iii. 248.
[2] *Amazed.*—He wonders that being turned to the east he should see the sun on his left, since in all the regions on this side of the tropic of Cancer it is seen on the right of one who turns his face towards the east; not recollecting that he was now antipodal to Europe, from whence he had seen the sun taking an opposite course.
[3] *Were Leda's offspring.*—"As the constellation of the Gemini is nearer the Bears than Aries is, it is certain that if the sun, instead of being in Aries, had been in Gemini, both the sun and that portion of the Zodiac made 'ruddy' by the sun, would have been seen to 'wheel nearer to the Bears.' Zodiac' must necessarily be understood the Zodiac affected or made red by th whole of the Zodiac never changes, r change, with respect to the remainder o —*Lombardi*.
[4] *The path.*—The ecliptic.
[5] *Thou wilt see.*—"If you consider t tain of Purgatory, and that of Sion, ar each other, you will perceive that the su opposite sides of the respective eminenc
[6] *That the mid orb.*—"That the equ always situated between that part where is, he causes summer, and the other whe produces winter) recedes from this mo the north, at the time when the Jews inh Sion saw it depart towards the south."—

How far we have to journey: for the hill
Mounts higher, than this sight of mine can mount."
 He thus to me: "Such is this steep ascent,
That it is ever difficult at first,
But more a man proceeds, less evil grows.[1]
When pleasant it shall seem to thee, so much
That upward going shall be easy to thee
As in a vessel to go down the tide,
Then of this path thou wilt have reach'd the end.
There hope to rest thee from thy toil. No more
I answer, and thus far for certain know."
As he his words had spoken, near to us
A voice there sounded: "Yet ye first perchance
May to repose you by constraint be led."
At sound thereof each turn'd; and on the left
A huge stone we beheld, of which nor I
Nor he before was ware. Thither we drew;
And there were some, who in the shady place
Behind the rock were standing, as a man
Through idleness might stand. Among them one,
Who seem'd to be much wearied, sat him down,
And with his arms did fold his knees about,
Holding his face between them downward bent.
 "Sweet Sir!" I cried, "behold that man who shows
Himself more idle than if laziness
Were sister to him." Straight he turn'd to us,
And, o'er the thigh lifting his face, observed,
Then in these accents spake: "Up then, proceed,
Thou valiant one." Straight who it was I knew;
Nor could the pain I felt (for want of breath
Still somewhat urged me) hinder my approach.
And when I came to him, he scarce his head
Uplifted, saying, "Well hast thou discern'd,
How from the left the sun his chariot leads."
 His lazy acts and broken words my lips
To laughter somewhat moved; when I began:
"Belacqua,[2] now for thee I grieve no more.

---

[1] *But more a man proceeds, less evil grows.*—Because in ascending he gets rid of the weight of his sins.

[2] *Belacqua.*—Concerning this man, the commentators afford no information, except that in the margin of the Monte Casino MS. there is found this brief notice

But tell, why thou art seated upright there.
Waitest thou escort to conduct thee hence?
Or blame I only thine accustom'd ways?"
Then he: "My brother! of what use to mount,
When, to my suffering, would not let me pass
The bird of God,[1] who at the portal sits?
Behoves so long that heaven first bear me round
Without its limits, as in life it bore;
Because I, to the end, repentant sighs
Delay'd; if prayer do not aid me first,
That riseth up from heart which lives in grace,
What other kind avails, not heard in heaven?"

Before me now the poet, up the mount
Ascending, cried: "Haste thee: for see the sun
Has touch'd the point meridian; and the night
Now covers with her foot Marocco's shore."[2]

---

of him: "Iste Belacqua fuit optimus magister cithararum, et leutorum, et pigrissimus homo in operibus mundi sicut in operibus animæ" ("This Belacqua was an excellent master of the harp and lute, but very negligent in his affairs, both spiritual and temporal").—*Lettera di Eustazio Dicearcheo ad Angelio Sidicino,* 4to, Roma, 1801.

[1] *The bird of God.*—Here are two other readings, "Uscier" and "Angel" ("Usher" and "Angel") of God.

[2] *Marocco's shore.*—" Cuopre la notte già col piè Marocco." Hence, perhaps, Milton:
"Damasco, or Marocco, or Trebisond."
Paradise Lost, b. i. 584.
Instead of Morocco, as he elsewhere calls it:
"Morocco, and Algiers, and Tremisen."
Paradise Lost, b. xi. 404.
If the vowels were to change places, the verse would in both instances be spoiled.

And there were some, who in the shady place
Behind the rock were standing, as a man
Through idleness might stand.

Canto IV., lines 100—102

CANTO V.

ARGUMENT.

They meet with others, who had deferred their repentance till they were overtaken by a violent death, when sufficient space being allowed them, they were then saved; and amongst these Giacopo del Cassero, Buonconte da Montefeltro, and Pia, a lady of Sienna.

NOW had I left those spirits, and pursued
The steps of my conductor; when behind,
Pointing the finger at me, one exclaim'd:
"See, how it seems as if the light not shone
From the left hand[1] of him beneath,[2] and he,
As living, seems to be led on." Mine eyes
I at that sound reverting, saw them gaze,
Through wonder, first at me; and then at me
And the light broken underneath, by turns.
"Why are thy thoughts thus riveted," my guide
Exclaim'd, "that thou hast slack'd thy pace? or how
Imports it thee, what thing is whisper'd here?
Come after me, and to their babblings leave
The crowd. Be as a tower,[3] that, firmly set,
Shakes not its top for any blast that blows.
He, in whose bosom thought on thought shoots out,
Still of his aim is wide, in that the one
Sicklies and wastes to nought the other's strength."
What other could I answer, save "I come"?
I said it, somewhat with that colour tinged,
Which oft-times pardon meriteth for man.
Meanwhile traverse along the hill there came,

---

[1] *See, how it seems as if the light not shone from the left hand.*—The sun was, therefore, on the right of our travellers. For, as before, when seated and looking to the east from whence they had ascended, the sun was on their left, so now that they have risen and are again going forward, it must be on the opposite side of them.

[2] *Of him beneath.*—Of Dante, who was following Virgil up the mountain, and, therefore, was the lower of the two.

[3] *Be as a tower.*—"Sta come torre ferma." So Berni, "Orlando Innamorato," lib. i., canto xvi., st. 48:
 "In quei due piedi sta fermo il gigante
  Com' una torre in mezzo d'un castello."
And Milton, "Paradise Lost," b. i. 591: "Stood like a tower."

A little way before us, some who sang
The "Miserere" in responsive strains.
When they perceived that through my body I
Gave way not for the rays to pass, their song
Straight to a long and hoarse exclaim they changed;
And two of them, in guise of messengers,
Ran on to meet us, and inquiring ask'd:
"Of your condition we would gladly learn."

To them my guide. "Ye may return, and bear
Tidings to them who sent you, that his frame
Is real flesh. If, as I deem, to view
His shade they paused, enough is answer'd them:
Him let them honour: they may prize him well."

Ne'er saw I fiery vapours[1] with such speed
Cut through the serene air at fall of night,
Nor August's clouds athwart the setting sun,
That upward these did not in shorter space
Return; and, there arriving, with the rest
Wheel back on us, as with loose rein a troop.

"Many," exclaim'd the bard, "are these, who throng
Around us: to petition thee they come.
Go therefore on, and listen as thou go'st."

"O spirit! who go'st on to blessedness,
With the same limbs that clad thee at thy birth,
Shouting they came: "a little rest thy step.
Look if thou any one amongst our tribe
Hast e'er beheld, that tidings of him there[2]
Thou mayst report. Ah, wherefore go'st thou on?
Ah, wherefore tarriest thou not? We all
By violence died, and to our latest hour
Were sinners, but then warn'd by light from heaven;
So that, repenting and forgiving, we
Did issue out of life at peace with God,
Who, with desire to see him, fills our heart."

Then I: "The visages of all I scan,

---

[1] *Ne'er saw I fiery vapours.*—Imitated by Tasso, "Gierusalemme Liberata," canto xix., st. 62:

"Tal suol fendendo liquido sereno
  Stella cader della gran madre in seno."

And by Milton, "Paradise Lost," b. iv. 558:

"Swift as a shooting star
In autumn thwarts the night, when vapours fired
Impress the air."

Compare Statius, "Thebais," i. 92: "Ilicet igne Jovis lapsisque citatior astris."

[2] *There.*—Upon the earth.

"Many," exclaim'd the bard, "are these, who throng
Around us: to petition thee they come.
Go therefore on, and listen as thou go'st."

Canto V., lines 42—44.

Yet none of ye remember. But if aught
That I can do may please you, gentle spirits!
Speak, and I will perform it; by that peace,
Which, on the steps of guide so excellent
Following, from world to world, intent I seek."

In answer he began: "None here distrusts
Thy kindness, though not promised with an oath;
So as the will fail not for want of power.
Whence I, who sole before the others speak,
Entreat thee, if thou ever see that land[1]
Which lies between Romagna and the realm
Of Charles, that of thy courtesy thou pray
Those who inhabit Fano, that for me
Their adorations duly be put up,
By which I may purge off my grievous sins.
From thence I came.[2] But the deep passages,
Whence issued out the blood[3] wherein I dwelt,
Upon my bosom in Antenor's land[4]
Were made, where to be more secure I thought.
The author of the deed was Este's prince,
Who, more than right could warrant, with his wrath
Pursued me. Had I towards Mira fled,
When overta'en at Oriaco, still
Might I have breathed. But to the marsh I sped;
And in the mire and rushes tangled there
Fell, and beheld my life-blood float the plain."

Then said another: "Ah! so may the wish,
That takes thee o'er the mountain, be fulfill'd,
As thou shalt graciously give aid to mine.
Of Montefeltro I;[5] Buonconte I:
Giovanna[6] nor none else have care for me;

---

[1] *If thou ever see that land.*—The Marca d'Ancona, between Romagna and Apulia, the kingdom of Charles of Anjou.

[2] *From thence I came.*—Giacopo del Cassero, a citizen of Fano, who having spoken ill of Azzo da Este, Marquis of Ferrara, was by his orders put to death. Giacopo was overtaken by the assassins at Oriaco, a place near the Brenta, from whence, if he had fled towards Mira, higher up on that river, instead of making for the marsh on the sea-shore, he might have escaped.

[3] *The blood.*—Supposed to be the seat of life.

[4] *Antenor's land.*—The city of Padua, said to be founded by Antenor. This implies a reflection on the Paduans. See "Hell," xxxii. 89. Thus G. Villani calls the Venetians "the perfidious descendants from the blood of Antenor, the betrayer of his country, Troy."—Lib. xi., cap. lxxxix.

[5] *Of Montefeltro I.*—Buonconte (son of Guido da Montefeltro, whom we have had in the twenty-seventh canto of "Hell") fell in the battle of Campaldino (1289), fighting on the side of the Aretini. In this engagement our poet took a distinguished part, as we have seen related in his Life. See Fazio degli Uberti, "Dittamondo," lib. ii., cap. xxix.

[6] *Giovanna.*—Either the wife or a kinswoman of Buonconte.

Sorrowing with these I therefore go." I thus:
"From Campaldino's field what force or chance
Drew thee, that ne'er thy sepulture was known?"

"Oh!" answer'd he, "at Casentino's foot
A stream there courseth, named Archiano, sprung
In Apennine above the hermit's seat.[1]
E'en where its name is cancel'd,[2] there came I,
Pierced in the throat,[3] fleeing away on foot,
And bloodying the plain. Here sight and speech
Fail'd me; and, finishing with Mary's name,
I fell, and tenantless my flesh remain'd.
I will report the truth; which thou again
Tell to the living. Me God's angel took,[4]
Whilst he of hell exclaim'd: 'O thou from heaven:
Say wherefore hast thou robb'd me? Thou of him
The eternal portion bear'st with thee away,
For one poor tear[5] that he deprives me of.
But of the other, other rule I make.'

"Thou know'st how in the atmosphere collects
That vapour dank, returning into water
Soon as it mounts where cold condenses it.
That evil will,[6] which in his intellect
Still follows evil, came; and raised the wind
And smoky mist, by virtue of the power
Given by his nature. Thence the valley, soon
As day was spent, he cover'd o'er with cloud,
From Pratomagno to the mountain range;[7]
And stretch'd the sky above; so that the air
Impregnate changed to water. Fell the rain:
And to the fosses came all that the land
Contain'd not; and, as mightiest streams are wont,
To the great river, with such headlong sweep,
Rush'd, that nought stay'd its course. My stiffen'd frame,

---

[1] *The hermit's seat.*—The hermitage of Camaldoli.
[2] *Where its name is cancel'd.*—That is, between Bibbiena and Poppi, where the Archiano falls into the Arno.
[3] *Throat.*—In the former editions it was printed "heart." Mr. Carlyle has observed the error.
[4] *Me God's angel took.*—"Cum autem finem vitæ explesset servus Dei aspiciens vidit diabolum simul et Angelum ad animam stantem ac unum quemque illam sibi tollere festinantem."—*Alberici Visio*, § 18.
[5] *For one poor tear.*—"Visum est quod angelus Domini lachrimas quas dives ille . . . fuderat ampulla teneret."—*Alberici Visio*, § 18.
[6] *That evil will.*—The devil. Lombardi refers to Albertus Magnus "De Potentiâ Dæmonum." Th notion of the Evil Spirit having power over t elements, appears to have arisen from his being term the "prince of the air" in the New Testament.
[7] *From Pratomagno to the mountain range.* From Pratomagno, now called Prato Vecchio (whi divides the Valdarno from Casentino), as far as to t Apennine.

From my breast
Loosening the cross, that of myself I made
When overcome with pain.

Canto V., lines 123—125

Laid at his mouth, the fell Archiano found,
And dash'd it into Arno ; from my breast
Loosening the cross, that of myself I made
When overcome with pain. He hurl'd me on,
Along the banks and bottom of his course ;
Then in his muddy spoils encircling wrapt."

"Ah ! when thou to the world shalt be return'd,
And rested after thy long road," so spake
Next the third spirit ; " then remember me.
I once was Pia.[1] Sienna gave me life ;
Maremma took it from me. That he knows,
Who me with jewel'd ring had first espoused."

---

[1] *Pia.*—She is said to have been a Siennese lady, of the family of Tolommei, secretly made away with by her husband, Nello della Pietra, of the same city, in Maremma, where he had some possessions.

CANTO VI.

ARGUMENT.

Many besides, who are in like case with those spoken of in the last Canto, beseech our Poet to obtain for them the prayers of their friends, when he shall be returned to this world. This moves him to express a doubt to his guide, how the dead can be profited by the prayers of the living; for the solution of which doubt he is referred to Beatrice. Afterwards he meets with Sordello, the Mantuan, whose affection, shown to Virgil, his countryman, leads Dante to break forth into an invective against the unnatural divisions with which Italy, and more especially Florence, was distracted.

WHEN from their game of dice men separate,
    He who hath lost remains in sadness fix'd,
Revolving in his mind[1] what luckless throws
He cast: but, meanwhile, all the company
Go with the other; one before him runs,
And one behind his mantle twitches, one
Fast by his side bids him remember him.
He stops not; and each one, to whom his hand
Is stretch'd, well knows he bids him stand aside;
And thus[2] he from the press defends himself.
E'en such was I in that close-crowding throng;
And turning so my face around to all,
And promising, I 'scaped from it with pains.
    Here of Arezzo him[3] I saw, who fell
By Ghino's cruel arm; and him beside,[4]
Who in his chase was swallow'd by the stream.

---

[1] *Revolving in his mind.*—
"Riman dolente
Ripetendo le volte, e triste impara."
Lombardi explains this: "That the loser remains by himself, and taking up the dice, casts them over again, as if to learn how he may throw the numbers he could wish to come up." There is something very natural in this; but whether the sense can be fairly deduced from the words is another question.

[2] *And thus.*—The late Archdeacon Fisher pointed out to me a passage in the "Novela de la Gitanilla" of Cervantes, ed. Valentia, 1797, p. 12, from which it appears that it was usual for money to be given to bystanders at play by winners; and as he well remarked: "Dante is therefore describing, with his usual power of observation, what he had often seen, the shuffling, boon-denying exit of the successful gamester."

[3] *Of Arezzo him.*—Benincasa of Arezzo, eminent for his skill in jurisprudence, who, having condemned to death Turrino da Turrita, brother of Ghino di Tacco, for his robberies in Maremma, was murdered by Ghino, in an apartment of his own house, in the presence of many witnesses. Ghino was not only suffered to escape in safety, but (as the commentators inform us) obtained so high a reputation by the liberality with which he was accustomed to dispense the fruits of his plunder, and treated those who fell into his hands with so much courtesy, that he was afterwards invited to Rome, and knighted by Boniface VIII. A story is told of him by Boccaccio, Giorn. x., Nov. 2.

[4] *Him beside.*—Cione, or Ciacco de' Tarlatti of Arezzo. He is said to have been carried by his horse into the Arno, and there drowned, while he was in pursuit of certain of his enemies.

"Then remember me.
I once was Pia."
Canto V., lines 130, 131.

Here Frederic Novello,[1] with his hand
Stretch'd forth, entreated; and of Pisa he,[2]
Who put the good Marzuco to such proof
Of constancy. Count Orso[3] I beheld;
And from its frame a soul dismiss'd for spite
And envy, as it said, but for no crime;
I speak of Peter de la Brosse:[4] and here,
While she yet lives, that Lady of Brabant,
Let her beware; lest for so false a deed
She herd with worse than these. When I was freed
From all those spirits, who pray'd for others' prayers
To hasten on their state of blessedness;
Straight I began: "O thou, my luminary!
It seems expressly in thy text[5] denied,
That heaven's supreme decree can ever bend
To supplication: yet with this design
Do these entreat. Can then their hope be vain?
Or is thy saying not to me reveal'd?"

He thus to me: "Both what I write is plain,
And these deceived not in their hope; if well
Thy mind consider, that the sacred height
Of judgment[6] doth not stoop, because love's flame
In a short moment all fulfils, which he,
Who sojourns here, in right should satisfy.
Besides, when I this point concluded thus,
By praying no defect could be supplied;
Because the prayer had none access to God.
Yet in this deep suspicion rest thou not

---

[1] *Frederic Novello.*—Son of the Conti Guido da Battifolle, and slain by one of the family of Bostoli.

[2] *Of Pisa he.*—Farinata de' Scornigiani of Pisa. His father Marzuco, who had entered the order of the Frati Minori, so entirely overcame the feelings of resentment, that he even kissed the hands of the slayer of his son, and, as he was following the funeral, exhorted his kinsmen to reconciliation. The eighteenth and thirtieth in the collection of Guittone d'Arezzo's Letters are addressed to Marzuco. The latter is in verse.

[3] *Count Orso.*—Son of Napoleone da Cerbaia, slain by Alberto da Mangona, his uncle.

[4] *Peter de la Brosse.*—Secretary of Philip III. of France. The courtiers, envying the high place which he held in the king's favour, prevailed on Mary of Brabant to charge him falsely with an attempt upon her person; for which supposed crime he suffered death. So say the Italian commentators. Henault represents the matter very differently: "Pierre de la Brosse, formerly barber to St. Louis, afterwards the favourite of Philip, fearing the too great attachment of the king for his wife Mary, accuses this princess of having poisoned Louis, eldest son of Philip, by his first marriage. This calumny is discovered by a nun of Nivelle in Flanders. La Brosse is hung."—*Abrégé Chron.*, 1275, &c. The Deputati, or those deputed to write annotations on the "Decameron," suppose that Boccaccio, in the Giornata ii., Novella 9, took the story from this passage in Dante, only concealing the real names and changing the incidents in some parts, in order not to wound the feelings of those whom, as it was believed, these incidents had so lately befallen. Ediz. Giunti, 1573, p. 40.

[5] *In thy text.*—He refers to Virgil, "Æneid," lib. vi. 376:
"Desine fata deûm flecti sperare precando."

[6] *The sacred height of judgment.*—So Shakespeare, "Measure for Measure," act ii., sc. 2:
"If he, which is the top of judgment."

Contented, unless she assure thee so,
Who betwixt truth and mind infuses light:
I know not if thou take me right; I mean
Beatrice. Her thou shalt behold above,[1]
Upon this mountain's crown, fair seat of joy."

Then I: "Sir! let us mend our speed; for now
I tire not as before: and lo! the hill[2]
Stretches its shadow far." He answer'd thus:
"Our progress with this day shall be as much
As we may now dispatch; but otherwise
Than thou supposest is the truth. For there
Thou canst not be, ere thou once more behold
Him back returning, who behind the steep
Is now so hidden, that, as erst, his beam
Thou dost not break. But lo! a spirit there
Stands solitary, and toward us looks:
It will instruct us in the speediest way."

We soon approach'd it. O thou Lombard spirit!
How didst thou stand, in high abstracted mood,
Scarce moving with slow dignity thine eyes.
It spoke not aught, but let us onward pass,
Eyeing us as a lion on his watch.[3]
But Virgil, with entreaty mild, advanced,
Requesting it to show the best ascent.
It answer to his question none return'd;
But of our country and our kind of life
Demanded. When my courteous guide began,
"Mantua," the shadow, in itself absorb'd,[4]
Rose towards us from the place in which it stood,
And cried, "Mantuan! I am thy countryman,
Sordello."[5] Each the other then embraced.

---

[1] *Above.*—See "Purgatory," c. xxx., v. 32.
[2] *The hill.*—It was now past the noon.
[3] *Eyeing us as a lion on his watch.*—"A guisa di leon quando si posa." A line taken by Tasso, "Gierusalemme Liberata," canto x., st. 56.
[4] *The shadow, in itself absorb'd*, I had before translated "the solitary shadow," and have made the alteration in consequence of Monti's just remark on the original, that "tutta in se romita" does not mean "solitary," but "collected, concentrated in itself." See his "Proposta" under "Romito." Vellutello had shown him the way to this interpretation, when he explained the words by "tutta in se raccolta e sola." Petrarch applies the expression to the spirit of Laura, when departing from the body. See his "Triumph of Death," cap. i., v. 152.

[5] *Sordello.*—The history of Sordello's life is wrapped in the obscurity of romance. That he distinguished himself by his skill in Provençal poetry is certain; and many feats of military prowess have been attributed to him. It is probable that he was born towards the end of the twelfth, and died about the middle of the succeeding century. Tiraboschi, who terms him the most illustrious of all the Provençal poets of his age, has taken much pains to sift all the notices he could collect relating to him, and has particularly exposed the fabulous narrative which Platina has introduced on this subject in his history of Mantua. Honourable mention of his name is made by our poet in the treatise "De Vulgari Eloquentia," lib. i., cap. 15, where it is said that, remarkable as he was for

Ah, slavish Italy; thou inn of grief![1]
Vessel without a pilot in loud storm!
Lady no longer of fair provinces,
But brothel-house impure! this gentle spirit,
Even from the pleasant sound of his dear land
Was prompt to greet a fellow-citizen
With such glad cheer: while now thy living ones[2]
In thee abide not without war; and one
Malicious gnaws another; ay, of those
Whom the same wall and the same moat contains.
Seek, wretched one! around thy sea-coasts wide;
Then homeward to thy bosom turn; and mark,
If any part of thee sweet peace enjoy.
What boots it, that thy reins Justinian's hand[3]
Refitted, if thy saddle be unprest?
Nought doth he now but aggravate thy shame.
Ah, people! thou obedient still shouldst live,
And in the saddle let thy Cæsar sit,
If well thou marked'st that which God commands.[4]

Look how that beast to fellness hath relapsed,
From having lost correction of the spur,
Since to the bridle thou hast set thine hand,
O German Albert![5] who abandon'st her
That is grown savage and unmanageable,
When thou shouldst clasp her flanks with forked heels
Just judgment from the stars fall on thy blood;
And be it strange and manifest to all;
Such as may strike thy successor[6] with dread;

eloquence, he deserted the vernacular language of his own country, not only in his poems, but in every other kind of writing. Tiraboschi had at first concluded him to be the same writer whom Dante elsewhere ("De Vulgari Eloquentia," lib. ii., c. 13) calls Gottus Mantuanus, but afterwards gave up that opinion to the authority of the Conte d'Arco and the Abate Bettinelli. By Bastero, in his "Crusca Provenzale," ediz. Roma, 1724, p. 94, amongst Sordello's MS. poems in the Vatican are mentioned "Canzoni, Tenzoni, Cobbole," and various "Serventesi," particularly one in the form of a funeral song on the death of Blancas, in which the poet reprehends all the reigning princes in Christendom. This last was well suited to attract the notice of our author. Mention of Sordello will recur in the notes to the "Paradise," c. ix., ver. 32. Since this note was written, many of Sordello's poems have been brought to light by the industry of M. Reynouard, in his "Choix des Poésies des Troubadours" and his "Lexique Roman."

[1] *Thou inn of grief.*—"S' io son d'ogni dolore ostello e chiave."—*Vita Nuova di Dante*, p. 225.
"Thou most beauteous inn,
Why should hard-favoured grief be lodged in thee?"
Shakespeare, Richard II., act v., sc. 1.
[2] *Thy living ones.*—Compare Milton, "Paradise Lost," b. ii. 496, &c.
[3] *Justinian's hand.*—"What avails it that Justinian delivered thee from the Goths and reformed thy laws, if thou art no longer under the control of his successors in the empire?"
[4] *That which God commands.*—He alludes to the precept, "Render unto Cæsar the things which are Cæsar's."
[5] *O German Albert!*—The Emperor Albert I. succeeded Adolphus in 1298, and was murdered in 1308. See "Paradise," canto xix. 114.
[6] *Thy successor.*—The successor of Albert was Henry of Luxemburgh, by whose interposition in the affairs of Italy our poet hoped to have been reinstated in his native city.

For that thy sire[1] and thou have suffer'd thus,
Through greediness of yonder realms detain'd,
The garden of the empire to run waste
Come, see the Capulets and Montagues,[2]
The Filippeschi and Monaldi,[3] man
Who carest for nought! those sunk in grief, and these
With dire suspicion rack'd. Come, cruel one!
Come, and behold the oppression of the nobles,
And mark their injuries; and thou mayst see
What safety Santafiore can supply.[4]
Come and behold thy Rome,[5] who calls on thee,
Desolate widow, day and night with moans,
"My Cæsar, why dost thou desert my side?"
Come, and behold what love among thy people:
And if no pity touches thee for us,
Come, and blush for thine own report. For me,
If it be lawful, O Almighty Power!
Who wast in earth for our sakes crucified,
Are thy just eyes turn'd elsewhere? or is this
A preparation, in the wondrous depth
Of thy sage counsel made, for some good end,
Entirely from our reach of thought cut off?
So are the Italian cities all o'erthrong'd
With tyrants, and a great Marcellus[6] made
Of every petty factious villager.

My Florence! thou mayst well remain unmoved
At this digression, which affects not thee;
Thanks to thy people, who so wisely speed.

---

[1] *Thy sire.*—The Emperor Rodolph, too intent on increasing his power in Germany to give much of his thoughts to Italy, "the garden of the empire."

[2] *Capulets and Montagues.*—Our ears are so familiarised to the names of these rival houses in the language of Shakespeare, that I have used them instead of the "Montecchi" and "Cappelletti." They were two powerful Ghibelline families of Verona. In some parts of that play in which they form the leading characters, our great dramatic poet seems to have been not a little indebted to the "Hadriana" of Luigi Groto, commonly called "Il cieco d'Adria." See Walker's "Historical Memoir on Italian Tragedy," 4to, 1799, § i., p. 49.

[3] *Filippeschi and Monaldi.*—Two other rival families in Orvieto.

[4] *What safety Santafiore can supply.*—A place between Pisa and Sienna. What he alludes to is so doubtful, that it is not certain whether we should not read "come si cura" ("how Santafiore is governed"). Perhaps the event related in the note to v. 58, canto xi., may be pointed at.

[5] *Come and behold thy Rome.*—Thus in the Latin Epistle to the Cardinals, which has been lately discovered in the Laurentian library, and has every appearance of being Dante's: "Romam urbem, nunc utroque lumine destitutam, nunc Hannibali nedum aliis miserandam, solam sedentem et viduam, prout superius proclamatur, qualis est, pro modulo nostræ imaginis, ante mortales oculos affigatis omnes."—*Opere minori di Dante*, tom. iii., parte ii., p. 270, 12mo, Fir., 1840.

[6] *Marcellus.*— "Un Marcel diventa
Ogni villan che parteggiando viene."

Repeated by Alamanni in his "Coltivazione," lib. i. He probably means the Marcellus who opposed Julius Cæsar.

Many have justice in their heart, that long
Waiteth for counsel to direct the bow,
Or ere it dart unto its aim: but thine
Have it on their lip's edge. Many refuse[1]
To bear the common burdens: readier thine
Answer uncall'd, and cry, "Behold I stoop!"

Make thyself glad, for thou hast reason now,
Thou wealthy! thou at peace! thou wisdom-fraught!
Facts best will witness if I speak the truth.
Athens and Lacedæmon, who of old
Enacted laws, for civil arts renown'd,
Made little progress in improving life
Towards thee, who usest such nice subtlety,
That to the middle of November scarce
Reaches the thread thou in October weavest.
How many times within thy memory,
Customs, and laws, and coins, and offices
Have been by thee renew'd, and people changed.

If thou remember'st well and canst see clear,
Thou wilt perceive thyself like a sick wretch,[2]
Who finds no rest upon her down, but oft
Shifting her side, short respite seeks from pain.

---

[1] *Many refuse.*—He appears to have been of Plato's mind, that in a commonwealth of worthy men, place and power would be as much declined as they are now sought after and coveted: κινδυνεύει πόλις ἀνδρῶν ἀγαθῶν εἰ γένοιτο, περιμαχητὸν ἂν εἶναι τὸ μὴ ἄρχειν ὥσπερ νῦν τὸ ἄρχειν. Πολιτ. Lib. A.

[2] *A sick wretch.*—Imitated by the Cardinal de Polignac:

"Ceu lectum peragrat membris languentibus æger,
In latus alterne lævum dextrumque recumbens:
Nec juvat: inde oculos tollit resupinus in altum:
Nusquam inventa quies; semper quæsita: quod illi
Primum in deliciis fuerat, mox torquet et angit:
Nec morbum sanat, nec fallit tædia morbi."
Anti-Lucretius, lib. i. 1052.

CANTO VII.

ARGUMENT.

The approach of night hindering further ascent, Sordello conducts our Poet apart to an eminence, from whence they behold a pleasant recess, in form of a flowery valley, scooped out of the mountain; where are many famous spirits, and among them the Emperor Rodolph, Ottocar, King of Bohemia, Philip III. of France, Henry of Navarre, Peter III. of Arragon, Charles I. of Naples, Henry III. of England, and William, Marquis of Montferrat.

AFTER their courteous greetings joyfully
Seven times exchanged, Sordello backward drew
Exclaiming, "Who are ye?"—"Before this mount
By spirits worthy of ascent to God
Was sought, my bones had by Octavius' care
Been buried. I am Virgil; for no sin
Deprived of heaven, except for lack of faith."
So answer'd him in few my gentle guide.
  As one, who aught before him suddenly
Beholding, whence his wonder riseth, cries,
"It is, yet is not," wavering in belief;
Such he appear'd; then downward bent his eyes,
And, drawing near with reverential step,
Caught him, where one of mean estate might clasp
His lord.[1] "Glory of Latium!" he exclaim'd,
"In whom our tongue its utmost power display'd;
Boast of my honour'd birth-place! what desert[2]
Of mine, what favour, rather, undeserved,
Shows thee to me? If I to hear that voice
Am worthy, say if from below thou comest,
And from what cloister's pale."—"Through every orb
Of that sad region," he replied, "thus far

---

[1] *Where one of mean estate might clasp his lord.*—
So Ariosto, "Orlando Furioso," c. xxiv., st. 19:
"E l'abbracciaro, ove il maggior s'abbraccia,
Col capo nudo e col ginocchio chino."

[2] *What desert.*—So Frezzi:
"Qual grazia, o qual destin m' ha fatto degno
Che io ti veggia."
Il Quadriregio, lib. iv., cap. 9.

"Through every orb
Of that sad region," he replied, "thus far
Am I arrived."

Canto VII., lines 21—23.

Am I arrived, by heavenly influence led:
And with such aid I come. Not for my doing,[1]
But for not doing, have I lost the sight
Of that high Sun, whom thou desirest, and who
By me too late was known. There is a place[2]
There underneath, not made by torments sad,
But by dun shades alone; where mourning's voice
Sounds not of anguish sharp, but breathes in sighs.
There I with little innocents abide,
Who by death's fangs were bitten, ere exempt
From human taint. There I with those abide,
Who the three holy virtues[3] put not on,
But understood the rest,[4] and without blame
Follow'd them all. But, if thou know'st, and canst,
Direct us how we soonest may arrive,
Where Purgatory its true beginning takes."

He answer'd thus: "We have no certain place
Assign'd us: upwards I may go, or round.
Far as I can, I join thee for thy guide.
But thou beholdest now how day declines;
And upwards to proceed by night, our power
Excels: therefore it may be well to choose
A place of pleasant sojourn. To the right
Some spirits sit apart retired. If thou
Consentest, I to these will lead thy steps:
And thou wilt know them, not without delight."

"How chances this?" was answer'd: "whoso wish'd
To ascend by night, would he be thence debarr'd
By other, or through his own weakness fail?"

The good Sordello then along the ground
Trailing his finger, spoke: "Only this line[5]
Thou shalt not overpass, soon as the sun
Hath disappear'd; not that aught else impedes
Thy going upwards, save the shades of night.
These, with the want of power, perplex the will.
With them thou haply mightst return beneath,

---

[1] *Not for my doing.*—I am indebted to the kindness of Mr. Lyell for pointing out to me that three lines of the original were here omitted in the former editions of this translation.

[2] *There is a place.*—Limbo. See "Hell," canto iv. 24.

[3] *The three holy virtues.*—Faith, Hope, and Charity.

[4] *The rest.*—Prudence, Justice, Fortitude, and Temperance.

[5] *Only this line.*—"Walk while ye have the light, lest darkness come upon you: for he that walketh in darkness knoweth not whither he goeth."—*John* xii. 35.

Or to and fro around the mountain's side
Wander, while day is in the horizon shut."

My master straight, as wondering at his speech,
Exclaim'd: "Then lead us quickly, where thou sayst
That, while we stay, we may enjoy delight."

A little space we were removed from thence,
When I perceived the mountain hollow'd out,
Even as large valleys[1] hollow'd out on earth.

"That way," the escorting spirit cried, "we go,
Where in a bosom the high bank recedes:
And thou await renewal of the day."

Betwixt the steep and plain, a crooked path
Led us traverse into the ridge's side,
Where more than half the sloping edge expires.
Refulgent gold, and silver thrice refined,
And scarlet grain and ceruse, Indian wood[2]
Of lucid dye serene, fresh emeralds[3]
But newly broken, by the herbs and flowers
Placed in that fair recess, in colour all
Had been surpass'd, as great surpasses less.
Nor nature only there lavish'd her hues,
But of the sweetness[4] of a thousand smells
A rare and undistinguish'd fragrance made.

"Salve Regina,"[5] on the grass and flowers,
Here chanting, I beheld those spirits sit,
Who not beyond the valley could be seen.

"Before the westering sun sink to his bed,"
Began the Mantuan, who our steps had turn'd,
"'Mid those, desire not that I lead ye on.
For from this eminence ye shall discern

---

[1] *As large valleys.*—"Viatores enim per viam rectam dum ambulant, campum juxta viam cernentes spatiosum et pulchrum, oblitique itineris, dicunt intra se, Iter per campum istum faciamus," &c.—*Alberici Visio*, § 28.

[2] *Indian wood.*—
"Indico legno lucido e sereno."
It is a little uncertain what is meant by this. Indigo, although it is extracted from a herb, seems the most likely. Monti, in his "Proposta," maintains it to be ebony.

[3] *Fresh emeralds.*—
"Under foot the violet,
Crocus, and hyacinth with rich inlay
Broider'd the ground, more colour'd than with stone
Of costliest emblem."
Milton, Paradise Lost, b. iv. 703.

"Zaffir, rubini, oro, topazj, e perle,
E diamanti, e crisoliti e giacinti
Potriano i fiori assimigliar, che per le
Liete piagge v'avea l'aura dipinti ;
Si verdi l'erbe, che potendo averle
Qua giù ne foran gli smeraldi vinti."
Ariosto, Orlando Furioso, canto xxxiv., st. 49.

[4] *The sweetness.*—
"E quella ai fiori, ai pomi, e alla verzura
Gli odor diversi depredando giva,
E di tutti faceva una mistura,
Che di soavità l'alma notriva."—*Ibid.,* st. 51.

[5] *Salve Regina.*—The beginning of a prayer to the Virgin. It is sufficient here to observe, that in similar instances I shall either preserve the original Latin words or translate them, as it may seem best to suit the purpose of the verse.

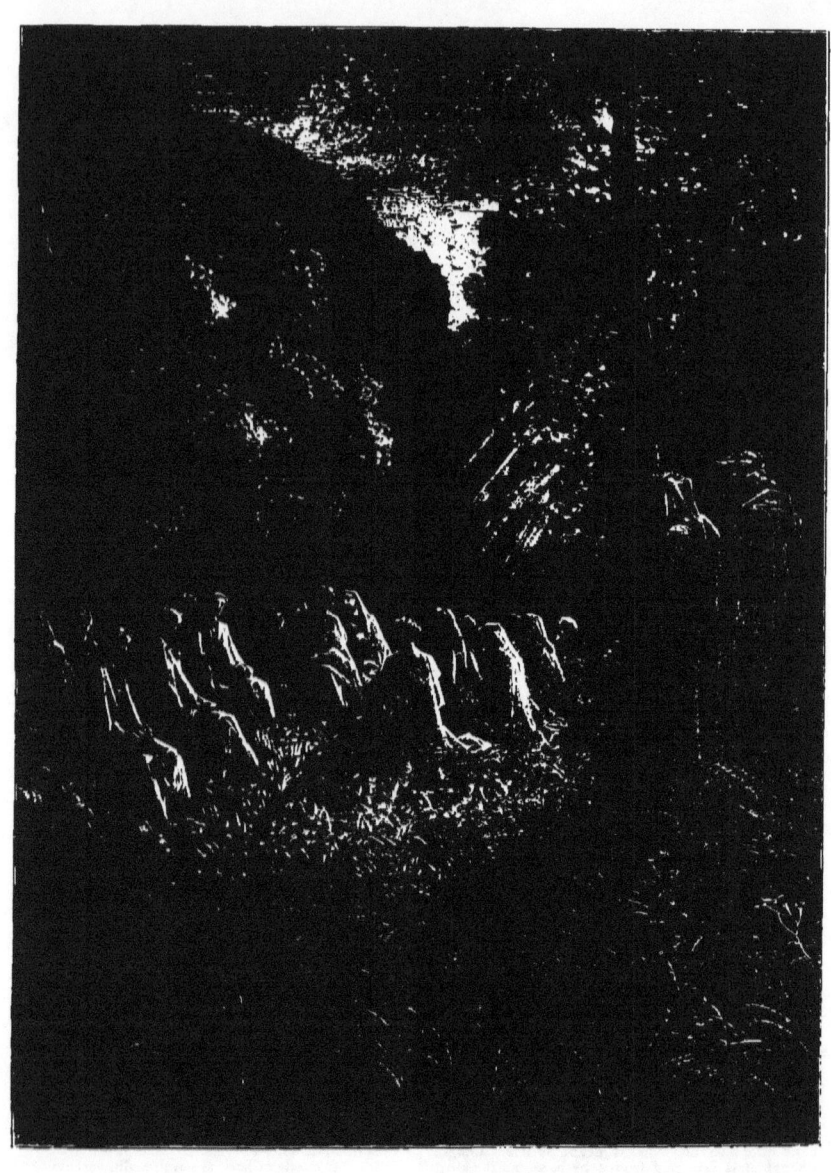

"Salve Regina," on the grass and flowers,
Here chanting, I beheld those spirits sit,
Who not beyond the valley could be seen.
Canto VII., lines 82—84.

Better the acts and visages of all,
Than, in the nether vale, among them mix'd.
He, who sits high above the rest, and seems
To have neglected that he should have done,
And to the others' song moves not his lip,
The Emperor Rodolph[1] call, who might have heal'd
The wounds whereof fair Italy hath died,
So that by others she revives but slowly.
He, who with kindly visage comforts him,
Sway'd in that country,[2] where the water springs,
That Moldaw's river to the Elbe, and Elbe
Rolls to the ocean: Ottocar[3] his name:
Who in his swaddling clothes was of more worth
Than Winceslaus his son, a bearded man,
Pamper'd with rank luxuriousness and ease.
And that one with the nose deprest,[4] who close
In counsel seems with him of gentle look,[5]
Flying expired, withering the lily's flower.
Look there, how he doth knock against his breast.
The other ye behold, who for his cheek
Makes of one hand a couch, with frequent sighs.
They are the father and the father-in-law
Of Gallia's bane:[6] his vicious life they know
And foul; thence comes the grief that rends them thus.

"He, so robust of limb,[7] who measure keeps
In song with him of feature prominent,[8]

---

[1] *The Emperor Rodolph.*—See the last canto, v. 104. He died in 1291.
[2] *That country.*—Bohemia.
[3] *Ottocar.*—King of Bohemia, who was killed in the battle of Marchfield, fought with Rodolph, August 26, 1278. Winceslaus II., his son, who succeeded him in the kingdom of Bohemia, died in 1305. The latter is again taxed with luxury in the "Paradise," xix. 123.
[4] *That one with the nose deprest.*—Philip III. of France, father of Philip IV. He died in 1285, at Perpignan, in his retreat from Arragon.
[5] *Him of gentle look.*—Henry of Navarre, father of Jane, married to Philip IV. of France, whom Dante calls "mal di Francia"—"Gallia's bane."
[6] *Gallia's bane.*—G. Villani, lib. vii., cap. cxlvi., speaks with equal resentment of Philip IV.: "In 1291, on the night of the calends of May, Philip le Bel, King of France, by advice of Biccio and Musciatto Franzesi, ordered all the Italians, who were in his country and realm, to be seized, under pretence of seizing the money-lenders, but thus he caused the good merchants also to be seized and ransomed, for which he was much blamed and held in great abhorrence; and from thenceforth the realm of France fell evermore into degradation and decline. And it is observable, that between the taking of Acre and this seizure in France, the merchants of Florence received great damage and ruin of their property."
[7] *He, so robust of limb.*—Peter III., called the Great, King of Arragon, who died in 1285, leaving four sons, Alonzo, James, Frederick, and Peter. The two former succeeded him in the kingdom of Arragon, and Frederick in that of Sicily. See G. Villani, lib. vii., cap. cii.; and Mariana, lib. xiv., cap. 9. He is enumerated among the Provençal poets by Millot, "Histoire Littéraire des Troubadours," tom. iii. p. 150.
[8] *Him of feature prominent.*—"Dal maschio naso" ("with the masculine nose"). Charles I., King of Naples, Count of Anjou, and brother of St. Louis. He died in 1284. The annalist of Florence remarks that "there had been no sovereign of the house of France since the time of Charlemagne, by whom Charles was surpassed either in military renown and prowess, or in the loftiness of his understanding" (G. Villani, lib. vii., cap. xciv.). We shall, however, find many of his actions severely reprobated in the twentieth canto.

With every virtue bore his girdle braced.
And if that stripling,[1] who behind him sits,
King after him had lived, his virtue then
From vessel to like vessel had been pour'd;
Which may not of the other heirs be said.
By James and Frederick[2] his realms are held;
Neither the better heritage obtains.
Rarely[3] into the branches of the tree
Doth human worth mount up: and so ordains
He who bestows it, that as his free gift
It may be call'd. To Charles[4] my words apply
No less than to his brother in the song;
Which Pouille and Provence now with grief confess.
So much that plant degenerates from its seed,
As, more than Beatrix and Margaret,
Costanza[5] still boasts of her valorous spouse.

"Behold the king of simple life and plain,
Harry of England[6] sitting there alone:
He through his branches better issue[7] spreads.

"That one, who, on the ground, beneath the rest,
Sits lowest, yet his gaze directs aloft,
Is William, that brave Marquis,[8] for whose cause,
The deed of Alexandria and his war
Makes Montferrat and Canavese weep."

---

[1] *That stripling.*—Either (as the old commentators suppose) Alonzo III., King of Arragon, the eldest son of Peter III., who died in 1291, at the age of twenty-seven; or, according to Venturi, Peter, the youngest son. The former was a young prince of virtue, sufficient to have justified the eulogium and the hopes of Dante. See Mariana, lib. xiv., cap. 14.

[2] *By James and Frederick.*—See note to canto iii.112.

[3] *Rarely.*—
"Full well can the wise poet of Florence,
That hight Dantes, speake in this sentence:
Lo! in such manner rime is Dantes tale.
Full selde upriseth by his branches smale
Prowesse of man, for God of his goodnesse
Woll that we claim of him our gentlenesse:
For of our elders may we nothing claime
But temporal thing, that men may hurt and maime."
Chaucer, *Wife of Bathe's Tale.*
Compare Homer, "Odyssey," b. ii., v. 276; Pindar, "Nem.," xi. 48; and Euripides, "Electra," 369.

[4] *To Charles.*—"Al Nasuto"—"Charles II., King of Naples, is no less inferior to his father Charles I. than James and Frederick to theirs, Peter III." See canto xx. 78, and "Paradise," canto xix. 125.

[5] *Costanza.*—Widow of Peter III. She has been already mentioned in the third canto, v. 112. By Beatrix and Margaret are probably meant two of the daughters of Raymond Berenger, Count of Provence; the latter married to St. Louis of France, the former to his brother Charles of Anjou, King of Naples. See "Paradise," canto vi. 135. Dante therefore considers Peter as the most illustrious of the three monarchs.

[6] *Harry of England.*—Henry III. The contemporary annalist speaks of this king in similar terms. G. Villani, lib. v., cap. iv.: "From Richard was born Henry, who reigned after him, who was a plain man and of good faith, but of little courage." Fazio degli Uberti, "Dittamondo," l. iv., cap. xxv., where he gives the characters of our Norman kings, speaks less respectfully of Henry. Capitoli xxiii.—xxv., lib. iv. of this neglected poem appear to deserve the notice of our antiquarians.

[7] *Better issue.*—Edward I., of whose glory our poet was perhaps a witness, in his visit to England: "From the said Henry was born the good king Edward, who reigns in our times, who has done great things, whereof we shall make mention in due place."—*G. Villani*, ibid.

[8] *William, that brave Marquis.*—William, Marquis of Montferrat, was treacherously seized by his own subjects, at Alessandria in Lombardy, A.D. 1290, and ended his life in prison. See G. Villani, lib. vii., cap. cxxxv. A war ensued between the people of Alessandria and those of Montferrat and the Canavese, now a part of Piedmont.

CANTO VIII.

ARGUMENT.

Two angels, with flaming swords broken at the points, descend to keep watch over the valley, into which Virgil and Dante entering by desire of Sordello, our Poet meets with joy the spirit of Nino, the judge of Gallura, one who was well known to him. Meantime three exceedingly bright stars appear near the pole, and a serpent creeps subtly into the valley, but flees at hearing the approach of those angelic guards. Lastly, Conrad Malaspina predicts to our Poet his future banishment.

NOW was the hour that wakens fond desire
In men at sea, and melts their thoughtful heart
Who in the morn have bid sweet friends farewell,
And pilgrim newly on his road with love
Thrills, if he hear the vesper bell from far[1]
That seems to mourn for the expiring day:[2]
When I, no longer taking heed to hear,
Began, with wonder, from those spirits to mark
One risen from its seat, which with its hand
Audience implored. Both palms it join'd and raised,
Fixing its stedfast gaze toward the east,
As telling God, "I care for nought beside."
"Te Lucis Ante,"[3] so devoutly then
Came from its lip, and in so soft a strain,
That all my sense[4] in ravishment was lost.
And the rest after, softly and devout,
Follow'd through all the hymn, with upward gaze
Directed to the bright supernal wheels.
Here, reader![5] for the truth make thine eyes keen:

---

[1] *Hear the vesper bell from far.*—.
"I hear the far-off curfeu sound."
                    Milton's Penseroso.
[2] *That seems to mourn for the expiring day.*—
"The curfew tolls the knell of parting day."
                    Gray's Elegy.
"Giorno—che si muore"
is from Statius: "Jam moriente die."
                    Sylvæ, l. iv. 6. 3.
[3] *Te Lucis Ante.*—"Te lucis ante terminum," says Lombardi, is the first verse of the hymn sung by the church in the last part of the sacred office termed compieta, a service which our Chaucer calls "complin."
[4] *All my sense.*—
"Fece me a me uscir di mente.
Me surpuerat mihi."
                    Horat., Carm., lib. iv., od. 13.
[5] *Here, reader!*—Lombardi's explanation of this passage, by which the commentators have been much perplexed, though it may be thought rather too subtle and fine-spun, like the veil itself spoken of in the text, cannot be denied the praise of extraordinary ingenuity. "This admonition of the poet to his reader," he observes, "seems to relate to what has been before said,

For of so subtle texture is this veil,
That thou with ease mayst pass it through unmark'd.
      I saw that gentle band silently next
Look up, as if in expectation held,
Pale and in lowly guise; and, from on high,
I saw, forth issuing descend beneath,
Two angels, with two flame-illumined swords,
Broken and mutilated of their points.
Green as the tender leaves but newly born,
Their vesture was, the which, by wings as green
Beaten, they drew behind them, fann'd in air.
A little over us one took his stand;
The other lighted on the opposing hill;
So that the troop were in the midst contain'd.
      Well I descried the whiteness on their heads;
But in their visages the dazzled eye
Was lost, as faculty[1] that by too much
Is overpower'd. "From Mary's bosom both
Are come," exclaim'd Sordello, "as a guard
Over the vale, 'gainst him, who hither tends,
The serpent." Whence, not knowing by which path
He came, I turn'd me round; and closely press'd,
All frozen, to my leader's trusted side.
      Sordello paused not: "To the valley now
(For it is time) let us descend; and hold
Converse with those great shadows: haply much
Their sight may please ye." Only three steps down
Methinks I measured, ere I was beneath,
And noted one who look'd as with desire
To know me. Time was now that air grew dim;
Yet not so dim, that, 'twixt his eyes and mine,

---

that these spirits sung the whole of the hymn 'Te lucis ante terminum' throughout, even that second strophe of it:—
    'Procul recedant somnia,
      Et noctium phantasmata,
      Hostemque nostrum comprime,
      Ne polluantur corpora;'
and he must imply that these souls, being incorporeal, did not offer up this petition on their own account. but on ours, who are yet in this world, as he afterwards makes those other spirits, who repeat the 'Pater Noster,' expressly declare, when after that prayer they add—
    'This last petition, dearest Lord! is made
      Not for ourselves,' &c.   Canto xi.

As, therefore, if we look through a very fine veil, the sight easily passes on, without perceiving it, to objects that lie on the other side, so here the poet fears that our mind's eye may insensibly pass on to contemplate these spirits, as if they were praying for the relief of their own wants; without discovering the veil of our wants, with which they invest themselves in the act of offering up this prayer."

[1] *As faculty.*—
  "My earthly by his heavenly overpower'd
     *   *   *   *   *   *   *
  As with an object, that excels the sense,
  Dazzled and spent."
        Milton, Paradise Lost, b. viii. 457.

It clear'd not up what was conceal'd before.
Mutually towards each other we advanced.
Nino, thou courteous judge![1] what joy I felt,
When I perceived thou wert not with the bad.
  No salutation kind on either part
Was left unsaid. He then inquired: "How long,
Since thou arrived'st at the mountain's foot,
Over the distant waves?"—"Oh!" answer'd I,
"Through the sad seats of woe this morn I came;
And still in my first life, thus journeying on,
The other strive to gain." Soon as they heard
My words, he and Sordello backward drew,
As suddenly amazed. To Virgil one,
The other to a spirit turn'd, who near
Was seated, crying: "Conrad![2] up with speed:
Come, see what of his grace high God hath will'd."
Then turning round to me: "By that rare mark
Of honour, which thou owest to him, who hides
So deeply his first cause it hath no ford;
When thou shalt be beyond the vast of waves,
Tell my Giovanna,[3] that for me she call
There, where reply to innocence is made.
Her mother,[4] I believe, loves me no more;
Since she has changed the white and wimpled folds,[5]
Which she is doom'd once more with grief to wish.
By her it easily may be perceived,
How long in woman lasts the flame of love,
If sight and touch do not relume it oft.
For her so fair a burial will not make
The viper,[6] which calls Milan to the field,

---

[1] *Nino, thou courteous judge.*—Nino di Gallura de' Visconti, nephew to Count Ugolino de' Gherardeschi, and betrayed by him. See notes to "Hell," canto xxxiii.

[2] *Conrad.*—Currado, father to Marcello Malaspina.

[3] *My Giovanna.*—The daughter of Nino, and wife of Riccardo da Camino of Trevigi, concerning whom see "Paradise," c. ix. 48.

[4] *Her mother.*—Beatrice, Marchioness of Este, wife of Nino, and after his death married to Galeazzo de' Visconti of Milan. It is remarked by Lombardi that the time which Dante assigns to this journey, and consequently to this colloquy with Nino Visconti—the beginning, that is, of April—is prior to the time which Bernardino Corio, in his history of Milan, part the second, fixes for the nuptials of Beatrice with Galeazzo; for he records her having been betrothed to that prince after the May of this year (1300), and her having been solemnly espoused at Modena on the 29th of June. Besides, however, the greater credit due to Dante, on account of his having lived at the time when these events happened, another circumstance in his favour is the discrepancy remarked by Giovambatista Giraldi ("Commentar. delle cose di Ferrara") in those writers by whom the history of Beatrice's life has been recorded. Nothing can set the general accuracy of our poet as to historical facts in a stronger point of view, than the difficulty there is in convicting him of even so slight a deviation from it as is here suspected.

[5] *The white and wimpled folds.*—The weeds of widowhood.

[6] *The viper.*—The arms of Galeazzo and the ensign of the Milanese

As had been made by shrill Gallura's bird."[1]

He spoke, and in his visage took the stamp
Of that right zeal, which with due temperature
Glows in the bosom. My insatiate eyes
Meanwhile to heaven had travel'd, even there
Where the bright stars are slowest, as a wheel
Nearest the axle; when my guide inquired:
"What there aloft, my son, has caught thy gaze?"

I answered: "The three torches,[2] with which here
The pole is all on fire." He then to me:
"The four resplendent stars, thou saw'st this morn,
Are there beneath; and these, risen in their stead.'

While yet he spoke, Sordello to himself
Drew him, and cried: "Lo there our enemy!"
And with his hand pointed that way to look.

Along the side, where barrier none arose
Around the little vale, a serpent lay,
Such haply as gave Eve the bitter food.[3]
Between the grass and flowers, the evil snake
Came on, reverting oft his lifted head;
And, as a beast that smooths its polish'd coat,
Licking his back. I saw not, nor can tell,
How those celestial falcons from their seat
Moved, but in motion each one well descried.
Hearing the air cut by their verdant plumes,
The serpent fled; and, to their stations, back
The angels up return'd with equal flight.

The spirit, (who to Nino, when he call'd,
Had come,) from viewing me with fixed ken,
Through all that conflict, loosen'd not his sight.

"So may the lamp, which leads thee up on high,[4]
Find, in thy free resolve, of wax so much,
As may suffice thee to the enamel'd height,"

---

[1] *Shrill Gallura's bird.*—The cock was the ensign of Gallura, Nino's province in Sardinia. "Hell," xxii. 80, and notes. It is not known whether Beatrice had any further cause to regret her nuptials with Galeazzo than a certain shame which appears, however unreasonably, to have attached to a second marriage.

[2] *The three torches.*—The three evangelical virtues, Faith, Hope, and Charity. These are supposed to rise in the evening, in order to denote their belonging to the contemplative, as the four others, which are made to rise in the morning, were probably intended to signify that the cardinal virtues belong to the active life: or perhaps it may mark the succession, in order of time, of the Gospel to the heathen system of morality.

[3] *Such haply as gave Eve the bitter food.*—Compare Milton's description of that serpent in the ninth book of the "Paradise Lost."

[4] *May the lamp, which leads thee up on high.*—"May the divine grace find so hearty a co-operation on the part of thy own will, as shall enable thee to ascend to the terrestrial paradise, which is on the top of this mountain."

It thus began: "If any certain news
Of Valdimagra[1] and the neighbour part
Thou know'st, tell me, who once was mighty there.
They call'd me Conrad Malaspina; not
That old one;[2] but from him I sprang. The love
I bore my people is now here refined."

"In your domains," I answer'd, "ne'er was I.
But, through all Europe, where do those men dwell,
To whom their glory is not manifest?
The fame, that honours your illustrious house,
Proclaims the nobles, and proclaims the land;
So that he knows it, who was never there.
I swear to you, so may my upward route
Prosper, your honour'd nation not impairs
The value of her coffer and her sword.
Nature and use give her such privilege,
That while the world is twisted from his course
By a bad head, she only walks aright,
And has the evil way in scorn." He then:
"Now pass thee on: seven times the tired sun
Revisits not the couch,[3] which with four feet
The forked Aries covers, ere that kind
Opinion shall be nail'd into thy brain
With stronger nails than others' speech can drive;
If the sure course of judgment be not stay'd."

---

[1] *Valdimagra.*—See "Hell," canto xxiv. 144, and notes.
[2] *That old one.*—An ancestor of Conrad Malaspina, who was also of that name.
[3] *Seven times the tired sun revisits not the couch.*—"The sun shall not enter into the constellation of Aries seven times more, before thou shalt have still better cause for the good opinion thou expressest of Valdimagra, in the kind reception thou shalt there meet with." Dante was hospitably received by the Marchese Marcello, or Moroello Malaspina, during his banishment, A.D. 1307.

CANTO IX.

ARGUMENT.

Dante is carried up the mountain, asleep and dreaming, by Lucia; and, on wakening, finds himself, two hours after sunrise, with Virgil, near the gate of purgatory, through which they are admitted by the angel deputed by St. Peter to keep it.

NOW the fair consort of Tithonus old,[1]
   Arisen from her mate's beloved arms,
Look'd palely o'er the eastern cliff; her brow,
Lucent with jewels, glitter'd, set in sign
Of that chill animal,[2] who with his train
Smites fearful nations: and where then we were,
Two steps of her ascent the night had past;
And now the third was closing up its wing,[3]
When I, who had so much of Adam with me,
Sank down upon the grass, o'ercome with sleep,
There where all five[4] were seated. In that hour,
When near the dawn the swallow her sad lay,
Remembering haply ancient grief,[5] renews;
And when our minds, more wanderers from the flesh,
And less by thought restrain'd, are, as 't were, full
Of holy divination in their dreams;
Then, in a vision, did I seem to view

---

[1] *Now the fair consort of Tithonus old.*—"La concubina di Titone antico." So Tassoni, "Secchia Rapita," c. viii., st. 15: "La puttanella del canuto amante." Venturi, after some of the old commentators, interprets this to mean an Aurora, or dawn of the moon; but this seems highly improbable. From what follows it may be conjectured that our poet intends us to understand that it was now near the break of day.

[2] *Of that chill animal.*—The scorpion.

[3] *The third was closing up its wing.*—The night being divided into four watches, I think he may mean that the third was past, and the fourth and last was begun, so that there might be some faint glimmering of morning twilight; and not merely, as Lombardi supposes, that the third watch was drawing towards its close, which would still leave an insurmountable difficulty in the first verse. At the beginning of canto xv our poet makes the evening commence three hours before sunset, and he may now consider the dawn as beginning at the same distance from sunrise. Those who would have the dawn, spoken of in the first verse of the present canto, to signify the rising of the moon, construe the "two steps of her ascent which the night had past" into as many hours, and not watches, so as to make it now about the third hour of the night. The old Latin annotator on the Monte Casino MS. alone, as far as I know, supposing the division made by St. Isidore ("Orig.," lib. 5) of the night into seven parts to be adopted by our poet, concludes that it was the third of these; and he too, therefore, is for the lunar dawn. Rosa Morando ingenuously confesses that to him the whole passage is "non esplicabile o almeno difficillimo," inexplicable, or, at best, extremely difficult.

[4] *All five.*—Virgil, Dante, Sordello, Nino, and Currado Malaspina.

[5] *Remembering haply ancient grief.*—Progne having been changed into a swallow after the outrage done her by Tereus. See Ovid, "Metamorphoses," lib. vi.

Now the fair consort of Tithonus old,
Arisen from her mate's beloved arms,
Look'd palely o'er the eastern cliff.
Canto IX., lines 1—3.

A golden-feather'd eagle[1] in the sky,
With open wings, and hovering for descent;
And I was in that place, methought, from whence
Young Ganymede, from his associates 'reft,
Was snatch'd aloft to the high consistory.
"Perhaps," thought I within me, "here alone
He strikes his quarry, and elsewhere disdains
To pounce upon the prey." Therewith, it seem'd,
A little wheeling in his aëry tour,
Terrible as the lightning, rush'd he down,
And snatch'd me upward even to the fire.
There both, I thought, the eagle and myself
Did burn; and so intense the imagined flames,
That needs my sleep was broken off. As erst
Achilles shook himself, and round he roll'd
His waken'd eyeballs, wondering where he was,
Whenas his mother had from Chiron fled
To Scyros, with him sleeping in her arms;
(There[2] whence the Greeks did after sunder him;)
E'en thus I shook me, soon as from my face
The slumber parted, turning deadly pale,
Like one ice-struck with dread. Sole at my side
My comfort stood: and the bright sun was now
More than two hours aloft: and to the sea
My looks were turn'd. "Fear not," my master cried,
"Assured we are at happy point. Thy strength
Shrink not, but rise dilated. Thou art come
To Purgatory now. Lo! there the cliff
That circling bounds it. Lo! the entrance there,
Where it doth seem disparted. Ere the dawn

---

[1] *A golden-feather'd eagle.*—So Chaucer, in the "House of Fame," at the conclusion of the first book and beginning of the second, represents himself carried up by the "grim pawes" of a golden eagle. Much of his description is closely imitated from Dante:—

"Methought I saw an eagle sore.
* * * * *
It was of golde and shone so bright,
That never sawe men soche a sight."
The House of Fame, b. i.

"This eagle, of which I have you tolde
That with fethirs shone al of golde,
Whiche that so hie gan to sore,
I gan beholdin more and more
To seen her beautee and the wonder,

But never was that dente of thonder,
Ne that thinge that men callin foudre,
That smite sometime a toure to poudre.
And in his swifte comminge brend,
That so swithe gan downwarde discende
As this foule whan that it behelde,
That I a roume was in the felde,
And with his grim pawes stronge,
Within his sharpe nailis longe,
Me fleyng at a swappe he hent," &c.
Ibid., b. ii.

"Avis candida columbæ similis adveniens . . . . per comam capitis suo me ore apprehendens ferre sublimem cepit."—*Alberici Visio*, § 1.

[2] *There.*—Mr. Darley has noted the omission of this line in the preceding editions.

Usher'd the day-light, when thy wearied soul
Slept in thee, o'er the flowery vale beneath
A lady came, and thus bespake me : ' I
Am Lucia.¹ Suffer me to take this man,
Who slumbers. Easier so his way shall speed.'
Sordello and the other gentle shapes
Tarrying, she bare thee up : and, as day shone,
This summit reach'd : and I pursued her steps.
Here did she place thee. First, her lovely eyes
That open entrance show'd me ; then at once
She vanish'd with thy sleep." Like one, whose doubts
Are chased by certainty, and terror turn'd
To comfort on discovery of the truth,
Such was the change in me : and as my guide
Beheld me fearless, up along the cliff
He moved, and I behind him, towards the height.

    Reader ! thou markest how my theme doth rise ;
Nor wonder therefore, if more artfully
I prop the structure. Nearer now we drew,
Arrived whence, in that part, where first a breach
As of a wall appear'd, I could descry
A portal, and three steps beneath, that led
For inlet there, of different colour each ;
And one who watch'd, but spake not yet a word.
As more and more mine eye did stretch its view,
I mark'd him seated on the highest step,
In visage such, as past my power to bear.
Grasp'd in his hand, a naked sword glanced back
The rays so towards me, that I oft in vain
My sight directed. " Speak, from whence ye stand ; "
He cried : " What would ye ? Where is your escort ?
Take heed your coming upward harm ye not."

    " A heavenly dame, not skilless of these things,"
Replied the instructor, " told us, even now,
' Pass that way : here the gate is.' "—" And may she,
Befriending, prosper your ascent," resumed
The courteous keeper of the gate : " Come then
Before our steps." We straightway thither came.

---

¹ *Lucia.*—See " Hell," c. ii. 97 ; and " Paradise," c. xxxii. 123.

There both, I thought, the eagle and myself
Did burn; and so intense the imagined flames,
That needs my sleep was broken off.
Canto IX., lines 29—31.

The lowest stair[1] was marble white, so smooth
And polish'd, that therein my mirror'd form
Distinct I saw. The next of hue more dark
Than sablest grain, a rough and singed block,
Crack'd lengthwise and across. The third, that lay
Massy above, seem'd porphyry, that flamed
Red as the life-blood spouting from a vein.
On this God's angel either foot sustain'd,
Upon the threshold seated, which appear'd
A rock of diamond. Up the trinal steps
My leader cheerly drew me. "Ask," said he,
"With humble heart, that he unbar the bolt."
    Piously at his holy feet devolved
I cast me, praying him for pity's sake
That he would open to me; but first fell
Thrice on my bosom prostrate. Seven times[2]
The letter, that denotes the inward stain,
He, on my forehead, with the blunted point
Of his drawn sword, inscribed. And "Look," he cried,
"When enter'd, that thou wash these scars away."
    Ashes, or earth ta'en dry out of the ground,
Were of one colour with the robe he wore.
From underneath that vestment forth he drew
Two keys,[3] of metal twain: the one was gold,
Its fellow silver. With the pallid first,
And next the burnish'd, he so ply'd the gate,
As to content me well. "Whenever one
Faileth of these, that in the key-hole straight
It turn not, to this alley then expect
Access in vain." Such were the words he spake.
"One is more precious:[4] but the other needs
Skill and sagacity, large share of each,

---

[1] *The lowest stair.*—By the white step is meant the distinctness with which the conscience of the penitent reflects his offences; by the burnt and cracked one, his contrition on their account; and by that of porphyry, the fervour with which he resolves on the future pursuit of piety and virtue. Hence, no doubt, Milton describing "the gate of heaven:"

    "Each stair mysteriously was meant."
              Paradise Lost, b. iii. 516.

[2] *Seven times.*—Seven P's, to denote the seven sins (Peccata) of which he was to be cleansed in his passage through Purgatory.

[3] *Two keys.*—Lombardi remarks that painters have usually drawn St. Peter with two keys, the one of gold and the other of silver; but that Niccolo Alemanni, in his "Dissertation de Parietinis Lateranensibus," produces instances of his being represented with one key, and with three. We have here, however, not St. Peter, but an angel deputed by him.

[4] *One is more precious.*—The golden key denotes the divine authority by which the priest absolves the sinners; the silver expresses the learning and judgment requisite for the due discharge of that office.

Ere its good task to disengage the knot
Be worthily perform'd. From Peter these
I hold, of him instructed that I err
Rather in opening, than in keeping fast;
So but the suppliant at my feet implore."

Then of that hallow'd gate he thrust the door,
Exclaiming, "Enter, but this warning hear:
He forth again departs who looks behind."

As in the hinges of that sacred ward
The swivels turn'd, sonorous metal strong,
Harsh was the grating;[1] nor so surlily
Roar'd the Tarpeian,[2] when by force bereft
Of good Metellus, thenceforth from his loss
To leanness doom'd. Attentively I turn'd,
Listening the thunder that first issued forth;
And "We praise thee, O God," methought I heard,
In accents blended with sweet melody.
The strains came o'er mine ear, e'en as the sound
Of choral voices, that in solemn chant
With organ[3] mingle, and, now high and clear
Come swelling, now float indistinct away.

---

[1] *Harsh was the grating.*—
"On a sudden open fly
With impetuous recoil and jarring sound
The infernal doors, and on their hinges grate
Harsh thunder."
  Milton, Paradise Lost, b. ii. 882.

[2] *The Tarpeian.*—
"Protinus abducto patuerunt templa Metello.
Tunc rupes Tarpeia sonat: magnoque reclusas
Testatur stridore fores: tunc conditus imo
Eruitur templo multis intactus ab annis
Romani census populi," &c.
  Lucan, Pharsalia, lib. iii. 157.

"The tribune with unwilling steps withdrew,
While impious hands the rude assault renew;
The brazen gates with thundering strokes resound,
And the Tarpeian mountain rings around.
At length the sacred storehouse, open laid,
The hoarded wealth of ages past displayed." *Rowe*.

[3] *Organ.*—Organs were used in Italy as early as in the sixth century. See Tiraboschi, "Storia della Lett. Ital.," 4to, vol. iii., lib. iii., cap i., § 11, where the following description of that instrument is quoted from Cassiodorus, in Ps. 150:—"Organum itaque est quasi turris diversis fistulis fabricata, quibus flatu follium vox copiosissima destinatur, et ut eam modulatio decora componat, linguis quibusdam ligneis ab interiore parte construitur, quas disciplinabiliter Magistrorum digiti reprimentes grandisonam efficiunt et suavisonam cantilenam." If I remember right, there is a passage in the Emperor Julian's writings which shows that the organ was not unknown in his time.

In visage such, as past my power to bear.
Canto IX., line 74

CANTO X.

ARGUMENT.

Being admitted at the gate of Purgatory, our Poets ascend a winding path up the rock till they reach an open and level space that extends each way round the mountain. On the side that rises, and which is of white marble, are seen artfully engraven many stories of humility, which whilst they are contemplating, there approach the souls of those who expiate the sin of pride, and who are bent down beneath the weight of heavy stones.

WHEN we had past the threshold of the gate,
(Which the soul's ill affection doth disuse,
Making the crooked seem the straighter path,)
I heard its closing sound. Had mine eyes turn'd,
For that offence what plea might have avail'd?
    We mounted up the riven rock, that wound[1]
On either side alternate, as the wave
Flies and advances. "Here some little art
Behoves us," said my leader, "that our steps
Observe the varying flexure of the path."
    Thus we so slowly sped, that with cleft orb
The moon once more o'erhangs her watery couch,
Ere we that strait have threaded. But when free,
We came, and open, where the mount above
One solid mass retires; I spent with toil,[2]
And both uncertain of the way, we stood,
Upon a plain more lonesome than the roads
That traverse desert wilds. From whence the brink
Borders upon vacuity, to foot
Of the steep bank that rises still, the space
Had measured thrice the stature of a man:
And, distant as mine eye could wing its flight,

---

[1] *That wound.*—Venturi justly observes that the Padre d'Aquino has misrepresented the sense of this passage in his translation:

    "Dabat ascensum tendentibus ultra
    Scissa tremensque silex, tenuique erratica motu."

The verb "muover" is used in the same signification in the "Inferno," canto xviii. 21:

    "Così da imo della roccia scogli
    Moven."
        "From the rock's low base
    Thus flinty paths advanced."

In neither place is actual motion intended to be expressed.

[2] *I spent with toil.*—Dante only was wearied, because he only had the weight of a bodily frame to encumber him.

To leftward now and now to right dispatch'd,
That cornice equal in extent appear'd.

 Not yet our feet had on that summit moved,
When I discover'd that the bank, around,
Whose proud uprising all ascent denied,
Was marble white; and so exactly wrought
With quaintest sculpture, that not there alone
Had Polycletus, but e'en nature's self
Been shamed. The angel (who came down to earth
With tidings of the peace so many years
Wept for in vain, that oped the heavenly gates
From their long interdict) before us seem'd,
In a sweet act, so sculptured to the life,
He look'd no silent image. One had sworn
He had said "Hail!"[1] for she was imaged there,
By whom the key did open to God's love;
And in her act as sensibly imprest
That word, "Behold the handmaid of the Lord,"
As figure seal'd on wax. "Fix not thy mind
On one place only," said the guide beloved,
Who had me near him on that part where lies
The heart of man. My sight forthwith I turn'd,
And mark'd, behind the virgin mother's form,
Upon that side where he that moved me stood,
Another story graven on the rock.

 I past athwart the bard, and drew me near,
That it might stand more aptly for my view.
There, in the self-same marble, were engraved
The cart and kine, drawing the sacred ark,
That from unbidden office awes mankind.[2]
Before it came much people; and the whole
Parted in seven quires. One sense cried "Nay,"
Another, "Yes, they sing." Like doubt arose
Betwixt the eye and smell, from the curl'd fume

---

[1] *Hail.*—
  "On whom the angel *Hail*
 Bestow'd, the holy salutation used
 Long after to blest Mary, second Eve."
   Milton, Paradise Lost, v. 387.

"The basso relievo on the border of the second rock in Purgatory furnished the idea of the "Annunziata," painted by Marcello Venusti from his (Michael Angelo's) design in the sacristy of St. Giovanni Lateran."—*Fuseli, Lecture* iii., note.

[2] *That from unbidden office awes mankind.*—
"And when they came to Nachon's threshing-floor, Uzzah put forth his hand to the ark of God, and took hold of it; for the oxen shook it. And the anger of the Lord was kindled against Uzzah; and God smote him there for his error; and there he died by the ark of God."—2 Sam. vi. 6, 7.

The wretch appear'd amid all these to say:
"Grant vengeance, Sire! for, woe beshrew this heart,
My son is murder'd."

Canto X., lines 74—76.

Of incense breathing up the well-wrought toil.
Preceding[1] the blest vessel, onward came,
With light dance leaping, girt in humble guise,
Israel's sweet harper: in that hap he seem'd
Less, and yet more, than kingly. Opposite,
At a great palace, from the lattice forth
Look'd Michol, like a lady full of scorn
And sorrow. To behold the tablet next,
Which, at the back of Michol, whitely shone,
I moved me. There, was storied on the rock
The exalted glory of the Roman prince,
Whose mighty worth moved Gregory[2] to earn
His mighty conquest, Trajan the Emperor.[3]
A widow at his bridle stood, attired
In tears and mourning. Round about them troop'd
Full throng of knights; and overhead in gold
The eagles floated,[4] struggling with the wind.
The wretch appear'd amid all these to say:
"Grant vengeance, Sire! for, woe beshrew this heart,
My son is murder'd." He replying seem'd:
"Wait now till I return." And she, as one
Made hasty by her grief: "O Sire! if thou
Dost not return?"—"Where I am, who then is,
May right thee."—"What to thee is other's good,
If thou neglect thy own?"—"Now comfort thee;"
At length he answers. "It beseemeth well
My duty be perform'd, ere I move hence:
So justice wills; and pity bids me stay."

He, whose ken nothing new surveys, produced
That visible speaking, new to us and strange,
The like not found on earth. Fondly I gazed

---

[1] *Preceding.*—"And David danced before the Lord with all his might; and David was girded with a linen ephod."—2 Sam. vi. 14.

[2] *Whose mighty worth moved Gregory.*—St. Gregory's prayers are said to have delivered Trajan from hell. See "Paradise," canto xx. 40.

[3] *Trajan the Emperor.*—For this story, Landino refers to two writers, whom he calls "Helinando," of France—by whom he means Elinand, a monk and chronicler in the reign of Philip Augustus—and "Polycrato," of England, by whom is meant John of Salisbury, author of the "Polycraticus de Curialium Nugis," in the twelfth century. The passage in the text I find nearly a translation from that work, lib. v., c. 8. The original appears to be in Dio Cassius, where it is told of the Emperor Hadrian, lib. lxix., ἀμέλει γυναικὸς, κ. τ. λ. "when a woman appeared to him with a suit, as he was on a journey, at first he answered her, 'I have no leisure;' but she crying out to him, 'then reign no longer,' he turned about, and heard her cause." Lombardi refers also to Johannes Diaconus. "Vita S. Gregor.," lib. ii., cap. 44; the Euchology of the Greeks, cap. 96; and St. Thomas Aquinas, "Supplem. Quæst." 73, art. 5 ad 5. Compare Fazio degli Uberti, "Dittamondo," lib. ii., cap. 6.

[4] *The eagles floated.*—See Perticari's Letter on this passage. Opere, vol. iii., p. 552, ed. Bol., 1823. The eagles were of metal; not worked on a standard, as Villani supposed.

G

Upon those patterns of meek humbleness,
Shapes yet more precious for their artist's sake;
When "Lo!" the poet whisper'd, "where this way
(But slack their pace) a multitude advance.
These to the lofty steps shall guide us on."

Mine eyes, though bent on view of novel sights,
Their loved allurement, were not slow to turn.

Reader! I would not that amazed thou miss
Of thy good purpose, hearing how just God
Decrees our debts be cancel'd. Ponder[1] not
The form of suffering. Think on what succeeds:
Think that, at worst, beyond the mighty doom
It cannot pass. "Instructor!" I began,
"What I see hither tending, bears no trace
Of human semblance, nor of aught beside
That my foil'd sight can guess." He answering thus:
"So courb'd to earth, beneath their heavy terms
Of torment stoop they, that mine eye at first
Struggled as thine. But look intently thither;
And disentangle with thy labouring view,
What, underneath those stones, approacheth: now,
E'en now, mayst thou discern the pangs of each."

Christians and proud! O poor and wretched ones!
That, feeble in the mind's eye, lean your trust
Upon unstaid perverseness: know ye not
That we are worms, yet made at last to form
The winged insect,[2] imp'd with angel plumes,
That to heaven's justice unobstructed soars?
Why buoy ye up aloft your unfledged souls?
Abortive[3] then and shapeless ye remain,

---

[1] *Ponder.*—This is, in truth, an unanswerable objection to the doctrine of Purgatory. It is difficult to conceive how the best can meet death without horror, if they believe it must be followed by immediate and intense suffering.

[2] *The winged insect.*—" L'angelica farfalla." The butterfly was an ancient and well-known symbol of the human soul. Venturi cites some lines from the "Canzoni Anacreontiche" of Magalotti, in which this passage is imitated.

[3] *Abortive.*—The word in the original is "entomata." Some critics, and Salvini amongst the rest, have supposed that Dante, finding in a vocabulary the Greek word ἔντομα with the article τὰ placed after it to denote its gender, mistook them for one word. From this error he is well exculpated by Rosa Mirando in a passage quoted by Lombardi from the "Osserv. Parad., III.," where it is shown that the Italian word is formed, for the sake of the verse, in analogy with some others used by our poet; and that Redi himself, an excellent Greek scholar, and a very accurate writer, has even in prose, where such licences are less allowable, thus lengthened it. It may be considered as some proof of our author's acquaintance with the Greek language, that in the "Convito," p. 26, he finds fault with the version of Aristotle's Ethics made by Taddeo d' Alderotto, the Florentine physician; and that in the treatise "De Monarchiâ," lib. i., p. 110, he quotes a Greek word from Aristotle himself. On the other hand, he speaks of a passage in the same writer being doubtful, on account of its being differently interpreted in two different translations, a new and an

Like the untimely embryon of a worm.

    As, to support incumbent floor or roof,
For corbel, is a figure[1] sometimes seen,
That crumples up its knees unto its breast;
With the feign'd posture, stirring ruth unfeign'd
In the beholder's fancy; so I saw
These fashion'd, when I noted well their guise.

    Each, as his back was laden, came indeed
Or more or less contracted; and it seem'd
As he, who show'd most patience in his look,
Wailing exclaim'd: "I can endure no more."

---

old one. "Convito," p. 75. And for the word "autentin," he refers to a vocabulary compiled by Uguccione Bentivegna of Pisa, a MS. that is perhaps still remaining, as Cinelli, in his MS. history of Tuscan writers referred to by Biscioni in the notes on the "Convito," p. 142, speaks of it as being preserved in the library of St. Francesco at Cesena. After all, Dante's knowledge of Greek must remain as questionable as Shakespeare's of that language and of Latin.

[1] *As, to support incumbent floor or roof, for corbel, is a figure.*—Chillingworth, cap vi., § 54, speaks of "those crouching anticks, which seem in great buildings to labour under the weight they bear." And Lord Shaftesbury has a similar illustration in his "Essay on Wit and Humour," p. 4, § 3.

CANTO XI.

ARGUMENT.

After a prayer uttered by the spirits who were spoken of in the last Canto, Virgil inquires the way upwards, and is answered by one, who declares himself to have been Omberto, son of the Count of Santafiore. Next our Poet distinguishes Oderigi, the illuminator, who discourses on the vanity of worldly fame, and points out to him the soul of Provenzano Salvani.

O THOU Almighty Father![1] who dost make
   The heavens thy dwelling, not in bounds confined,
But that, with love intenser, there thou view'st
Thy primal effluence; hallow'd be thy name:
Join, each created being, to extol
Thy might; for worthy humblest thanks and praise
Is thy blest Spirit. May thy kingdom's peace
Come unto us; for we, unless it come,
With all our striving, thither tend in vain.
As, of their will, the angels unto thee
Tender meet sacrifice, circling thy throne
With loud hosannas; so of theirs be done
By saintly men on earth. Grant us, this day,
Our daily manna, without which he roams
Through this rough desert retrograde, who most
Toils to advance his steps. As we to each
Pardon the evil done us, pardon thou
Benign, and of our merit take no count.
'Gainst the old adversary, prove thou not
Our virtue, easily subdued; but free
From his incitements, and defeat his wiles.
This last petition, dearest Lord! is made
Not for ourselves; since that were needless now:
But for their sakes who after us remain."

---

[1] *O thou Almighty Father!*—The first four lines are borrowed by Pulci, "Morgante Maggiore," c. vi. Dante, in his "Credo," has again versified the Lord's Prayer, if, indeed, the "Credo" be Dante's, which some have doubted; and in the preface to Allacci's Collection it is ascribed to Antonio di Ferrara.

Thus for themselves and us good speed imploring,
Those spirits went beneath a weight like that
We sometimes feel in dreams; all, sore beset,
But with unequal anguish; wearied all;
Round the first circuit; purging as they go
The world's gross darkness off. In our behoof
If their vows still be offer'd, what can here
For them be vow'd and done by such, whose wills
Have root of goodness in them?[1] Well beseems
That we should help them wash away the stains
They carried hence; that so, made pure and light,
They may spring upward to the starry spheres.

"Ah! so may mercy-temper'd justice rid
Your burdens speedily; that ye have power
To stretch your wing, which e'en to your desire
Shall lift you; as ye show us on which hand
Toward the ladder leads the shortest way.
And if there be more passages than one,
Instruct us of that easiest to ascend:
For this man, who comes with me, and bears yet
The charge of fleshly raiment Adam left him,
Despite his better will, but slowly mounts."
From whom the answer came unto these words,
Which my guide spake, appear'd not; but 'twas said
"Along the bank to rightward come with us;
And ye shall find a pass that mocks not toil
Of living man to climb: and were it not
That I am hinder'd by the rock, wherewith
This arrogant neck is tamed, whence needs I stoop
My visage to the ground; him, who yet lives,
Whose name thou speak'st not, him I fain would view;
To mark if e'er I knew him, and to crave
His pity for the fardel that I bear.
I was of Latium;[2] of a Tuscan born,
A mighty one: Aldobrandesco's name,
My sire's, I know not if ye e'er have heard.
My old blood and forefathers' gallant deeds

---

[1] *Root of goodness in them.*—The poet has before told us that there are no others on earth whose prayers avail to shorten the pains of those who are in Purgatory.

[2] *I was of Latium.*—Omberto, the son of Guglielmo Aldobrandesco, Count of Santafiore, in the territory of Sienna. His arrogance provoked his countrymen to such a pitch of fury against him that he was murdered by them at Campagnatico.

Made me so haughty, that I clean forgot
The common mother; and to such excess
Wax'd in my scorn of all men, that I fell,
Fell therefore; by what fate, Sienna's sons,
Each child in Campagnatico, can tell.
I am Omberto: not me, only, pride
Hath injured, but my kindred all involved
In mischief with her. Here my lot ordains
Under this weight to groan, till I appease
God's angry justice, since I did it not
Amongst the living, here amongst the dead."

  Listening I bent my visage down: and one
(Not he who spake) twisted beneath the weight
That urged him, saw me, knew me straight, and call'd;
Holding his eyes with difficulty fix'd
Intent upon me, stooping as I went
Companion of their way. "O!" I exclaim'd,
"Art thou not Oderigi?[1] art not thou
Agobbio's glory, glory of that art
Which they of Paris call the limner's skill?"

  "Brother!" said he, "with tints, that gayer smile,
Bolognian Franco's[2] pencil lines the leaves.
His all the honour now; my light obscured.
In truth, I had not been thus courteous to him
The whilst I lived, through eagerness of zeal
For that pre-eminence my heart was bent on.
Here, of such pride, the forfeiture is paid.[3]
Nor were I even here, if, able still
To sin, I had not turn'd me unto God.
O powers of man! how vain your glory, nipt
E'en in its height of verdure, if an age
Less bright succeed not.[4] Cimabue[5] thought

---

[1] *Oderigi.*—The illuminator, or miniature painter, a friend of Giotto and Dante.
[2] *Bolognian Franco.*—Franco of Bologna, who is said to have been a pupil of Oderigi's.
[3] *The forfeiture is paid.*—
 "Di tal superbia qui si paga il fio."
So in the "Inferno," c. xxvii. 135:
 "In che si paga il fio."
And Ariosto, "Orlando Furioso," c. xxii. 59:
 "Prestate olà, che qui si paga il fio."
[4] *If an age less bright succeed not.*—If a generation of men do not follow, among whom none exceeds or equals those who have immediately preceded them. "Etati grosse;" to which Volpi remarks a similar expression in Boileau:
 "Villon sût le premier, dans ces siècles grossiers,
 Debrouiller l'art confus de nos vieux romanciers."
     Art Poétique, ch. I.

[5] *Cimabue.*—Giovanni Cimabue, the restorer of painting, was born at Florence, of a noble family, in 1240, and died in 1300. The passage in the text is an allusion to his epitaph:
 "Credidit ut Cimabos picturæ castra tenere,
  Sic tenuit vivens: nunc tenet astra poli."

> To lord it over painting's field; and now
> The cry is Giotto's,[1] and his name eclipsed.
> Thus hath one Guido from the other[2] snatch'd

[1] *The cry is Giotto's.*—In Giotto we have a proof of how early a period the fine arts were encouraged in Italy. His talents were discovered by Cimabue, while he was tending sheep for his father in the neighbourhood of Florence, and he was afterwards patronised by Pope Benedict XI. and Robert King of Naples; and enjoyed the society and friendship of Dante, whose likeness he has transmitted to posterity. He died in 1336, at the age of 60.

[2] *One Guido from the other.*—Guido Cavalcanti, the friend of our poet (see "Hell," canto x. 59), had eclipsed the literary fame of Guido Guinicelli, of a noble family in Bologna, whom we shall meet with in the twenty-sixth canto, and of whom frequent and honourable mention is made by our poet in his treatise "De Vulgari Eloquentia." Guinicelli died in 1276, as is proved by Fantuzzi, on the Bolognian writers, tom. iv., p. 345. See Mr. Mathias's "Tiraboschi," tom. i., p. 110. There are more of Guinicelli's poems to be found in Allacci's Collection, than Tiraboschi, who tells us he had not seen it, supposed. From these I have selected two which appear to me singularly pathetic. It must, however, be observed that the former of them is attributed in the Vatican MS. 3213, to Cino da Pistoia, as Bottari informs us in the notes to "Lettere di Fra Guittone d'Arezzo," p. 171. Many of Cavalcanti's writings, hitherto in MS., are said to be publishing at Florence. See "Esprit des Journaux," Jan., 1813. [They were edited there in that year, but not for sale, by Antonio Cicciaporci, as I learn from Gamba's "Testi di Lingua Ital." 272.]

" Noi provamo ch' in questo cieco mondo
Ciascun si vive in angosciosa doglia,
Ch' in onni avversita ventura 'l tira.
Beata l' alma che lassa tal pondo.
E va nel ciel, dove è compita zoglia,
Zoglioso cor far de corrotto e d' ira.
Or dunque di chel vostro cor sospira
Che rallegrar si dè del suo migliore,
Che Dio, nostro signore,
Volse di lei, come avea l'angel detto,
Fare il ciel perfetto.
Per nuova cosa ogni santo la mira :
Ed ella sta d'avante alla salute ;
Ed in ver lei parla ogni vertute."
Allacci, Ediz. Napoli, 1661, p. 378.

" By proof, in this blind mortal world, we know,
That each one lives in grief and sore annoy ;
Such ceaseless strife of fortune we sustain.
Blessed the soul, that leaves this weight below,
And goes its way to heaven, where it hath joy
Entire, without a touch of wrath or pain.
Now then what reason hath thy heart to sigh,
That should be glad, as for desire fulfill'd,
That God, our Sovereign, will'd
She, as He told His angel, should be given
To bless and perfect heaven ?
Each saint looks on her with admiring eye ;
And she stands ever in salvation's sight ;
And every virtue bends on her its light."

" Conforto già conforto l'amor chiama,
E pietà prega per Dio, fatti resto ;
Or v' inchinate a sì dolce preghiera ;
Spogliatevi di questa vesta grama,
Da che voi sete per ragion richiesto.
Che l'uomo per dolor more e dispera.
Con voi vedeste poi la bella ciera,

Se v' accogliesse morte in disperanza,
De sì grave pesanza
Traete il vostro cor ormai per Dio,
Che non sia così rio
Ver l'alma vostra che ancora spiera
Vederla in ciel e star nelle sue braccia,
Dunque spene dè confortar vi piaccia."
Allacci, Ediz. Napoli, 1661, p. 380.

"' Comfort thee, comfort thee,' exclaimeth Love ;
And Pity by thy God adjures thee 'rest :'
Oh then incline ye to such gentle prayer ;
Nor Reason's plea should ineffectual prove,
Who bids ye lay aside this dismal vest :
For man meets death through sadness and despair.
Amongst you ye have seen a face so fair :
Be this in mortal mourning some relief.
And, for more balm of grief,
Rescue thy spirit from its heavy load.
Remembering thy God ;
And that in heaven thou hopest again to share
In sight of her, and with thine arms to fold :
Hope then ; nor of this comfort quit thy hold."

To these I will add a sonnet by the same writer, from the poems printed with the "Bella Mano" of Giusto de' Conti. Ediz. 1715, p. 167 :

" Io vo dal ver la mia donna laudare,
E rassembrarla alla rosa, ed al giglio.
Più che stella Diana splende, e pare,
Ciò che lassù è bello a lei somiglio.
Verdi rivere a lei rassembro, l'are,
Tutto color di porpora, e vermiglio,
Oro, ed argento, e ricche gioie preclare ;
Medesmo amor per lei raffina miglio.
Passa per via adorna, e sì gentile,
Cui bassa orgoglio, a cui dona salute,
E fal di nostra fe, se non la crede.
E non le può appressare, uom che sia vile,
Ancor ve ne dirò maggior vertute,
Nullo uom può mai pensar finchè la vede."

" I would from truth my lady's praise supply,
Resembling her to lily and to rose ;
Brighter than morning's lucid star she shows,
And fair as that which fairest is on high.
To the blue wave, I liken her, and sky,
All colour that with pink and crimson glows,
Gold, silver, and rich stones : nay lovelier grows
E'en love himself, when she is standing by.
She passeth on so gracious and so mild,
One's pride is quench'd, and one of sick is well :
And they believe, who from the faith did err ;
And none may near her come by harm defiled.
A mightier virtue have I yet to tell ;
No man may think of evil, seeing her."

The two following sonnets of Guido Cavalcanti may enable the reader to form some judgment whether Dante had sufficient reason for preferring him to his predecessor Guinicelli :

" Io temo che la mia disavventura
Non faccia sì ch' io dico io mi dispero,
Però ch' io sento nel cor un pensiero,
Che fa tremar la mente di paura.
E par ch' ei dica : Amor non t'assicura
In guisa che tu possa di leggiero
Alla tua donna sì contare il vero,
Che morte non ti ponga in sua figura.
Della gran doglia, che l'anima sente,
Si parte dallo core un tal sospiro

The letter'd prize : and he, perhaps, is born,[1]
Who shall drive either from their nest. The noise
Of worldly fame is but a blast of wind,
That blows from diverse points, and shifts its name,
Shifting the point it blows from. Shalt thou more
Live in the mouths of mankind, if thy flesh
Part shrivel'd from thee, than if thou hadst died
Before the coral and the pap were left ;
Or e'er some thousand years have past ? and that
Is, to eternity compared, a space
Briefer than is the twinkling of an eye
To the heaven's slowest orb. He there, who treads
So leisurely before me, far and wide
Through Tuscany resounded once ; and now
Is in Sienna scarce with whispers named :
There was he sovereign, when destruction caught
The maddening rage of Florence, in that day
Proud as she now is loathsome. Your renown
Is as the herb, whose hue doth come and go ;
And his might withers it, by whom it sprang
Crude from the lap of earth." I thus to him :
" True are thy sayings : to my heart they breathe
The kindly spirit of meekness, and allay

Che va dicendo : Spiritei fuggite ;
Allor null' uom, che sia pietoso, miro ;
Che consolasse mia vita dolente,
Dicendo : Spiritei non vi partite."
  Anecdota Literaria ex MSS. Codicibus eruta.
    Ediz. Roma (no year), v. iii., p. 452.
" I fear lest my mischance may so prevail,
That it may make me of myself despair.
For, my heart searching, I discover there
A thought that makes the mind with terror quail.
It says, meseemeth, ' Love shall not avail
To strengthen thee so much, that thou shalt dare
Tell her thou lovest, thy passion, or thy prayer,
To save from power of death thy visage pale.'
Through the dread sorrow that o'erwhelms my soul,
There issues from my bosom such a sigh,
As passeth, crying, ' Spirits, flee away.'
And then, when I am fainting in my dole,
No man so merciful there standeth by,
To comfort me, and answer, ' Spirits, stay.' "

" Beltà di donna, e di saccente core,
E cavalieri armati, che sian genti,
Cantar d'augelli, e ragionar d'amore,
Adorni legni in mar, forti e correnti ;
Aria serena, quando appar l'albore,
E bianca neve scender senza venti,
Rivera d'acqua, e prato d'ogni fiore,
Oro, e argento, azzurro in ornamenti :

Ciò che può la beltate, e la valenza
Della mia donna in suo gentil coraggio,
Par che rassembra vile a chi ciò guarda.
E tanto ha più d'ogni altra conoscenza,
Quanto lo Ciel di questa terra è maggio,
A simil di natura ben non tarda."
  La Bella Mano e Rime Antiche.
    Ediz. Fir., 1715, p. 128.
" Whatso is fair in lady's face or mind,
And gentle knights caparison'd and gay,
Singing of sweet birds unto love inclined,
And gallant barks that cut the watery way ;
The white snow falling without any wind,
The cloudless sky at break of early day,
The crystal stream, with flowers the meadow lined,
Silver, and gold, and azure for array :
To him that sees the beauty and the worth
Whose power doth meet and in my lady dwell,
All seem as vile, their price and lustre gone.
And, as the heaven is higher than the earth,
So she in knowledge doth each one excel,
Not slow to good in nature like her own."

[1] *He, perhaps, is born.*—Some imagine, with much probability, that Dante here augurs the greatness of his own poetical reputation. Others have absurdly fancied that he prophesies the glory of Petrarch : but Petrarch was not yet born. Lombardi doubts whether it is not spoken generally of human vicissitudes.

What tumours[1] rankle there. But who is he,
Of whom thou spakest but now?" "This," he replied,
"Is Provenzano. He is here, because
He reach'd with grasp presumptuous at the sway
Of all Sienna. Thus he still hath gone,
Thus goeth never-resting, since he died.
Such is the acquittance render'd back of him,
Who, in the mortal life, too much hath dared."
I then: "If soul, that to life's verge delays
Repentance, linger in that lower space,
Nor hither mount (unless good prayers befriend),
Or ever time, long as it lived, be past;[2]
How chanced admittance was vouchsafed to him?"

"When at his glory's topmost height," said he,
"Respect of dignity all cast aside,
Freely he fix'd him on Sienna's plain,
A suitor[3] to redeem his suffering friend,
Who languish'd in the prison-house of Charles;
Nor, for his sake, refused through every vein
To tremble. More I will not say; and dark,
I know, my words are; but thy neighbours soon[4]
Shall help thee to a comment on the text.
This is the work, that from these limits freed him."

---

[1] *What tumours.—*
"Apt words have power to swage
The tumours of a troubled mind."
Milton, Samson Agonistes.

[2] *Or ever time, long as it lived, be past.—*This line was omitted in the former editions, as Mr. Lyell has pointed out to me.

[3] *A suitor.—*Provenzano Salvani humbled himself so far for the sake of one of his friends, who was detained in captivity by Charles I. of Sicily, as personally to supplicate the people of Sienna to contribute the sum required by the king for his ransom; and this act of self-abasement atoned for his general ambition and pride. He fell in the battle of Val d' Elsa, wherein the Florentines discomfited the Siennese in June, 1269. G. Villani relates some curious particulars of his fate: "Messer Provenzano Salvani, the lord and conductor of the army, was taken, and his head cut off and carried through all the camp, fixed upon a lance. And well was accomplished the prophecy and revelation made to him by the devil by way of witchcraft, but he understood it not; for having compelled him to answer how he should succeed in the said engagement, he told him, lyingly—'Thou shalt go, fight, conquer not, die in the battle, and thy head shall be the highest in the camp.' And he thought to have the victory, and from these words hoped to remain master of all, and noted not the fallacy, where he said, 'Conquer not, die.' And therefore it is great folly to trust such counsel as that of the devil."—Lib. vii., cap. xxxi.

[4] *Thy neighbours soon.—*"Thou wilt know in the time of thy banishment, which is near at hand, what it is to solicit favours of others, and 'tremble through every vein,' lest they should be refused thee."

CANTO XII.

ARGUMENT.

Dante being desired by Virgil to look down on the ground which they are treading, observes that it is wrought over with imagery exhibiting various instances of pride recorded in history and fable. They leave the first cornice, and are ushered to the next by an angel who points out the way.

WITH equal pace, as oxen in the yoke,
    I, with that laden spirit, journey'd on,
Long as the mild instructor suffer'd me ;
But, when he bade me quit him, and proceed
(For " Here," said he, " behoves with sail and oars
Each man, as best he may, push on his bark "),
Upright, as one disposed for speed, I raised
My body, still in thought submissive bow'd.
    I now my leader's track not loth pursued ;
And each had shown how light we fared along,
When thus he warned me : " Bend thine eyesight down :
For thou, to ease the way, shalt find it good
To ruminate the bed beneath thy feet."
    As, in memorial of the buried, drawn
Upon earth-level tombs, the sculptured form
Of what was once, appears (at sight whereof
Tears often stream forth, by remembrance waked,
Whose sacred stings the piteous often feel),
So saw I there, but with more curious skill
Of portraiture o'erwrought, whate'er of space
From forth the mountain stretches. On one part
Him I beheld, above all creatures erst·
Created noblest, lightning fall from heaven :
On the other side, with bolt celestial pierced,
Briareus ; cumbering earth he lay, through dint
Of mortal ice-stroke. The Thymbræan god,[1]

---

[1] *The Thymbræan god.*—Apollo. " Si modo, quem perhibes, pater est Thymbræus Apollo." *Virgil, Georgics,* iv. 323.

With equal pace, as oxen in the yoke,
I, with that laden spirit, journey'd on,
Long as the mild instructor suffer'd me.
Canto XII., lines 1—3.

With Mars,[1] I saw, and Pallas, round their sire,
Arm'd still, and gazing on the giants' limbs
Strewn o'er the ethereal field. Nimrod I saw:
At foot of the stupendous work he stood,
As if bewilder'd, looking on the crowd
Leagued in his proud attempt on Sennaar's plain.[2]

O Niobe! in what a trance of woe
Thee I beheld, upon that highway drawn,
Seven sons on either side thee slain. O Saul!
How ghastly didst thou look, on thine own sword
Expiring, in Gilboa, from that hour
Ne'er visited with rain from heaven, or dew.

O fond Arachne! thee I also saw,
Half spider now, in anguish, crawling up
The unfinish'd web thou weaved'st to thy bane.

O Rehoboam![3] here thy shape doth seem
Louring no more defiance; but fear-smote,
With none to chase him, in his chariot whirl'd.

Was shown beside upon the solid floor
How dear Alcmæon[4] forced his mother rate
That ornament, in evil hour received:
How, in the Temple, on Sennacherib[5] fell
His sons, and how a corpse they left him there.
Was shown the scath, and cruel mangling made
By Tomyris[6] on Cyrus, when she cried,
"Blood thou didst thirst for: take thy fill of blood."
Was shown how routed in the battle fled
The Assyrians, Holofernes[7] slain, and e'en
The relics of the carnage. Troy I mark'd
In ashes and in caverns. Oh! how fallen,
How abject, Ilion, was thy semblance there.

What master of the pencil or the style[8]

---

[1] *Mars.*—
"With such a grace,
The giants that attempted to scale heaven,
When they lay dead on the Phlegrœan plain,
Mars did appear to Jove."
Beaumont and Fletcher, The Prophetess,
act ii., sc. 3.

[2] *Sennaar's plain.*—
"The builders such of Babel on the plain
Of Sennaar." *Milton, Paradise Lost,* b. iii. 467.

[3] *O Rehoboam.*—1 Kings xii. 18.

[4] *Alcmæon.*—Virgil, "Æneid," lib. vi. 445; and Homer, "Odyssey," xi. 325.

[5] *Sennacherib.*—2 Kings xix. 37.

[6] *Tomyris.*—"Caput Cyri amputatum in utrem humano sanguine repletum conjici Regina jubet cum hac exprobatione crudelitatis, Satia te, inquit, sanguine quem sitisti, cujusque insatiabilis semper fuisti."—*Justin,* lib. i., cap. 8.

[7] *Holofernes.*—Judith xiii.

[8] *What master of the pencil or the style.*—
"Inimitable on earth
By model, or by shading pencil drawn."
Milton, Paradise Lost, b. iii. 509.

Had traced the shades and lines, that might have made
The subtlest workman wonder? Dead, the dead;
The living seem'd alive: with clearer view,
His eye beheld not, who beheld the truth,
Than mine what I did tread on, while I went
Low bending. Now swell out, and with stiff necks
Pass on, ye sons of Eve! vale not your looks,
Lest they descry the evil of your path.

I noted not (so busied was my thought)
How much we now had circled of the mount;
And of his course yet more the sun had spent;
When he, who with still wakeful caution went,
Admonish'd: "Raise thou up thy head: for know
Time is not now for slow suspense. Behold,
That way, an angel hasting towards us. Lo,
Where duly the sixth handmaid[1] doth return
From service on the day. Wear thou, in look
And gesture, seemly grace of reverent awe;
That gladly he may forward us aloft.
Consider that this day ne'er dawns again."

Time's loss he had so often warn'd me 'gainst,
I could not miss the scope at which he aim'd.

The goodly shape approach'd us, snowy white
In vesture, and with visage casting streams
Of tremulous lustre like the matin star.
His arms he open'd, then his wings; and spake:
"Onward! the steps, behold, are near; and now
The ascent is without difficulty gain'd."

A scanty few are they, who, when they hear
Such tidings, hasten. O ye race of men!
Though born to soar, why suffer ye a wind
So slight to baffle ye? He led us on
Where the rock parted; here, against my front,
Did beat his wings; then promised I should fare
In safety on my way. As to ascend
That steep, upon whose brow the chapel stands[2]

---

[1] *Where duly the sixth handmaid.*—Compare canto xxii. 116.
[2] *The chapel stands.*—The church of San Miniato in Florence, situated on a height that overlooks the Arno, where it is crossed by the bridge Rubaconte, so called from Messer Rubaconte da Mandella of Milan, chief magistrate of Florence, by whom the bridge was founded in 1237. See G. Villani, lib. vi., cap. xxvii.

O fond Arachne! thee I also saw,
Half spider now, in anguish, crawling up
The unfinish'd web thou weaved'st to thy bane.
Canto XII., lines 39—41.

(O'er Rubaconte, looking lordly down
On the well-guided city[1]), up the right
The impetuous rise is broken by the steps
Carved in that old and simple age, when still
The registry[2] and label rested safe;
Thus is the acclivity relieved, which here,
Precipitous, from the other circuit falls:
But, on each hand, the tall cliff presses close.

    As, entering, there we turn'd, voices, in strain
Ineffable, sang: "Blessed[3] are the poor
In spirit." Ah! how far unlike to these
The straits of hell: here songs to usher us,
There shrieks of woe. We climb the holy stairs:
And lighter to myself by far I seem'd
Than on the plain before; whence thus I spake:
"Say, master, of what heavy thing have I
Been lighten'd; that scarce aught the sense of toil
Affects me journeying?" He in few replied:
"When sin's broad characters,[4] that yet remain
Upon thy temples, though well nigh effaced,
Shall be, as one is, all clean razed out;
Then shall thy feet by heartiness of will
Be so o'ercome, they not alone shall feel
No sense of labour, but delight much more
Shall wait them, urged along their upward way."

    Then like to one, upon whose head is placed
Somewhat he deems not of, but from the becks
Of others, as they pass him by; his hand
Lends therefore help to assure him, searches, finds,
And well performs such office as the eye
Wants power to execute; so stretching forth
The fingers of my right hand, did I find
Six only of the letters, which his sword,
Who bare the keys, had traced upon my brow.
The leader, as he mark'd mine action, smiled.

---

[1] *The well-guided city.*—This is said ironically of Florence.

[2] *The registry.*—In allusion to certain instances of fraud committed in Dante's time with respect to the public accounts and measures. See "Paradise," canto xvi. 103.

[3] *Blessed.*—" Blessed are the poor in spirit, for theirs is the kingdom of heaven." — Matt. v. 3.

[4] *Sin's broad characters.*—Of the seven P's, that denoted the same number of sins (Peccata) whereof he was to be cleansed (see canto ix. 100), the first had now vanished, in consequence of his having passed the place where the sin of pride, the chief of them, was expiated.

CANTO XIII.

ARGUMENT.

They gain the second cornice, where the sin of envy is purged; and having proceeded a little to the right, they hear voices uttered by invisible spirits recounting famous examples of charity, and next behold the shades, or souls, of the envious clad in sackcloth, and having their eyes sewed up with an iron thread. Amongst these Dante finds Sapia, a Siennese lady, from whom he learns the cause of her being there.

WE reach'd the summit of the scale, and stood
    Upon the second buttress of that mount
Which healeth him who climbs. A cornice there,
Like to the former, girdles round the hill;
Save that its arch, with sweep less ample, bends.
    Shadow, nor image there, is seen: all smooth
The rampart and the path, reflecting nought
But the rock's sullen hue. "If here we wait,
For some to question," said the bard, "I fear
Our choice may haply meet too long delay."
    Then fixedly upon the sun his eyes
He fasten'd; made his right the central point
From whence to move; and turn'd the left aside.
"O pleasant light, my confidence and hope!
Conduct us thou," he cried, "on this new way,
Where now I venture; leading to the bourn
We seek. The universal world to thee
Owes warmth and lustre. If[1] no other cause
Forbid, thy beams should ever be our guide."
    Far, as is measured for a mile on earth,
In brief space had we journey'd; such prompt will
Impell'd; and towards us flying, now were heard
Spirits invisible, who courteously
Unto love's table bade the welcome guest.
The voice that first flew by, call'd forth aloud,
"They have no wine,"[2] so on behind us past,

---

[1] *If.*—"Unless there be some urgent necessity for travelling by night, the daylight should be preferred for that purpose."

[2] *They have no wine.*—John, chap. ii. ver. 3. These words of the Virgin are referred to as an instance of charity.

E'en thus the blind and poor,
Near the confessionals, to crave an alms,
Stand, each his head upon his fellow's sunk;
So most to stir compassion, not by sound
Of words alone, but that which moves not less,
The sight of misery.

Canto XIII., lines 55—60.

Those sounds reiterating, nor yet lost
In the faint distance, when another came
Crying, "I am Orestes,"[1] and alike
Wing'd its fleet way. "O father!" I exclaim'd,
"What tongues are these?" and as I question'd, lo!
A third exclaiming, "Love ye those have wrong'd you."[2]
   "This circuit," said my teacher, "knots the scourge[3]
For envy; and the cords are therefore drawn
By charity's correcting hand. The curb
Is of a harsher sound; as thou shalt hear
(If I deem rightly) ere thou reach the pass,
Where pardon sets them free. But fix thine eyes
Intently through the air; and thou shalt see
A multitude before thee seated, each
Along the shelving grot." Then more than erst
I oped mine eyes; before me view'd; and saw
Shadows with garments dark as was the rock;
And when we pass'd a little forth, I heard
A crying, "Blessed Mary! pray for us,
Michael and Peter! all ye saintly host!"
   I do not think there walks on earth this day
Man so remorseless, that he had not yearn'd
With pity at the sight that next I saw.
Mine eyes a load of sorrow teem'd, when now
I stood so near them, that their semblances
Came clearly to my view. Of sackcloth vile
Their covering seem'd; and, on his shoulder, one
Did stay another, leaning; and all lean'd
Against the cliff. E'en thus the blind and poor,
Near the confessionals, to crave an alms,
Stand, each his head upon his fellow's sunk;
So most to stir compassion, not by sound
Of words alone, but that which moves not less,
The sight of misery. And as never beam
Of noon-day visiteth the eyeless man,
E'en so was heaven a niggard unto these

---

[1] *Orestes.*—Alluding to his friendship with Pylades.
[2] *Love ye those have wrong'd you.*—"But I say unto you, Love your enemies, bless them that curse you, do good to them that hate you, and pray for them which despitefully use you and persecute you."—Matt. v. 44.
[3] *The scourge.*—"The chastisement of envy consists in hearing examples of the opposite virtue, charity. As a curb and restraint on this vice, you will presently hear very different sounds, those of threatening and punishment."

Of his fair light: for through the orbs of all,
A thread of wire, impiercing, knits them up,
As for the taming of a haggard hawk.

 It were a wrong, methought, to pass and look
On others, yet myself the while unseen.
To my sage counsel therefore did I turn.
He knew the meaning of the mute appeal,
Nor waited for my questioning, but said:
"Speak, and be brief, be subtile in thy words."

 On that part of the cornice, whence no rim
Engarlands its steep fall, did Virgil come;
On the other side me were the spirits, their cheeks
Bathing devout with penitential tears,
That through the dread impalement forced a way.

 I turn'd me to them, and "O shades!" said I,
"Assured that to your eyes unveil'd shall shine
The lofty light, sole object of your wish,
So may heaven's grace[1] clear whatsoe'er of foam
Floats turbid on the conscience, that thenceforth
The stream of mind roll limpid from its source;
As ye declare (for so shall ye impart
A boon I dearly prize) if any soul
Of Latium dwell among ye: and perchance
That soul may profit, if I learn so much."

 "My brother! we are, each one, citizens
Of one true city.[2] Any, thou wouldst say,
Who lived a stranger in Italia's land."

 So heard I answering, as appear'd, a voice,
That onward came some space from whence I stood.

 A spirit I noted, in whose look was mark'd
Expectance. Ask ye how? The chin was raised
As in one reft of sight. "Spirit," said I,
"Who for thy rise art tutoring (if thou be
That which didst answer to me), or by place,
Or name, disclose thyself, that I may know thee."

---

[1] *So may heaven's grace.—*

"Se tosto grazia risolva le schiume
Di vostra coscienza, sì che chiaro
Per esso scenda della mente il fiume."

This is a fine moral, and finely expressed. Unless the conscience be cleared from its impurity, which it can only thoroughly be by an influence from above, the mind itself cannot act freely and clearly. "If ye will do his will, ye shall know of the doctrine."—John vii. 17.

[2] *Citizens of one true city.—*"For here we have no continuing city, but we seek one to come."—Heb. xiii. 14.

"Who then, amongst us here aloft,
Hath brought thee, if thou weenest to return?"
Canto XIII., lines 129, 130.

"I was," it answer'd, "of Sienna: here
I cleanse away with these the evil life,
Soliciting with tears that He, who is,
Vouchsafe him to us. Though Sapia[1] named,
In sapience I excell'd not; gladder far
Of other's hurt, than of the good befel me.
That thou mayst own I now deceive thee not,
Hear, if my folly were not as I speak it.
When now my years sloped waning down the arch,
It so bechanced, my fellow-citizens
Near Colle met their enemies in the field;
And I pray'd God to grant what He had will'd.[2]
There were they vanquish'd, and betook themselves
Unto the bitter passages of flight.
I mark'd the hunt; and waxing out of bounds
In gladness, lifted up my shameless brow,
And, like the merlin[3] cheated by a gleam,
Cried, 'It is over. Heaven! I fear thee not,
Upon my verge of life I wish'd for peace
With God; nor yet repentance had supplied
What I did lack of duty, were it not
The hermit Piero,[4] touch'd with charity,
In his devout oraisons thought on me.
But who art thou that question'st of our state,
Who go'st, as I believe, with lids unclosed,
And breathest in thy talk?"—"Mine eyes," said I,
"May yet be here ta'en from me; but not long;
For they have not offended grievously
With envious glances. But the woe beneath[5]
Urges my soul with more exceeding dread.
That nether load already weighs me down."

She thus: "Who then, amongst us here aloft,
Hath brought thee, if thou weenest to return?"

"He," answered I, "who standeth mute beside me.

---

[1] *Sapia.*—A lady of Sienna, who, living in exile at Colle, was so overjoyed at a defeat which her countrymen sustained near that place, that she declared nothing more was wanting to make her die contented. The Latin annotator on the Monte Casino MS. says of this lady: "Fuit uxor D. Cinii de Pigezo de Senis."

[2] *And I pray'd God to grant what He had will'd.*—That her countrymen should be defeated in battle.

[3] *The merlin.*—The story of the merlin is, that having been induced by a gleam of fine weather in the winter to escape from his master, he was soon oppressed by the rigour of the season.

[4] *The hermit Piero.*—Piero Pettinagno, a holy hermit of Florence.

[5] *The woe beneath.*—Dante felt that he was much more subject to the sin of pride, than to that of envy; and this is just what we should have concluded of a mind such as his.

I live: of me ask therefore, chosen spirit!
If thou desire I yonder yet should move
For thee my mortal feet."—"Oh!" she replied,
This is so strange a thing, it is great sign
That God doth love thee. Therefore with thy prayer
Sometime assist me: and, by that I crave,
Which most thou covetest, that if thy feet
E'er tread on Tuscan soil, thou save my fame
Amongst my kindred. Them shalt thou behold
With that vain multitude,[1] who set their hope
On Telamone's haven; there to fail
Confounded, more than when the fancied stream
They sought, of Dian call'd: but they, who lead[2]
Their navies, more than ruin'd hopes shall mourn."

---

[1] *Them shalt thou behold with that vain multitude.*—The Siennese. See "Hell," c. xxix. 118. "Their acquisition of Telamone, a seaport on the confines of the Maremma, has led them to conceive hopes of becoming a naval power: but this scheme will prove as chimerical as their former plan for the discovery of a subterraneous stream under their city." Why they gave the appellation of Diana to the imagined stream, Venturi says he leaves it to the antiquaries of Sienna to conjecture.

[2] *They who lead.*—The Latin note to the Monte Casino MS. informs us, that those who were to command the fleets of the Siennese, in the event of their becoming a naval power, lost their lives during their employment at Telamone, through the pestilent air of the Maremma, which lies near that place.

CANTO XIV.

ARGUMENT.

Our Poet on this second cornice finds also the souls of Guido del Duca of Brettinoro, and Rinieri da Calboli of Romagna; the latter of whom, hearing that he comes from the banks of the Arno, inveighs against the degeneracy of all those who dwell in the cities visited by that stream; and the former, in like manner, against the inhabitants of Romagna. On leaving these, our Poets hear voices recording noted instances of envy.

"SAY,[1] who is he around our mountain winds,
   Or ever death has pruned his wings for flight
That opes his eyes, and covers them at will?"
   "I know not who he is, but know thus much;
He comes not singly. Do thou ask of him,
For thou art nearer to him; and take heed,
Accost him[2] gently, so that he may speak."
   Thus on the right two spirits, bending each
Toward the other, talk'd of me; then both
Addressing me, their faces backward lean'd,
And thus the one[3] began: "O soul, who yet
Pent in the body, tendest towards the sky!
For charity, we pray thee, comfort us;
Recounting whence thou comest, and who thou art:
For thou dost make us, at the favour shown thee,
Marvel, as at a thing that ne'er hath been."
   "There stretches through the midst of Tuscany,"
I straight began, "a brooklet,[4] whose well-head
Springs up in Falterona; with his race
Not satisfied, when he some hundred miles
Hath measured. From his banks bring I this frame.
To tell you who I am were words mis-spent:

---

[1] *Say.*—The two spirits who thus speak to each other are Guido del Duca of Brettinoro, and Rinieri da Calboli of Romagna.

[2] *Accost him.*—It is worthy of remark, that the Latin annotator on the Monte Casino MS. agrees with Landino in reading "a colo," instead of "accolo," and interprets it as he does: "Nil aliud vult auctor dicere de colo, nisi quod cum interroget ita dulciter ut respondeat (sic) eum ad colum, id est quod tantum respondeat auctor eis quod animus eorum remaneat in quiete et non in suspenso" ("The author means to say, that the spirit should interrogate him courteously, that he may return such an answer as shall put a *period* to their suspense"). Still I have retained my translation of the common reading generally supposed to be put by syncope for "accoglilo," "accost him."

[3] *The one.*—Guido del Duca.

[4] *A brooklet.*—The Arno, that rises in Falterona, a mountain in the Apennine. Its course is a hundred and twenty miles, according to G. Villani, who traces it accurately.

For yet my name scarce sounds on rumour's lip."
"If well I do incorporate with my thought
The meaning of thy speech," said he, who first
Address'd me, "thou dost speak of Arno's wave."
　　To whom the other:[1] "Why hath he conceal'd
The title of that river, as a man
Doth of some horrible thing?" The spirit, who
Thereof was question'd, did acquit him thus:
"I know not: but 'tis fitting well the name
Should perish of that vale; for from the source,[2]
Where teems so plenteously the Alpine steep
Maim'd of Pelorus,[3] (that doth scarcely pass
Beyond that limit,)[4] even to the point
Where unto ocean is restored what heaven
Drains from the exhaustless store for all earth's streams.
Throughout the space is virtue worried down,
As 't were a snake, by all, for mortal foe;
Or through disastrous influence on the place,
Or else distortion of misguided wills
That custom goads to evil: whence in those,
The dwellers in that miserable vale,
Nature is so transform'd, it seems as they
Had shared of Circe's feeding. 'Midst brute swine,[5]
Worthier of acorns than of other food
Created for man's use, he shapeth first
His obscure way; then, sloping onward, finds
Curs,[6] snarlers more in spite than power, from whom
He turns with scorn aside: still journeying down,
By how much more the curst and luckless foss[7]
Swells out to largeness, e'en so much it finds
Dogs turning into wolves.[8] Descending still
Through yet more hollow eddies, next he meets
A race of foxes,[9] so replete with craft,

---

[1] *The other.*—Rinieri da Calboli.
[2] *From the source.*—"From the rise of the Arno in that 'Alpine steep,' the Apennine, from whence Pelorus in Sicily was torn by a convulsion of the earth, even to the point where the same river unites its waters to the ocean, Virtue is persecuted by all."
[3] *Maim'd of Pelorus.*—Virgil, "Æneid," lib. iii. 414; Lucan, "Pharsalia," lib. ii. 438.
　　"A hill
　　Torn from Pelorus."
　　Milton, *Paradise Lost*, b. i. 232.
[4] *That doth scarcely pass beyond that limit.*—"Pelorus is in few places higher than Falterona, where the Arno springs." Lombardi explains this differently, and, I think, erroneously.
[5] *'Midst brute swine.*—The people of Casentino.
[6] *Curs.*—The Arno leaves Arezzo about four miles to the left.
[7] *The curst and luckless foss.*—So in his anger he terms the Arno.
[8] *Wolves.*—The Florentines.
[9] *Foxes.*—The Pisans.

They do not fear that skill can master it.
Nor will I cease because my words are heard[1]
By other ears than thine. It shall be well
For this man,[2] if he keep in memory
What from no erring spirit I reveal.
Lo! I behold thy grandson,[3] that becomes
A hunter of those wolves, upon the shore
Of the fierce stream; and cows them all with dread.
Their flesh, yet living, sets he up to sale,
Then, like an aged beast, to slaughter dooms.
Many of life he reaves, himself of worth
And goodly estimation. Smear'd with gore,
Mark how he issues from the rueful wood;
Leaving such havoc, that in thousand years
It spreads not to prime lustihood again."

As one, who tidings hears of woe to come,
Changes his looks perturb'd, from whate'er part
The peril grasp him; so beheld I change
That spirit, who had turn'd to listen; struck
With sadness, soon as he had caught the word.

His visage, and the other's speech, did raise
Desire in me to know the names of both;
Whereof, with meek entreaty, I inquired.

The shade, who late address'd me, thus resumed:
"Thy wish imports, that I vouchsafe to do
For thy sake what thou wilt not do[4] for mine.
But, since God's will is that so largely shine
His grace in thee, I will be liberal too.
Guido of Duca know then that I am.
Envy so parch'd my blood, that had I seen
A fellow-man made joyous, thou had'st mark'd
A livid paleness overspread my cheek.
Such harvest reap I of the seed I sow'd.
O man! why place[5] thy heart where there doth need
Exclusion of participants in good?

---

[1] *My words are heard.*—It should be recollected that Guido still addresses himself to Rinieri.
[2] *For this man.*—"For Dante, who has told us that he comes from the banks of the Arno."
[3] *Thy grandson.*—Fulcieri da Calboli, grandson of Rinieri da Calboli who is here spoken to. The atrocities predicted came to pass in 1302. See G. Villani, lib. viii., c. lix.
[4] *What thou wilt not do.*—Dante having declined telling him his name. See v. 22.
[5] *Why place.*—This will be explained in the ensuing canto.

This is Rinieri's spirit; this, the boast
And honour of the house of Calboli;
Where of his worth no heritage remains.
Nor his the only blood, that hath been stript
('Twixt Po, the mount, the Reno, and the shore[1])
Of all that truth or fancy[2] asks for bliss:
But, in those limits, such a growth has sprung
Of rank and venom'd roots, as long would mock
Slow culture's toil. Where is good Lizio?[3] where
Manardi, Traversaro, and Carpigna?[4]
O bastard slips of old Romagna's line!
When in Bologna the low artisan,[5]
And in Faenza yon Bernardin[6] sprouts,
A gentle cyon from ignoble stem.
Wonder not, Tuscan, if thou see me weep,
When I recall to mind those once loved names,
Guido of Prata,[7] and of Azzo him[8]
That dwelt with us;[9] Tignoso[10] and his troop,
With Traversaro's house and Anastagio's[11]
(Each race disherited); and beside these,
The ladies[12] and the knights, the toils and ease,

---

[1] *'Twixt Po, the mount, the Reno, and the shore.*—The boundaries of Romagna.

[2] *Fancy.*—"Trastullo." Quadrio, in the notes on the second of the "Salmi Penitenziali" of our author, understands this in a higher sense, as meaning that joy which results from an easy and constant practice of virtue. See "Opere di Dante," Zatta ediz., tom. iv., part ii., p. 193. And he is followed by Lombardi.

[3] *Lizio.*—Lizio da Valbona introduced into Boccaccio's "Decameron," Giorn v., Nov. 4.

[4] *Manardi, Traversaro, and Carpigna.*—Arrigo Manardi of Faenza, or, as some say, of Brettinoro; Pier Traversaro, lord of Ravenna; and Guido di Carpigna of Montefeltro.

[5] *In Bologna the low artisan.*—One who had been a mechanic, named Lambertaccio, arrived at almost supreme power in Bologna.

"Quando in Bologna un Fabbro si ralligna:
Quando in Faenza un Bernardin di Fosco."

The pointing and the marginal note of the Monte Casino MS. entirely change the sense of these two lines. There is a mark of interrogation added to each; and by way of answer to both there is written, "Quasi dicat numquam." Fabbro is made a proper name, and it is said of him: "Iste fuit Dom. Faber de Lambertaciis de Bononia;" and Benvenuto da Imola calls him "Nobilis Miles." I have not ventured to alter the translation so as to make it accord with this interpretation, as it must have been done in the face, I believe, of nearly all the editions, and, as far as may be gathered from the silence of Lombardi, of the MSS. also which that commentator had consulted. But those who wish to see more on the subject are referred to Monti's "Proposta," tom. iii., parte 2, under the word "Rallignare."

[6] *Yon Bernardin.*—Bernardin di Fosco, a man of low origin, but great talents, who governed at Faenza.

[7] *Prata.*—A place between Faenza and Ravenna.

[8] *Of Azzo him.*—Ugolino, of the Ubaldini family in Tuscany.

[9] *With us.*—Lombardi claims the reading, "nosco," instead of "vosco," "with us," instead of "with you," for his favourite edition; but it is also in Landino's of 1488.

[10] *Tignoso.*—Federigo Tignoso of Rimini.

[11] *Traversaro's house and Anastagio's.*—Two noble families of Ravenna. See v. 100. She, to whom Dryden has given the name of Honoria, in the fable so admirably paraphrased from Boccaccio, was of the former: her lover and the spectre were of the Anastagi family. See canto xxviii. 20.

[12] *The ladies, &c.*—

"Le donne, e i cavalier, gli affanni, e gli agi
Che ne 'nvogliava amore e cortesia."

These two lines express the true spirit of Chivalry. "Agi" is understood, by the commentators whom I have consulted, to mean "the ease procured for others by the exertions of knight-errantry." But surely it signifies the alternation of ease with labour. Venturi is of opinion that the opening of the "Orlando Furioso"—

"Le donne, i cavalier, l'arme, gli amori,
Le cortesie, l'audaci imprese io canto,"

originates in this passage.

That witch'd us into love and courtesy;[1]
Where now such malice reigns in miscreant hearts.
O Brettinoro![2] wherefore tarriest still,
Since forth of thee thy family hath gone,
And many, hating evil, join'd their steps?
Well doeth he, that bids his lineage cease,
Bagnacavallo;[3] Castracaro ill,
And Conio worse,[4] who care to propagate
A race of Counties[5] from such blood as theirs.
Well shall ye also do, Pagani,[6] then
When from amongst you hies your demon child;
Not so, howe'er,[7] that thenceforth there remain
True proof of what ye were. O Hugolin,[8]
Thou sprung of Fantolini's line! thy name
Is safe; since none is look'd for after thee
To cloud its lustre, warping from thy stock.
But, Tuscan! go thy ways; for now I take
Far more delight in weeping, than in words.
Such[9] pity for your sakes hath wrung my heart."

We knew those gentle spirits, at parting, heard
Our steps. Their silence therefore, of our way,
Assured us. Soon as we had quitted them,

---

[1] *Courtesy.*—"Cortesia e onestade," &c., "Convito," p. 65. "Courtesy and honour are all one; and because anciently virtue and good manners were usual in courts, as the contrary now is, this term was derived from thence: courtesy was as much as to say, custom of courts; which word, if it were taken from courts, especially those of Italy, would be no other than turpitude," "turpezza."

"Courtesy,
Which oft is sooner found in lowly sheds
With smoky rafters, than in tapestry halls
And courts of princes, where it first was named,
And yet is most pretended."
          Milton, Comus.

Marino has exceeded his usual extravagance in his play on this word:

"Ma come può vero diletto? ò come
Vera quiete altrui donar la Corte?
Le diè la Cortesia del proprio nome
Solo il principio, il fine ha della Morte."
          Adone, c. ix., st. 77.

[2] *O Brettinoro.*—A beautifully situated castle in Romagna, the hospitable residence of Guido del Duca, who is here speaking. Landino relates, that there were several of this family, who, when a stranger arrived amongst them, contended with one another by whom he should be entertained; and that in order to end this dispute, they set up a pillar with as many rings as there were fathers of families among them, a ring being assigned to each, and that accordingly as a stranger on his arrival hung his horse's bridle on one or other of these, he became his guest to whom the ring belonged.

[3] *Bagnacavallo.*—A castle between Imola and Ravenna.

[4] *Castracaro ill, and Conio worse.*—Both in Romagna.

[5] *Counties.*—I have used this word here for "Counts," as it is in Shakespeare.

[6] *Pagani.*—The Pagani were lords of Faenza and Imola. One of them, Machinardo, was named *the Demon,* from his treachery. See "Hell," canto xxvii. 47, and note.

[7] *Not so, howe'er.*—"Yet your offspring will be stained with some vice, and will not afford true proof of the worth of your ancestors."

[8] *Hugolin.*—Ugolino Ubaldini, a noble and virtuous person in Faenza, who, on account of his age probably, was not likely to leave any offspring behind him. He is enumerated among the poets by Crescimbeni, and by Tiraboschi, Mr. Mathias's edit., vol. i., p. 143; and Perticari cites a beautiful little poem by him in the "Apologia di Dante," parte ii., c. 27, but with so little appearance of antiquity that nothing less than the assurance of so able a critic could induce one for a moment to receive it as genuine.

[9] *Such.*—Here again the Nidobeatina edition adopted by Lombardi, and the Monte Casino MS. differ from the common reading, and both have—

"Si m' ha nostra region la mente stretta,"
"Our country's sorrow has so wrung my heart," instead of
"Si m' ha vostra ragion," &c.

Advancing onward, lo! a voice, that seem'd
Like volley'd lightning, when it rives the air,
Met us, and shouted, "Whosoever finds
Will slay me;"[1] then fled from us, as the bolt
Lanced sudden from a downward-rushing cloud.
When it had given short truce unto our hearing,
Behold the other with a crash as loud
As the quick-following thunder: "Mark in me
Aglauros,[2] turn'd to rock." I, at the sound
Retreating, drew more closely to my guide.

Now in mute stillness rested all the air;
And thus he spake: "There was the galling bit,[3]
Which[4] should keep man within his boundary.
But your old enemy so baits the hook,
He drags you eager to him. Hence nor curb
Avails you, nor reclaiming call. Heaven calls,[5]
And, round about you wheeling, courts your gaze
With everlasting beauties. Yet your eye
Turns with fond doting still upon the earth.
Therefore He smites you who discerneth all."

---

[1] *Whosoever finds will slay me.*—The words of Cain, Gen. iv. 14.

[2] *Aglauros.*—Ovid, "Metamorphoses," lib. ii., fab. 12.

[3] *There was the galling bit.*—Referring to what had been before said, canto xiii. 35. The commentators remark the unusual word "camo," which occurs here in the original; but they have not observed, I believe, that Dante himself uses it in the "De Monarchiâ," lib. iii., p. 155. For the Greek word χάμον see a fragment by S. Petrus Alex. in Routh's "Reliquiæ Sacræ," vol. iii., p. 342, and note.

[4] *Which.*—Mr. Darley has noticed the omission of this line in the former editions.

[5] *Heaven calls.*—

"Or ti solleva a più beata speme,
Mirando il ciel, che ti si volve intorno
Immortal ed adorno."
Petrarca, Canzone. I'vo pensando.

CANTO XV.

ARGUMENT.

An angel invites them to ascend the next steep. On their way Dante suggests certain doubts, which are resolved by Virgil; and, when they reach the third cornice, where the sin of anger is purged, our Poet, in a kind of waking dream, beholds remarkable instances of patience; and soon after they are enveloped in a dense fog.

As much[1] as 'twixt the third hour's close and dawn,
Appeareth of heaven's sphere, that ever whirls
As restless as an infant in his play;
So much appear'd remaining to the sun
Of his slope journey towards the western goal.

Evening was there, and here the noon of night;
And full upon our forehead smote the beams.
For round the mountain, circling, so our path
Had led us, that toward the sun-set now
Direct we journey'd; when I felt a weight
Of more exceeding splendour than before,
Press on my front. The cause unknown, amaze
Possess'd me! and both hands[2] against my brows
Lifting, I interposed them, as a screen,
That of its gorgeous superflux of light
Clips the diminish'd orb. As when the ray,[3]
Striking on water or the surface clear
Of mirror, leaps unto the opposite part,
Ascending at a glance,[4] e'en as it fell,
And as much[5] differs from the stone, that falls

---

[1] *As much.*—"It wanted three hours of sunset."
[2] *Both hands.*—
"Raising his hand to save the dazzled sense."
              Southey, Thalaba, b. xii.
[3] *As when the ray.*—
"Sicut aquæ tremulum labris ubi lumen aënis
Sole repercussum, aut radiantis imagine lunæ,
Omnia pervolitat late loca, jamque sub auras
Erigitur, summique ferit laquearia tecti."
              Æn. lib. viii. 25.
Compare Apollonius Rhodius, lii. 755.

[4] *Ascending at a glance.*—
"Quod simul ac primum sub divo splendor aquai
Ponitur: extemplo, cœlo stellante, serena
Sidera respondent in aquâ radiantia mundi.
Jamne vides igitur, quam parvo tempore imago
Ætheris ex oris ad terrarum accidat oras."
              Lucretius, lib. iv. 215.

[5] *And as much.*—Lombardi, I think justly, observes that this does not refer to the length of time which a stone is in falling to the ground, but to the perpendicular line which it describes when falling, as contrasted

Through equal space (so practic skill hath shown);
Thus, with refracted light, before me seem'd
The ground there smitten; whence, in sudden haste,
My sight recoil'd. "What is this, sire beloved!
'Gainst which I strive to shield the sight in vain?"
Cried I, "and which toward us moving seems?"

"Marvel not, if the family of heaven,"
He answer'd, "yet with dazzling radiance dim
Thy sense. It is a messenger who comes,
Inviting man's ascent. Such sights ere long,
Not grievous, shall impart to thee delight,
As thy perception is by nature wrought
Up to their pitch." The blessed angel, soon
As we had reach'd him, hail'd us with glad voice:
"Here enter on a ladder far less steep
Than ye have yet encounter'd." We forthwith
Ascending, heard behind us chanted sweet,
"Blessed the merciful,"[1] and "Happy thou,
That conquer'st." Lonely each, my guide and I,
Pursued our upward way; and as we went,
Some profit from his words I hoped to win,
And thus of him inquiring, framed my speech:
"What meant Romagna's spirit,[2] when he spake
Of bliss exclusive, with no partner shared?"

He straight replied: "No wonder, since he knows
What sorrow waits on his own worst defect,
If he chide others, that they less may mourn.
Because ye point your wishes at a mark,
Where, by communion of possessors, part
Is lessen'd, envy bloweth up men's sighs.
No fear of that might touch ye, if the love
Of higher sphere exalted your desire.
For there,[3] by how much more they call it *ours*,

---

with the angle of incidence formed by light reflected from water or from a mirror.

[1] *Blessed the merciful.*—Matt. v. 7.

[2] *What meant Romagna's spirit.*—Guido del Duca of Brettinoro, whom we have seen in the preceding canto.

[3] *For there.*—Landino has here cited, in addition to Seneca and Boetius, the two following apposite passages from Augustine and Saint Gregory: "Nullo modo fit minor accedente consortio possessio bonitatis, quam tanto latius quanto concordius individua sociorum possidet caritas."—*Augustin., De Civitate Dei.*
"Qui facibus invidiæ carere desiderat, illam posses-

So much propriety of each in good
Increases more, and heighten'd charity
Wraps that fair cloister in a brighter flame."
"Now lack I satisfaction more," said I,
"Than if thou hadst been silent at the first;
And doubt more gathers on my labouring thought.
How can it chance, that good distributed,
The many, that possess it, makes more rich,
Than if 't were shared by few?" He answering thus:
"Thy mind, reverting still to things of earth,
Strikes darkness from true light. The highest good
Unlimited, ineffable, doth so speed
To love, as beam to lucid body darts,
Giving as much of ardour as it finds.
The sempiternal effluence streams abroad,
Spreading, wherever charity extends.
So that the more aspirants to that bliss
Are multiplied, more good is there to love,
And more is loved; as mirrors, that reflect,
Each unto other, propagated light.
If these my words avail not to allay
Thy thirsting, Beatrice thou shalt see,
Who of this want, and of all else thou hast,
Shall rid thee to the full. Provide but thou,[1]
That from thy temples may be soon erased,
E'en as the two already, those five scars,
That, when they pain thee worst, then kindliest heal."
"Thou," I had said, "content'st me;" when I saw
The other round was gain'd, and wondering eyes
Did keep me mute. There suddenly I seem'd
By an ecstatic vision wrapt away;
And in a temple saw, methought, a crowd
Of many persons; and at the entrance stood
A dame,[2] whose sweet demeanour did express
A mother's love, who said, "Child! why hast thou
Dealt with us thus? Behold thy sire and I
Sorrowing have sought thee;" and so held her peace;

---

sionem appetat, quam numerus possidentium non angustat."
[1] *Provide but thou.*—"Take heed that thou be healed of the five remaining sins, as thou already art of the two—namely, pride and envy."
[2] *A dame.*—Luke ii. 48.

And straight the vision fled. A female next
Appear'd before me, down whose visage coursed
Those waters, that grief forces out from one
By deep resentment stung, who seem'd to say:
"If thou, Pisistratus, be lord indeed
Over this city,[1] named with such debate
Of adverse gods, and whence each science sparkles,
Avenge thee of those arms, whose bold embrace
Hath clasp'd our daughter;" and to her, meseem'd,
Benign and meek, with visage undisturb'd,
Her sovran spake: "How shall we those requite[2]
Who wish us evil, if we thus condemn
The man that loves us?" After that I saw
A multitude, in fury burning, slay
With stones a stripling youth,[3] and shout amain
"Destroy, destroy;" and him I saw, who bow'd
Heavy with death unto the ground, yet made
His eyes, unfolded upward, gates to heaven,
Praying forgiveness of the Almighty Sire,
Amidst that cruel conflict, on his foes,
With looks that win compassion to their aim.

    Soon as my spirit, from her airy flight
Returning, sought again the things whose truth
Depends not on her shaping, I observed
She had not roved to falsehood in her dreams.

    Meanwhile the leader, who might see I moved
As one who struggles to shake off his sleep,
Exclaim'd: "What ails thee, that thou canst not hold
Thy footing firm; but more than half a league
Hast travel'd with closed eyes and tottering gait,
Like to a man by wine or sleep o'ercharged?"

    "Beloved father! so thou deign," said I,
"To listen, I will tell thee what appear'd
Before me, when so fail'd my sinking steps."

    He thus: "Not if thy countenance were mask'd

---

[1] *Over this city.*—Athens, named after Ἀθήνη, Minerva, in consequence of her having produced a more valuable gift for it in the olive, than Neptune had done in the horse.

[2] *How shall we those requite.*—The answer of Pisistratus the tyrant to his wife, when she urged him to inflict the punishment of death on a young man, who, inflamed with love for his daughter, had snatched a kiss from her in public. The story is told by Valerius Maximus, lib. v. 1.

[3] *Slay with stones a stripling youth.*—The protomartyr Stephen.

After that I saw
A multitude, in fury burning, slay
With stones a stripling youth, and shout amain
"Destroy, destroy."

Canto XV., lines 103—106.

With hundred vizards, could a thought of thine,
How small soe'er, elude me. What thou saw'st
Was shown, that freely thou mightst ope thy heart
To the waters of peace, that flow diffused
From their eternal fountain. I not ask'd,
What ails thee? for such cause as he doth, who
Looks only with that eye, which sees no more,
When spiritless the body lies; but ask'd,
To give fresh vigour to thy foot. Such goads,
The slow and loitering need; that they be found
Not wanting, when their hour of watch returns."

So on we journey'd, through the evening sky
Gazing intent, far onward as our eyes,
With level view, could stretch against the bright
Vespertine ray: and lo! by slow degrees
Gathering, a fog made towards us, dark as night.
There was no room for 'scaping; and that mist
Bereft us, both of sight and the pure air.

CANTO XVI.

ARGUMENT.

As they proceed through the mist, they hear the voices of spirits praying. Marco Lombardo, one of these, points out to Dante the error of such as impute our actions to necessity; explains to him that man is endued with free will; and shows that much of human depravity results from the undue mixture of spiritual and temporal authority in rulers.

HELL'S dunnest gloom, or night unlustrous, dark,
Of every planet 'reft, and pall'd in clouds,
Did never spread before the sight a veil
In thickness like that fog, nor to the sense
So palpable and gross. Entering its shade,
Mine eye endured not with unclosed lids;
Which marking, near me drew the faithful guide,
Offering me his shoulder for a stay.
As the blind man behind his leader walks,
Lest he should err, or stumble unawares
On what might harm him or perhaps destroy;
I journey'd through that bitter air and foul,
Still listening to my escort's warning voice,
"Look that from me thou part not." Straight I heard
Voices, and each one seem'd to pray for peace,
And for compassion, to the Lamb of God
That taketh sins away. Their prelude still
Was "Agnus Dei;" and through all the choir,
One voice, one measure ran, that perfect seem'd
The concord of their song. "Are these I hear
Spirits, O master?" I exclaim'd; and he,
"Thou aim'st aright: these loose the bonds of wrath."
"Now who art thou, that through our smoke dost cleave,
And speak'st of us, as thou thyself e'en yet
Dividedst time by calends?"[1] So one voice
Bespake me; whence my master said, "Reply;
And ask, if upward hence the passage lead."
"O being! who doth make thee pure, to stand
Beautiful once more in thy Maker's sight;
Along with me: and thou shalt hear and wonder."
Thus I, whereto the spirit answering spake:

---

[1] *As thou thyself e'en yet dividedst time by calends.*—" As if thou wert still living."

"Now who art thou, that through our smoke dost cleave,
And speak'st of us, as thou thyself e'en yet
Dividedst time by calends?"

Canto XVI., lines 23—25.

"Long as 'tis lawful for me, shall my steps
Follow on thine; and since the cloudy smoke
Forbids the seeing, hearing in its stead
Shall keep us join'd." I then forthwith began:
"Yet in my mortal swathing, I ascend
To higher regions; and am hither come
Through the fearful agony of hell.
And, if so largely God hath doled his grace,
That, clean beside all modern precedent,
He wills me to behold his kingly state;
From me conceal not who thou wast, ere death
Had loosed thee; but instruct me: and instruct
If rightly to the pass I tend; thy words
The way directing, as a safe escort."

"I was of Lombardy, and Marco call'd:[1]
Not inexperienced of the world, that worth
I still affected, from which all have turn'd
The nerveless bow aside. Thy course tends right
Unto the summit:" and, replying thus,
He added, "I beseech thee pray for me,
When thou shalt come aloft." And I to him:
"Accept my faith for pledge I will perform
What thou requirest. Yet one doubt remains,
That wrings me sorely, if I solve it not.
Singly before it urged me, doubled now
By thine opinion, when I couple that
With one elsewhere[2] declared; each strengthening other.
The world indeed is even so forlorn
Of all good, as thou speak'st it, and so swarms
With every evil. Yet, beseech thee, point
The cause out to me, that myself may see,
And unto others show it: for in heaven
One places it, and one on earth below."

---

[1] *I was of Lombardy, and Marco call'd.*—A Venetian gentleman. "Lombardo," both was his surname and denoted the country to which he belonged. G. Villani, lib. vii., cap. cxx., terms him "a wise and worthy courtier." Benvenuto da Imola, says Landino, relates of him, that being imprisoned and not able to pay the price of his ransom, he applied by letter to his friend Riccardo da Camino, lord of Trevigi, for relief. Riccardo set on foot a contribution among several nobles of Lombardy for the purpose; of which, when Marco was informed, he wrote back with much indignation to Riccardo, that he had rather die than remain under obligations to so many benefactors. It is added that Riccardo then paid the whole out of his own purse. Of this generous man I have occasion to speak again in the notes to canto viii. 71, and to "Paradise," canto ix. 48.

[2] *When I couple that with one elsewhere.*—He refers to what Guido del Duca had said in the fourteenth canto, concerning the degeneracy of his countrymen.

Then heaving forth a deep and audible sigh,
"Brother!" he thus began, "the world is blind;
And thou in truth comest from it. Ye, who live,
Do so each cause refer to heaven above.
E'en as its motion, of necessity,
Drew with it all that moves. If this were so,[1]
Free choice in you were none; nor justice would
There should be joy for virtue, woe for ill.
Your movements have their primal bent from heaven;
Not all: yet said I all; what then ensues?
Light have ye still to follow evil or good,
And of the will free power, which, if it stand
Firm and unwearied in Heaven's first essay,
Conquers at last, so it be cherish'd well,
Triumphant over all. To mightier force,[2]
To better nature subject, ye abide
Free, not constrain'd by that which forms in you
The reasoning mind uninfluenced of the stars.
If then the present race of mankind err,
Seek in yourselves the cause, and find it there.
Herein thou shalt confess me no false spy.

"Forth from his plastic hand, who charm'd beholds
Her image ere she yet exist, the soul
Comes like a babe, that wantons sportively,[3]
Weeping and laughing in its wayward moods;
As artless, and as ignorant of aught,
Save that her Maker being one who dwells
With gladness ever, willingly she turns
To whate'er yields her joy. Of some slight good

---

[1] *If this were so.*—Mr. Crowe, in his "Lewesdon Hill," has expressed similar sentiments with much energy:

"Of this be sure,
Where freedom is not, there no virtue is:
If there be none, this world is all a cheat,
And the divine stability of heaven
(That assured seat for good men after death)
Is but a transient cloud, display'd so fair
To cherish virtuous hope, but at our need
Eludes the sense, and fools our honest faith,
Vanishing in a lie," &c.

So, also, Frezzi, in his "Quadriregio:"

"Or sappi ben che Dio ha dato il freno
A voi di voi; e, se non fosse questo,
Libero arbitrio in voi sarebbe meno."
Lib. ii., cap. 1.

There is much more on this subject at the conclusion of the eighth Capitolo of this book. Compare also Origen in "Genesin. Patrum Græcor," vol. xi., p. 14, Werceburgi, 1783, 8vo; and Tertullian, "Contra Marcionem," lib. ii., p. 458, Lutetiæ, 1641, fol. A very noble passage on the freedom of the will occurs in the first book "De Monarchiâ," beginning "Et humanum genus, potissimum liberum, optime se habet" ("The human race, when most completely free, is in its highest state of excellence").

[2] *To mightier force.*—"Though ye are subject to a higher power than that of the heavenly constellations. even to the power of the great Creator himself, yet ye are still left in the possession of liberty."

[3] *Like a babe, that wantons sportively.*—This reminds us of the Emperor Hadrian's verses to his departing soul:

"Animula vagula blandula," &c.

"Long as 'tis lawful for me, shall my steps
Follow on thine; and since the cloudy smoke
Forbids the seeing, hearing in its stead
Shall keep us join'd."

Canto XVI., lines 32—35.

The flavour soon she tastes; and, snared by that,
With fondness she pursues it; if no guide
Recal, no rein direct her wandering course.
Hence it behoved, the law should be a curb;
A sovereign hence behoved, whose piercing view
Might mark at least the fortress[1] and main tower
Of the true city. Laws indeed there are:
But who is he observes them? None; not he,
Who goes before, the shepherd of the flock,
Who[2] chews the cud but doth not cleave the hoof.
Therefore the multitude, who see their guide
Strike at the very good they covet most,
Feed there and look no further. Thus the cause
Is not corrupted nature in yourselves,
But ill-conducting, that hath turn'd the world
To evil. Rome, that turn'd it unto good,
Was wont to boast two suns,[3] whose several beams
Cast light on either way, the world's and God's.
One since hath quench'd the other; and the sword
Is grafted on the crook; and, so conjoin'd,
Each must perforce decline to worse, unawed
By fear of other. If thou doubt me, mark
The blade: each herb is judged of by its seed.
That land,[4] through which Adice and the Po
Their waters roll, was once the residence
Of courtesy and valour, ere the day[5]
That frown'd on Frederick; now secure may pass
Those limits, whosoe'er hath left, for shame,
To talk with good men, or come near their haunts.
Three aged ones are still found there, in whom

---

[1] *The fortress.*—Justice, the most necessary virtue in the chief magistrate, as the commentators for the most part explain it; and it appears manifest from all our poet says in his book "De Monarchiâ," concerning the authority of the temporal monarch and concerning justice, that they are right. Yet Lombardi understands the law here spoken of to be the law of God; *the sovereign,* a spiritual ruler, and *the true city*, the society of true believers; so that *the fortress*, according to him, denotes the principal parts of Christian duty.

[2] *Who.*—He compares the Pope, on account of the union of the temporal with the spiritual power in his person, to an unclean beast in the Levitical law. "The camel, because he cheweth the cud, but divideth not the hoof; he is unclean unto you."—Lev. xi. 4.

[3] *Two suns.*—The Emperor and the Bishop of Rome. There is something similar to this in the "De Monarchiâ," lib. iii., p. 138. "They say first, according to that text in Genesis, that God made two great lights, the greater light and the lesser, the one to rule the day, and the other the night; then, that as the moon, which is the lesser light, has no brightness, except as she receives it from the sun, so neither has the temporal kingdom authority, except what it receives from the spiritual government." The fallacy of which reasoning (if such it can be called) he proceeds to prove.

[4] *That land.*—Lombardy.

[5] *The day.*—Before the Emperor Frederick II. was defeated before Parma, in 1248. G. Villani, lib. vi., cap. xxxv.

The old time[1] chides the new: these deem it long
Ere God restore them to a better world:
The good Gherardo;[2] of Palazzo he,
Conrad;[3] and Guido of Castello,[4] named
In Gallic phrase more fitly the plain Lombard.
On this at last conclude. The church of Rome,
Mixing two governments that ill assort,
Hath miss'd her footing, fallen into the mire,[5]
And there herself and burden much defiled."

"O Marco!" I replied, "thine arguments
Convince me: and the cause I now discern,
Why of the heritage no portion came
To Levi's offspring. But resolve me this:
Who that Gherardo is, that as thou say'st
Is left a sample of the perish'd race,
And for rebuke to this untoward age?"

"Either thy words," said he, "deceive, or else
Are meant to try me; that thou, speaking Tuscan,
Appear'st not to have heard of good Gherardo;
The sole addition that, by which I know him;
Unless I borrow'd from his daughter Gaïa[6]
Another name to grace him. God be with you.
I bear you company no more. Behold
The dawn with white ray glimmering through the mist.
I must away—the angel comes—ere he
Appear." He said, and would not hear me more.

---

[1] *The old time.*—"L'antica età."

"It is silly sooth,
And dallies with the innocence of love,
Like the old age."
Shakespeare, Twelfth Night, act ii., sc. 4.

[2] *The good Gherardo.*—Gherardo de Camino, of Trevigi. He is honourably mentioned in our poet's "Convito," p. 173: "Let us suppose that Gherardo da Camino had been the grandson of the meanest hind that ever drank of the Sile or the Cagnano, and that his grandfather was not yet forgotten; who will dare to say that Gherardo da Camino was a mean man, and who will not agree with me in calling him noble? Certainly no one, however presumptuous, will deny this; for such he was, and as such let him ever be remembered." Tiraboschi supposes him to have been the same Gherardo with whom the Provençal poets were used to meet a hospitable reception. "This is probably that same Gherardo, who, together with his sons, so early as before the year 1254, gave a kind and hospitable reception to the Provençal poets." Mr. Mathias's edition, tom. i., p. 137.

[3] *Conrad.*—Currado da Palazzo, a gentleman of Brescia.

[4] *Guido of Castello.*—Of Reggio. All the Italians were called Lombards by the French.

[5] *Fallen into the mire.*—There is a passage resembling this in the "De Vulgari Eloquentia," lib. ii., cap. 4: "Ante omnia ergo dicimus unumquemque debere materiæ pondus propriis humeris excipere æquale, ne forte humerorum nimio gravatam virtutem in cœnum cespitare necesse sit."

[6] *His daughter Gaïa.*—A lady equally admired for her modesty, the beauty of her person, and the excellency of her talents. Gaïa, says Tiraboschi, may perhaps lay claim to the praise of having been the first among the Italian ladies by whom the vernacular poetry was cultivated. This appears (although no one has yet named her as a poetess) from the MS. Commentary on the "Commedia" of Dante, by Giovanni da Serravalle, afterwards Bishop of Fermo, where, commenting on canto xvi. of the "Purgatory," he says: "De istâ Gajâ filiâ dicti boni Gerardi, possent dici multæ laudes, quia fuit prudens domina, literata, magni consilii, et magnæ prudentiæ, maximæ pulchritudinis, quæ scivit bene loqui rhythmatice in vulgari."

CANTO XVII.

ARGUMENT.

The Poet issues from that thick vapour; and soon after his fancy represents to him in lively portraiture some noted examples of anger. This imagination is dissipated by the appearance of an angel, who marshals them onward to the fourth cornice, on which the sin of gloominess or indifference is purged; and here Virgil shows him that this vice proceeds from a defect of love, and that all love can be only of two sorts, either natural, or of the soul; of which sorts the former is always right, but the latter may err either in respect of object or of degree.

CALL to remembrance, reader, if thou e'er
    Hast on an Alpine height[1] been ta'en by cloud,
Through which thou saw'st no better than the mole
Doth through opacous membrane; then, whene'er
The watery vapours dense began to melt
Into thin air, how faintly the sun's sphere
Seem'd wading through them: so thy nimble thought
May image, how at first I rebeheld
The sun, that bedward now his couch o'erhung.
    Thus, with my leader's feet still equaling pace,
From forth that cloud I came, when now expired
The parting beams from off the nether shores.
    O quick and forgetive power! that sometimes dost
So rob us of ourselves, we take no mark
Though round about us thousand trumpets clang;
What moves thee, if the senses stir not? Light
Moves thee from heaven, spontaneous, self-inform'd;
Or, likelier, gliding down with swift illapse
By will divine. Portray'd before me came
The traces of her dire impiety,
Whose form was changed into the bird, that most
Delights itself in song:[2] and here my mind

---

[1] *On an Alpine height.*—" Nell' alpe." Although the Alps, as Landino remarks, are properly those mountains which divide Italy from France, yet from them all high mountains are in the Tuscan language, though not in the Latin, termed Alps. Milton uses the word thus generally in the "Samson Agonistes":
"Nor breath of vernal air from snowy Alp."
And this is a sufficient answer to the charge of impropriety, which is brought by Dr. Johnson, on the introduction of it into that drama. See the *Rambler*, No. 140.

[2] *The bird, that most delights itself in song.*—I cannot think, with Vellutello, that the swallow is here meant. Dante probably alludes to the story of Philomela, as it is found in Homer's "Odyssey," b. xix. 518, rather than as later poets have told it. "She

Was inwardly so wrapt, it gave no place
To aught that ask'd admittance from without.
Next shower'd into my fantasy a shape
As of one crucified,[1] whose visage spake
Fell rancour, malice deep, wherein he died;
And round him Ahasuerus the great king;
Esther his bride; and Mordecai the just,
Blameless in word and deed. As of itself
That unsubstantial coinage of the brain
Burst, like a bubble,[2] when the water fails
That fed it; in my vision straight uprose
A damsel[3] weeping loud, and cried, "O queen!
O mother! wherefore has intemperate ire
Driven thee to loathe thy being? Not to lose
Lavinia, desperate thou hast slain thyself.
Now hast thou lost me. I am she, whose tears
Mourn, ere I fall, a mother's timeless end."

  E'en as a sleep breaks off, if suddenly
New radiance strike upon the closed lids,
The broken slumber quivering ere it dies;[4]
Thus, from before me, sunk that imagery,
Vanishing, soon as on my face there struck
The light, outshining far our earthly beam.
As round I turn'd me to survey what place
I had arrived at, "Here ye mount:" exclaim'd

---

intended to slay the son of her husband's brother Amphion, incited to it by the envy of his wife, who had six children, while herself had only two, but through mistake slew her own son Itylus, and for her punishment was transformed by Jupiter into a nightingale." Cowper's note on this passage. In speaking of the nightingale, let me observe, that while some have considered its song as melancholy, and others as a cheerful one, Chiabrera appears to have come nearest the truth, when he says, in the "Alcippo," act i., sc. 1:—

"Non mai si stanca d'iterar le note,
O gioconde o dogliose,
Al sentir dilettose."

"Unwearied still reiterates her lays,
Jocund or sad, delightful to the ear."

See a very pleasing letter on this subject by a late illustrious statesman, "*Address to the reader prefixed to Fox's History of James II.*," edit. 1808, p. xii.; and a beautiful poem by Mr. Coleridge. I know not whether the following lines by a neglected poet have yet been noticed, as showing the diversity of opinions that have prevailed respecting the song of this bird:

"The cheerful birds
With sweetest notes to sing their Maker's praise,
Among the which, the merrie
With swete and swete, her br
Ringes out all night."
   Vallans, 7

[1] *One crucified.*—Haman. S c. vii. "In the Lunetta of Ham lime conception of his figure (b this passage."—*Fuseli*, Lecture

[2] *Like a bubble.*—

"The earth hath bubbles, a
And these are of them."
   Shakespeare,

[3] *A damsel.*—Lavinia, mour Amata, who impelled by grief the supposed death of Turnus, *Æneid*, lib. xii. 595.

[4] *The broken slumber quive* Venturi suggests that this bold a may have been formed on that in

"Tempus erat quo prima q
Incipit, et dono divûm gra

A voice, that other purpose left me none
Save will so eager to behold who spake,
I could not chuse but gaze. As 'fore the sun,
That weighs our vision down, and veils his form
In light transcendent, thus my virtue fail'd
Unequal. "This is Spirit from above,
Who marshals us our upward way, unsought;
And in his own light shrouds him. As a man
Doth for himself, so now is done for us.
For whoso waits imploring, yet sees need
Of his prompt aidance, sets himself prepared
For blunt denial, ere the suit be made.
Refuse we not to lend a ready foot
At such inviting: haste we to ascend,
Before it darken: for we may not then,
Till morn again return." So spake my guide;
And to one ladder both address'd our steps;
And the first stair approaching, I perceived
Near me as 't were the waving of a wing,
That fann'd my face, and whisper'd: "Blessed they,
The peacemakers:[1] they know not evil wrath."

Now to such height above our heads were raised
The last beams, follow'd close by hooded night,
That many a star on all sides through the gloom
Shone out. "Why partest from me, O my strength?"
So with myself I communed; for I felt
My o'ertoil'd sinews slacken. We had reach'd
The summit, and were fix'd like to a bark
Arrived at land. And waiting a short space,
If aught should meet mine ear in that new round,
Then to my guide I turn'd, and said: "Loved sire!
Declare what guilt is on this circle purged.
If our feet rest, no need thy speech should pause."

He thus to me: "The love[2] of good, whate'er
Wanted of just proportion, here fulfils.
Here plies afresh the oar, that loiter'd ill.
But that thou mayst yet clearlier understand,

---

[1] *The peacemakers.*—"Blessed are the peacemakers; they shall be called the children of God."—Matt. v. 9.

[2] *The love.*—"A defect in our love towards God, or lukewarmness in piety, is here removed."

Give ear unto my words; and thou shalt cull
Some fruit may please thee well, from this delay.
"Creator, nor created being, e'er,
My son," he thus began, "was without love,
Or natural,[1] or the free spirit's growth.
Thou hast not that to learn. The natural still
Is without error: but the other swerves,
If on ill object bent, or through excess
Of vigour, or defect. While e'er it seeks[2]
The primal blessings,[3] or with measure due
The inferior,[4] no delight, that flows from it,
Partakes of ill. But let it warp to evil,
Or with more ardour than behoves, or less,
Pursue the good; the thing created then
Works 'gainst its Maker. Hence thou must infer,
That love is germin of each virtue in ye,
And of each act no less, that merits pain.
Now[5] since it may not be, but love intend
The welfare mainly of the thing it loves,
All from self-hatred are secure; and since
No being can be thought to exist apart,
And independent of the first, a bar
Of equal force restrains from hating that.
"Grant the distinction just; and it remains
The evil must be another's, which is loved.
Three ways such love is gender'd in your clay.
There is[6] who hopes (his neighbour's worth deprest)
Pre-eminence himself; and covets hence,
For his own greatness, that another fall.
There is[7] who so much fears the loss of power,
Fame, favour, glory (should his fellow mount
Above him), and so sickens at the thought,
He loves their opposite: and there is he,

---

[1] *Or natural.*—Lombardi refers to the "Convito," Canz. i., Tratt. 2, cap. 3, where this subject is diffusely treated by our poet.
[2] *While e'er it seeks.*—So Frezzi:
"E s'egli è ben, che d'altro ben dipenda,
Non s'ami quasi per se esistente,
Se vuoi, che quando è tolto, non t'offenda."
Il Quadriregio, lib. ii., cap. 14.
This Capitolo, which describes the punishment of those who give way to inordinate grief for the loss of their kindred, is marked by much power of imagination and a sublime morality.
[3] *The primal blessings.*—Spiritual good.
[4] *The inferior.*—Temporal good.
[5] *Now.*—"It is impossible for any being, either to hate itself, or to hate the First Cause of all, by which it exists. We can, therefore, only rejoice in the evil which befals others."
[6] *There is.*—The proud.
[7] *There is.*—The envious.

Whom wrong or insult seems to gall and shame,[1]
That he doth thirst for vengeance; and such needs
Must dote on other's evil. Here beneath,
This threefold love is mourn'd.[2] Of the other sort
Be now instructed; that which follows good,
But with disorder'd and irregular course.

"All indistinctly apprehend a bliss,
On which the soul may rest; the hearts of all
Yearn after it; and to that wished bourn
All therefore strive to tend. If ye behold,
Or seek it, with a love remiss and lax;
This cornice, after just repenting, lays
Its penal torment on ye. Other good
There is, where man finds not his happiness:
It is not true fruition; not that blest
Essence, of every good the branch and root
The love too lavishly bestow'd on this,
Along three circles[3] over us, is mourn'd.
Account of that division tripartite
Expect not, fitter for thine own research."

---

[1] *There is he, whom wrong or insult seems to gall and shame.*—The resentful.

[2] *This threefold love is mourn'd.*—Frezzi alludes to this distinction:

"Superbia puote essere in tre modi;
Sì come si dimostra dalla Musa,
La qual hai letta, e che tu tanto lodi."
Il Quadriregio, lib. iii., cap. 2.

[3] *Along three circles.*—According to the allegorical ommentators, as Venturi has observed, Reason is represented under the person of Virgil, and Sense under that of Dante. The former leaves to the latter to discover for itself the three carnal sins—avarice, gluttony, and libidinousness; having already declared the nature of the spiritual sins—pride, envy, anger, and indifference, or lukewarmness in piety, which the Italians call *accidia*, from the Greek word ἀκηδία, and which Chaucer vainly endeavoured to naturalise in our language. See the "Persone's Tale." Lombardi refers to Thomas Aquinas, lib. i., Quest. 72, Art. 2, for the division here made by our poet.

CANTO XVIII.

ARGUMENT.

Virgil discourses further concerning the nature of love. Then a multitude of spirits rush by; two of whom, in van of the rest, record instances of zeal and fervent affection, and another, who was abbot of San Zeno in Verona, declares himself to Virgil and Dante; and lastly follow other spirits, shouting forth memorable examples of the sin for which they suffer. The Poet, pursuing his meditations, falls into a dreamy slumber.

THE teacher ended,[1] and his high discourse
    Concluding, earnest in my looks inquired
If I appear'd content; and I, whom still
Unsated thirst to hear him urged, was mute,
Mute outwardly, yet inwardly I said:
"Perchance my too much questioning offends."
But he, true father, mark'd the secret wish
By diffidence restrain'd; and, speaking, gave
Me boldness thus to speak: "Master! my sight
Gathers so lively virtue from thy beams,
That all, thy words convey, distinct is seen.
Wherefore I pray thee, father, whom this heart
Holds dearest, thou wouldst deign by proof t' unfold
That love, from which, as from their source, thou bring'st
All good deeds and their opposite." He then:
"To what I now disclose be thy clear ken
Directed; and thou plainly shalt behold
How much those blind have err'd, who make themselves
The guides of men. The soul, created apt
To love, moves versatile which way soe'er
Aught pleasing prompts her, soon as she is waked
By pleasure into act. Of substance true
Your apprehension[2] forms its counterfeit;

---

[1] *The teacher ended.*—Compare Plato, "Protagoras," v. iii., p. 123, Bip. edit: Πρωταγόρας μὲν τοσαῦτα κ.τ.λ. Apollonius Rhodius, l. i. 513; and Milton, "Paradise Lost," b. viii. 1:
"The angel ended, and in Adam's ear
So charming left his voice, that he awhile
Thought him still speaking, still stood fix'd to hear."

[2] *Your apprehension.*—It is literally, "Your apprehensive faculty derives intension from a thing really existing, and displays that intension within you, so that it makes the soul turn to it." The commentators labour in explaining this; but whatever sense they have elicited, may, I think, be resolved into the words of the translation in the text.

And, in you the ideal shape presenting,
Attract the soul's regard. If she, thus drawn,
Incline toward it; love is that inclining,
And a new nature knit by pleasure in ye.
Then, as the fire points up, and mounting seeks
His birth-place and his lasting-seat, e'en thus
Enters the captive soul into desire,
Which is a spiritual motion, that ne'er rests
Before enjoyment of the thing it loves.
Enough to show thee, how the truth from those
Is hidden, who aver all love a thing
Praise-worthy in itself; although perhaps[1]
Its matter still seem good. Yet if the wax
Be good, it follows not the impression must."

"What love is," I return'd, "thy words, O guide!
And my own docile mind, reveal. Yet thence
New doubts have sprung. For, from without, if love
Be offer'd to us, and the spirit knows
No other footing; tend she right or wrong,
Is no desert of hers." He answering thus:
"What reason here discovers, I have power
To show thee: that which lies beyond, expect
From Beatrice, faith not reason's task.
Spirit,[2] substantial form, with matter join'd,
Not in confusion mix'd, hath in itself
Specific virtue of that union born,
Which is not felt except it work, nor proved
But through effect, as vegetable life
By the green leaf. From whence his intellect
Deduced its primal notices of things,

---

[1] *Perhaps.* — "Our author," Venturi observes, "uses the language of the Peripatetics, which denominates the *kind* of things, as determinable by many differences, *matter*. Love then, in kind perhaps, appears good; and it is said *perhaps*, because, strictly speaking, *in kind* there is neither good nor bad, neither praiseworthy nor blameable." To this Lombardi adds, that what immediately follows —namely, that "every mark is not good although the wax be so," answers to this interpretation. For the wax is precisely as the determinable matter, and the mark or impression as the determining form; and even as the wax, which is either good or at least not bad, may, by being imprinted by a bad figure, acquire the name of bad; so may love be said generally to be good or at least not bad, and acquire the name of bad by being determined to an unfit object. "As the wax takes all shapes, and yet is wax still at the bottom; the τὸ ὑποκείμενον still is wax; so the soul transported in so many several passions of joy, fear, hope, sorrow, anger, and the like, has for its general groundwork of all this, Love."—*Henry More*, Discourse xvi. This passage in the most philosophical of our theologians, may serve for an answer to the objection of those who blame Collins for not having brought in Love among the "Passions" in his exquisite ode.

[2] *Spirit.*—The human soul, which differs from that of brutes, inasmuch as though united with the body, it has a separate existence of its own.

Man therefore knows not, or his appetites
Their first affections; such in you, as zeal
In bees to gather honey; at the first,
Volition, meriting nor blame nor praise.
But o'er each lower faculty supreme,
That, as she list, are summon'd to her bar,
Ye have that virtue[1] in you, whose just voice
Uttereth counsel, and whose word should keep
The threshold of assent. Here is the source,
Whence cause of merit in you is derived;
E'en as the affections, good or ill, she takes,
Or severs,[2] winnow'd as the chaff. Those men,[3]
Who, reasoning, went to depth profoundest, mark'd
That innate freedom; and were thence induced
To leave their moral teaching to the world.
Grant then, that from necessity arise
All love that glows within you; to dismiss
Or harbour it, the power is in yourselves.
Remember, Beatrice, in her style,
Denominates free choice by eminence
The noble virtue; if in talk with thee
She touch upon that theme." The moon, well nigh
To midnight hour belated, made the stars
Appear to wink and fade; and her broad disk
Seem'd like a crag[4] on fire, as up the vault[5]
That course she journey'd, which the sun then warms;
When they of Rome behold him at his set
Betwixt Sardinia and the Corsic isle.
And now the weight, that hung upon my thought,
Was lighten'd by the aid of that clear spirit,

---

[1] *That virtue.*—Reason.

[2] *Or severs.*—Lest the reader of the original should be misled, it is right to warn him that the word "vigliare" must not be confounded with "vagliare" to winnow, and strictly means "to separate from the straw what remains of the grain after the threshing." The process is distinctly described in the notes on the "Decameron," p. 77, ediz. Giunti, 1573, where this passage is referred to.

[3] *Those men.*—The great moral philosophers among the heathens.

[4] *A crag.*—I have preferred the reading of Landino, *scheggion,* "crag," conceiving it to be more poetical than *secchion,* "bucket," which is the common reading. The same cause, the vapours, which the commentators say might give the appearance of increased magnitude to the moon, might also make her seem broken at her rise. Lombardi explains it differently. The moon being, as he says, in the fifth night of her wane, has exactly the figure of a brazen bucket, round at the bottom and open at top; and, if we suppose it to be all on fire, we shall have, besides the form of the moon, her colour also. There is a simile in one of Fielding's novels very like this, but so ludicrous that I am unwilling to disturb the reader's gravity by inserting it.

[5] *Up the vault.*—The moon passed with a motion opposite to that of the heavens, through the constellation of the Scorpion, in which the sun is, when to those who are in Rome he appears to set between the isles of Corsica and Sardinia.

But not long
Slumber'd; for suddenly a multitude,
The steep already turning from behind,
Rush'd on.

Canto XVIII., lines 87—90.

Who raiseth Andes[1] above Mantua's name.
I therefore, when my questions had obtain'd
Solution plain and ample, stood as one
Musing in dreamy slumber; but not long
Slumber'd; for suddenly a multitude,
The steep already turning from behind,
Rush'd on. With fury and like random rout,
As echoing on their shores at midnight heard
Ismenus and Asopus,[2] for his Thebes
If Bacchus' help were needed; so came these
Tumultuous, curving each his rapid step,
By eagerness impell'd of holy love.

    Soon they o'ertook us; with such swiftness moved
The mighty crowd. Two spirits at their head
Cried, weeping, "Blessed Mary[3] sought with haste
The hilly region. Cæsar,[4] to subdue
Ilerda, darted in Marseilles his sting,
And flew to Spain."—"Oh, tarry not: away!"
The others shouted; "let not time be lost
Through slackness of affection. Hearty zeal
To serve reanimates celestial grace."

    "O ye! in whom intenser fervency
Haply supplies, where lukewarm erst ye fail'd,
Slow or neglectful, to absolve your part
Of good and virtuous; this man, who yet lives
(Credit my tale, though strange), desires to ascend,
So morning rise to light us. Therefore say
Which hand leads nearest to the rifted rock."

    So spake my guide; to whom a shade return'd:
"Come after us, and thou shalt find the cleft.
We may not linger: such resistless will
Speeds our unwearied course. Vouchsafe us then
Thy pardon, if our duty seem to thee
Discourteous rudeness. In Verona I

---

[1] *Andes.*—Andes, now Pietola, made more famous than Mantua, near which it is situated, by having been the birth-place of Virgil.

[2] *At midnight heard Ismenus and Asopus.*—Rivers near Thebes.

[3] *Mary.*—"And Mary arose in those days, and went into the hill-country with haste, into a city of Judah; and entered into the house of Zacharias, and saluted Elizabeth."—Luke i. 39, 40.

[4] *Cæsar.*—See Lucan, "Pharsalia," lib. iii. and iv.; and Cæsar, "De Bello Civili," lib. i. Cæsar left Brutus to complete the siege of Marseilles, and hastened on to the attack of Afranius and Petreius, the generals of Pompey, at Ilerda (Lerida) in Spain.

Was abbot[1] of San Zeno, when the hand
Of Barbarossa grasp'd Imperial sway,
That name ne'er utter'd without tears in Milan.
And there is he,[2] hath one foot in his grave,
Who for that monastery ere long shall weep,
Ruing his power misused: for that his son,
Of body ill compact, and worse in mind,
And born in evil, he hath set in place
Of its true pastor." Whether more he spake,
Or here was mute, I know not: he had sped
E'en now so far beyond us. Yet thus much
I heard, and in remembrance treasured it.

He then, who never fail'd me at my need,
Cried, "Hither turn. Lo! two with sharp remorse
Chiding their sin." In rear of all the troop
These shouted: "First they died,[3] to whom the sea
Open'd, or ever Jordan saw his heirs:
And they,[4] who with Æneas to the end
Endured not suffering, for their portion chose
Life without glory." Soon as they had fled
Past reach of sight, new thought within me rose
By others follow'd fast, and each unlike
Its fellow: till led on from thought to thought,
And pleasured with the fleeting train, mine eye
Was closed, and meditation changed to dream.

---

[1] *Abbot.*—Alberto, abbot of San Zeno in Verona, when Frederick I. was emperor, by whom Milan was besieged and reduced to ashes, in 1162.

[2] *There is he.*—Alberto della Scala, Lord of Verona, who had made his natural son abbot of San Zeno.

[3] *First they died.*—The Israelites, who on account of their disobedience died before reaching the promised land.

[4] *And they.*—Those Trojans, who wearied with their voyage, chose rather to remain in Sicily with Acestes, than accompany Æneas to Italy. Virgil, "Æneid," lib. v.

CANTO XIX.

ARGUMENT.

The Poet, after describing his dream, relates how, at the summoning of an angel, he ascends with Virgil to the fifth cornice, where the sin of avarice is cleansed, and where he finds Pope Adrian V

IT was the hour,[1] when of diurnal heat
   No reliques chafe the cold beams of the moon,
O'erpower'd by earth, or planetary sway
Of Saturn; and the geomancer[2] sees
His Greater Fortune up the east ascend,
Where grey dawn checkers first the shadowy cone;
When, 'fore me in my dream, a woman's shape[3]
There came, with lips that stammer'd, eyes aslant,
Distorted feet, hands maim'd, and colour pale.
   I look'd upon her: and, as sunshine cheers
Limbs numb'd by nightly cold, e'en thus my look
Unloosed her tongue; next, in brief space, her form
Decrepit raised erect, and faded face
With love's own hue[4] illumed. Recovering speech,
She forthwith, warbling, such a strain began,
That I, how loth soe'er, could scarce have held
Attention from the song. "I," thus she sang,
"I am the Syren, she, whom mariners
On the wide sea are wilder'd when they hear:
Such fulness of delight the listener feels.

---

[1] *The hour.*—Near the dawn.

[2] *The geomancer.*—The geomancers, says Landino, when they divined, drew a figure consisting of sixteen marks, named from so many stars which constitute the end of Aquarius and the beginning of Pisces. One of these they called "the greater fortune." Chaucer has imitated this in a description of morning ("Troilus and Creseide," b. iii.), for he did not find it in his original, Boccaccio's "Filostrato:"

"But when the cocke, commune astrologer,
Gan on his brest to bete, and after crowe,
And Lucifer the dayis-messanger
Gan for to rise, and out his bemis throwe,
And estward rose, to him that could it knowe.
Fortuna Major."

[3] *When, 'fore me in my dream, a woman's shape.*—Worldly happiness. This allegory reminds us of the "Choice of Hercules."

[4] *Love's own hue.*—

"A smile that glow'd
Celestial rosy red, love's proper hue."
Milton, Paradise Lost, b. viii. 619.

"Facies pulcherrima tunc est,
Quum porphyriaco variatur candida rubro.
Quid color hic roseus sibi vult? designat amorem:
Quippe amor est igni similis; flammasque rubentes
Ignis habere solet."
Palingenii Zodiacus Vitæ, lib. xii.

I, from his course, Ulysses[1] by my lay
Enchanted drew. Whoe'er frequents me once,
Parts seldom : so I charm him, and his heart
Contented knows no void." Or ere her mouth
Was closed, to shame her, at my side appear'd
A dame[2] of semblance holy. With stern voice
She utter'd : "Say, O Virgil! who is this?"
Which hearing, he approach'd, with eyes still bent
Toward that goodly presence : the other seized her,
And, her robes tearing, open'd her before,
And show'd the belly to me, whence a smell,
Exhaling loathsome, waked me. Round I turn'd
Mine eyes : and thus the teacher : "At the least
Three times my voice hath call'd thee. Rise, begone.
Let us the opening find where thou mayst pass."

    I straightway rose. Now day, pour'd down from high,
Fill'd all the circuits of the sacred mount;
And, as we journey'd, on our shoulder smote
The early ray. I follow'd stooping low
My forehead, as a man, o'ercharged with thought,
Who bends him to the likeness of an arch
That midway spans the flood; when thus I heard,
"Come, enter here," in tone so soft and mild,
As never met the ear on mortal strand.

    With swan-like wings dispred and pointing up,
Who thus had spoken marshal'd us along,
Where, each side of the solid masonry,
The sloping walls retired; then moved his plumes,
And fanning us, affirm'd that those, who mourn[3]
Are blessed, for that comfort shall be theirs.

    "What aileth thee, that still thou look'st to earth?"
Began my leader; while the angelic shape
A little over us his station took.

    "New vision," I replied, "hath raised in me
Surmisings strange and anxious doubts, whereon

---

[1] *Ulysses.*—It is not easy to determine why Ulysses, contrary to the authority of Homer, is said to have been drawn aside from his course by the song of the Syren. No improbable way of accounting for the contradiction is, to suppose that she is here represented as purposely deviating from the truth. Or Dante may have followed some legend of the middle ages, in which the wanderings of Ulysses were represented otherwise than in Homer.
[2] *A dame.*—Philosophy, or perhaps Truth.
[3] *Who mourn.*—"Blessed are they that mourn : for they shall be comforted."—Matt. v. 4.

"What aileth thee, that still thou look'st to earth?"
Began my leader; while the angelic shape
A little over us his station took.

Canto XIX., lines 51—53.

My soul intent allows no other thought
Or room, or entrance."—"Hast thou seen," said he,
"That old enchantress, her, whose wiles alone
The spirits o'er us weep for? Hast thou seen
How man may free him of her bonds? Enough.
Let thy heels spurn the earth;[1] and thy raised ken
Fix on the lure, which heaven's eternal King
Whirls in the rolling spheres." As on his feet
The falcon[2] first looks down, then to the sky
Turns, and forth stretches eager for the food,
That wooes him thither; so the call I heard:
So onward, far as the dividing rock
Gave way, I journey'd, till the plain was reach'd.

On the fifth circle when I stood at large,
A race appear'd before me, on the ground
All downward lying prone and weeping sore.
"My soul[3] hath cleaved to the dust," I heard
With sighs so deep, they well nigh choked the words.

"O ye elect of God! whose penal woes
Both hope and justice mitigate, direct
Towards the steep rising our uncertain way."

"If ye approach secure from this our doom,
Prostration, and would urge your course with speed,
See that ye still to rightward keep the brink."

So them the bard besought; and such the words,
Beyond us some short space, in answer came.
I noted what remain'd yet hidden from them:[4]
Thence to my liege's eyes mine eyes I bent,
And he, forthwith interpreting their suit,
Beckon'd his glad assent. Free then to act
As pleased me, I drew near, and took my stand
Over that shade whose words I late had mark'd,

---

[1] *Let thy heels spurn the earth.*—This is a metaphor from hawking, though less apparent than in the lines that follow.

[2] *The falcon.*—
"Poi come fa 'l falcon, quando si move,
Cosi Umiltà al cielo alzò la vista."
Frezzi, Il Quadriregio, lib. iv., cap. v.

"Io vidi poi color tutti levare
Inverso il cielo, come fa 'l falcone,
Quando la preda sua prende in su l'arc."
Ibid., cap. xiii.

One of our periodical critics has remarked that Dante must have loved hawking; and "that he paints his bird always to the life."—*Edinburgh Review,* No. lviii., p. 472. In the same manner Mr. Blomfield supposes that Æschylus was addicted to fishing, because he often takes his metaphors from fishing-nets. See that gentleman's notes to the Persæ, Glossar., v. 430.

[3] *My soul.*—"My soul cleaveth to the dust: quicken thou me according to thy word."—Ps. cxix. 25.

[4] *I noted what remain'd yet hidden from them.*—They were ignorant, it appeared, whether Dante was come there to be purged of his sins.

And, "Spirit!" I said, "in whom repentant tears
Mature that blessed hour when thou with God
Shalt find acceptance, for a while suspend
For me that mightier care. Say who thou wast;
Why thus ye grovel on your bellies prone;
And if, in aught, ye wish my service there,
Whence living I am come." He answering spake:
"The cause why Heaven our back toward his cope
Reverses, shalt thou know: but me know first,
The successor of Peter,[1] and the name
And title of my lineage, from that stream
That 'twixt Chiaveri and Siestri draws
His limpid waters[2] through the lowly glen.
A month and little more by proof I learnt,
With what a weight that robe of sovereignty
Upon his shoulder rests, who from the mire
Would guard it; that each other fardel seems
But feathers in the balance. Late, alas!
Was my conversion: but, when I became
Rome's pastor, I discern'd at once the dream
And cozenage of life; saw that the heart
Rested not there, and yet no prouder height
Lured on the climber: wherefore, of that life
No more enamour'd, in my bosom love
Of purer being kindled. For till then
I was a soul in misery, alienate
From God, and covetous of all earthly things;
Now, as thou seest, here punish'd for my doting.
Such cleansing from the taint of avarice
Do spirits, converted, need. This mount inflicts
No direr penalty. E'en as our eyes
Fasten'd below, nor e'er to loftier clime
Were lifted;[3] thus hath justice level'd us,
Here on the earth. As avarice quench'd our love
Of good, without which is no working; thus

---

[1] *The successor of Peter.*—Ottobuono, of the family of Fieschi, Counts of Lavagno, died thirty-nine days after he became pope, with the title of Adrian V., in 1276.
[2] *That stream that 'twixt Chiaveri and Siestri draws his limpid waters.*—The river Lavagno, in the Genoese territory; to the east of which territory are situated Siestri and Chiaveri.
[3] *Were lifted.*—Rosa Morando and Lombardi are very severe on Venturi's perplexity occasioned by the word "aderse." They have none of them noticed Landino's reading of "aperse." Ediz. 1484.

"Up," he exclaim'd, "brother! upon thy feet
Arise; err not: thy fellow servant I
(Thine and all others'), of one Sovran Power."
Canto XIX., lines 131—133.

Here justice holds us prison'd, hand and foot
Chain'd down and bound, while heaven's just Lord shall please,
So long to tarry, motionless, outstretch'd."

My knees I stoop'd, and would have spoke; but he,
Ere my beginning, by his ear perceived
I did him reverence; and "What cause," said he,
"Hath bow'd thee thus?"—"Compunction," I rejoin'd,
"And inward awe of your high dignity."

"Up," he exclaim'd, "brother! upon thy feet
Arise; err not:[1] thy fellow servant I
(Thine and all others'), of one Sovran Power.
If thou hast ever mark'd those holy sounds
Of gospel truth, 'nor shall be given in marriage,'[2]
Thou mayst discern the reasons of my speech.
Go thy ways now; and linger here no more.
Thy tarrying is a let unto the tears,
With which I hasten that whereof thou spakest.[3]
I have on earth a kinswoman;[4] her name
Alagia, worthy in herself, so ill
Example of our house corrupt her not:
And she is all remaineth of me there."

---

[1] *Err not.*—"And I fell at his feet to worship him. And he said unto me, See thou do it not: I am thy fellow servant, and of thy brethren that have the testimony of Jesus."—Rev. xix. 10.

[2] *Nor shall be given in marriage.*—"Since in this state we neither marry nor are given in marriage, I am no longer the spouse of the church, and therefore no longer retain my former dignity."—See Matt. xxii. 30.

[3] *That whereof thou spakest.*—See ver. 89.

[4] *A kinswoman.*—Alagia is said to have been the wife of the Marchese Marcello Malaspina, one of the poet's protectors during his exile. See canto viii. 133.

CANTO XX.

ARGUMENT.

Among those on the fifth cornice, Hugh Capet records illustrious examples of voluntary poverty and of bounty; then tells who himself is, and speaks of his descendants on the French throne; and, lastly, adds some noted instances of avarice. When he has ended, the mountain shakes, and all the spirits sing "Glory to God."

ILL strives the will, 'gainst will more wise that strives:
  His pleasure therefore to mine own preferr'd,
I drew the sponge[1] yet thirsty from the wave.
  Onward I moved: he also onward moved,
Who led me, coasting still, wherever place
Along the rock was vacant; as a man
Walks near the battlements on narrow wall.
For those on the other part, who drop by drop
Wring out their all-infecting malady,
Too closely press the verge. Accurst be thou,
Inveterate wolf![2] whose gorge ingluts more prey
Than every beast beside, yet is not fill'd;
So bottomless thy maw.—Ye spheres of heaven!
To whom there are, as seems, who attribute
All change in mortal state, when is the day
Of his appearing,[3] for whom fate reserves
To chase her hence?—With wary steps and slow
We pass'd; and I attentive to the shades,
Whom piteously I heard lament and wail;
And, 'midst the wailing, one before us heard
Cry out, "O blessed Virgin!" as a dame
In the sharp pangs of childbed; and "How poor
Thou wast," it added, "witness that low roof
Where thou didst lay thy sacred burden down.
O good Fabricius![4] thou didst virtue chuse
With poverty, before great wealth with vice."

---

[1] *I drew the sponge.*—"I did not persevere in my inquiries from the spirit, though still anxious to learn more."

[2] *Wolf.*—Avarice.

[3] *Of his appearing.*—He is thought to allude to Can Grande della Scala. See "Hell," canto i. 98.

[4] *Fabricius.*—So our author in the second book of the " De Monarchiâ," p. 121, " Nonne Fabricium," &c.

With wary steps and slow
We pass'd; and I attentive to the shades,
Whom piteously I heard lament and wail.
Canto XX., lines 17—19.

The words so pleased me, that desire to know
The spirit, from whose lip they seem'd to come,
Did draw me onward. Yet it spake the gift
Of Nicholas,[1] which on the maidens he
Bounteous bestow'd, to save their youthful prime
Unblemish'd. "Spirit! who dost speak of deeds
So worthy, tell me who thou wast," I said,
"And why thou dost with single voice renew
Memorial of such praise. That boon vouchsafed
Haply shall meet reward; if I return
To finish the short pilgrimage of life,
Still speeding to its close on restless wing."

"I," answer'd he, "will tell thee; not for help,
Which thence I look for; but that in thyself
Grace so exceeding shines, before thy time
Of mortal dissolution. I was root[2]
Of that ill plant whose shade such poison sheds
O'er all the Christian land, that seldom thence
Good fruit is gather'd. Vengeance soon should come,
Had Ghent and Douay, Lille and Bruges power;[3]
And vengeance I of heaven's great Judge implore.
Hugh Capet was I hight; from me descend
The Philips and the Louis, of whom France
Newly is govern'd: born of one, who plied
The slaughterer's trade[4] at Paris. When the race
Of ancient kings had vanish'd (all save one[5]

"Has not Fabricius given us another example of resisting avarice, when, poor as he was, he preserved his faith to the republic, and rejected with scorn a great sum of gold that was offered him?" Our poet, in the sixth book, records this when he says:

"Parvoque potentem
 Fabricium."

Compare Petrarch, "Tr. della Fama," c. i.:

"Un Curio ed un Fabricio assai più belli
Con la lor povertà, che Mida e Crasso
Con l'oro ond' a virtù furon rubelli."

[1] *Nicholas.*—The story of Nicholas is, that an angel having revealed to him that the father of a family was so impoverished as to resolve on exposing the chastity of his three daughters to sale, he threw in at the window of their house three bags of money, containing a sufficient portion for each of them.

[2] *Root.*—Hugh Capet, ancestor of Philip IV.

[3] *Had Ghent and Douay, Lille and Bruges power.*—These cities had lately been seized by Philip IV. The spirit is made to intimate the approaching defeat of the French army by the Flemings in the battle of Courtrai, which happened in 1302.

[4] *The slaughterer's trade.*—This reflection on the birth of his ancestor induced Francis I. to forbid the reading of Dante in his dominions. Hugh Capet, who came to the throne of France in 987, was, however, the grandson of Robert, who was the brother of Eudes, King of France in 888; and it may, therefore, well be questioned whether by *Beccaio di Parigi* is meant literally one who had carried on the trade of a butcher at Paris, and whether the sanguinary disposition of Hugh Capet's father is not stigmatised by this opprobrious appellation. See Cancellieri, "Osservazioni," &c., Roma, 1814, p. 6.

[5] *All save one.*—The posterity of Charlemagne, the second race of French monarchs, had failed, with the exception of Charles of Lorraine, who is said, on account of the melancholy temper of his mind, to have always clothed himself in black. Venturi suggests that Dante may have confounded him with Childeric III., the last of the Merovingian, or first race, who was deposed and made a monk in 751.

Wrapt up in sable weeds) within my gripe
I found the reins of empire, and such powers
Of new acquirement, with full store of friends,
That soon the widow'd circlet of the crown
Was girt upon the temples of my son,[1]
He, from whose bones the anointed race begins.
Till the great dower of Provence[2] had removed
The stains,[3] that yet obscured our lowly blood,
Its sway indeed was narrow; but howe'er
It wrought no evil: there, with force and lies,
Began its rapine: after, for amends,[4]
Poitou it seized, Navarre and Gascony.[5]

---

[1] *My son.*—Hugh Capet caused his son Robert to be crowned at Orleans.

[2] *The great dower of Provence.*—Louis IX. and his brother Charles of Anjou married two of the four daughters of Raymond Berenger, Count of Provence. See "Paradise," c. vi. 135.

[3] *The stains.*—Lombardi understands this differently from all the other commentators with whom I am acquainted. The word "vergogna" he takes in the sense of "a praise-worthy shame of doing ill;" and according to him the translation should run thus:

"The shame that yet restrain'd my race from ill."

By "Provenza" he understands the estates of Toulouse, the dowry of the only daughter of Raymond, Count of Toulouse, married to a brother of Louis IX.

[4] *For amends.*—This is ironical.

[5] *Poitou it seized, Navarre and Gascony.*—I venture to read—

"Potti e Navarra prese e Guascogna,"

instead of

"Ponti e Normandia prese e Guascogna."

"Seized Ponthieu, Normandy, and Gascogny."
Landino has "Potti," and he is probably right; for Poitou was annexed to the French Crown by Philip IV. See Henault, "Abrégé Chron.," A.D. 1283, &c. Normandy had been united to it long before by Philip Augustus, a circumstance of which it is difficult to imagine that Dante should have been ignorant; but Philip IV., says Henault, ibid., took the title of King of Navarre, and the subjugation of Navarre is also alluded to in the "Paradise," canto xix. 140. In 1293, Philip IV. summoned Edward I. to do him homage for the duchy of Gascogny, which he had conceived the design of seizing. See G. Villani, lib. viii., cap. iv. The whole passage has occasioned much perplexity. I cannot withhold from my readers the advantage of an attempt made to unravel it by the late Archdeacon Fisher, which that gentleman, though a stranger, had the goodness to communicate to me in the following terms: "I am encouraged to offer you an elucidation of a passage, with the interpretation of which I was never yet satisfied. As it goes to establish the accuracy of two very happy conjectures which you have made at 'Purgatory,' xx. 66, you will perhaps forgive me, if my notion a little militates against your solution of the difficulty. The passage is as follows:

'I' fui radice della mala pianta,
Che la terra Cristiana tutta aduggia,
Si che buon frutto rado se ne schianta.

Ma se Doagio, Guanto, Lilla, e Bruggia
Potesser, tosto ne saria vendetta:
Ed io la cheggio a lui, che tutto giuggia.

Mentre che la gran dote Provenzale
Al sangue mio non tolse la vergogna,
Poco valea, ma pur non facea male.
Li cominciò con forza e con menzogna
La sua rapina; e poscia, per ammenda
Potti e Navarra prese, e Guascogna.'

It is my persuasion that the stanzas I have copied are *one* passage, continuous in its sense, interrupted only by a parenthesis of four stanzas, which are introduced as necessary to the political solution of the meaning. Again, I think that my quoted stanzas refer to only one person, and that Philip IV., of France. He is depicted by both the phrases, 'mala pianta,' and 'sangue mio.' I do not find that Louis IX. obtained any part of Provence by dowry, owing to his marriage with the daughter of the prince of that country; at least, nothing equivalent to the words 'la gran dote Provenzale.' I suppose the stanzas quoted to depict the three great events in the life of Philip IV. He married, during the life of his father, the heiress of the kingdom of Navarre, and also of the duchy of Champagne. Philip obtained at once the sovereignty of both these dowries, and left to his son Philip V. the title of King of France and Navarre. On the accession of Philip IV. to the throne, he became embroiled with the English respecting the duchy of Guienne, which, after having changed masters frequently, was then in the possession of Edward I. The word Guienne included Poitou and Gascony, and was generally the country termed by Cæsar, Aquitania. By perfidy, and the childish ignorance of Edmund, the brother of Edward I., Philip got possession of Guienne. . . . The duchy of Champagne, now annexed to the crown of France, lying adjacent to that of Flanders, Philip next endeavoured to lay hands on that fief: and failing in treacherous negotiation, he carried a cruel and murderous war into the low countries, and laid them desolate. His progress was stopped by the Flemings at the battle of Courtrai, and he was soon after compelled to surrender Guienne to the English king, and to make peace with his numerous enemies. Now, to these three leading epochs of Philip's life, the poet seems to allude. 'Doagio, Guanto, Lilla e Bruggia' refer to his desolating war in Flanders; 'Vendetta,' to the battle of Courtrai; 'la gran dote Provenzale,' to the dowry of the kingdom of Navarre and the duchy of Champagne; 'forza e

To Italy came Charles ; and for amends,
Young Conradine,[1] an innocent victim, slew ;
And sent the angelic teacher[2] back to heaven,
Still for amends. I see the time at hand,
That forth from France invites another Charles[3]
To make himself and kindred better known.
Unarm'd he issues, saving with that lance,
Which the arch-traitor tilted with ;[4] and that
He carries with so home a thrust, as rives
The bowels of poor Florence. No increase
Of territory hence, but sin and shame
Shall be his guerdon ; and so much the more
As he more lightly deems of such foul wrong.
I see the other[5] (who a prisoner late
Had stept on shore) exposing to the mart
His daughter, whom he bargains for, as do
The Corsairs for their slaves. O avarice !
What canst thou more, who hast subdued our blood
So wholly to thyself, they feel no care
Of their own flesh ? To hide with direr guilt
Past ill and future, lo ! the flower-de-luce[6]

---

menzogna,' to his conduct respecting Guienne with its two sister provinces, as you so convincingly conjectured, ' Potti e Guascogna.' "

[1] *Young Conradine.*—Charles of Anjou put Conradino to death in 1268, and became King of Naples. See " Hell," canto xxviii. 16, and note. Compare Fazio degli Uberti, " Dittamondo," lib. ii., cap. xxix.

[2] *The angelic teacher.*—Thomas Aquinas. He was reported to have been poisoned by a physician, who wished to ingratiate himself with Charles of Anjou. " In the year 1323, at the end of July, by the said Pope John and by his cardinals, was canonised at Avignon Thomas Aquinas, of the order of Saint Dominic, a master in divinity and philosophy, a man most excellent in all science, and who expounded the sense of Scripture better than any one since the time of Augustin. He lived in the time of Charles I. King of Sicily ; and going to the council at Lyons, it is said that he was killed by a physician of the said king, who put poison for him into some sweetmeats, thinking to ingratiate himself with King Charles, because he was of the lineage of the lords of Aquino, who had rebelled against the king, and doubting lest he should be made cardinal : whence the church of God received great damage. He died at the abbey of Fossanova, in Campagna."—G. Villani, lib. ix., cap. ccxviii. We shall find him in the " Paradise," canto x.

[3] *Another Charles.*—Charles of Valois, brother of Philip IV., was sent by Pope Boniface VIII. to settle the disturbed state of Florence. In consequence of the measures he adopted for that purpose, our poet and his friends were condemned to exile and death. See G. Villani, lib. viii., c. xlviii.

[4] *With that lance, which the arch-traitor tilted with.*—

" Con la lancia
Con la qual giostro Giuda."

If I remember right, in one of the old romances, Judas is represented tilting with our Saviour.

[5] *The other.*—Charles, King of Naples, the eldest son of Charles of Anjou, having, contrary to the directions of his father, engaged with Ruggier de Lauria, the admiral of Peter of Arragon, was made prisoner, and carried into Sicily, June, 1284. He afterwards, in consideration of a large sum of money, married his daughter to Azzo VIII., Marquis of Ferrara. I take Lauria to be the hero meant by Petrarch in his Triumph of Fame :

" Quel di Luria seguiva il Saladino."
Cap. ii., v. 151.

Of whom Biagioli says in a note, " Non so chi sia, e non trovo nè vivo nè morto chi mel dica," " I know not who he is, and I find no one alive or dead to tell me." Mariana, lib. xiv., cap. 10, calls Lauria "a brave captain, signalised by his former victories." See also the seventh book of G. Villani's history, and Boccaccio's " Decameron," Giorn. 5, Nov. 6 ; where he is named Ruggieri dell' Oria.

[6] *The flower-de-luce.*—Boniface VIII. was seized at Alagna in Campagna, by the order of Philip IV., in the year 1303, and soon after died of grief. G. Villani, lib. viii., cap. lxiii. " As it pleased God, the heart of Boniface being petrified with grief, through the injury he had sustained, when he came to Rome, he fell into a strange malady, for he gnawed himself as one

Enters Alagna; in his Vicar Christ
Himself a captive, and his mockery
Acted again. Lo! to his holy lip
The vinegar and gall once more applied;
And he 'twixt living robbers doom'd to bleed.
Lo! the new Pilate, of whose cruelty
Such violence cannot fill the measure up,
With no decree to sanction, pushes on
Into the temple his yet eager sails.[1]

"O sovran Master![2] when shall I rejoice
To see the vengeance, which thy wrath, well-pleased,
In secret silence broods?—While daylight lasts,
So long what thou didst hear[3] of her, sole spouse
Of the Great Spirit, and on which thou turn'dst
To me for comment, is the general theme
Of all our prayers: but, when it darkens, then
A different strain we utter; then record
Pygmalion,[4] whom his gluttonous thirst of gold
Made traitor, robber, parricide: the woes
Of Midas, which his greedy wish ensued,
Mark'd for derision to all future times:
And the fond Achan,[5] how he stole the prey,
That yet he seems by Joshua's ire pursued.
Sapphira with her husband next we blame;
And praise the forefeet, that with furious ramp
Spurn'd Heliodorus.[6] All the mountain round
Rings with the infamy of Thracia's king,[7]
Who slew his Phrygian charge: and last a shout

---

frantic, and in this state expired." His character is strongly drawn by the annalist in the next chapter. Thus, says Landino, was verified the prophecy of Celestine respecting him, that he should enter on the popedom like a fox, reign like a lion, and die like a dog.

[1] *Into the temple his yet eager sails.*—It is uncertain whether our poet alludes still to the event mentioned in the preceding note, or to the destruction of the order of the Templars in 1310, but the latter appears more probable.

[2] *O sovran Master.*—Lombardi, who rightly corrects Venturi's explanation of this passage, with which I will not trouble the reader, should have acknowledged, if he was conscious of it, that his own interpretation of it was the same as that before given by Vellutello: "When, O Lord, shall I behold that vengeance accomplished, which being already determined in thy secret judgment, thy retributive justice even now contemplates with delight?"

[3] *While daylight lasts, so long what thou didst hear.*—See ver. 21.

[4] *Pygmalion.*— " Ille Sychæum
Impius ante aras, atque auri cæcus amore,
Clam ferro incautum superat."
Virgil, Æneid, l. 1, 350.

[5] *Achan.*—Joshua vii.

[6] *Heliodorus.*—" For there appeared unto them an horse, with a terrible rider upon him, and adorned with a very fair covering, and he ran fiercely and smote at Heliodorus with his fore feet."—2 Maccabees iii. 25.

[7] *Thracia's king.*—Polymnestor, the murderer of Polydorus. " Hell," canto xxx. 19.

Ascends: 'Declare, O Crassus!¹ for thou know'st,
The flavour of thy gold.' The voice of each
Now high, now low, as each his impulse prompts,
Is led through many a pitch, acute or grave.
Therefore, not singly, I erewhile rehearsed
That blessedness we tell of in the day:
But near me, none, beside, his accent raised."

From him we now had parted, and essay'd
With utmost efforts to surmount the way;
When I did feel, as nodding to its fall,
The mountain tremble; whence an icy chill
Seized on me, as on one to death convey'd.
So shook not Delos, when Latona there
Couch'd to bring forth the twin-born eyes of heaven.

Forthwith from every side a shout arose
So vehement, that suddenly my guide
Drew near, and cried: "Doubt not, while I conduct thee."
"Glory!" all shouted (such the sounds mine ear
Gather'd from those, who near me swell'd the sounds),
"Glory in the highest be to God." We stood
Immovably suspended, like to those,
The shepherds, who first heard in Bethlehem's field
That song: till ceased the trembling, and the song
Was ended: then our hallow'd path resumed,
Eying the prostrate shadows, who renew'd
Their custom'd mourning. Never in my breast
Did ignorance so struggle with desire
Of knowledge, if my memory do not err,
As in that moment; nor through haste dared I
To question, nor myself could aught discern.
So on I fared, in thoughtfulness and dread.

---

¹ *Crassus.*—Marcus Crassus, who fell miserably in the Parthian war. See Appian, "Parthica:"
"E vidi Ciro più di sangue avaro,
Che Crasso d'oro, e l'uno e l'altro n'ebbe
Tanto, che parve a ciascheduno amaro."
Petrarca.

CANTO XXI.

ARGUMENT.

The two Poets are overtaken by the spirit of Statius, who, being cleansed, is on his way to Paradise, and who explains the cause of the mountain shaking, and of the hymn; his joy at beholding Virgil.

THE natural thirst, ne'er quench'd but from the well[1]
  Whereof the woman of Samaria craved
Excited; haste, along the cumber'd path,
After my guide, impell'd; and pity moved
My bosom for the 'vengeful doom though just.
When lo! even as Luke[2] relates, that Christ
Appear'd unto the two upon their way,
New-risen from his vaulted grave; to us
A shade appear'd, and after us approach'd,
Contemplating the crowd beneath its feet.
We are not ware of it; so first it spake,
Saying, "God give you peace, my brethren!" then
Sudden we turn'd: and Virgil such salute,
As fitted that kind greeting, gave; and cried:
"Peace in the blessed council be thy lot,
Awarded by that righteous court which me
To everlasting banishment exiles."

"How!" he exclaim'd, nor from his speed meanwhile
Desisting;[3] "If that ye be spirits whom God
Vouchsafes not room above; who up the height
Has been thus far your guide?" To whom the bard:
"If thou observe the tokens,[4] which this man,
Traced by the finger of the angel, bears;
'Tis plain that in the kingdom of the just

---

[1] *The well.*—"The woman saith unto him, Sir, give me this water, that I thirst not."—John iv. 15.

[2] *Luke.*—Chapter xxiv. 13.

[3] *Nor from his speed meanwhile desisting.*—The unintelligible reading of almost all the editions here (but not of all, as Lombardi would lead us to suppose, except his favourite Nidobeatina) is "E perchè andate forte?"
Vellutello has also that which is no doubt the right: "E parte andava forte."

[4] *The tokens.*—The letter P for Peccata, sins, inscribed upon his forehead by the Angel, in order to his being cleared of them in his passage through Purgatory to Paradise.

He needs must share. But sithence she,[1] whose wheel
Spins day and night, for him not yet had drawn
That yarn, which on the fatal distaff piled,
Clotho apportions to each wight that breathes;
His soul, that sister is to mine and thine,
Not of herself could mount; for not like ours
Her ken: whence I, from forth the ample gulf
Of hell, was ta'en, to lead him, and will lead
Far as my lore avails. But, if thou know,
Instruct us for what cause, the mount erewhile
Thus shook, and trembled: wherefore all at once
Seem'd shouting, even from his wave-wash'd foot"

   That questioning so tallied with my wish,
The thirst did feel abatement of its edge
E'en from expectance. He forthwith replied:
"In its devotion, nought irregular
This mount can witness, or by punctual rule
Unsanction'd; here from every change exempt,
Other than that, which heaven in itself
Doth of itself receive,[2] no influence
Can reach us. Tempest none, shower, hail, or snow,
Hoar frost, or dewy moistness, higher falls
Than that brief scale of threefold steps: thick clouds,
Nor scudding rack, are ever seen: swift glance
Ne'er lightens; nor Thaumantian[3] Iris gleams,
That yonder often shifts on each side heaven.
Vapour adust doth never mount above
The highest of the trinal stairs, whereon
Peter's vicegerent stands. Lower perchance,
With various motion rock'd, trembles the soil:
But here, through wind in earth's deep hollow pent,
I know not how, yet never trembled: then
Trembles, when any spirit feels itself
So purified, that it may rise, or move
For rising; and such loud acclaim ensues.

---

[1] *She.*—Lachesis, one of the three fates.
[2] *That which heaven in itself doth of itself receive.*—Venturi, I think rightly, interprets this to be light.
[3] *Thaumantian.*—Figlia di Taumante.
Θαύμαντος θυγάτηρ.—*Hesiod, Theogony,* 780.

Compare Plato, "Theæt." v. ii., p. 76, Bip. edit.; Virgil, "Æneid," ix. 5; and Spenser, "Faery Queen," b. v., c. iii., st. 25.

"Fair is Thaumantias in her crystal gown."
Drummond.

Purification, by the will alone,
Is proved, that free to change society
Seizes the soul rejoicing in her will.
Desire of bliss is present from the first;
But strong propension hinders, to that wish[1]
By the just ordinance of heaven opposed;
Propension now as eager to fulfil
The allotted torment, as erewhile to sin.
And I, who in this punishment had lain
Five hundred years and more, but now have felt
Free wish for happier clime. Therefore thou felt'st
The mountain tremble; and the spirits devout
Heard'st, over all his limits, utter praise
To that liege Lord, whom I entreat their joy
To hasten." Thus he spake: and, since the draught
Is grateful ever as the thirst is keen,
No words may speak my fulness of content.

"Now," said the instructor sage, "I see the net[2]
That takes ye here: and how the toils are loosed;
Why rocks the mountain, and why ye rejoice.
Vouchsafe, that from thy lips I next may learn
Who on the earth thou wast; and wherefore here,
So many an age, were prostrate."—"In that time,
When the good Titus,[3] with Heaven's King to help,
Avenged those piteous gashes, whence the blood
By Judas sold did issue; with the name[4]
Most lasting and most honour'd, there, was I
Abundantly renown'd," the shade replied,
"Not yet with faith endued. So passing sweet
My vocal spirit; from Tolosa,[5] Rome
To herself drew me, where I merited

---

[1] *To that wish.*—Lombardi here alters the sense by reading with the Nidobeatina, "con tal voglia," instead of "contra voglia," and explains it: "With the same ineffectual will with which man was contrary to sin while he resolved on sinning, even with the same, would he wish to rise from his torment in Purgatory, at the same time that through inclination to satisfy the divine justice he yet remains there."

[2] *I see the net.*—" I perceive that ye are detained here by your wish to satisfy the divine justice."

[3] *When the good Titus.*—When it was so ordered by the divine Providence that Titus, by the destruction of Jerusalem, should avenge the death of our Saviour on the Jews.

[4] *The name.*—The name of poet.

[5] *From Tolosa.*—Dante, as many others have done, confounds Statius the poet, who was a Neapolitan, with a rhetorician of the same name, who was of Tolosa, or Thoulouse. Thus Chaucer, " Temple of Fame," b. iii.:

"The Tholason, that height Stace."

And Boccaccio, as cited by Lombardi:

" E Stazio di Tolosa ancora caro."

Amorosa Visio, cant. 5.

A myrtle garland[1] to inwreathe my brow.
Statius they name me still. Of Thebes I sang,
And next of great Achilles; but i' the way
Fell[2] with the second burthen. Of my flame
Those sparkles were the seeds, which I derived
From the bright fountain of celestial fire
That feeds unnumber'd lamps ; the song I mean
Which sounds Æneas' wanderings: that the breast
I hung at ; that the nurse, from whom my veins
Drank inspiration: whose authority
Was ever sacred with me. To have lived
Co-eval with the Mantuan, I would bide
The revolution of another sun
Beyond my stated years in banishment."

    The Mantuan, when he heard him, turn'd to me;
And holding silence, by his countenance
Enjoin'd me silence : but the power, which wills,
Bears not supreme control : laughter and tears
Follow so closely on the passion prompts them,
They wait not for the motions of the will
In natures most sincere. I did but smile,
As one who winks ;[3] and thereupon the shade
Broke off, and peer'd into mine eyes, where best
Our looks interpret. "So to good event
Mayst thou conduct such great emprize," he cried,
"Say, why across thy visage beam'd, but now,
The lightning of a smile." On either part
Now am I straiten'd ; one conjures me speak,
The other to silence binds me : whence a sigh
I utter, and the sigh is heard. "Speak on,"
The teacher cried : "and do not fear to speak ;
But tell him what so earnestly he asks."
Whereon I thus : "Perchance, O ancient spirit !
Thou marvel'st at my smiling. There is room
For yet more wonder. He, who guides my ken

---

[1] *A myrtle garland.*—
"Et vos, O lauri, carpam, et te, proxima myrte."
                      Virgil, Ecl. ii.
"Qual vaghezza di lauro ? o qual di mirto ?"
                      Petrarca.
"Yet once more, O ye laurels, and once more,
  Ye myrtles brown."   *Milton, Lycidas.*

[2] *Fell.*—Statius lived to write only a small part of the "Achilleid."

[3] *I did but smile, as one who winks.*—"I smiled no more than one would do who wished by a smile to intimate his consciousness of anything to another person."

On high, he is that Mantuan, led by whom
Thou didst presume of men and gods to sing.
If other cause thou deem'dst for which I smiled,
Leave it as not the true one: and believe
Those words, thou spakest of him, indeed the cause."

    Now down he bent to embrace my teacher's feet;
But he forbade him: "Brother! do it not:
Thou art a shadow, and behold'st a shade."
He, rising, answer'd thus: "Now hast thou proved
The force and ardour of the love I bear thee,
When I forget we are but things of air,
And, as a substance, treat an empty shade."

CANTO XXII.

ARGUMENT.

Dante, Virgil, and Statius mount to the sixth cornice, where the sin of gluttony is cleansed, the two Latin Poets discoursing by the way. Turning to the right, they find a tree hung with sweet-smelling fruit, and watered by a shower that issues from the rock. Voices are heard to proceed from among the leaves, recording examples of temperance.

NOW we had left the angel, who had turn'd
To the sixth circle our ascending step;
One gash from off my forehead razed; while they,
Whose wishes tend to justice, shouted forth,
"Blessed!"[1] and ended with "I thirst:" and I,
More nimble than along the other straits,
So journey'd, that, without the sense of toil,
I follow'd upward the swift-footed shades;
When Virgil thus began: "Let its pure flame
From virtue flow, and love can never fail
To warm another's bosom, so the light
Shine manifestly forth. Hence, from that hour,
When, 'mongst us in the purlieus of the deep,
Came down the spirit of Aquinum's bard,[2]
Who told of thine affection, my good will
Hath been for thee of quality as strong
As ever link'd itself to one not seen.
Therefore these stairs will now seem short to me.
But tell me: and, if too secure, I loose
The rein with a friend's licence, as a friend
Forgive me, and speak now as with a friend:
How chanced it covetous desire could find
Place in that bosom, 'midst such ample store
Of wisdom, as thy zeal had treasured there?"

---

[1] *Blessed.*—"Blessed be they which do hunger and thirst after righteousness, for they shall be filled."—Matt. v. 6.

[2] *Aquinum's bard.*—Juvenal had celebrated his contemporary, Statius, Sat. vii. 82; though some critics imagine that there is a secret derision couched under his praise.

First somewhat moved to laughter by his words,
Statius replied: "Each syllable of thine
Is a dear pledge of love. Things oft appear,
That minister false matter to our doubts,
When their true causes are removed from sight.
Thy question doth assure me, thou believest
I was on earth a covetous man; perhaps
Because thou found'st me in that circle placed.
Know then I was too wide of avarice:
And e'en for that excess, thousands of moons
Have wax'd and waned upon my sufferings.
And were it not that I with heedful care
Noted, where thou exclaim'st as if in ire
With human nature, 'Why,[1] thou cursed thirst
Of gold! dost not with juster measure guide
The appetite of mortals?' I had met
The fierce encounter[2] of the voluble rock.
Then was I ware that, with too ample wing,
The hands may haste to lavishment; and turn'd,
As from my other evil, so from this,
In penitence. How many from their grave
Shall with shorn locks[3] arise, who living, ay,
And at life's last extreme, of this offence,
Through ignorance, did not repent! And know
The fault, which lies direct from any sin
In level opposition, here, with that,
Wastes its green rankness on one common heap.
Therefore, if I have been with those, who wail
Their avarice, to cleanse me; through reverse
Of their transgression, such hath been my lot."

To whom the sovran of the pastoral song:
"While thou didst sing that cruel warfare waged
By the twin sorrow of Jocasta's womb,[4]
From thy discourse with Clio[5] there, it seems

---

[1] *Why.—*
"Quid non mortalia pectora cogis,
Auri sacra fames?"
Virgil, Æneid, lib. iii. 57.
Venturi supposes that Dante might have mistaken the meaning of the word *sacra,* and construed it "holy," instead of "cursed." But I see no necessity for having recourse to so improbable a conjecture.

[2] *The fierce encounter.*—See "Hell," canto vii. 26.
[3] *With shorn locks.*—See "Hell," canto vii. 58.
[4] *The twin sorrow of Jocasta's womb.*—Eteocles and Polynices.
[5] *With Clio.—*
"Quem prius heroum Clio dabis? immodicum iræ
Tydea? laurigeri subitos an vatis hiatus?"
Statius, Thebaid, i. 42.

As faith had not been thine; without the which,
Good deeds suffice not. And if so, what sun
Rose on thee, or what candle pierced the dark,
That thou didst after see to hoise the sail,
And follow where the fisherman had led?"

He answering thus: "By thee conducted first,
I enter'd the Parnassian grots, and quaff'd
Of the clear spring: illumined first by thee,
Open'd mine eyes to God. Thou didst, as one,
Who, journeying through the darkness, bears a light
Behind, that profits not himself, but makes
His followers wise, when thou exclaimedst, 'Lo!
A renovated world,[1] Justice return'd,
Times of primeval innocence restored,
And a new race descended from above.'
Poet and Christian both to thee I owed.
That thou mayst mark more clearly what I trace,
My hand shall stretch forth to inform the lines
With livelier colouring. Soon o'er all the world,
By messengers from heaven, the true belief
Teem'd now prolific; and that word of thine,
Accordant, to the new instructors chimed.
Induced by which agreement, I was wont
Resort to them; and soon their sanctity
So won upon me, that, Domitian's rage
Pursuing them, I mix'd my tears with theirs,
And, while on earth I stay'd, still succour'd them;
And their most righteous customs made me scorn
All sects besides. Before[2] I led the Greeks,
In tuneful fiction, to the streams of Thebes,
I was baptised: but secretly, through fear,
Remain'd a Christian, and conform'd long time
To Pagan rites. Four centuries and more,
I, for that lukewarmness, was fain to pace
Round the fourth circle. Thou then, who hast raised
The covering which did hide such blessing from me,

---

[1] *A renovated world.*—
"Magnus ab integro sæclorum nascitur ordo.
Jam redit et Virgo; redeunt Saturnia regna;
Jam nova progenies cœlo demittitur alto."
Virgil, Ecl., iv. 5.

For the application of Virgil's prophecy to the incarnation, see Natalis Alexander, "Hist. Eccl.," Sæc. i., Dissert. 1. Paris, 1679, v. i., p. 166.

[2] *Before.*—Before I had composed the "Thebaid."

Whilst much of this ascent is yet to climb,
Say, if thou know, where our old Terence[1] bides,
Cæcilius,[2] Plautus, Varro:[3] if condemn'd
They dwell, and in what province of the deep."
"These," said my guide, "with Persius and myself,
And others many more, are with that Greek,[4]
Of mortals, the most cherish'd by the nine,
In the first ward[5] of darkness. There, oft-times,
We of that mount hold converse, on whose top
For aye our nurses live. We have the bard
Of Pella,[6] and the Teian,[7] Agatho,[8]
Simonides, and many a Grecian else
Ingarlanded with laurel. Of thy train,[9]
Antigone is there, Deïphile,
Argia, and as sorrowful as erst
Ismene, and who show'd Langia's wave:[10]
Deïdamia with her sisters there,
And blind Tiresias' daughter,[11] and the bride

---

[1] *Our old Terence.*—"Antico," which is found in many of the old editions, seems preferable to "amico."

[2] *Cæcilius.*—Cæcilius Statius, a Latin comic poet, of whose works some fragments only remain. Our poet had Horace in his eye:

"Decitur Afrani toga convenisse Menandro,
Plautus ad exemplar Siculi properare Epicharmi,
Vincere Cæcilius gravitate, Terentius arte."
Epist., lib. ii. I.

[3] *Varro.*—"Quam multa pene omnia tradidit Varro."—*Quintilian, Institutiones Oratoricæ*, lib. xii. "Vix aperto ad philosophiam aditu, primus M. Varro veterum omnium doctissimus."—*Sadolet. de liberis recte instit.* Edit. Lugd. 1533, p. 137.

[4] *That Greek.*—Homer.

[5] *In the first ward.*—In Limbo.

[6] *The bard of Pella.*—Euripides.

[7] *The Teian.*—

"Euripide v' è nosco e Anacreonte."

The Monte Casino MS. reads "Antifonte," "Antipho," instead of "Anacreonte." Dante probably knew little more of these Greek writers than the names.

[8] *Agatho.*—Chaucer, speaking of the Daisy as a representation of Alcestis, refers to Agaton:

"No wonder is though Jove her stellifie,
As tellith Agaton for her goodnesse."
Legende of Good Women.

And Mr. Tyrwhitt tells us that "he has nothing to say of this writer except that one of the same name is quoted in the Prol. to the tragedie of Cambises, by Thomas Preston. There is no reason," he adds, "for supposing with Gloss. Ur. that a philosopher of Samos is meant, or any of the Agathoes of antiquity." I am inclined, however, to believe that Chaucer must have meant Agatho, the dramatic writer, whose name, at least, appears to have been familiar in the middle ages; for, besides the mention of him in the text, he is quoted by Dante in the "Treatise De Monarchiâ," lib. iii.:

"Deus per nuncium facere non potest, genita non esse, genita, juxta sententiam Agathonis." The original is to be found in Aristotle, "Ethic. Nicom.," lib. vi., c. 2:

Μόνου γὰρ αὐτοῦ καὶ θεὸς στερίσκεται,
Ἀγένητα ποιεῖν ἄσσ' ἂν ᾖ πεπραγμένα.

Agatho is mentioned by Xenophon in his "Symposium;" by Plato in the "Protagoras," and in the "Banquet," a favourite book with our author; and by Aristotle in his "Art of Poetry," where the following remarkable passage occurs respecting him, from which I will leave it to the reader to decide whether it is possible that the allusion in Chaucer might have arisen: ἐν ἐνίαις μὲν ἓν ἢ δύο τῶν γνωρίμων ἐστὶν ὀνομάτων τὰ δὲ ἄλλα πεποιημένα· ἐν ἐνίαις δὲ οὐθέν· οἷον ἐν τῷ Ἀγάθωνος "Ἄνθει. ὁμοίως γὰρ ἐν τούτῳ τά τε πράγματα καὶ τὰ ὀνόματα πεποίηται, καὶ οὐδὲν ἧττον εὐφραίνει.—Edit. 1794. p. 33. "There are, however, some tragedies, in which one or two of the names are historical, and the rest feigned; there are even some, in which none of the names are historical; such is Agatho's tragedy called 'The Flower;' for in that all is invention, both incidents and names; and yet it pleases."—*Aristotle's Treatise on Poetry*, by Thomas Twining, 8vo Edit. 1812, vol. i., p. 128.

[9] *Of thy train.*—"Of those celebrated in thy poem."

[10] *Who show'd Langia's wave.*—Hypsipyle. See note to canto xxvi., v. 87.

[11] *Tiresias' daughter.*—Dante, as some have thought, had forgotten that he had placed Manto, the daughter of Tiresias, among the sorcerers. See "Hell," canto xx. Vellutello endeavours, rather awkwardly, to reconcile the apparent inconsistency, by observing, that although she was placed there as a sinner, yet, as one of famous memory, she had also a place among the worthies in Limbo. Lombardi, or rather the Della Crusca academicians, excuse our author better, by observing that Tiresias had a

Sea-born of Peleus."[1] Either poet now
Was silent; and no longer by the ascent
Or the steep walls obstructed, round them cast
Inquiring eyes. Four handmaids[2] of the day
Had finish'd now their office, and the fifth
Was at the chariot-beam, directing still
Its flamy point aloof; when thus my guide:
"Methinks, it well behoves us to the brink
Bend the right shoulder, circuiting the mount,
As we have ever used." So custom there
Was usher to the road; the which we chose
Less doubtful, as that worthy shade[3] complied.

 They on before me went: I sole pursued,
Listening their speech, that to my thoughts convey'd
Mysterious lessons of sweet poesy.
But soon they ceased; for midway of the road
A tree we found, with goodly fruitage hung,
And pleasant to the smell: and as a fir,
Upward from bough to bough, less ample spreads;
So downward this less ample spread;[4] that none,
Methinks, aloft may climb. Upon the side,
That closed our path, a liquid crystal fell
From the steep rock, and through the sprays above
Stream'd showering. With associate step the bards
Drew near the plant; and, from amidst the leaves,
A voice was heard: "Ye shall be chary of me;"
And after added: "Mary took more thought[5]
For joy and honour of the nuptial feast,
Than for herself, who answers now for you.
The women of old Rome[6] were satisfied

---

daughter named Daphne. See Diodorus Siculus, lib. iv., § 66. I have here to acknowledge a communication made to me by the learned writer of an anonymous letter, who observes that Manto and Daphne are only different names for the same person; and that Servius, in his Commentary on the "Æneid," x. 198, says, that some make Manto the prophetess to be a daughter of Hercules.

[1] *The bride sea-born of Peleus.*—Thetis.
[2] *Four handmaids.*—Compare canto xii., v. 74.
[3] *That worthy shade.*—Statius.
[4] *Downward this less ample spread.*—The early commentators understand that this tree had its root upward and the boughs downward; and this opinion, however derided by their successors, is not a little countenanced by the imitation of Frezzi, who lived so near the time of our poet:

"Su dentro al cielo avea la sua radice,
E giù inverso terra i rami spande."
   Il Quadriregio, lib. iv., cap. 1.

"It had in heaven
Its root above, and downward to the earth
Stretch'd forth the branches."

[5] *Mary took more thought.*—"The blessed Virgin, who answers for you now in heaven, when she said to Jesus, at the marriage in Cana of Galilee, 'They have no wine,' regarded not the gratification of her own taste, but the honour of the nuptial banquet."

[6] *The women of old Rome.*—See Valerius Maximus, l. ii., c. 1.

With water for their beverage. Daniel[1] fed
On pulse, and wisdom gain'd. The primal age
Was beautiful as gold: and hunger then
Made acorns tasteful; thirst, each rivulet
Run nectar. Honey and locusts were the food,
Whereon the Baptist in the wilderness
Fed, and that eminence of glory reach'd
And greatness, which the Evangelist records."

---

[1] *Daniel.*—" Then said Daniel to Melzar, whom the prince of the eunuchs had set over Daniel, Hananiah, Mishael, and Azariah, Prove thy servants, I beseech thee, ten days; and let them give us pulse to eat, and water to drink."—Dan. i. 11, 12. "Thus Melzar took away the portion of their meat, and the wine that they should drink; and gave them pulse. As for these four children, God gave them knowledge and skill in all learning and wisdom: and Daniel had understanding in all visions and dreams."—*Ibid.* 16, 17.

CANTO XXIII.

ARGUMENT.

They are overtaken by the spirit of Forese, who had been a friend of our Poet's on earth, and who now inveighs bitterly against the immodest dress of their countrywomen at Florence.

ON the green leaf mine eyes were fix'd, like his
    Who throws away his days in idle chase
Of the diminutive birds, when thus I heard
The more than father warn me : "Son ! our time
Asks thriftier using. Linger not : away."
    Thereat my face and steps at once I turn'd
Toward the sages, by whose converse cheer'd
I journey'd on, and felt no toil : and lo !
A sound of weeping, and a song : "My lips,[1]
O Lord !" and these so mingled, it gave birth
To pleasure and to pain. "O Sire beloved !
Say what is this I hear." Thus I inquired.
    "Spirits," said he, "who, as they go, perchance,
Their debt of duty pay." As on their road
The thoughtful pilgrims, overtaking some
Not known unto them, turn to them, and look,
But stay not ; thus, approaching from behind
With speedier motion, eyed us, as they pass'd,
A crowd of spirits, silent and devout.
The eyes[2] of each were dark and hollow ; pale
Their visage, and so lean withal, the bones
Stood staring through the skin. I do not think
Thus dry and meagre Erisicthon show'd,
When pinch'd by sharp-set famine to the quick.
    "Lo !" to myself I mused, "the race, who lost
Jerusalem, when Mary[3] with dire beak
Prey'd on her child." The sockets seem'd as rings,[4]

---

[1] *My lips.*—"O Lord, open thou my lips ; and my mouth shall show forth thy praise."—Ps. li. 15.

[2] *Eyes.*—Compare Ovid, "Metamorphoses," lib. viii. 801 :

"Hirtus erat crinis ; cava lumina, pallor in ore :

*   *   *   *   *   *

Dura cutis, per quam spectari viscera possent ·
Ossa sub incurvis exstabant arida lumbis."

[3] *When Mary.*—Josephus, "De Bello Jud.," lib. vii., c. xxi., p. 954, ed. Genev, fol. 1611. The shocking story is well told.

[4] *Rings.*

"Senza fior prato o senza gemma anello."
    Petrarca, Son. Lasciata hai, morte.

"O ring of which the rubie is outfall."
    Chaucer, Troilus and Creseide, b. v.

From which the gems were dropt. Who reads the name[1]
Of man upon his forehead, there the M
Had traced most plainly. Who would deem, that scent
Of water and an apple could have proved
Powerful to generate such pining want,
Not knowing how it wrought? While now I stood,
Wondering what thus could waste them (for the cause
Of their gaunt hollowness and scaly rind
Appear'd not), lo! a spirit turn'd his eyes
In their deep-sunken cells, and fasten'd them
On me, then cried with vehemence aloud:
"What grace is this vouchsafed me?" By his looks
I ne'er had recognised him: but the voice
Brought to my knowledge what his cheer conceal'd.
Remembrance of his altered lineaments
Was kindled from that spark; and I agnized
The visage of Forese.[2] "Ah! respect
This wan and leprous-wither'd skin," thus he
Suppliant implored, "this macerated flesh.
Speak to me truly of thyself. And who
Are those twain spirits, that escort thee there?
Be it not said thou scorn'st to talk with me."

"That face of thine," I answer'd him, "which dead
I once bewail'd, disposes me not less
For weeping, when I see it thus transform'd.
Say then, by Heaven, what blasts ye thus? The whilst
I wonder, ask not speech from me: unapt
Is he to speak, while other will employs."

He thus: "The water and the plant, we pass'd,
With power are gifted, by the eternal will
Infused; the which so pines me. Every spirit,
Whose song bewails his gluttony indulged
Too grossly, here in hunger and in thirst
Is purified. The odour, which the fruit,

"In this habit
Met I my father with his bleeding rings,
Their precious stones new lost."
   Shakespeare, Lear, act. v., sc. 3.
[1] *Who reads the name.*—"He who pretends to distinguish the letters which form OMO in the features of the human face, might easily have traced out the M on their emaciated countenances." The temples, nose, and forehead are supposed to represent this letter; and the eyes the two O's placed within each side of it.

[2] *Forese.*—One of the brothers of Piccarda; he who is again spoken of in the next canto, and introduced in the "Paradise," canto iii. Cionacci, in his "Storia della Beata Umiliana," parte iv., cap. i., is referred to by Lombardi, in order to show that Forese was also the brother of Corso Donati, our author's political enemy. See next canto, v. 81. Tiraboschi, after Crescimbeni, enumerates him among the Tuscan poets, "Storia della Poes. It.," v. i., p. 139.

"And who
Are those twain spirits, that escort thee there?
Be it not said thou scorn'st to talk with me."
Canto XXIII., lines 47—49.

And spray that showers upon the verdure, breathe,
Inflames us with desire to feed and drink.
Nor once alone, encompassing our route,
We come to add fresh fuel to the pain:
Pain, said I? solace rather: for that will,
To the tree, leads us, by which Christ was led
To call on Eli, joyful, when he paid
Our ransom from his vein." I answering thus:
" Forese! from that day, in which the world
For better life thou changedst, not five years
Have circled. If the power[1] of sinning more
Were first concluded in thee, ere thou knew'st
That kindly grief which re-espouses us
To God, how hither art thou come so soon?
I thought to find thee lower,[2] there, where time
Is recompense for time." He straight replied:
"To drink up the sweet wormwood of affliction
I have been brought thus early, by the tears
Stream'd down my Nella's[3] cheeks. Her prayers devout,
Her sighs have drawn me from the coast, where oft
Expectance lingers; and have set me free
From the other circles. In the sight of God
So much the dearer is my widow prized,
She whom I loved so fondly, as she ranks
More singly eminent for virtuous deeds.
The tract, most barbarous of Sardinia's isle,[4]
Hath dames more chaste, and modester by far,
Than that wherein I left her. O sweet brother!
What wouldst thou have me say?[5] A time to come
Stands full within my view, to which this hour
Shall not be counted of an ancient date,
When from the pulpit shall be loudly warn'd
The unblushing dames of Florence,[6] lest they bare

---

[1] *If the power.*—" If thou didst delay thy repentance to the last, when thou hadst lost the power of sinning, how happens it thou art arrived here so early?"

[2] *Lower.*—In the Ante-Purgatory. See canto ii.

[3] *My Nella.*—The wife of Forese.

[4] *The tract, most barbarous of Sardinia's isle.*—The *Barbagia* is a part of Sardinia, to which that name was given, on account of the uncivilised state of its inhabitants, who are said to have gone nearly naked.

[5] *What wouldst thou have me say?*—The interrogative, which Lombardi would dismiss from this place, as unmeaning and superfluous, appears to me to be the natural result of a deep feeling, and to prepare us for the invective that follows.

[6] *The unblushing dames of Florence.*—Landino's note exhibits a curious instance of the changeableness of his countrywomen. He even goes beyond the acrimony of the original. "In those days," says the commentator, " no less than in ours, the Florentine ladies exposed the neck and bosom, a dress, no doubt, more suitable to a harlot than a matron. But, as they changed soon after, insomuch that they wore collars

Unkerchief'd bosoms to the common gaze.
What savage women hath the world e'er seen,
What Saracens,[1] from whom there needed scourge
Of spiritual or other discipline,
To force them walk with covering on their limbs?
But did they see, the shameless ones, what Heaven
Wafts on swift wing toward them while I speak,
Their mouths were oped for howling: they shall taste
Of sorrow (unless foresight cheat me here)
Or e'er the cheek of him be clothed with down,
Who is now rock'd with lullaby[2] asleep.
Ah! now, my brother, hide thyself no more:
Thou seest[3] how not I alone, but all,
Gaze, where thou veil'st the intercepted sun."

Whence I replied: "If thou recall to mind
What we were once together, even yet
Remembrance of those days may grieve thee sore.
That I forsook that life, was due to him
Who there precedes me, some few evenings past,
When she was round, who shines with sister lamp
To his that glisters yonder," and I show'd
The sun. "'Tis he, who through profoundest night
Of the true dead has brought me, with this flesh
As true, that follows. From that gloom the aid
Of his sure comfort drew me on to climb,
And, climbing, wind along this mountain-steep,
Which rectifies in you whate'er the world
Made crooked and depraved. I have his word,
That he will bear me company as far
As till I come where Beatrice dwells:
But there must leave me. Virgil is that spirit,
Who thus hath promised," and I pointed to him;
"The other is that shade, for whom so late
Your realm, as he arose, exulting, shook
Through every pendent cliff and rocky bound."

---

up to the chin, covering the whole of the neck and throat, so have I hopes they will change again; not indeed so much from motives of decency, as through that fickleness which pervades every action of their lives."

[1] *Saracens.*—"This word, during the middle ages, was indiscriminately applied to Pagans and Mahometans; in short, to all nations (except the Jews) who did not profess Christianity."—*Mr.* Ellis's *Specimens of Early English Metrical Romances*, vol. i., p. 196 (a note). Lond. 8vo, 1805.

[2] *With lullaby.*—"Colui che mo si consola con nanna." "Nanna" is said to have been the sound with which the Florentine women hushed their children to sleep.

[3] *Thou seest.*—Thou seest how we wonder that thou art here in a living body.

> The shadowy forms,
> That seem'd things dead and dead again, drew in
> At their deep-delved orbs rare wonder of me,
> Perceiving I had life.
>
> *Canto XXIV., lines 4—7.*

CANTO XXIV.

ARGUMENT.

Forese points out several others by name who are here, like himself, purifying themselves from the vice of gluttony; and amongst the rest, Buonaggiunta of Lucca, with whom our Poet converses. Forese then predicts the violent end of Dante's political enemy, Corso Donati; and when he has quitted them, the Poet, in company with Statius and Virgil, arrives at another tree, from whence issue voices that record ancient examples of gluttony; and proceeding forwards, they are directed by an angel which way to ascend to the next cornice of the mountain.

OUR journey was not slacken'd by our talk,
    Nor yet our talk by journeying. Still we spake,
And urged our travel stoutly, like a ship
When the wind sits astern. The shadowy forms,
That seem'd things dead and dead again, drew in
At their deep-delved orbs rare wonder of me,
Perceiving I had life; and I my words
Continued, and thus spake: "He journeys[1] up
Perhaps more tardily than else he would,
For others' sake. But tell me, if thou know'st
Where is Piccarda?[2] Tell me, if I see
Any of mark, among this multitude
Who eye me thus."—" My sister (she for whom,
'Twixt beautiful and good,[3] I cannot say
Which name was fitter) wears e'en now her crown,
And triumphs in Olympus." Saying this,
He added: "Since spare diet[4] hath so worn
Our semblance out, 'tis lawful here to name
Each one. This," and his finger then he raised,
" Is Buonaggiunta,[5]—Buonaggiunta, he

---

[1] *He journeys.*—The soul of Statius perhaps proceeds more slowly, in order that he may enjoy as long as possible the company of Virgil.
[2] *Piccarda.*—See "Paradise," canto iii.
[3] *'Twixt beautiful and good.*—
    " Tra bella e onesta
  Qual fu più, lasciò in dubbio."
      Petrarca, Son. Ripensaudo a quel.
[4] *Diet.*—Dieta.
" And dieted with fasting every day."
    Spenser, Faery Queen, b. i., c. i., st. 26.

"Spare fast that oft with gods doth diet."
    Milton, Il Penseroso.
[5] *Buonaggiunta.*—Buonaggiunta Urbiciani, of Lucca. "There is a canzone by this poet, printed in the collection made by the Giunti (p. 209), and a sonnet to Guido Guinicelli in that made by Corbinelli (p. 169), from which we collect that he lived not about 1230, as Quadrio supposes (t. ii., p. 159), but towards the end of the thirteenth century. Concerning other poems by Buonaggiunta, that are preserved in MS. in some libraries, Crescimbeni may be consulted."—*Tiraboschi, Mr. Mathias's ed.,* v. i., p. 115. Three

Of Lucca: and that face beyond him, pierced
Unto a leaner fineness than the rest,
Had keeping of the church; he was of Tours,[1]
And purges by wan abstinence away
Bolsena's eels and cups of muscadel."[2]

He show'd me many others, one by one:
And all, as they were named, seem'd well content;
For no dark gesture I discern'd in any.
I saw, through hunger, Ubaldino[3] grind
His teeth on emptiness; and Boniface,[4]
That waved the crozier[5] o'er a numerous flock:
I saw the Marquis,[6] who had time erewhile
To swill at Forli with less drought; yet so,
Was one ne'er sated. I howe'er, like him
That, gazing 'midst a crowd, singles out one,
So singled him of Lucca; for methought

---

of these, a canzone, a sonnet, and a ballata, have been published in the "Anecdota Literaria ex MSS. Codicibus eruta," 8vo, Roma (no year), v. iii., p. 453. He is thus mentioned by our author in his "Treatise de Vulgari Eloquentia," lib. i., cap. xiii.: Next let us come to the Tuscans, who, made senseless by their folly, arrogantly assume to themselves the title of a vernacular diction, more excellent than the rest; nor are the vulgar alone misled by this wild opinion, but many famous men have maintained it, as Guittone d'Arezzo, who never addicted himself to the polished style of the court, Buonaggiunta of Lucca, Gallo of Pisa, Mino Mocato of Sienna, and Brunetto of Florence, whose compositions, if there shall be leisure for examining them, will be found not to be in the diction of the court, but in that of their respective cities." As a specimen of Buonaggiunta's manner, the reader will take the following Sonnet from Corbinelli's Collection added to the "Bella Mano:"—

"Qual uomo è in su la rota per Ventura,
   Non si rallegri, perchè sia innalzato;
   Che quando più si mostra chiara, e pura,
   Allor si gira, ed hallo disbassato.
E nullo prato ha sì fresca verdura,
   Che li suoi fiori non cangino stato;
   E questo saccio, che avvien per natura;
   Più grave cade, chi più è montato.
Non si dee uomo troppo rallegrare
   Di gran grandezza, nè tenere spene;
   Che egli è gran doglia, allegrezza fallire:
Anzi si debbe molto umiliare;
   Non far soperchio, perchè aggia gran bene;
   Che ogni monte a valle dee venire."

La Bella Mano e Rime Antiche, ed. Firenze, 1715, p. 170.

"What man is raised on Fortune's wheel aloft,
Let him not triumph in his bliss elate;
For when she smiles with visage fair and soft,
Then whirls she round, reversing his estate.
Fresh was the verdure in the sunny croft,
Yet soon the wither'd flowerets met their fate;
And things exalted most, as chanceth oft,
Fall from on high to earth with ruin great.
Therefore ought none too greatly to rejoice
In greatness, nor too fast his hope to hold:
For one, that triumphs, great pain is to fail
But lowly meekness is the wiser choice;
And he must down, that is too proud and bold:
For every mountain stoopeth to the vale."

[1] *He was of Tours.*—Simon of Tours became Pope with the title of Martin IV. in 1281, and died in 1285.

[2] *Bolsena's eels and cups of muscadel.*—The Nidobeatina edition and the Monte Casino MS. agree in reading

"L'anguille di Bolsena in la vernaccia;"

from which it would seem, that Martin IV. refined so much on epicurism as to have his eels killed by being put into the wine called vernaccia, in order to heighten their flavour. The Latin annotator on the MS. relates that the following epitaph was inscribed on the sepulchre of the pope:

"Gaudent anguillæ, quod mortuus hic jacet ille,
Qui quasi morte reas excoriabat eas."

[3] *Ubaldino.*—Ubaldino degli Ubaldini, of Pila, in the Florentine territory.

[4] *Boniface.*—Archbishop of Ravenna. By Venturi he is called Bonifazio de' Fieschi, a Genoese; by Vellutello, the son of the above-mentioned Ubaldini and by Landino, Francioso, a Frenchman.

[5] *Crozier.*—It is uncertain whether the word "rocco," in the original, means a "crozier" or a "bishop's rochet," that is, his episcopal gown. In support of the latter interpretation Lombardi cites Du Fresne's Glossary, article Roccus: "Rochettum hodie vocant vestem linteam episcoporum . . . quasi parvum roccum;" and explains the verse,

"Che pasturò col rocco molte genti:"

"who, from the revenues of his bishopric, supported in luxury a large train of dependents." If the reader wishes to learn more on the subject, he is referred to Monti's "Proposta," under the word "Rocco."

[6] *The Marquis.*—The Marchese de' Rigogliosi, of Forli. When his butler told him it was commonly reported in the city that he did nothing but drink, he is said to have answered, "And do you tell them that I am always thirsty."

Was none amongst them took such note of me.
Somewhat I heard him whisper of Gentucca:[1]
The sound was indistinct, and murmur'd there,[2]
Where justice, that so strips them, fix'd her sting.

"Spirit!" said I, "it seems as thou wouldst fain
Speak with me. Let me hear thee. Mutual wish
To converse prompts, which let us both indulge."

He, answering, straight began: "Woman is born,
Whose brow no wimple shades yet,[3] that shall make
My city please thee, blame it as they may.[4]
Go then with this forewarning. If aught false
My whisper too implied, the event shall tell.
But say, if of a truth I see the man
Of that new lay the inventor, which begins
With 'Ladies, ye that con the lore of love.'"[5]

To whom I thus: "Count of me but as one,
Who am the scribe of love; that, when he breathes,
Take up my pen, and, as he dictates, write."

"Brother!" said he, "the hindrance, which once held
The notary,[6] with Guittone[7] and myself,

---

[1] *Gentucca.*—Of this lady it is thought that our poet became enamoured during his exile. See note to canto xxxi. 56.

[2] *There.*—In the throat, the part in which they felt the torment inflicted by the divine justice.

[3] *Whose brow no wimple shades yet.*—"Who has not yet assumed the dress of a woman."

[4] *Blame it as they may.*—See "Hell," canto xxi. 39.

[5] *Ladies, ye that con the lore of love.*—
"Donne ch' avete intelletto d'amore."
The first verse of a canzone in our author's "Vita Nuova."

[6] *The notary.*—Jacopo da Lentino, called the Notary, a poet of these times. He was probably an Apulian: for Dante ("De Vulgari Eloquentia," lib. i., cap. 12), quoting a verse which belongs to a canzone of his, published by the Giunti, without mentioning the writer's name, terms him one of "the illustrious Apulians," præfulgentes Apuli. See Tiraboschi, Mr. Mathias's edit., vol. i., p. 137. Crescimbeni (lib. i. "Della Volgar. Poesia," p. 72, 4to ed., 1698) gives an extract from one of his poems, printed in Allacci's Collection, to show that the whimsical compositions called "Ariette," are not of modern invention. His poems have been collected among the "Poeti del primo secolo della Lingua Italiana," 2 vols. 8vo, Firenze, 1816. They extend from p. 249 to p. 319 of the first volume.

[7] *Guittone.*—Fra Guittone, of Arezzo, holds a distinguished place in Italian literature, as, besides his poems printed in the Collection of the Giunti, he has left a collection of letters, forty in number, which afford the earliest specimen of that kind of writing in the language. They were published at Rome in 1743, with learned illustrations by Giovanni Bottari. He was also the first who gave to the sonnet its regular and legitimate form, a species of composition in which not only his own countrymen, but many of the best poets in all the cultivated languages of modern Europe, have since so much delighted. Guittone, a native of Arezzo, was the son of Viva di Michele. He was of the order of the "Frati Godenti," of which an account may be seen in the notes to "Hell," canto xxiii. In the year 1293 he founded a monastery of the order of Camaldoli, in Florence, and died in the following year. Tiraboschi, ibid., p. 119. Dante, in the "Treatise de Vulgari Eloquentia," lib. i., cap. 13 (see note to v. 20 of this canto), and lib. ii., cap. 6, blames him for preferring the plebeian to the more courtly style; and Petrarch twice places him in the company of our poet, "Triumph of Love," cap. iv., and "Sonnets," part second, "Sennuccio mio." The eighth book in the collection of the old poets published by the Giunti in 1527 consists of sonnets and canzoni by Guittone. They are marked by a peculiar solemnity of manner, of which the ensuing sonnet will afford a proof and an example.

" Gran placer Signor mio, e gran desire
  Harei d'essere avanti al divin trono,
  Dove si prenderà pace e perdono
  Di suo ben fatto e d'ogni suo fallire:
E gran piacer harei hor di sentire
  Quella sonante tromba e quel gran suono,
  E d'udir dire: hora venuti sono,
  A chi dar pace, a chi crudel martire.
Questo tutto vorrei caro Signore ;
  Perchè fia scritto a ciaschedun nel volto
  Quel chè già tenne ascoso dentro al core:
Allhor vedrete a la mia fronte avvolto
  Un brieve, che dirà ; che 'l crudo amore
  Per voi me prese, e mai non m' ha disciolto."

Short of that new and sweeter style[1] I hear,
Is now disclosed: I see how ye your plumes
Stretch, as the inditer guides them; which, no question,
Ours did not. He that seeks a grace beyond,
Sees not the distance parts one style from other.
And, as contented, here he held his peace.

Like as the birds, that winter near the Nile,[2]
In squared regiment direct their course,
Then stretch themselves in file for speedier flight;
Thus all the tribe of spirits, as they turn'd
Their visage, faster fled, nimble alike
Through leanness and desire. And as a man,
Tired with the motion of a trotting steed,[3]
Slacks pace, and stays behind his company,
Till his o'erbreathed lungs keep temperate time;
E'en so Forese let that holy crew
Proceed, behind them lingering at my side,
And saying: "When shall I again behold thee?"

"How long my life may last," said I, "I know not:
This know, how soon soever I return,
My wishes will before me have arrived:
Sithence the place,[4] where I am set to live,
Is, day by day, more scoop'd of all its good;
And dismal ruin seems to threaten it."

"Go now," he cried: "lo! he,[5] whose guilt is most,
Passes before my vision, dragg'd at heels

"Great joy it were to me to join the throng,
That thy celestial throne, O Lord, surround,
Where perfect peace and pardon shall be found,
Peace for good doings, pardon for the wrong:
Great joy to hear the vault of heaven prolong
That everlasting trumpet's mighty sound,
That shall to each award their final bound,
Wailing to these, to those the blissful song.
All this, dear Lord, were welcome to my soul.
For on his brow then every one shall bear
Inscribed, what late was hidden in the heart;
And round my forehead wreathed a letter'd scroll
Shall in this tenor my sad fate declare:
'Love's bondman I from him might never part.'"

Bottari doubts whether some of the sonnets attributed to Guittone in the "Rime Antiche" are by that writer. See his notes to " Lettere di Fra Guittone," p. 135.

[1] *That new and sweeter style.*—He means the style introduced in our poet's time.

[2] *Like as the birds, that winter near the Nile.*—"Hell," canto v. 46. Euripides, "Helena," 1495, and Statius, "Thebais," lib. v. 12.

[3] *Tired with the motion of a trotting steed.*—I have followed Venturi's explanation of this passage. Others understand

" Di trottare è lasso "

of the fatigue produced by running.

[4] *The place.*—Florence.

[5] *He.*—Corso Donati was suspected of aiming at the sovereignty of Florence. To escape the fury of his fellow citizens, he fled away on horseback, but falling, was overtaken and slain, A.D. 1308. The contemporary annalist, after relating at length the circumstances of his fate, adds, "that he was one of the wisest and most valorous knights, the best speaker, the most expert statesman, the most renowned and enterprising man of his age in Italy, a comely knight and of graceful carriage, but very worldly, and in his time had formed many conspiracies in Florence, and entered into many scandalous practices for the sake of attaining state and lordship."—G. *Villani,* lib. viii., cap. xcvi. The character of Corso is forcibly drawn by another of his contemporaries, Dino Compagni, lib. iii. Muratori, "Rerum Italicarum Scriptores," tom. ix., p. 523. Guittone d'Arezzo's seventh letter is addressed to him. It is in verse.

At length, as undeceived, they went their way:
And we approach the tree, whom vows and tears
Sue to in vain; the mighty tree.
Canto XXIV., lines 112—114.

Of an infuriate beast. Toward the vale,
Where guilt hath no redemption, on it speeds,
Each step increasing swiftness on the last;
Until a blow it strikes, that leaveth him
A corse most vilely shatter'd. No long space
Those wheels have yet to roll" (therewith his eyes
Look'd up to heaven), "ere thou shalt plainly see
That which my words may not more plainly tell.
I quit thee: time is precious here: I lose
Too much, thus measuring my pace with thine."

As from a troop of well rank'd chivalry,
One knight, more enterprising than the rest,
Pricks forth at gallop, eager to display
His prowess in the first encounter proved;
So parted he from us, with lengthen'd strides;
And left me on the way with those twain spirits,
Who were such mighty marshals of the world.

When he beyond us had so fled, mine eyes
No nearer reach'd him, than my thought his words;
The branches of another fruit, thick hung,
And blooming fresh, appear'd. E'en as our steps
Turn'd thither: not far off, it rose to view.
Beneath it were a multitude, that raised
Their hands, and shouted forth I know not what
Unto the boughs; like greedy and fond brats,
That beg, and answer none obtain from him,
Of whom they beg; but more to draw them on,
He, at arm's length, the object of their wish
Above them holds aloft, and hides it not.

At length, as undeceived, they went their way:
And we approach the tree, whom vows and tears
Sue to in vain; the mighty tree. "Pass on,
And come not near. Stands higher up the wood,
Whereof Eve tasted: and from it was ta'en
This plant." Such sounds from midst the thickets came.
Whence I, with either bard, close to the side
That rose, pass'd forth beyond. "Remember," next
We heard, "those unblest creatures of the clouds,[1]

---

[1] *Creatures of the clouds.*—The Centaurs. Ovid, "Metamorphoses," lib. xii., fab. 4.

How they their twyfold bosoms, overgorged,
Opposed in fight to Theseus : call to mind
The Hebrews, how, effeminate, they stoop'd[1]
To ease their thirst ; whence Gideon's ranks were thinn'd,
As he to Madian[2] march'd adown the hills."

Thus near one border coasting, still we heard
The sins of gluttony, with woe erewhile
Reguerdon'd. Then along the lonely path,
Once more at large, full thousand paces on
We travel'd, each contemplative and mute.

"Why pensive journey so ye three alone?"
Thus suddenly a voice exclaim'd : whereat
I shook, as doth a scared and paltry beast ;
Then raised my head, to look from whence it came.

Was ne'er, in furnace, glass, or metal, seen
So bright and glowing red, as was the shape
I now beheld. "If ye desire to mount,"
He cried ; "here must ye turn. This way he goes
Who goes in quest of peace." His countenance
Had dazzled me ; and to my guides I faced
Backward, like one who walks as sound directs.

As when, to harbinger the dawn, springs up
On freshen'd wing the air of May, and breathes
Of fragrance, all impregn'd with herb and flowers ;
E'en such a wind I felt upon my front
Blow gently, and the moving of a wing
Perceived, that, moving, shed ambrosial smell ;
And then a voice : "Blessed are they, whom grace
Doth so illume, that appetite in them
Exhaleth no inordinate desire,
Still hungering as the rule of temperance wills.

---

[1] *Call to mind the Hebrews, how, effeminate, they stoop'd.*—Judges vii.
[2] *To Madian.*—

"The matchless Gideon in pursuit
Of Madian and her vanquisht kings."
Milton, Samson Agonistes.

CANTO XXV.

ARGUMENT.

Virgil and Statius resolve some doubts that have arisen in the mind of Dante from what he had just seen. They all arrive on the seventh and last cornice, where the sin of incontinence is purged in fire; and the spirits of those suffering therein are heard to record illustrious instances of chastity.

IT was an hour, when he who climbs, had need
To walk uncrippled: for the sun[1] had now
To Taurus the meridian circle left,
And to the Scorpion left the night. As one,
That makes no pause, but presses on his road,
Whate'er betide him, if some urgent need
Impel; so enter'd we[2] upon our way,
One before other; for, but singly, none
That steep and narrow scale admits to climb.

E'en as the young stork lifteth up his wing
Through wish to fly, yet ventures not to quit
The nest, and drops it; so in me desire
Of questioning my guide arose, and fell,
Arriving even to the act that marks
A man prepared for speech. Him all our haste
Restrain'd not; but thus spake the sire beloved:
"Fear not to speed the shaft,[3] that on thy lip
Stands trembling for its flight." Encouraged thus,
I straight began: "How there can leanness come,[4]
Where is no want of nourishment to feed?"
"If thou," he answer'd, "hadst remember'd thee,

---

[1] *The sun.*—The sun had passed the meridian two hours, and that meridian was now occupied by the constellation of Taurus, to which, as the Scorpion is opposite, the latter constellation was consequently at the meridian of night.

[2] *So enter'd we.*—
"Davanti a me andava la mia guida:
E poi io dietro per una via stretta
Seguendo lei come mia scorta fida."
Frezzi, Il Quadriregio, lib. ii., cap. 3.
The good prelate of Foligno has followed our poet so closely throughout this Capitolo, that it would be necessary to transcribe almost the whole of it in order to show how much he has copied. These verses of his own may well be applied to him on the occasion.

[3] *Fear not to speed the shaft.*—"Fear not to utter the words that are already at the tip of thy tongue."

Πολλὰ μὲν ἀρτιεπὴς
Γλῶσσα μοι τοξεύματ' ἔχει περὶ κείνων
Κελαδῆσαι.   *Pindar, Isthm.*, v. 60.

"Full many a shaft of sounding rhyme
Stands trembling on my lip
Their glory to declare."

[4] *How there can leanness come.*—"How can spirits that need not corporeal nourishment, be subject to leanness?" This question gives rise to the following explanation of Statius respecting the formation of the human body from the first, its junction with the soul, and the passage of the latter to another world.

How Meleager[1] with the wasting brand
Wasted alike, by equal fires consumed;
This would not trouble thee: and hadst thou thought,
How in the mirror[2] your reflected form
With mimic motion vibrates; what now seems
Hard, had appear'd no harder than the pulp
Of summer-fruit mature. But that thy will
In certainty may find its full repose,
Lo Statius here! on him I call, and pray
That he would now be healer of thy wound."

"If, in thy presence, I unfold to him
The secrets of heaven's vengeance, let me plead
Thine own injunction to exculpate me."
So Statius answer'd, and forthwith began:
"Attend my words, O son, and in thy mind
Receive them; so shall they be light to clear
The doubt thou offer'st. Blood, concocted well,
Which by the thirsty veins is ne'er imbibed,
And rests as food superfluous, to be ta'en
From the replenish'd table, in the heart
Derives effectual virtue, that informs
The several human limbs, as being that
Which passes through the veins itself to make them.
Yet more concocted it descends, where shame
Forbids to mention: and from thence distils
In natural vessels on another's blood.
There each unite together; one disposed
To endure, to act the other, through that power
Derived from whence it came;[3] and being met,
It 'gins to work, coagulating first;
Then vivifies what its own substance made
Consist. With animation now indued,
The active virtue (differing from a plant
No further, than that this is on the way,
And at its limit that) continues yet
To operate, that now it moves, and feels,

---

[1] *Meleager.*—Virgil reminds Dante that, as Meleager was wasted away by the decree of the fates, and not through want of blood, so, by the divine appointment, there may be leanness where there is no need of nourishment.

[2] *In the mirror.*—As the reflection of a form in a mirror is modified in agreement with the modification of the form itself, so the soul, separated from the earthly body, impresses the image or ghost of that body with its own affections.

[3] *From whence it came.*—"From the heart," as Lombardi rightly interprets it.

Here the rocky precipice
Hurls forth redundant flames; and from the rim
A blast up-blown, with forcible rebuff
Driveth them back, sequester'd from its bound.
Canto XXV., lines 107—110.

As sea-sponge[1] clinging to the rock : and there
Assumes the organic powers its seed convey'd,
This is the moment, son ! at which the virtue,
That from the generating heart proceeds,
Is pliant and expansive ; for each limb
Is in the heart by forgeful nature plann'd.
How babe[2] of animal becomes, remains
For thy considering. At this point, more wise,
Than thou, has err'd,[3] making the soul disjoin'd
From passive intellect, because he saw
No organ for the latter's use assign'd.

"Open thy bosom to the truth that comes.
Know, soon as in the embryo, to the brain
Articulation is complete, then turns
The primal Mover with a smile of joy
On such great work of nature ; and imbreathes
New spirit replete with virtue, that what here
Active it finds, to its own substance draws :
And forms an individual soul, that lives,
And feels, and bends reflective on itself.
And that thou less mayst marvel at the word,
Mark the sun's heat ;[4] how that to wine doth change,
Mix'd with the moisture filter'd through the vine.

"When Lachesis hath spun the thread,[5] the soul
Takes with her both the human and divine,
Memory, intelligence, and will, in act
Far keener than before ; the other powers
Inactive all and mute. No pause allow'd,
In wondrous sort self-moving, to one strand
Of those, where the departed roam, she falls :
Here learns her destined path. Soon as the place
Receives her, round the plastic virtue beams,

---

[1] *As sea-sponge.*—The fœtus is in this stage a zoöphyte.

[2] *Babe.*—By "fante," which is here rendered "babe," is meant "the human creature." "The creature that is distinguished from others by its faculty of speech," just as Homer calls men—
γενεαὶ μερόπων ἀνθρώπων.

[3] *More wise, than thou, has err'd.*—Averroes is said to be here meant. Venturi refers to his commentary on Aristotle, "De Anim.," lib. iii., cap. 5, for the opinion that there is only one universal intellect or mind pervading every individual of the human race. Much of the knowledge displayed by our poet in the present canto appears to have been derived from the medical work of Averroes called the "Colliget," lib. ii., f. 10, Ven., 1490, fol.

[4] *Mark the sun's heat.*—Redi and Tiraboschi (Mr. Mathias's ed., v. ii., p. 36) have considered this as an anticipation of a profound discovery of Galileo's in natural philosophy ; but it is in reality taken from a passage in Cicero, "De Senectute," where, speaking of the grape, he says, " Quæ, et succo terræ et calore solis augescens, primo est peracerba gustatu, deinde maturata dulcescit."

[5] *When Lachesis had spun the thread*—When a man's life on earth is at an end.

Distinct as in the living limbs before:
And as the air, when saturate with showers,
The casual beam refracting, decks itself
With many a hue; so here the ambient air
Weareth that form, which influence of the soul
Imprints on it: and like the flame, that where
The fire moves, thither follows; so, henceforth,
The new form on the spirit follows still:
Hence hath it semblance, and is shadow call'd,
With each sense, even to the sight, endued:
Hence speech is ours, hence laughter, tears, and sighs,
Which thou mayst oft have witness'd on the mount.
The obedient shadow fails not to present
Whatever varying passion moves within us.
And this the cause of what thou marvel'st at."

 Now the last flexure of our way we reach'd;
And to the right hand turning other care
Awaits us. Here the rocky precipice
Hurls forth redundant flames; and from the rim
A blast up-blown, with forcible rebuff
Driveth them back, sequester'd from its bound.

 Behoved us, one by one, along the side,
That border'd on the void, to pass; and I
Fear'd on one hand the fire, on the other fear'd
Headlong to fall: when thus the instructor warn'd;
"Strict rein must in this place direct the eyes.
A little swerving and the way is lost."

 Then from the bosom of the burning mass,
"O God of mercy!"[1] heard I sung, and felt
No less desire to turn. And when I saw
Spirits along the flame proceeding, I
Between their footsteps and mine own was fain
To share by turns my view. At the hymn's close
They shouted loud, "I do not know a man;"[2]
Then in low voice again took up the strain;
Which once more ended, "To the wood," they cried,
"Ran Dian, and drave forth Callisto[3] stung

---

[1] "*O God of mercy.*"—"Summæ Deus clementiæ." The beginning of the hymn sung on the Sabbath at matins, as it stands in the ancient breviaries; for in the modern it is "summæ parens clementiæ."—*Lombardi.*

[2] *At the hymn's close they shouted loud,* "*I do not know a man.*"—Luke i. 34.

[3] *Callisto.*—See Ovid, "Metamorphoses," lib. ii., fab. 5.

Then from the bosom of the burning mass,
"O God of mercy!" heard I sung, and felt
No less desire to turn.
Canto XXV., lines 117—119.

With Cytherea's poison:" then return'd
Unto their song; then many a pair extoll'd,
Who lived in virtue chastely and the bands
Ot wedded love. Nor from that task, I ween,
Surcease they; whilesoe'er the scorching fire
Enclasps them. Of such skill appliance needs,
To medicine the wound that healeth last.[1]

---

[1] *The wound that healeth last.*—The marginal note in the Monte Casino MS. on this passage is: "Id est ultima litera quæ denotat ultimum peccatum mortale;" and the editor remarks that Dante in these last two verses admonishes himself, and in himself all those guilty of carnal sin, in what manner the wound inflicted by it, and expressed by the last P. on his forehead, may be healed.

CANTO XXVI.

ARGUMENT.

The spirits wonder at seeing the shadow cast by the body of Dante on the flame as he passes it. This moves one of them to address him. It proves to be Guido Guinicelli, the Italian poet, who points out to him the spirit of Arnault Daniel, the Provençal, with whom he also speaks.

WHILE singly thus along the rim we walk'd,
    Oft the good master warn'd me: "Look thou well.
Avail it that I caution thee." The sun
Now all the western clime irradiate changed
From azure tinct to white; and, as I pass'd,
My passing shadow made the umber'd flame
Burn ruddier. At so strange a sight I mark'd
That many a spirit marvel'd on his way.
    This bred occasion first to speak of me.
"He seems," said they, "no insubstantial frame:"
Then, to obtain what certainty they might,
Stretch'd towards me, careful not to overpass
The burning pale. "O thou! who followest
The others, haply not more slow than they,
But moved by reverence; answer me, who burn
In thirst and fire: nor I alone, but these
All for thine answer do more thirst, than doth
Indian or Æthiop for the cooling stream.
Tell us, how is it that thou makest thyself
A wall against the sun, as thou not yet
Into the inextricable toils of death
Hadst enter'd?" Thus spake one: and I had straight
Declared me, if attention had not turn'd
To new appearance. Meeting these, there came,
Midway the burning path, a crowd, on whom
Earnestly gazing, from each part I view
The shadows all press forward, severally
Each snatch a hasty kiss, and then away.
E'en so the emmets, 'mid their dusky troops,

And when I saw
Spirits along the flame proceeding, I
Between their footsteps and mine own was fain
To share by turns my view.
Canto XXV., lines 119—122.

Peer closely one at other, to spy out
Their mutual road perchance, and how they thrive.
  That friendly greeting parted, ere dispatch
Of the first onward step, from either tribe
Loud clamour rises: those, who newly come,
Shout "Sodom and Gomorrah!" these, "The cow
Pasiphae enter'd, that the beast she woo'd
Might rush unto her luxury." Then as cranes,
That part towards the Riphæan mountains fly,
Part towards the Lybic sands, these to avoid
The ice, and those the sun; so hasteth off
One crowd, advances the other; and resume
Their first song, weeping, and their several shout.[1]
  Again drew near my side the very same,
Who had erewhile besought me; and their looks
Mark'd eagerness to listen. I, who twice
Their will had noted, spake: "O spirits! secure,
Whene'er the time may be, of peaceful end;
My limbs, nor crude, nor in mature old age,
Have I left yonder: here they bear me, fed
With blood, and sinew-strung. That I no more
May live in blindness, hence I tend aloft.
There is a dame on high, who wins for us
This grace, by which my mortal through your realm
I bear. But may your utmost wish soon meet
Such full fruition, that the orb of Heaven,
Fullest of love, and of most ample space,
Receive you: as ye tell (upon my page
Henceforth to stand recorded) who ye are;
And what this multitude, that at your backs
Have past behind us." As one, mountain-bred,
Rugged and clownish, if some city's walls
He chance to enter, round him stares agape,
Confounded and struck dumb; e'en such appear'd
Each spirit. But when rid of that amaze
(Not long the inmate of a noble heart),[2]

---

[1] *Their first song, weeping, and their several shout.*
—See the last canto, v. 118 and 123.

[2] *Amaze (not long the inmate of a noble heart).*—
  "Stupore
Lo qual negli alti cor tosto s'attuta."

Thus Speroni: "Lo stupore
  Lo qual dagli alti cor tosto si parte."
               Canace.
He does not say that wonder is not natural to a lofty mind, for it is the very principle of knowledge (μάλα

He, who before had question'd, thus resumed:
"O blessed! who, for death preparing, takest
Experience of our limits, in thy bark;
Their crime, who not with us proceed, was that
For which, as he did triumph, Cæsar[1] heard
The shout of 'queen,' to taunt him. Hence their cry
Of 'Sodom,' as they parted; to rebuke
Themselves, and aid the burning by their shame.
Our sinning was Hermaphrodite: but we,
Because the law of human kind we broke,
Following like beasts our vile concupiscence,
Hence parting from them, to our own disgrace
Record the name of her, by whom the beast
In bestial tire was acted. Now our deeds
Thou know'st, and how we sinn'd. If thou by name
Wouldst haply know us, time permits not now
To tell so much, nor can I. Of myself
Learn what thou wishest. Guinicelli[2] I;
Who having truly sorrow'd ere my last,
Already cleanse me." With such pious joy,
As the two sons upon their mother gazed
From sad Lycurgus[3] rescued; such my joy
(Save that I more repress'd it) when I heard
From his own lips the name of him pronounced,
Who was a father to me, and to those
My betters, who have ever used the sweet
And pleasant rhymes of love. So nought I heard,
Nor spake; but long time thoughtfully I went
Gazing on him; and, only for the fire,
Approach'd not nearer. When my eyes were fed
By looking on him; with such solemn pledge,

γὰρ φιλοσόφου τοῦτο τὸ πάθος, τὸ θαυμάζειν, οὐ γὰρ ἄλλη ἀρχὴ φιλοσοφίας ἢ αὑτή.—*Plato, Theæt.*, edit. Bipont., tom. ii., p. 76), but that it is not of long continuance in such a mind. On this subject it is well said by Dr. Horsley: "Wonder, connected with a principle of rational curiosity, is the source of all knowledge and discovery, and it is a principle even of piety: but wonder, which ends in wonder, and is satisfied with wonder, is the quality of an idiot."—*Sermons*, vol. i., p. 227. Compare Aristotle, "Metaph.," lib. i., p. 335. edit. Sylb. The above passage from Plato is adduced by Clemens Alexandrinus, "Strom.," lib. ii., sect. 9.

[1] *Cæsar.*—For the opprobrium cast on Cæsar's effeminacy, see Suetonius, "Julius Cæsar," c. 49.

[2] *Guinicelli.*—See note to canto xi. 96.

[3] *Lycurgus.*—Statius, "Thebais," lib. iv. and v. Hypsipyle had left her infant charge, the son of Lycurgus, on a bank, where it was destroyed by a serpent, when she went to show the Argive army the river of Langia; and, on her escaping the effects of Lycurgus's resentment, the joy her own children felt at the sight of her was such as our poet felt on beholding his predecessor Guinicelli. The incidents are beautifully described in Statius, and seem to have made an impression on Dante, for he before (canto xxii. 110) characterises Hypsipyle as her—

"Who show'd Langia's wave."

As forces credence, I devoted me
Unto his service wholly. In reply
He thus bespake me: "What from thee I hear
Is graved so deeply on my mind, the waves
Of Lethe shall not wash it off, nor make
A whit less lively. But as now thy oath
Has seal'd the truth, declare what cause impels
That love, which both thy looks and speech bewray."

"Those dulcet lays," I answer'd; "which, as long
As of our tongue the beauty does not fade,
Shall make us love the very ink that traced them."

"Brother!" he cried, and pointed at the shade
Before him, "there is one, whose mother speech
Doth owe to him a fairer ornament.
He[1] in love ditties, and the tales of prose,
Without a rival stands; and lets the fools

---

[1] *He.*—The united testimony of Dante and of Petrarch places Arnault Daniel at the head of the Provençal poets:
"Poi v'era un drappello
Di portamenti e di volgari strani:
Fra tutti il primo Arnaldo Daniello
Gran maestro d'amor ch' a la sua terra
Ancor fa onor col suo dir nuovo e bello."
Petrarca, Trionfo d'Amore, c. iv.

That he was born of poor but noble parents, at the castle of Ribeyrac in Périgord, and that he was at the English court, is the amount of Millot's information concerning him (tom. ii., p. 479). The account there given of his writings is not much more satisfactory, and the criticism on them must go for little better than nothing. It is to be regretted that we have not an opportunity of judging for ourselves of his "love ditties and his tales of prose"—

"Versi d'amore e prose di romanzi."

Our poet frequently cites him in the work "De Vulgari Eloquio." In the second chapter of the second book, he is instanced as one "who had treated of love;" and in the tenth chapter, he is said to have used in almost all his canzoni a particular kind of stanza, the sestine, which Dante had followed in one of his own canzoni, beginning,

"Al poco giorno ed al gran cerchio d'ombra."

This stanza is termed by Gray, "both in sense and sound, a very mean composition."—*Gray's Works*, 4to, Lond., 1814, vol. ii., p. 23. According to Crescimbeni ("Della Volgar Poesia," lib. i., p. 7, ed. 1698), he died in 1189. Arnault Daniel was not soon forgotten; for Ausias March, a Catalonian, who was himself distinguished as a Provençal poet in the middle of the fifteenth century, makes honourable mention of him in some verses, which are quoted by Bastero in his "Crusca Provenzale," ediz. Roma, 1724, p. 75:

"Envers alguns aço miracle par;
Mas sin's membram d'en Arnau Daniel
E de aquels que la terra los es vel,
Sabrem Amor vers nos que pot donar."

"To some this seems a miracle to be;
But if we Arnault Daniel call to mind,
And those beside, whom earthly veil doth bind,
We then the mighty power of love shall see."

Since this note was written, M. Raynouard has made us better acquainted with the writings and history of the Provençal poets. I have much pleasure in citing the following particulars respecting Arnault Daniel from his "Choix des Poésies des Troubadours," tom. ii., pp. 318, 319: "L'autorité de Dante suffirait pour nous convaincre qu' Arnaud Daniel avait composé plusieurs romans. Mais il reste une preuve positive de l'existence d'un roman d'Arnaud Daniel; c'est celui de Lancelot du Lac, dont la traduction fut faite, vers la fin du treizième siècle, en allemand, par Ulrich de Zatchitschoven, qui nomme Arnaud Daniel comme l'auteur original."[*] "Le Tasse, dans l'un de ses ouvrages,[†] s'exprime en ces termes, au sujet des romans composés par les troubadours: E romanzi furono detti quei poemi, o più tosto quelle istorie favolose, che furono scritte nella lingua de' Provenzali o de' Castigliani; le quali non si scrivevano in versi, ma in prosa, come alcuni hanno osservato prima da me, perchè Dante, parlando d'Arnaldo Daniello, disse:

'Versi d'amore e prose di romanzi,' &c.

Enfin Pulci, dans son 'Morgante Maggiore,' nomme Arnaud Daniel comme auteur d'un roman de Renaud:

'Dopo costui venne il famoso Arnaldo
Che molto diligentemente ha scritto,
E investigò le opre di Rinaldo,
De le gran cose che fece in Egitto,' &c."
Morgante Maggiore, canto xxvii., ott. 80.
See also Raynouard, tom. v. 30.

[*] Des extraits de cette traduction allemande ont été publiés.
[†] Discorso sopra il parere fatto del Signor Fr. Patricio, &c., edit. fol., tom. iv., p. 210.

Talk on, who think the songster of Limoges[1]
O'ertops him. Rumour and the popular voice
They look to, more than truth; and so confirm
Opinion, ere by art or reason taught.
Thus many of the elder time cried up
Guittone,[2] giving him the prize, till truth
By strength of numbers vanquish'd. If thou own
So ample privilege, as to have gain'd
Free entrance to the cloister, whereof Christ
Is Abbot of the college; say to him
One paternoster for me, far as needs[3]
For dwellers in this world, where power to sin
No longer tempts us." Haply to make way
For one that follow'd next, when that was said,
He vanish'd through the fire, as through the wave
A fish, that glances diving to the deep.

 I, to the spirit he had shown me, drew
A little onward, and besought his name,
For which my heart, I said, kept gracious room.
He frankly thus began: "Thy courtesy[4]

---

[1] *The songster of Limoges.*—Giraud de Borneil, of Sideuil, a castle in Limoges. He was a Troubadour, much admired and caressed in his day, and appears to have been in favour with the monarchs of Castile, Leon, Navarre, and Arragon. Giraud is mentioned by Dante in a remarkable passage of the "De Vulgari Eloquentia," lib. ii., cap. 2: "As man is endowed with a triple soul—vegetable, animal, and rational—so he walks in a triple path. Inasmuch as he is vegetable, he seek utility, in which he has a common nature with plants; inasmuch as he is animal, he seeks for pleasure, in which he participates with brutes; inasmuch as he is rational, he seeks for honour, in which he is either alone, or is associated with the angels. Whatever we do, appears to be done through these three principles," &c.,—"With respect to utility, we shall find on a minute inquiry that the primary object with all who seek it, is safety; with regard to pleasure, love is entitled to the first place; and as to honour, no one will hesitate in assigning the same pre-eminence to virtue. These three, then—safety, love, virtue—appear to be three great subjects, which ought to be treated with most grandeur; that is, those things which chiefly pertain to these, as courage in arms, ardency of love, and the direction of the will: concerning which alone we shall find on inquiry that illustrious men have composed their poems in the vernacular tongues; Bertrand de Born, of arms; Arnault Daniel, of love; Giraud de Borneil, of rectitude; Cino da Pistoia, of love; his friend" (by whom he means himself) "of rectitude; but I find no Italian as yet who has treated of arms." Giraud is again quoted in the sixth chapter of this book. The following notice respecting him is found in Gray's posthumous works, 4to, Lond., 1814, vol. ii., p. 23:—"The canzone is of very ancient date, the invention of it being ascribed to Girard de Borneil, of the school of Provence, who died in 1178. He was of Limoges, and was called 'Il Maestro de' Trovatori.'" That he was distinguished by this title (a circumstance that, perhaps, induced Dante to vindicate the superior claims of Arnault Daniel) is mentioned by Bastero in his "Crusca Provenzale," ediz. Roma, p. 84, where we find the following list of his MSS. poems preserved in the Vatican, and in the library of S. Lorenzo at Florence: "Una tenzone col Re d'Aragona; e un Serventese contra Cardaillac, e diverse Canzoni massimamente tre pel ricuperamento del S. Sepolcro, o di Terra Santa, ed alcune col titolo di Canterete, cioe picciole cantari, ovvero canzonette." The light which these and similar writings might cast, not only on the events, but still more on the manners of a most interesting period of history, would surely, without taking into the account any merit they may possess as poetical compositions, render them objects well deserving of more curiosity than they appear to have hitherto excited in the public mind. Many of his poems are still remaining in MS. According to Nostradamus he died in 1278. Millot, " Hist. Littéraire des Troubadours," tom. ii., p. 1 and 23. But I suspect that there is some error in this date, and that he did not live to so late a period. Some of his poems have since been published by Raynouard, "Poésies des Troubadours," tom. iii., p. 304, &c.

[2] *Guittone.*—See canto xxiv. 56.

[3] *Far as needs.*—See canto xi. 23.

[4] *Thy courtesy.*—Arnault is here made to speak in his own tongue, the Provençal. According to Dante ("De Vulgari Eloquentia," lib. i., c. 8), the Provençal was one language with the Spanish. What he says

So wins on me, I have nor power, nor will
To hide me. I am Arnault; and with songs,
Sorely waymenting for my folly past,
Thorough this ford of fire I wade, and see
The day, I hope for, smiling in my view.
I pray ye by the worth that guides ye up
Unto the summit of the scale, in time
Remember ye my sufferings." With such words
He disappear'd in the refining flame.

---

on this subject is so curious, that the reader will perhaps not be displeased if I give an abstract of it. He first makes three great divisions of the European languages. "One of these extends from the mouths of the Danube, or the lake of Mæotis, to the western limits of England, and is bounded by the limits of the French and Italians, and by the ocean. One idiom obtained over the whole of this space: but was afterwards subdivided into the Sclavonian, Hungarian, Teutonic, Saxon, English, and the vernacular tongues of several other people, one sign remaining to all, that they use the affirmative *io* (our English *ay*). The whole of Europe, beginning from the Hungarian limits and stretching towards the east, has a second idiom, which reaches still further than the end of Europe, into Asia. This is the Greek. In all that remains of Europe, there is a third idiom, subdivided into three dialects, which may be severally distinguished by the use of the affirmatives, *oc*, *oil*, and *si*; the first spoken by the Spaniards, the next by the French, the third by the Latins (or Italians). The first occupy the western part of southern Europe, beginning from the limits of the Genoese. The third occupy the eastern part from the said limits, as far that is, as to the promontory of Italy, where the Adriatic sea begins, and to Sicily. The second are in a manner northern, with respect to these, for they have the Germans to the east and north, on the west they are bounded by the English sea and the mountains of Arragon, and on the south by the people of Provence and the declivity of the Apennine.'—Ibid., c. x. 'Each of these three," he observes, "has its own claims to distinction. The excellency of the French anguage consists in its being best adapted, on account of its facility and agreeableness, to prose narration (quicquid redactum, sive inventum est ad vulgare prosaicum, suum est); and he instances the books compiled on the gests of the Trojans and Romans, and the delightful Adventures of King Arthur, with many other histories and works of instruction. The Spanish (or Provençal) may boast of its having produced such as first cultivated in this, as in a more perfect and sweet language, the vernacular poetry: among whom are Pierre d'Auvergne, and others more ancient. The privileges of the Latin, or Italian, are two; first, that it may reckon for its own those writers who have adopted a more sweet and subtile style of poetry, in the number of whom are Cino da Pistoia and his friend; and the next, that its writers seem to adhere to certain general rules of grammar, and in so doing give it, in the opinion of the intelligent, a very weighty pretension to preference." Since the last edition of this book, it has appeared that Mr. Gray understood by the words "Grammaticæ, quæ communis est," "the Latin or mother-tongue," and not, as I have rendered them, " general rules of grammar." In this latter sense, however, the word "Grammatica," has been used twice before in the " Treatise de Vulgari Eloquentia," though it is certainly afterwards applied in the sense in which Gray took it. See the edition of Gray's works, for which we are so much indebted to Mr. Mathias, 4to, London, 1814, vol. ii., p. 35. We learn from our author's "Vita Nuova," p. 258, that there were no poetic compositions in the Provençal or Italian more than one hundred and fifty years before the " Vita Nuova " was written; and that the first who wrote in the vernacular languages wrote to make himself understood by a lady. M. Raynouard supposed the text of all the editions to be miserably corrupted in this place, and took much pains to restore it. I will add the passage as that learned writer concluded it to have come from the hand of Dante :

 "Tan m'abellis vostre cortes deman,
  Ch' ieu non me puese ni m voil a vos cobrire ;
  Jeu sui Arnautz, che plor e vai cantan ;
  Consiros, vei la passada follor,
  E vei jauzen lo joi qu'esper denan ;
  Aras vos prec, per aquella valor
  Que us guida al som sens freich e sens calina,
  Sovegna vos atenprar ma dolor."

" Tant me plaît votre courtoise demande,—que je ne puis ni ne me veux à vous cacher ;—je suis Arnaud, qui pleure et va chantant ;—soucieux, je vois la passée folie,—et vois joyeux le bonheur, que j'espère à l'avenir ; —maintenant je vous prie, par cette vertu—qui vous guide au sommet, sans froid et sans chaud ; qu'il souvienne à vous de soulager ma douleur. Il n'est pas un des nombreux manuscrits de la Divina Commedia, pas une des éditions multipliées qui en ont été données, qui ne présente dans les vers que Dante prête au troubadour Arnaud Daniel, un texte défiguré et devenu, de copie en copie, presque inintelligible. Cependant j'ai pensé qu'il n'était pas impossible de rétablir le texte de ces vers, en comparant avec soin, dans les manuscrits de Dante que possèdent les dépôts publics de Paris, toutes les variantes qu'ils pouvaient fournir, et en les choisissant d'après les régles grammaticales et les notions lexicographiques de la langue des troubadours. Mon espoir n'a point été trompé, et sans aucun secours conjectural, sans aucun déplacement ni changement de mots, je suis parvenu par le simple choix des variantes, à retrouver le texte primitif, tel qu'il a dû être produit par Dante."—*Raynouard, Lexique Roman*, tom. i., p. xlii., 8vo, Par., 1830.

CANTO XXVII.

ARGUMENT.

An angel sends them forward through the fire to the last ascent, which leads to the terrestrial Paradise, situated on the summit of the mountain. They have not proceeded many steps on their way upward, when the fall of night hinders them from going further; and our Poet, who has lain down with Virgil and Statius to rest, beholds in a dream two females, figuring the active and contemplative life. With the return of morning, they reach the height; and here Virgil gives Dante full liberty to use his own pleasure and judgment in the choice of his way, till he shall meet with Beatrice.

NOW was the sun[1] so station'd, as when first
His early radiance quivers on the heights,
Where stream'd his Maker's blood; while Libra hangs
Above Hesperian Ebro; and new fires,
Meridian, flash on Ganges' yellow tide.
So day was sinking, when the angel of God
Appear'd before us. Joy was in his mien.
Forth of the flame he stood upon the brink;
And with a voice, whose lively clearness far
Surpass'd our human, "Blessed[2] are the pure
In heart," he sang: then near him as we came,
"Go ye not further, holy spirits!" he cried,
"Ere the fire pierce you: enter in; and list
Attentive to the song ye hear from thence."
I, when I heard his saying, was as one
Laid in the grave.[3] My hands together clasp'd,
And upward stretching, on the fire I look'd;
And busy fancy conjured up the forms
Erewhile beheld alive consumed in flames.
The escorting spirits turn'd with gentle looks

---

[1] *The sun.*—At Jerusalem it was dawn, in Spain midnight, and in India noonday, while it was sunset in Purgatory.
[2] *Blessed.*—Matt. v. 8.
[3] *As one laid in the grave.*—
"Quale è colui che nella fossa è messo."
Lombardi understands this of a man who is taken to execution in the manner described in "Hell," c. xix. 52. "Colui," he thinks, cannot be properly applied to a corse. Yet Boccaccio's imitation confirms the opinion of the other commentators:
"Essa era tale, a guardarla nel viso,
Qual donna morta alla fossa portata."
Il Filostrato, p. v., st. 83.
Which Chaucer has thus translated:
"She was right soche to sene in her visage,
As is that wight that men on bere ybinde."
Troilus and Creseide, b. iv.

Toward me; and the Mantuan spake: "My son,
Here torment thou mayst feel, but canst not death.
Remember thee, remember thee, if I
Safe e'en on Geryon brought thee; now I come
More near to God, wilt thou not trust me now?
Of this be sure; though in its womb that flame
A thousand years contain'd thee, from thy head
No hair should perish. If thou doubt my truth,
Approach; and with thy hands thy vesture's hem
Stretch forth, and for thyself confirm belief.
Lay now all fear, oh! lay all fear aside.
Turn hither, and come onward undismay'd."

    I still, though conscience urged, no step advanced.
When still he saw me fix'd and obstinate,
Somewhat disturb'd he cried: "Mark now, my son,
From Beatrice thou art by this wall
Divided." As at Thisbe's name the eye
Of Pyramus was open'd (when life ebb'd
Fast from his veins), and took one parting glance,
While vermeil[1] dyed the mulberry; thus I turn'd
To my sage guide, relenting, when I heard
The name that springs for ever in my breast.

    He shook his forehead; and, "How long," he said,
"Linger we now?" then smiled, as one would smile
Upon a child that eyes the fruit and yields.
Into the fire before me then he walk'd;
And Statius, who erewhile no little space
Had parted us, he pray'd to come behind.

    I would have cast me into molten glass
To cool me, when I enter'd; so intense
Raged the conflagrant mass. The sire beloved,
To comfort me, as he proceeded, still
Of Beatrice talk'd. "Her eyes," saith he,
"E'en now I seem to view." From the other side
A voice, that sang, did guide us; and the voice
Following, with heedful ear, we issued forth,
There where the path led upward. "Come," we heard,
"Come, blessed of my Father."[2] Such the sounds

---

[1] *While vermeil.*—Ovid, "Metamorphoses," lib. iv. 125.   [2] "*Come, blessed of my Father.*"—Matt. xxv. 34.

That hail'd us from within a light, which shone
So radiant, I could not endure the view.
"The sun," it added, "hastes: and evening comes.
Delay not: ere the western sky is hung
With blackness, strive ye for the pass." Our way
Upright within the rock arose, and faced
Such part of heaven, that from before my steps
The beams were shrouded of the sinking sun.

    Nor many stairs were overpast, when now
By fading of the shadow we perceived
The sun behind us couch'd; and ere one face
Of darkness o'er its measureless expanse
Involved the horizon, and the night her lot
Held individual, each of us had made
A stair his pallet; not that will, but power,
Had fail'd us, by the nature of that mount
Forbidden further travel. As the goats,
That late have skipt and wanton'd rapidly
Upon the craggy cliffs, ere they had ta'en
Their supper on the herb, now silent lie
And ruminate beneath the umbrage brown,
While noon-day rages; and the goatherd leans
Upon his staff, and leaning watches them:
And as the swain, that lodges out all night
In quiet by his flock, lest beast of prey
Disperse them: even so all three abode,
I as a goat, and as the shepherds they,
Close pent on either side by shelving rock.

    A little glimpse of sky was seen above;
Yet by that little I beheld the stars,
In magnitude and lustre shining forth
With more than wonted glory. As I lay,
Gazing on them, and in that fit of musing,
Sleep overcame me, sleep, that bringeth oft
Tidings of future hap. About the hour,
As I believe, when Venus from the east
First lighten'd on the mountain, she whose orb
Seems alway glowing with the fire of love,
A lady young and beautiful, I dream'd,
Was passing o'er a lea; and, as she came,

A lady young and beautiful, I dream'd,
Was passing o'er a lea; and, as she came,
Methought I saw her ever and anon
Bending to cull the flowers.
Canto XXVII., lines 97—100.

Methought I saw her ever and anon
Bending to cull the flowers; and thus she sang:
"Know ye, whoever of my name would ask,
That I am Leah:[1] for my brow to weave
A garland, these fair hands unwearied ply.
To please me[2] at the crystal mirror, here
I deck me. But my sister Rachel, she
Before her glass abides the livelong day,[3]
Her radiant eyes beholding, charm'd no less,
Than I with this delightful task. Her joy
In contemplation, as in labour mine."

And now as glimmering dawn appear'd, that breaks
More welcome to the pilgrim still, as he
Sojourns less distant on his homeward way,
Darkness from all sides fled, and with it fled
My slumber; whence I rose, and saw my guide
Already risen. "That delicious fruit,
Which through so many a branch the zealous care
Of mortals roams in quest of, shall this day
Appease thy hunger." Such the words I heard
From Virgil's lip; and never greeting heard,
So pleasant as the sounds. Within me straight
Desire so grew upon desire to mount,
Thenceforward at each step I felt the wings
Increasing for my flight. When we had run
O'er all the ladder to its topmost round,
As there we stood, on me the Mantuan fix'd
His eyes, and thus he spake: "Both fires, my son,
The temporal and eternal, thou hast seen;
And art arrived, where of itself my ken
No further reaches. I, with skill and art,
Thus far have drawn thee. Now thy pleasure take
For guide. Thou hast o'ercome the steeper way,
O'ercome the straiter. Lo! the sun, that darts

—By Leah is understood the active figures the contemplative. Michel de these allegorical personages the atues on the monument of Julius II. of S. Pietro in Vincolo. See Mr. of Michel Angelo," sculpture viii. and

[2] *To please me.*—"For the sake of that enjoyment which I shall have in beholding my God face to face, I thus exercise myself in good works."

[3] *She before her glass abides the livelong day.*—"Her delight is in admiring in her mirror, that is, in the Supreme Being, the light, or knowledge, that He vouchsafes her."

His beam upon thy forehead: lo! the herb,[1]
The arborets and flowers, which of itself
This land pours forth profuse. Till those bright eyes[2]
With gladness come, which, weeping, made me haste
To succour thee, thou mayst or seat thee down,
Or wander where thou wilt. Expect no more
Sanction of warning voice or sign from me,
Free of thy own arbitrement to chuse,
Discreet, judicious. To distrust thy sense
Were henceforth error. I invest thee then
With crown and mitre, sovereign o'er thyself."

---

[1] *Lo! the herb.*—" In alium campum transit amœnissimum.—Ipse vero campus splendidus, suavis ac decorus quantæ magnitudinis, quantæ gloriæ, quantæque sit pulchritudinis, nulla lingua, nullusque sermo, potest enarrare: plenus est enim omni jucunditate, et gaudio, et lætitia. Ibi liliorum, et rosarum odor, ibi odoramentorum omnium redolet fragrantia, ibi mannæ, omniumque eternarum deliciarum redundat abundantia. In hujus campi medio paradisus est."—*Alberici Visio*, § 20.

[2] *Those bright eyes.*—The eyes of Beatrice.

CANTO XXVIII.

ARGUMENT.

Dante wanders through the forest of the terrestrial Paradise, till he is stopped by a stream, on the other side of which he beholds a fair lady, culling flowers. He speaks to her; and she, in reply, explains to him certain things touching the nature of that place, and tells that the water, which flows between them, is here called Lethe, and in another place has the name of Eunoe.

THROUGH that celestial forest, whose thick shade
With lively greenness the new-springing day
Attemper'd, eager now to roam, and search
Its limits round, forthwith I left the bank;
Along the champain leisurely my way
Pursuing, o'er the ground, that on all sides
Delicious odour breathed. A pleasant air,[1]
That intermitted never, never veer'd,
Smote on my temples, gently, as a wind
Of softest influence: at which the sprays,
Obedient all, lean'd trembling to that part[2]
Where first the holy mountain casts his shade;
Yet were not so disorder'd, but that still
Upon their top the feather'd quiristers[3]
Applied their wonted art, and with full joy
Welcomed those hours of prime, and warbled shrill
Amid the leaves, that to their jocund lays
Kept tenour; even as from branch to branch,
Along the piny forests on the shore
Of Chiassi,[4] rolls the gathering melody,

---

[1] *A pleasant air.—*
"Cantan fra i rami gli augelletti vaghi,
Azzurri, e bianchi, e verdi, e rossi, e gialli;
Mormoranti ruscelli, e cheti laghi
Di limpidezza vincono i cristalli.
Una dolc' aura, che ti par che vaghi
A un modo sempre, e dal suo stil non falli,
Facea sì l'aria tremolar d'intorno,
Che non potea nojar calor del giorno."
Ariosto, Orlando Furioso, c. xxxiv., st. 50.
"Therewith a winde, unnethe it might be less,

Made in the levis grene a noise soft,
Accordant to the foulis song on loft."
Chaucer, The Assemble of Foules.

[2] *To that part.—*The west.

[3] *The feather'd quiristers.—*Imitated by Boccaccio, "Fiammetta," lib. iv.: "Odi i queruli uccelli," &c.— "Hear the querulous birds plaining with sweet songs, and the boughs trembling, and moved by a gentle wind, as it were keeping tenour to their notes."

[4] *Chiassi.—*This is the wood where the scene of Boccaccio's sublimest story (taken entirely from

When Eolus hath from his cavern loosed
The dripping south. Already had my steps,
Though slow, so far into that ancient wood
Transported me, I could not ken the place
Where I had enter'd; when, behold! my path
Was bounded by a rill, which, to the left,
With little rippling waters bent the grass
That issued from its brink. On earth no wave,
How clean soe'er, that would not seem to have
Some mixture in itself, compared with this,
Transpicuous clear; yet darkly on it roll'd,
Darkly beneath perpetual gloom, which ne'er
Admits or sun or moon-light there to shine.

My feet advanced not; but my wondering eyes
Pass'd onward, o'er the streamlet, to survey
The tender may-bloom, flush'd through many a hue,
In prodigal variety: and, there,
As object, rising suddenly to view,
That from our bosom every thought beside
With the rare marvel chases, I beheld
A lady[1] all alone, who, singing, went,
And culling flower from flower, wherewith her way
Was all o'er painted. "Lady beautiful!
Thou, who (if looks, that use to speak the heart,
Are worthy of our trust) with love's own beam
Dost warm thee," thus to her my speech I framed;
"Ah! please thee hither towards the streamlet bend
Thy steps so near, that I may list thy song.
Beholding thee and this fair place, methinks,
I call to mind where wander'd and how look'd
Proserpine, in that season, when her child
The mother lost, and she the bloomy spring."

As when a lady, turning in the dance,

Elinaud, as I learn in the notes to the "Decameron," ediz. Giunti, 1573, p. 62) is laid. See "Decameron," Giorn. 5, Nov. 8, and Dryden's "Theodore and Honoria." Our poet perhaps wandered in it during his abode with Guido Novello da Polenta.

[1] *A lady.*—Most of the commentators suppose that by this lady, who in the last canto is called Matilda, is to be understood the Countess Matilda, who endowed the holy see with the estates called the Patrimony of St. Peter, and died in 1115. See G. Villani, lib. iv., cap. xx. But it seems more probable that she should be intended for an allegorical personage. Venturi accordingly supposes that she represents the active life. But, as Lombardi justly observes, we have had that already shadowed forth in the character of Leah; and he therefore suggests, that by Matilda may be understood that affection which we ought to bear towards the holy church, and for which the lady above mentioned was so remarkable.

Already had my steps,
Though slow, so far into that ancient wood
Transported me, I could not ken the place
Where I had enter'd.

Canto XXVIII., lines 22—25

Doth foot it featly, and advances scarce
One step before the other to the ground;
Over the yellow and vermilion flowers
Thus turn'd she at my suit, most maiden-like,
Valing her sober eyes; and came so near,
That I distinctly caught the dulcet sound.
Arriving where the limpid waters now
Laved the green swerd, her eyes she deign'd to raise,
That shot such splendour on me, as I ween
Ne'er glanced from Cytherea's, when her son
Had sped his keenest weapon to her heart.
Upon the opposite bank she stood and smiled;
As through her graceful fingers shifted still
The intermingling dyes, which without seed
That lofty land unbosoms. By the stream
Three paces only were we sunder'd: yet,
The Hellespont, where Xerxes pass'd it o'er
(A curb for ever[1] to the pride of man),
Was by Leander not more hateful held
For floating, with inhospitable wave,
'Twixt Sestus and Abydos, than by me
That flood, because it gave no passage thence.

"Strangers ye come; and haply in this place,
That cradled human nature in her birth,
Wondering, ye not without suspicion view
My smiles: but that sweet strain of psalmody,
'Thou, Lord! hast made me glad,'[2] will give ye light,
Which may uncloud your minds. And thou, who stand'st
The foremost, and didst make thy suit to me,
Say if aught else thou wish to hear: for I
Came prompt to answer every doubt of thine."

She spake; and I replied: "I know not how
To reconcile this wave,[3] and rustling sound
Of forest leaves, with what I late have heard
Of opposite report." She answering thus:
"I will unfold the cause, whence that proceeds,

---

[1] *A curb for ever.*—Because Xerxes had been so humbled, when he was compelled to repass the Hellespont in one small bark, after having a little before crossed with a prodigious army, in the hopes of subduing Greece.

[2] *But that sweet strain of psalmody,* 'Thou, Lord! hast made me glad.'—Ps. xcii. 4.

[3] *I know not how to reconcile this wave.*—See canto xxi. 45.

Which makes thee wonder; and so purge the cloud
That hath enwrapt thee. The First Good, whose joy
Is only in himself, created man,
For happiness; and gave this goodly place,
His pledge and earnest of eternal peace.
Favour'd thus highly, through his own defect
He fell; and here made short sojourn; he fell,
And, for the bitterness of sorrow, changed
Laughter unblamed and ever-new delight.
That vapours none, exhaled from earth beneath,
Or from the waters (which, wherever heat
Attracts them, follow), might ascend thus far
To vex man's peaceful state, this mountain rose
So high toward the heaven, nor fears the rage
Of elements contending;[1] from that part
Exempted, where the gate his limit bars.
Because the circumambient air, throughout,
With its first impulse circles still, unless
Aught interpose to check or thwart its course;
Upon the summit, which on every side
To visitation of the impassive air
Is open, doth that motion strike, and makes
Beneath its sway the umbrageous wood resound:
And in the shaken plant such power resides,
That it impregnates with its efficacy
The voyaging breeze, upon whose subtle plume
That, wafted, flies abroad; and the other land,[2]
Receiving (as 'tis worthy in itself,
Or in the clime that warms it), doth conceive;
And from its womb produces many a tree
Of various virtue. This when thou hast heard,
The marvel ceases, if in yonder earth
  ome plant, without apparent seed, be found
To fix its fibrous stem. And further learn,
That with prolific foison of all seeds

---

[1] *Of elements contending.*—In the "Dittamondo," of Fazio degli Uberti, l. i., cap. xi., there is a description of the terrestrial Paradise, in which the poet has had Dante before him.

[2] *The other land.*—The continent, inhabited by the living, and separated from Purgatory by the ocean, is affected (and that diversely, according to the nature of the soil, or the climate) by a virtue, or efficacy, conveyed to it by the winds from plants growing in the terrestrial Paradise, which is situated on the summit of Purgatory; and this is the cause why some plants are found on earth without any apparent seed to produce them.

This holy plain is fill'd, and in itself
Bears fruit that ne'er was pluck'd on other soil.
    "The water, thou behold'st, springs not from vein,
Restored by vapour, that the cold converts;
As stream that intermittently repairs
And spends his pulse of life; but issues forth
From fountain, solid, undecaying, sure:
And, by the will omnific, full supply
Feeds whatsoe'er on either side it pours;
On this, devolved with power to take away
Remembrance of offence; on that, to bring
Remembrance back of every good deed done.
From whence its name of Lethe on this part;
On the other, Eunoe: both of which must first
Be tasted, ere it work; the last exceeding
All flavours else. Albeit thy thirst may now
Be well contented, if I here break off,
No more revealing; yet a corollary
I freely give beside: nor deem my words
Less grateful to thee, if they somewhat pass
The stretch of promise. They, whose verse of yore
The golden age recorded and its bliss,
On the Parnassian mountain,[1] of this place
Perhaps had dream'd. Here was man guiltless; here
Perpetual spring,[2] and every fruit; and this
The far-famed nectar." Turning to the bards,
When she had ceased, I noted in their looks
A smile at her conclusion; then my face
Again directed to the lovely dame.

---

[1] *On the Parnassian mountain.*—
    "In bicipiti somniasse Parnasso."
                            Persius, Prol.

[2] *Perpetual spring.*—
    "Ver erat æternum, placidique tepentibus auris

Mulcebant zephyri natos sine semine flores.
  *   *   *   *   *   *
Flumina jam lactis, jam flumina nectaris ibant."
                    Ovid, Metamorphoses,
                            lib. i., v. III.

CANTO XXIX.

ARGUMENT.

The lady, who in a following canto is called Matilda, moves along the side of the stream in a contrary direction to the current, and Dante keeps equal pace with her on the opposite bank. A marvellous sight, preceded by music, appears in view.

SINGING,[1] as if enamour'd, she resumed
And closed the song, with "Blessed they whose sins
Are cover'd."[2] Like the wood-nymphs then, that tripp'd
Singly across the sylvan shadows; one
Eager to view, and one to escape the sun;
So moved she on, against the current, up
The verdant rivage. I, her mincing step
Observing, with as tardy step pursued.

Between us not an hundred paces trod,
The bank, on each side bending equally,
Gave me to face the orient. Nor our way
Far onward brought us, when to me at once
She turn'd, and cried: "My brother! look, and hearken."
And lo! a sudden lustre ran across
Through the great forest on all parts, so bright,
I doubted whether lightning were abroad;
But that, expiring ever in the spleen
That doth unfold it, and this during still,
And waxing still in splendour, made me question
What it might be: and a sweet melody
Ran through the luminous air. Then did I chide,
With warrantable zeal, the hardihood
Of our first parent; for that there, where earth
Stood in obedience to the heavens, she only,
Woman, the creature of an hour, endured not
Restraint of any veil, which had she borne
Devoutly, joys, ineffable as these,
Had from the first, and long time since, been mine.

While, through that wilderness of primy sweets
That never fade, suspense I walk'd, and yet
Expectant of beatitude more high;
Before us, like a blazing fire, the air

---

[1] *Singing.*—"Cantava come fosse innamorata." Guido Cavalcanti, *Poeti del primo secolo*, v. 2, p. 283.

[2] *And closed the song, with "Blessed they whose sins are cover'd."*—Ps. xxxii. 1.

Beneath a sky
So beautiful, came four and twenty elders,
By two and two, with flower-de-luces crown'd.
Canto XXIX., lines 80—82.

Under the green boughs glow'd; and, for a song,
Distinct the sound of melody was heard.
　　O ye thrice holy virgins! for your sakes
If e'er I suffer'd hunger, cold, and watching,
Occasion calls on me to crave your bounty.
Now through my breast let Helicon his stream
Pour copious, and Urania[1] with her choir
Arise to aid me; while the verse unfolds
Things, that do almost mock the grasp of thought.
　　Onward a space, what seem'd seven trees of gold
The intervening distance to mine eye
Falsely presented; but, when I was come
So near them, that no lineament was lost
Of those, with which a doubtful object, seen
Remotely, plays on the misdeeming sense;
Then did the faculty, that ministers
Discourse to reason, these for tapers of gold[2]
Distinguish; and i' the singing trace the sound
"Hosanna." Above, their beauteous garniture
Flamed with more ample lustre, than the moon
Through cloudless sky at midnight, in her noon.
　　I turn'd me, full of wonder, to my guide;
And he did answer with a countenance
Charged with no less amazement: whence my view
Reverted to those lofty things, which came
So slowly moving towards us, that the bride[3]
Would have outstript them on her bridal day.
　　The lady call'd aloud: "Why thus yet burns
Affection in thee for these living lights,
And dost not look on that which follows them?"
　　I straightway mark'd a tribe behind them walk,
As if attendant on their leaders, clothed
With raiment of such whiteness, as on earth
Was never. On my left, the watery gleam

---

[1] *Urania.*—Landino observes, that intending to ing of heavenly things, he rightly invokes Urania. Thus Milton:
"Descend from Heaven, Urania, by that name
If rightly thou art call'd."
　　　　　　　　　Paradise Lost, b. vii. 1.

[2] *Tapers of gold.*—See Rev. i. 12. The commentitors are not agreed whether the seven sacraments of the Church or the seven gifts of the Spirit are intended. n his "Convito," our author says: "Because these gifts proceed from ineffable charity, and divine charity is appropriated to the Holy Spirit, hence, also, it is that they are called gifts of the Holy Spirit, the which, as Isaiah distinguishes them, are seven."—Page 189.

[3] *The bride.*—
"E come va per via sposa novella
A passi rari, e porta gli occhi bassi
Con faccia vergognosa, e non favella."
　　　　Frezzi, Il Quadriregio, lib. i., cap. 16.

Borrow'd, and gave me back, when there I look'd,
As in a mirror, my left side portray'd.
    When I had chosen on the river's edge
Such station, that the distance of the stream
Alone did separate me; there I stay'd
My steps for clearer prospect, and beheld
The flames go onward, leaving,[1] as they went,
The air behind them painted as with trail
Of liveliest pencils;[2] so distinct were mark'd
All those seven listed colours,[3] whence the sun
Maketh his bow, and Cynthia her zone.
These streaming gonfalons did flow beyond
My vision; and ten paces,[4] as I guess,
Parted the outermost. Beneath a sky
So beautiful, came four and twenty elders,[5]
By two and two, with flower-de-luces crown'd.
All sang one song: "Blessed be thou[6] among
The daughters of Adam! and thy loveliness
Blessed for ever!" After that the flowers,
And the fresh herblets, on the opposite brink,
Were free from that elected race; as light
In heaven doth second light, came after them
Four[7] animals, each crown'd with verdurous leaf.
With six wings each was plumed; the plumage full
Of eyes; and the eyes of Argus would be such,
Were they endued with life. Reader! more rhymes
I will not waste in shadowing forth their form:
For other need so straitens, that in this

---

[1] *Leaving.—*
"Lasciando dietro a se l'aer dipinto.
Che lascia dietro a se l'aria dipinta."
Mr. Mathias's *Ode to Mr. Nichols, Gray's Works*,
vol. i., p. 532.

[2] *Pencils.—*Since this translation was made, Perticari has affixed another sense to the word "pennelli," which he interprets "pennons" or "streamers." Monti, in his "Proposta," highly applauds the discovery. The conjecture loses something of its probability, if we read the whole passage, not as Monti gives it, but as it stands in Landino's edition of 1484:
"Et vidi le fiamelle andar dàvante
  lasciando drieto a se laire dipinto
  che di tratti pennegli havea sembiante
Siche li sopra rimanea distinto
  di sette liste tutte in que colori
  onde fa larcho el sole & della elcinto."

[3] *Listed colours.—*
"Di sette liste tutte in quel colori," &c.
  "A bow
Conspicuous with three listed colours gay."
    Milton, Paradise Lost, b. xi. 865.

[4] *Ten paces.—*For an explanation of the allegorical meaning of this mysterious procession, Venturi refers those, "who would see in the dark," to the commentaries of Landino, Vellutello, and others: and adds, that it is evident the poet has accommodated to his own fancy many sacred images in the Apocalypse. In Vassari's life of Giotto, we learn that Dante recommended that book to his friend, as affording fit subjects for his pencil.

[5] *Four and twenty elders.—*"Upon the seats I saw four and twenty elders sitting."—Rev. iv. 4.

[6] *Blessed be thou.—*"Blessed art thou among women, and blessed is the fruit of thy womb."—Luke i. 42.

[7] *Four.—*The four evangelists.

>   Three nymphs,
> At the right wheel, came circling in smooth dance:
> The one so ruddy, that her form had scarce
> Been known within a furnace of clear flame;
> The next did look, as if the flesh and bones
> Were emerald; snow new-fallen seem'd the third.
>   *Canto XXIX., lines 110—121.*

I may not give my bounty room. But read
Ezekiel;[1] for he paints them, from the north
How he beheld them come by Chebar's flood,
In whirlwind, cloud, and fire; and even such
As thou shalt find them character'd by him,
Here were they; save as to the pennons: there,
From him departing, John[2] accords with me.

The space, surrounded by the four, enclosed
A car triumphal:[3] on two wheels it came,
Drawn at a Gryphon's[4] neck; and he above
Stretch'd either wing uplifted, 'tween the midst
And the three listed hues, on each side, three;
So that the wings did cleave or injure none;
And out of sight they rose. The members, far
As he was bird, were golden; white the rest,
With vermeil inter vein'd. So beautiful[5]
A car, in Rome, ne'er graced Augustus' pomp,
Or Africanus'; e'en the sun's itself
Were poor to this; that chariot of the sun,
Erroneous, which in blazing ruin fell
At Tellus' prayer[6] devout, by the just doom
Mysterious of all-seeing Jove. Three nymphs,
At the right wheel, came circling in smooth dance:[7]
The one so ruddy, that her form had scarce
Been known within a furnace of clear flame;
The next did look, as if the flesh and bones

---

[1] *Ezekiel.*—"And I looked, and, behold, a whirlwind came out of the north, a great cloud, and a fire infolding itself, and a brightness was about it, and out of the midst thereof as the colour of amber, out of the midst of the fire. Also out of the midst thereof came the likeness of four living creatures. And this was their appearance; they had the likeness of a man. And every one had four faces, and every one had four wings."—Ezek. i. 4, 5, 6.

[2] *John.*—"And the four beasts had each of them six wings about him."—Rev. iv. 8. "Aliter senas alas propter senarii numeri perfectionem positum arbitror; quia in sexta ætate, id est adveniente plenitudine temporum, hæc Apostolus peracta commemorat; in novissimo enim animali conclusit omnia."—*Primasii, Augustini discipuli, Episcopi Comment. lib. quinque in Apocal.*, ed. Basil, 1544. "With this interpretation it is very consonant that Ezekiel discovered in these animals only four wings, because his prophecy does not extend beyond the fourth age; beyond that is the end of the synagogue and the calling of the Gentiles: whereas Dante beholding them in the sixth age, saw them with six wings, as did Saint John."—*Lombardi.*

[3] *A car triumphal.*—Either the Christian church, or perhaps the Papal chair.

[4] *Gryphon.*—Under the gryphon, an imaginary creature, the fore-part of which is an eagle, and the hinder a lion, is shadowed forth the union of the divine and the human nature in Jesus Christ.

[5] *So beautiful.*—
"E certo quando Roma più onore
Di carro trionfale a Scipione
Fece, non fu cotal, nè di splendore
Passato fu da quello, il qual Fetone
Abbandonò per soverchio tremore."
Boccaccio, Teseide, lib. ix., st. 31.
Thus in the "Quadriregio," lib. i., cap. 5:
"Mai vide Roma carro trionfante
Quanto era questo bel, ne vedrà unquanco."

[6] *Tellus' prayer.*—Ovid, "Metamorphoses," lib. ii., v. 279.

[7] *Three nymphs, at the right wheel, came circling in smooth dance.*—The three evangelical virtues: the first Charity, the next Hope, and the third Faith. Faith may be produced by charity, or charity by faith, but the inducements to hope must arise either from one or other of these.

Were emerald; snow new-fallen seem'd the third.
Now seem'd the white to lead, the ruddy now;
And from her song who led, the others took
Their measure, swift or slow. At the other wheel,
A band quaternion,[1] each in purple clad,
Advanced with festal step, as, of them, one
The rest conducted;[2] one, upon whose front
Three eyes were seen. In rear of all this group,
Two old men[3] I beheld, dissimilar
In raiment, but in port and gesture like,
Solid and mainly grave; of whom, the one
Did show himself some favour'd counsellor
Of the great Coan,[4] him, whom nature made
To serve the costliest creature of her tribe:
His fellow mark'd an opposite intent;
Bearing a sword, whose glitterance and keen edge,
E'en as I view'd it with the flood between,
Appall'd me. Next, four others[5] I beheld
Of humble seeming: and, behind them all,
One single old man,[6] sleeping as he came,
With a shrewd visage. And these seven, each
Like the first troop were habited; but wore
No braid of lilies on their temples wreathed.
Rather, with roses and each vermeil flower,
A sight, but little distant, might have sworn,
That they were all on fire[7] above their brow.

Whenas the car was o'er against me, straight
Was heard a thundering, at whose voice it seem'd
The chosen multitude were stay'd; for there,
With the first ensigns, made they solemn halt.

---

[1] *A band quaternion.*—The four moral or cardinal virtues, of whom Prudence directs the others.
[2] *One the rest conducted.*—Prudence, described with three eyes, because she regards the past, the present, and the future.
[3] *Two old men.*—St. Luke, the physician, characterised as the writer of the Acts of the Apostles, and St. Paul, represented with a sword, on account, as it should seem, of the power of his style.
[4] *Of the great Coan.*—Hippocrates, "whom nature made for the benefit of her favourite creature, man."
[5] *Four others.*—"The commentators," says Venturi, "suppose these four to be the four evangelists; but I should rather take them to be four principal doctors of the church." Yet both Landino and Vellutello expressly call them the authors of the epistles, James, Peter, John, and Jude.

[6] *One single old man.*—As some say, St. John, under the character of the author of the Apocalypse. But, in the poem attributed to Giacopo, the son of our poet, which in some MSS., and in one of the earliest editions, accompanies the original of this work, and is descriptive of its plan, this old man is said to be Moses:
"E'l vecchio, ch' era dietro a tutti loro,
Fu Moyse."
"And the old man, who was behind them all,
Was Moses."
See No. 3,459 of the Harleian MSS. in the British Museum.
[7] *All on fire.*—So Giles Fletcher:
"The wood's late wintry head
With flaming primroses set all on fire."
Christ's Triumph after Death.

CANTO XXX.

ARGUMENT.

Beatrice descends from heaven, and rebukes the poet.

SOON as that polar light,[1] fair ornament
Of the first heaven, which hath never known
Setting nor rising, nor the shadowy veil
Of other cloud than sin, to duty there
Each one convoying, as that lower doth
The steersman to his port, stood firmly fixed;
Forthwith the saintly tribe, who in the van
Between the Gryphon and its radiance came,
Did turn them to the car, as to their rest:
And one, as if commission'd from above,
In holy chant thrice shouted forth aloud;
"Come, spouse! from Libanus:"[2] and all the rest
Took up the song.—At the last audit, so
The blest shall rise, from forth his cavern each
Uplifting lightly his new-vested flesh;
As, on the sacred litter, at the voice
Authoritative of that elder, sprang
A hundred ministers and messengers
Of life eternal. "Blessed[3] thou, who comest!"
And, "Oh!" they cried, "from full hands[4] scatter ye
Unwithering lilies:" and, so saying, cast
Flowers over head and round them on all sides.
    I have beheld, ere now, at break of day,
The eastern clime all roseate; and the sky
Opposed, one deep and beautiful serene;
And the sun's face so shaded, and with mists

---

[1] *That polar light.*—The seven candlesticks of gold, which he calls the polar light of heaven itself, because they perform the same office for Christians that the polar star does for mariners, in guiding them to their port.

[2] *Come, spouse! from Libanus.*—"Come with me from Lebanon, my spouse, with me, from Lebanon."—Song of Solomon iv. 8.

[3] *Blessed.*—"Blessed is he that cometh in the name of the Lord."—Matt. xxi. 9.

[4] *From full hands.*—"Manibus date lilia plenis." Virgil, *Æneid*, lib. vi. 884.

Attemper'd, at his rising, that the eye
Long while endured the sight: thus, in a cloud
Of flowers,[1] that from those hands angelic rose,
And down within and outside of the car
Fell showering, in white veil with olive wreathed,
A virgin in my view appear'd, beneath
Green mantle, robed in hue of living flame:
And[2] o'er my spirit, that so long a time
Had from her presence felt no shuddering dread,
Albeit mine eyes discern'd her not, there moved
A hidden virtue from her, at whose touch
The power of ancient love[3] was strong within me.

No sooner on my vision streaming, smote
The heavenly influence, which, years past, and e'en
In childhood, thrill'd me, than towards Virgil I
Turn'd me to leftward; panting, like a babe,
That flees for refuge to his mother's breast,
If aught have terrified or work'd him woe:
And would have cried, "There is no dram of blood,
That doth not quiver in me. The old flame[4]
Throws out clear tokens of reviving fire."
But Virgil had bereaved us of himself;
Virgil, my best-loved father; Virgil, he
To whom I gave me up for safety: nor[5]
All, our prime mother lost, avail'd to save

---

[1] *In a cloud of flowers.—*
"Dentro una nuvola di fiori.
* * * Ninguntque rosarum.
Floribus, umbrantes matrem," &c.
Lucretius, lib. ii.
Thus Milton:
"Eve separate he spies,
Veil'd in a cloud of fragrance, where she stood."
Paradise Lost, b. ix., v. 425.
And Thomson, in his Invocation to Spring:
"Veil'd in a shower
Of shadowing roses, on our plains descend."

[2] *And.—*In the first edition it stood thus:
"And o'er my spirit, that in former days
Within her presence had abode so long,
No shuddering terror crept. Mine eyes no more
Had knowledge of her; yet there moved from her
A hidden virtue, at whose touch awaked," &c.
And this was a translation of the common reading, which has "con la sua presenza," instead of "che alla sua presenza," and a full stop instead of a comma after "infranto." As I have little doubt but that the reading of the Nidobeatina edition and that of many MSS.
is right in this instance, I have altered the version as it now stands in the text, which still perhaps needs some explanation. His spirit, which had been so long unawed by the presence of Beatrice (for she had been ten years dead), now felt, through a secret influence proceeding from her, its ancient love revived, though his sight had not yet distinguished her.

[3] *The power of ancient love.—*
"D'antico amor sentì la gran potenza.
Io sento si d'amor la gran possanza."
Dante, Canzone vi.
"Sveglia d'antico amor la gran possanza."
Mr. Mathias's Ode to Mr. Nichols, Gray's Works,
4to, 1814, vol. i., p. 532.

[4] *The old flame.—*"Agnosco veteris vestigia flammæ."
Virgil, Æneid, lib. iv. 23.
"Conosco i segni dell' antico fuoco."
Giusto de' Conti, La Bella Mano.

[5] *Nor.—*"Not all the beauties of the terrestrial Paradise, in which I was, were sufficient to allay my grief."

>   Thus, in a cloud
> Of flowers, that from those hands angelic rose,
> And down within and outside of the car
> Fell showering, in white veil with olive wreathed,
> A virgin in my view appear'd, beneath
> Green mantle, robed in hue of living flame.
>   *Canto XXX., lines 28—33.*

My undew'd cheeks from blur of soiling tears.
  "Dante! weep not that Virgil leaves thee; nay
Weep thou not yet: behoves thee feel the edge
Of other sword; and thou shalt weep for that."
  As to the prow or stern, some admiral
Paces the deck, inspiriting his crew,
When 'mid the sail-yards all hands ply aloof;
Thus, on the left side of the car, I saw
(Turning me at the sound of mine own name,
Which here I am compell'd to register)
The virgin station'd, who before appear'd
Veil'd in that festive shower angelical.
  Towards me, across the stream, she bent her eyes;
Though from her brow the veil descending, bound
With foliage of Minerva, suffer'd not
That I beheld her clearly: then with act
Full royal, still insulting o'er her thrall,
Added, as one who, speaking, keepeth back
The bitterest saying, to conclude the speech:
"Observe me well. I am, in sooth, I am
Beatrice. What! and hast thou deign'd at last
Approach the mountain? Knewest not, O man!
Thy happiness is here?" Down fell mine eyes
On the clear fount; but there, myself espying,
Recoil'd, and sought the greenswerd; such a weight
Of shame was on my forehead. With a mien
Of that stern majesty, which doth surround
A mother's presence to her awe-struck child,
She look'd; a flavour of such bitterness
Was mingled in her pity. There her words
Brake off; and suddenly the angels sang,
"In thee, O gracious Lord! my hope hath been:"
But[1] went no further than, "Thou, Lord! hast set
My feet in ample room." As snow, that lies,
Amidst the living rafters[2] on the back
Of Italy, congeal'd, when drifted high

---

[1] *But.*—They sang the thirty-first Psalm, to the end of the eighth verse. What follows in that Psalm would not have suited the place or the occasion.

[2] *The living rafters.*—" Vive travi." The leafless woods on the Apennine.

"Fraxineæque trabes."
  Virgil, Æneid, lib. vi. 181.
and—
"Trabibusque obscurus acernis."
  Ibid., lib. ix. 87.

And closely piled by rough Sclavonian blasts;
Breathe but the land whereon no shadow falls,[1]
And straightway melting it distils away,
Like a fire-wasted taper: thus was I,
Without a sigh or tear, or ever these
Did sing, that, with the chiming of heaven's sphere,
Still in their warbling chime: but when the strain
Of dulcet symphony express'd for me
Their soft compassion, more than could the words,
"Virgin! why so consumest him?" then, the ice,[2]
Congeal'd about my bosom, turn'd itself
To spirit and water; and with anguish forth
Gush'd, through the lips and eyelids, from the heart.

Upon the chariot's same edge[3] still she stood,
Immovable; and thus address'd her words
To those bright semblances with pity touch'd:
"Ye in the eternal day your vigils keep;
So that nor night nor slumber, with close stealth,
Conveys from you a single step, in all
That goings on of time: thence, with more heed
I shape mine answer, for his ear intended,
Who there stands weeping; that the sorrow now
May equal the transgression. Not alone
Through operation of the mighty orbs,
That mark each seed to some predestined aim,
As with aspect or fortunate or ill
The constellations meet; but through benign
Largess of heavenly graces, which rain down
From such a height as mocks our vision, this man
Was, in the freshness of his being,[4] such,
So gifted virtually, that in him
All better habits wondrously had thrived.
The more of kindly strength is in the soil,
So much doth evil seed and lack of culture

---

[1] *The land whereon no shadow falls.*—"When the wind blows from off Africa, where, at the time of the equinox, bodies, being under the equator, cast little or no shadow; or, in other words, when the wind is south"

[2] *The ice.*—Milton has transferred this conceit, though scarcely worth the pains of removing, into one of his Italian poems, Son. v.

[3] *Same edge*—The Nidobeatina edition, and many MSS., here read "*detta* coscia," instead of "destra," or "dritta coscia;" and it is probable from what has gone before, that the former is the right reading. See v. 60.

[4] *In the freshness of his being.*—"Nella sua vita nuova." Some suppose our poet alludes to the work so called, written in his youth.

Mar it the more, and make it run to wildness.
These looks sometime upheld him; for I show'd
My youthful eyes, and led him by their light
In upright walking. Soon as I had reach'd
The threshold of my second age,[1] and changed
My mortal for immortal; then he left me,
And gave himself to others. When from flesh
To spirit I had risen, and increase
Of beauty and of virtue circled me,
I was less dear to him, and valued less.
His steps were turn'd into deceitful ways,
Following false images of good, that make
No promise perfect. Nor avail'd me aught
To sue for inspirations, with the which,
I, both in dreams of night, and otherwise,
Did call him back; of them, so little reck'd him.
Such depth he fell, that all device was short
Of his preserving, save that he should view
The children of perdition. To this end
I visited the purlieus of the dead:
And one, who hath conducted him thus high,
Received my supplications urged with weeping.
It were a breaking of God's high decree,
If Lethe should be past, and such food[2] tasted,
Without the cost of some repentant tear."

---

[1] *The threshold of my second age.* — In the "Convito," our poet makes a division of human life into four ages, the first of which lasts till the twenty-fifth year. Beatrice, therefore, passed from this life to a better about that period.

[2] *If Lethe should be past, and such food.*—The oblivion of sins.

CANTO XXXI.

ARGUMENT.

Beatrice continues her reprehension of Dante, who confesses his error, and falls to the ground. Coming to himself again, he is by Matilda drawn through the waters of Lethe, and presented first to the four virgins who figure the cardinal virtues; these in their turn lead him to the Gryphon, a symbol of our Saviour; and the three virgins representing the evangelical virtues intercede for him with Beatrice, that she would display to him her second beauty.

"O THOU!" her words she thus without delay
    Resuming, turn'd their point on me, to whom
They, with but lateral edge,[1] seem'd harsh before:
    Say thou, who stand'st beyond the holy stream,
If this be true. A charge, so grievous, needs
Thine own avowal." On my faculty
Such strange amazement hung, the voice expired
Imperfect, ere its organs gave it birth.
    A little space refraining, then she spake:
"What dost thou muse on? Answer me. The wave
On thy remembrances of evil yet
Hath done no injury." A mingled sense
Of fear and of confusion, from my lips
Did such a "Yea" produce, as needed help
Of vision to interpret. As when breaks,
In act to be discharged, a cross-bow bent
Beyond its pitch, both nerve and bow o'erstretch'd;
The flagging weapon feebly hits the mark:
Thus, tears and sighs forth gushing, did I burst,
Beneath the heavy load: and thus my voice
Was slacken'd on its way. She straight began:
"When my desire invited thee to love
The good, which sets a bound to our aspirings;
What bar of thwarting foss or linked chain
Did meet thee, that thou so shouldst quit the hope
Of further progress? or what bait of ease,
Or promise of allurement, led thee on

---

[1] *To whom they, with but lateral edge.*—The words of Beatrice, when not addressed directly to himself, but spoken to the angel of him, Dante had thought sufficiently harsh.

Elsewhere, that thou elsewhere shouldst rather wait?"
  A bitter sigh I drew, then scarce found voice
To answer; hardly to these sounds my lips
Gave utterance, wailing: "Thy fair looks withdrawn,
Things present, with deceitful pleasures, turn'd
My steps aside." She answering spake: "Hadst thou
Been silent, or denied what thou avow'st,
Thou hadst not hid thy sin the more; such eye
Observes it. But whene'er the sinner's cheek
Breaks forth into the precious-streaming tears
Of self-accusing, in our court the wheel
Of justice doth run counter to the edge.[1]
Howe'er, that thou mayst profit by thy shame
For errors past, and that henceforth more strength
May arm thee, when thou hear'st the Syren-voice;
Lay thou aside the motive to this grief,
And lend attentive ear, while I unfold
How opposite a way my buried flesh
Should have impell'd thee. Never didst thou spy,
In art or nature, aught so passing sweet,
As were the limbs that in their beauteous frame
Enclosed me, and are scatter'd now in dust.
If sweetest thing thus fail'd thee with my death,
What, afterward, of mortal, should thy wish
Have tempted? When thou first hadst felt the dart
Of perishable things, in my departing
For better realms, thy wing thou shouldst have pruned
To follow me; and never stoop'd again,
To 'bide a second blow, for a slight girl,[2]
Or other gaud as transient and as vain.

---

[1] *Counter to the edge.*—" The weapons of divine justice are blunted by the confession and sorrow of the offender."

[2] *For a slight girl.*—" Daniello and Venturi say that this alludes to Gentucca of Lucca, mentioned in the twenty-fourth canto. They did not, however, observe that Dante knew not if Gentucca were then in the world, and that Beatrice is now reprehending him for past and not for future errors." Thus Lombardi. Pelli (" Memor.," p. 57) acquaints us that Corbinelli, in the Life of Dante added to the edition of the " De Vulgari Eloquentia," says the name of this lady was "Pargoletta." But the intimation, as Pelli justly remarks, can scarcely be deemed authentic. The annotator on the Monte Casino MS. gives a very different turn to the allusion. "Quæ proca fuit," &c. " This was either a mistress; or else it is put for the poetic art, as when he says in a certain song:

 ' Io mi son pargoletta bella e nuova
  E son venuta;'

which rebuke of Beatrice's may be delivered in the person of many theologians dissuading from poetry and other worldly sciences; a rebuke that should be directed against those who read the poets to gratify their own inclination, and not for the sake of instruction, that they may defeat the errors of the Gentiles." It remains to be considered whether our poet's marriage with Gemma de' Donati, and the difficulties in which that engagement involved him, may not be the object of Beatrice's displeasure.

The new and inexperienced bird[1] awaits,
Twice it may be, or thrice, the fowler's aim;
But in the sight of one whose plumes are full,
In vain the net is spread, the arrow wing'd."

   I stood, as children silent and ashamed
Stand, listening, with their eyes upon the earth,
Acknowledging their fault, and self-condemn'd.
And she resumed: "If, but to hear, thus pains thee;
Raise thou thy beard, and lo! what sight shall do."

   With less reluctance yields a sturdy holm,
Rent from its fibres by a blast, that blows
From off the pole, or from Iarbas' land,[2]
Than I at her behest my visage raised:
And thus the face denoting by the beard,[3]
I mark'd the secret sting her words convey'd.

   No sooner lifted I mine aspect up,
Than I perceived[4] those primal creatures cease
Their flowery sprinkling; and mine eyes beheld
(Yet unassured and wavering in their view)
Beatrice; she, who towards the mystic shape,
That joins two natures in one form, had turn'd:
And, even under shadow of her veil,
And parted by the verdant rill that flow'd
Between, in loveliness she seem'd as much
Her former self surpassing, as on earth
All others she surpass'd. Remorseful goads
Shot sudden through me. Each thing else, the more
Its love had late beguiled me, now the more
Was loathsome. On my heart so keenly smote
The bitter consciousness, that on the ground
O'erpower'd I fell: and what my state was then,
She knows, who was the cause. When now my strength
Flow'd back, returning outward from the heart,

---

[1] *Bird.*—"Surely in vain the net is spread in the sight of any bird."—Prov. i. 17.
[2] *From Iarbas' land.*—The south.
[3] *The beard.*—"I perceived, that when she desired me to raise my beard, instead of telling me to lift up my head, a severe reflection was implied on my want of that wisdom which should accompany the age of manhood."
[4] *Than I perceived.*—I had before translated this differently, and in agreement with those editions which read—

" Posarsi quelle belle creature
  Da loro apparsion,"

instead of

" Posarsi quelle prime creature
  Da loro aspersion;"

for which reading I am indebted to Lombardi, who derives it from the Nidobeatina edition. By the " primal creatures " are meant the angels, who were scattering the flowers on Beatrice.

The beauteous dame, her arms expanding, clasp'd
My temples, and immerged me where 'twas fit
The wave should drench me.
Canto XXXI., lines 100—102.

The lady,[1] whom alone I first had seen,
I found above me. "Loose me not," she cried:
"Loose not thy hold:" and lo! had dragg'd me high
As to my neck into the stream; while she,
Still as she drew me after, swept along,
Swift as a shuttle, bounding o'er the wave.
　　The blessed shore approaching, then was heard
So sweetly, "Tu asperges me,"[2] that I
May not remember, much less tell the sound.
　　The beauteous dame, her arms expanding, clasp'd
My temples, and immerged me where 'twas fit
The wave should drench me: and, thence raising up,
Within the fourfold dance of lovely nymphs
Presented me so laved; and with their arm
They each did cover me. "Here are we nymphs,
And in the heaven are stars.[3] Or ever earth
Was visited of Beatrice, we
Appointed for her handmaids, tended on her.
We to her eyes will lead thee: but the light
Of gladness, that is in them, well to scan,
Those yonder three,[4] of deeper ken than ours,
Thy sight shall quicken." Thus began their song:
And then they led me to the Gryphon's breast,
Where, turn'd toward us, Beatrice stood.
"Spare not thy vision. We have station'd thee
Before the emeralds,[5] whence love, erewhile,
Hath drawn his weapons on thee." As they spake
A thousand fervent wishes riveted
Mine eyes upon her beaming eyes, that stood,
Still fix'd toward the Gryphon, motionless.
As the sun strikes a mirror, even thus
Within those orbs the twyfold being shone;

---

[1] *The lady.*—Matilda.
[2] *Tu asperges me.*—"Purge me with hyssop, and I shall be clean; wash me, and I shall be whiter than snow."—Ps. li. 7. Sung by the choir, while the priest is sprinkling the people with holy water.
[3] *Here are we nymphs, and in the heaven are stars.* —See canto i. 24.
[4] *Well to scan, those yonder three.*—Faith, Hope, and Charity.
[5] *We have station'd thee before the emeralds.*—The eyes of Beatrice. The author of "Illustrations of Shakespeare," 8vo, 1807, vol. ii., p. 193, has referred to old writers, by whom the epithet green is given to eyes, as by the early French poets, and by Shakespeare, "Romeo and Juliet," act. iii., sc. 5:

"An eagle, madam,
Hath not so green, so quick, so fair an eye."

Mr. Douce's conjecture, that eyes of this colour are much less common now than formerly, is not so probable as that writers, and especially poets, should at times be somewhat loose and general in applying terms expressive of colour, whereof an instance may be seen in some ingenious remarks by Mr. Blomfield on the word κυάνεος.—*Æschyli Persæ*, edit. 1814, Glossar., p. 107.

For ever varying, in one figure now
Reflected, now in other. Reader! muse
How wondrous in my sight it seem'd, to mark
A thing, albeit stedfast in itself,
Yet in its imaged semblance mutable.

    Full of amaze, and joyous, while my soul
Fed on the viand, whereof still desire
Grows with satiety; the other three,
With gesture that declared a loftier line,
Advanced: to their own carol, on they came
Dancing, in festive ring angelical.

    "Turn, Beatrice!" was their song: "Oh! turn
Thy saintly sight on this thy faithful one,
Who, to behold thee, many a wearisome pace
Hath measured. Gracious at our prayer, vouchsafe
Unveil to him thy cheeks: that he may mark
Thy second beauty, now conceal'd." O splendour!
O sacred light eternal! who is he,
So pale with musing in Pierian shades,
Or with that fount so lavishly imbued,
Whose spirit should not fail him in the essay
To represent thee such as thou didst seem,
When under cope of the still-chiming heaven
Thou gavest to open air thy charms reveal'd?

CANTO XXXII.

ARGUMENT.

Dante is warned not to gaze too fixedly on Beatrice. The procession moves on, accompanied by Matilda, Statius, and Dante, till they reach an exceeding lofty tree, where divers strange chances befall.

MINE eyes with such an eager coveting
Were bent to rid them of their ten years' thirst,[1]
No other sense was waking: and e'en they
Were fenced on either side from heed of aught;
So tangled, in its custom'd toils, that smile
Of saintly brightness drew me to itself:
When forcibly, toward the left, my sight
The sacred virgins turn'd; for from their lips
I heard the warning sounds: "Too fix'd a gaze![2]
Awhile my vision labour'd; as when late
Upon the o'erstrain'd eyes the sun hath smote:
But soon,[3] to lesser object, as the view
Was now recover'd (lesser in respect
To that excess of sensible, whence late
I had perforce been sunder'd), on their right
I mark'd that glorious army wheel, and turn,
Against the sun and sevenfold lights, their front
As when, their bucklers for protection raised,
A well-ranged troop, with portly banners curl'd,
Wheel circling, ere the whole can change their ground;
E'en thus the goodly regiment of heaven,
Proceeding, all did pass us ere the car
Had sloped his beam. Attendant at the wheels
The damsels turn'd; and on the Gryphon moved
The sacred burden, with a pace so smooth,

---

[1] *Their ten years' thirst.*—Beatrice had been dead ten years.

[2] *Too fix'd a gaze.*—The allegorical interpretation of Vellutello, whether it be considered as justly inferable from the text or not, conveys so useful a lesson, that it deserves our notice. "The understanding is sometimes so intently engaged in contemplating the light of divine truth in the Scriptures, that it becomes dazzled, and is made less capable of attaining such knowledge, than if it had sought after it with greater moderation."

[3] *But soon.*—As soon as his sight was recovered, so as to bear the view of that glorious procession, which, splendid as it was, was yet less so than Beatrice, by whom his vision had been overpowered, &c.

No feather on him trembled. The fair dame,
Who through the wave had drawn me, companied
By Statius and myself, pursued the wheel,
Whose orbit, rolling, mark'd a lesser arch.

Through the high wood, now void (the more her blame,
Who by the serpent was beguil'd), I pass'd,
With step in cadence to the harmony
Angelic. Onward had we moved, as far,
Perchance, as arrow at three several flights
Full wing'd had sped, when from her station down
Descended Beatrice. With one voice
All murmur'd "Adam;" circling next a plant[1]
Despoil'd of flowers and leaf, on every bough.
Its tresses[2] spreading more as more they rose,
Were such, as 'midst their forest wilds, for height,
The Indians[3] might have gazed at. "Blessed thou,
Gryphon![4] whose beak hath never pluck'd that tree
Pleasant to taste: for hence the appetite
Was warp'd to evil." Round the stately trunk
Thus shouted forth the rest, to whom return'd
The animal twice gender'd: "Yea! for so
The generation of the just are saved."
And turning to the chariot pole, to foot
He drew it of the widow'd branch, and bound
There, left unto the stock[5] whereon it grew.

As when large floods of radiance[6] from above
Stream, with that radiance mingled, which ascends

---

[1] *A plant.*—Lombardi has conjectured, with much probability, that this tree is not (as preceding commentators had supposed) merely intended to represent the tree of knowledge of good and evil, but that the Roman empire is figured by it. Among the maxims maintained by our poet, as the same commentator observes, were these: that one monarchy had been willed by Providence, and was necessary for universal peace; and that this monarchy, by right of justice and by the divine ordinance, belonged to the Roman people only. His "Treatise de Monarchiâ" was written, indeed, to inculcate these maxims, and to prove that the temporal monarchy depends immediately on God, and should be kept as distinct as possible from the authority of the Pope.

[2] *Its tresses.*—"I saw, and behold, a tree in the midst of the earth, and the height thereof was great."—Dan. iv. 10.

[3] *The Indians.*—
"Quos oceano proprior gerit India lucos."
Virgil, Georgics, lib. ii. 122.

"Such as at this day to Indians known."
Milton, Paradise Lost, b. ix. 1102.

[4] *Blessed thou, Gryphon!*—Our Saviour's submission to the Roman empire appears to be intended, and particularly His injunction, " to render unto Cæsar the things that are Cæsar's."

[5] *There, left unto the stock.*—Dante here seems, I think, to intimate what he has attempted to prove at the conclusion of the second book "De Monarchiâ;" namely, that our Saviour, by His suffering under the sentence, not of Herod, but of Pilate, who was the delegate of the Roman emperor, acknowledged and confirmed the supremacy of that emperor over the whole world; for if, as he argues, all mankind were become sinners through the sin of Adam, no punishment, that was inflicted by one who had a right of jurisdiction over less than the whole human race, could have been sufficient to satisfy for the sins of all men. See note to "Paradise," c. vi. 89.

[6] *When large floods of radiance.*—When the sun enters into Aries, the constellation next to that of the Fish.

Next after setting of the scaly sign,
Our plants then burgein, and each wears anew
His wonted colours, ere the sun have yoked
Beneath another star his flamy steeds ;
Thus putting forth a hue more faint than rose,
And deeper than the violet, was renew'd
The plant, erewhile in all its branches bare.
Unearthly was the hymn, which then arose.
I understood it not, nor to the end
Endured the harmony. Had I the skill
To pencil forth how closed the unpitying eyes[1]
Slumbering, when Syrinx warbled (eyes that paid
So dearly for their watching), then, like painter,
That with a model paints, I might design
The manner of my falling into sleep.
But feign who will the slumber cunningly,
I pass it by to when I waked ; and tell,
How suddenly a flash of splendour rent
The curtain of my sleep, and one cries out,
"Arise: what dost thou?" As the chosen three,
On Tabor's mount admitted to behold
The blossoming of that fair tree,[2] whose fruit
Is coveted of angels, and doth make
Perpetual feast in heaven ; to themselves
Returning, at the word whence deeper sleeps[3]
Were broken, they their tribe diminish'd saw ;
Both Moses and Elias gone, and changed
The stole their master wore ; thus to myself
Returning, over me beheld I stand
The piteous one,[4] who, cross the stream, had brought
My steps. "And where," all doubting, I exclaim'd,
"Is Beátrice?"—"See her," she replied,
"Beneath the fresh leaf, seated on its root.
Behold the associate choir, that circles her.
The others, with a melody more sweet
And more profound, journeying to higher realms,

---

[1] *The unpitying eyes.*—See Ovid, "Metamorphoses," lib. i. 689.
[2] *Blossoming of that fair tree.*—Our Saviour's transfiguration. "As the apple-tree among the trees of the wood, so is my beloved among the sons."—Solomon's Song ii. 3.
[3] *Whence deeper sleeps.*—The sleep of death, in the instance of the ruler of the Synagogue's daughter and of Lazarus.
[4] *Returning, over me beheld I stand the piteous one.*—Matilda.

Upon the Gryphon tend." If there her words
Were closed, I know not; but mine eyes had now
Ta'en view of her, by whom all other thoughts
Were barr'd admittance. On the very ground
Alone she sat, as she had there been left
A guard upon the wain, which I beheld
Bound to the twyform beast. The seven nymphs
Did make themselves a cloister round about her;
And, in their hands, upheld those lights[1] secure
From blast septentrion and the gusty south.

"A little while thou shalt be forester here;
And citizen shalt be, for ever with me,
Of that true Rome,[2] wherein Christ dwells a Roman.
To profit the misguided world, keep now
Thine eyes upon the car; and what thou seest,
Take heed thou write, returning to that place."[3]

Thus Beatrice: at whose feet inclined
Devout, at her behest, my thought and eyes,
I, as she bade, directed. Never fire,
With so swift motion, forth a stormy cloud
Leap'd downward from the welkin's furthest bound,
As I beheld the bird of Jove[4] descend
Down through the tree; and, as he rush'd, the rind
Disparting crush beneath him; buds much more,
And leaflets. On the car, with all his might
He struck; whence, staggering, like a ship it reel'd,
At random driven, to starboard now, o'ercome,
And now to larboard, by the vaulting waves.

Next, springing up into the chariot's womb,
A fox[5] I saw, with hunger seeming pined
Of all good food. But, for his ugly sins
The saintly maid rebuking him, away
Scampering he turn'd, fast as his hide-bound corpse
Would bear him. Next, from whence before he came,
I saw the eagle dart into the hull
O' the car, and leave it with his feathers lined:[6]

---

[1] *And, in their hands, upheld those lights.*—The tapers of gold.
[2] *And citizen shalt be, for ever with me, of that true Rome.*—Of heaven.
[3] *To that place.*—To the earth.
[4] *The bird of Jove.*—This, which is imitated from Ezek. xvii. 3, 4, is typical of the persecutions which the church sustained from the Roman emperors.
[5] *A fox.*—By the fox probably is represented the treachery of the heretics.
[6] *With his feathers lined.*—In allusion to the donations made by Constantine to the church.

At her side,
As 'twere that none might bear her off, I saw
A giant stand; and ever and anon
They mingled kisses.
          Canto XXXII., lines 148—151.

And then a voice, like that which issues forth
From heart with sorrow rived, did issue forth
From heaven, and, "O poor bark of mine!" it cried,
"How badly art thou freighted." Then it seem'd
That the earth open'd, between either wheel;
And I beheld a dragon[1] issue thence,
That through the chariot fix'd his forked train;
And like a wasp, that draggeth back the sting,
So drawing forth his baleful train, he dragg'd
Part of the bottom forth; and went his way,
Exulting. What remain'd, as lively turf
With green herb, so did clothe itself with plumes,[2]
Which haply had, with purpose chaste and kind,
Been offer'd; and therewith were clothed the wheels,
Both one and other, and the beam, so quickly,
A sigh were not breathed sooner. Thus transform'd,
The holy structure, through its several parts,
Did put forth heads;[3] three on the beam, and one
On every side: the first like oxen horn'd;
But with a single horn upon their front,
The four. Like monster, sight hath never seen.
O'er it[4] methought there sat, secure as rock
On mountain's lofty top, a shameless whore,
Whose ken roved loosely round her. At her side,
As 'twere that none might bear her off, I saw
A giant stand; and ever and anon
They mingled kisses. But, her lustful eyes
Chancing on me to wander, that fell minion
Scourged her from head to foot all o'er; then full
Of jealousy, and fierce with rage, unloosed
The monster, and dragg'd on,[5] so far across
The forest, that from me its shades alone
Shielded the harlot and the new-form'd brute.

---

[1] *A dragon.*—Probably Mahomet; for what Lombardi offers to the contrary is far from satisfactory.

[2] *With plumes.*—The increase of wealth and temporal dominion, which followed the supposed gift of Constantine.

[3] *Heads.*—By the seven heads, it is supposed with sufficient probability, are meant the seven capital sins: by the three with two horns, pride, anger, and avarice, injurious both to man himself and to his neighbour: by the four with one horn, gluttony, gloominess, concupiscence, and envy, hurtful, at least in their primary effects, chiefly to him who is guilty of them. Vellutello refers to Rev. xvii. Landino, who is followed by Lombardi, understands the seven heads to signify the seven sacraments, and the ten horns the ten commandments. Compare "Hell," c. xix. 112.

[4] *O'er it.*—The harlot is thought to represent the state of the church under Boniface VIII., and the giant to figure Philip IV. of France.

[5] *Dragg'd on.*—The removal of the Pope's residence from Rome to Avignon is pointed at.

CANTO XXXIII.

ARGUMENT.

After a hymn sung, Beatrice leaves the tree, and takes with her the seven virgins, Matilda, Statius, and Dante. She then darkly predicts to our Poets some future events. Lastly, the whole band arrive at the fountain, from whence the two streams, Lethe and Eunoe, separating, flow different ways; and Matilda, at the desire of Beatrice, causes our Poet to drink of the latter stream.

"THE heathen,[1] Lord! are come:" responsive thus,
The trinal now, and now the virgin band
Quaternion, their sweet psalmody began,
Weeping; and Beatrice listen'd, sad
And sighing, to the song, in such a mood,
That Mary, as she stood beside the cross,
Was scarce more changed. But when they gave her place
To speak, then, risen upright on her feet,
She, with a colour glowing bright as fire,
Did answer: "Yet a little while,[2] and ye
Shall see me not; and, my beloved sisters!
Again a little while, and ye shall see me."
Before her then she marshal'd all the seven;
And, beckoning only, motion'd me, the dame,
And that remaining sage,[3] to follow her.
So on she pass'd; and had not set, I ween,
Her tenth step to the ground, when, with mine eyes,
Her eyes encounter'd; and, with visage mild,
"So mend thy pace," she cried, "that if my words
Address thee, thou mayst still be aptly placed
To hear them." Soon as duly to her side
I now had hasten'd: "Brother!" she began,
"Why makest thou no attempt at questioning,
As thus we walk together?" Like to those
Who, speaking with too reverent an awe
Before their betters, draw not forth the voice

---

[1] *The heathen.*—"O God, the heathen are come into thine inheritance."—Ps. lxxix. 1.
[2] *Yet a little while.*—"A little while, and ye shall not see me; and again a little while, and ye shall see me."—John xvi. 16.
[3] *That remaining sage.*—Statius.

Alive unto their lips, befell me then
That I in sounds imperfect thus began:
"Lady! what I have need of, that thou know'st;
And what will suit my need." She answering thus:
"Of fearfulness and shame, I will that thou
Henceforth do rid thee; that thou speak no more,
As one who dreams.[1] Thus far be taught of me:
The vessel which thou saw'st the serpent break,
Was, and is not:[2] let him, who hath the blame,
Hope not to scare God's vengeance with a sop.[3]
Without an heir for ever shall not be
That eagle,[4] he, who left the chariot plumed,
Which monster made it first and next a prey.
Plainly I view, and therefore speak, the stars
E'en now approaching, whose conjunction, free
From all impediment and bar, brings on
A season, in the which, one sent from God
(Five hundred, five, and ten, do mark him out),
That foul one, and the accomplice of her guilt,
The giant, both, shall slay. And if perchance
My saying, dark as Themis or as Sphinx,
Fail to persuade thee (since like them it foils
The intellect with blindness), yet erelong
Events shall be the Naïads,[5] that will solve
This knotty riddle; and no damage light[6]

---

[1] *As one who dreams.*—Imitated by Petrarch, L. i., s. 41:

"Se parole fai,
Sono imperfette e quasi d'uom che sogna."

[2] *Was, and is not.*—"The beast that was and is not."—Rev. xvii. 11.

[3] *Hope not to scare God's vengeance with a sop.*—"Let not him who hath occasioned the destruction of the church, that vessel which the serpent brake, hope to appease the anger of the Deity by any outward acts of religious, or rather superstitious ceremony; such as was that, in our poet's time, performed by a murderer at Florence, who imagined himself secure from vengeance, if he ate a sop of bread in wine upon the grave of the person murdered, within the space of nine days."

[4] *That eagle.*—He prognosticates that the Emperor of Germany will not always continue to submit to the usurpations of the Pope, and foretells the coming of Henry VII., Duke of Luxemburgh, signified by the numerical figures DVX; or, as Lombardi supposes, of Can Grande della Scala, appointed the leader of the Ghibelline forces. It is unnecessary to point out the imitation of the Apocalypse in the manner of this prophecy. Troya assigns reasons for applying the prediction to Uguccione della Faggiola rather than to Henry or Can Grande. "Veltro Allegorico di Dante," ediz. 1826, p. 143. But see my note "Hell," i. 102.

[5] *The Naïads.*—Dante, it is observed, has been led into a mistake by a corruption in the text of Ovid's "Metamorphoses," l. vii. 757, where he found—

"Carmina Naïades non intellecta priorum
Solvunt,"

instead of—

"Carmina Laïades non intellecta priorum
Solverat,"

as it has been since corrected by Heinsius. Lombardi, after Rosa Morando, questions the propriety of this emendation, and refers to Pausanias, where "the Nymphs" are spoken of as expounders of oracles, for a vindication of the poet's accuracy. Should the reader blame me for not departing from the error of the original (if error it be), he may substitute:

"Events shall be the Œdipus will solve," &c.

[6] *No damage light.*—

"Protinus Aoniis immissa est bellua Thebis,
Cessit et exitio multis; pecorique sibique
Ruricolæ pavere feram."

Ovid, Metamorphoses.

On flock or field. Take heed; and as these words
By me are utter'd, teach them even so
To those who live that life, which is a race
To death: and when thou writest them, keep in mind
Not to conceal how thou hast seen the plant,
That twice[1] hath now been spoil'd. This whoso robs,
This whoso plucks, with blasphemy of deed
Sins against God, who for his use alone
Creating hallow'd it. For taste of this,
In pain and in desire, five thousand years[2]
And upward, the first soul did yearn for him
Who punish'd in himself the fatal gust.

"Thy reason slumbers, if it deem this height,
And summit thus inverted,[3] of the plant,
Without due cause: and were not vainer thoughts,
As Elsa's numbing waters,[4] to thy soul,
And their fond pleasures had not dyed it dark
As Pyramus the mulberry; thou hadst seen,[5]
In such momentous circumstance alone,
God's equal justice morally implied
In the forbidden tree. But since I mark thee,
In understanding, harden'd into stone,
And, to that hardness, spotted too and stain'd,
So that thine eye is dazzled at my word;
I will, that, if not written, yet at least
Painted thou take it in thee, for the cause,
That one brings home his staff inwreathed with palm."[6]

---

[1] *Twice.*—First by the eagle and next by the giant. See the last canto, v. 110 and v. 154.

[2] *Five thousand years.*—That such was the opinion of the church, Lombardi shows by a reference to Baronius, "Martyr. Rom.," Dec. 25: "Anno a creatione mundi, quando a principio creavit Deus cœlum et terram, quinquies millesimo centesimo nonagesimo—Jesus Christus—conceptus."—Edit. Col. Agripp., 4to., 1610, p. 858.

[3] *Inverted.*—The branches, unlike those of other trees, spreading more widely the higher they rose. See the last canto, v. 39.

[4] *Elsa's numbing waters.*—The Elsa, a little stream which flows into the Arno about twenty miles below Florence, is said to possess a petrifying quality. Fazio degli Uberti, at the conclusion of cap. viii., l. 3, of the "Dittamondo," mentions a successful experiment he had himself made of the property here attributed to it.

[5] *Thou hadst seen.*—This is obscure. But it would seem as if he meant to inculcate his favourite doctrine of the inviolability of the empire, and of the care taken by Providence to protect it.

[6] *That one brings home his staff inwreathed with palm.*—"For the same cause that the *palmer*, returning from Palestine, brings home his staff, or bourdon, bound with palm," that is, to show where he has been.

"Che si reca 'l bordon di palma cinto."

"It is to be understood," says our poet in the "Vita Nuova," "that people who go on the service of the Most High, are probably named in three ways. They are named *palmers*, inasmuch as they go beyond sea, from whence they often bring back the palm. Inasmuch as they go to the house of Galicia, they are called pilgrims; because the sepulchre of St. James was further from his country than that of any other Apostle. They are called Romei" (for which I know of no other word we have in English except *Roamers*), "inasmuch as they go to Rome."—Page 275. "In regard to the word *bourdon*, why it has been applied to a pilgrim's staff it is not easy to guess. I believe, however, that this name has been given to such sort of staves, because pilgrims usually travel and perform their pilgrimages on foot, their staves serving them

I thus: "As wax by seal, that changeth not
Its impress, now is stamp'd my brain by thee.
But wherefore soars thy wish'd-for speech so high
Beyond my sight, that loses it the more,
The more it strains to reach it?"—"To the end
That thou mayst know," she answer'd straight, "the school,
That thou hast follow'd; and how far behind,
When following my discourse, its learning halts:
And mayst·behold your art,[1] from the divine
As distant, as the disagreement is
'Twixt earth and heaven's most high and rapturous orb."

"I not remember," I replied, "that e'er
I was estranged from thee; nor for such fault
Doth conscience chide me." Smiling she return'd:
"If thou canst not remember, call to mind
How lately thou hast drunk of Lethe's wave;
And, sure as smoke doth indicate a flame,
In that forgetfulness itself conclude
Blame from thy alienated will incurr'd.
From henceforth, verily, my words shall be
As naked, as will suit them to appear
In thy unpractised view." More sparkling now,
And with retarded course, the sun possess'd
The circle of mid-day, that varies still
As the aspect varies of each several clime;
When, as one, sent in vaward of a troop
For escort, pauses, if perchance he spy
Vestige of somewhat strange and rare; so paused[2]
The sevenfold band, arriving at the verge
Of a dun umbrage hoar, such as is seen,
Beneath green leaves and gloomy branches, oft
To overbrow a bleak and alpine cliff.
And, where they stood, before them, as it seem'd,

---

instead of horses or mules, then called *bourdons* and *burdones*, by writers in the middle ages."—Mr. Johnes's Translation of *Joinville's Memoirs*, Dissertation xv., by M. du Cange, p. 152, 4to edit. The word is thrice used by Chaucer in the "Romaunt of the Rose."

[1] *Mayst behold your art.*—The second persons, singular and plural, are here used intentionally by our author, the one referring to himself alone, the second to mankind in general. Compare "Hell," xi. 107.

But I will follow the example of Brunck, who in a note on the passage in the "Philoctetes" of Sophocles, v. 369, where a similar distinction requires to be made, says that it would be ridiculous to multiply instances in a matter so well known.

[2] *So paused.*—Lombardi imagines that the seven nymphs, who represent the four cardinal and the three evangelical virtues, are made to stop at the verge of the shade, because retirement is the friend of every virtuous quality and spiritual gift.

I, Tigris and Euphrates[1] both, beheld
Forth from one fountain issue; and, like friends,
Linger at parting. "O enlightening beam!
O glory of our kind! beseech thee say
What water this, which, from one source derived,
Itself removes to distance from itself?"

To such entreaty answer thus was made:
"Entreat Matilda, that she teach thee this."
And here, as one who clears himself of blame
Imputed, the fair dame return'd: "Of me
He this and more hath learnt; and I am safe
That Lethe's water hath not hid it from him."

And Beatrice: "Some more pressing care,
That oft the memory 'reaves, perchance hath made
His mind's eye dark. But lo, where Eunoe flows!
Lead thither; and, as thou art wont, revive
His fainting virtue." As a courteous spirit,
That proffers no excuses, but as soon
As he hath token of another's will,
Makes it his own; when she had ta'en me, thus
The lovely maiden moved her on, and call'd
To Statius, with an air most lady-like:
"Come thou with him." Were further space allow'd,
Then, reader! might I sing, though but in part,
That beverage, with whose sweetness I had ne'er
Been sated. But, since all the leaves are full,
Appointed for this second strain, mine art
With warning bridle checks me. I return'd
From the most holy wave, regenerate,
E'en as new plants renew'd[2] with foliage new
Pure and made apt for mounting to the stars.

---

[1] *I, Tigris and Euphrates.*—
"Quaque caput rapido tollit cum Tigride magnus
Euphrates, quos non diversis fontibus edit
Persis." *Lucan, Pharsalia*, lib. iii. 258.
"Tigris et Euphrates uno se fonte resolvunt."
  Boëtius, De Consol. Philosoph., lib. v., Metr. 1.
  "Là oltre ond' esce
D'un medesimo fonte Eufrate e Tigre."
  Petrarca, Son. Mie Venture, &c.

[2] *Renew'd.*— "Come piante novelle
Rinnovellate da novella fronda."
  Spenser, Faery Queene, b. i., c. xi., st. 34.
"So new this new-borne knight to battle new did rise."
"Rinnovellate" is another of those words which Chaucer in vain endeavoured to introduce into our language from the Italian, unless it be supposed that he rather borrowed it from the French. "Certes ones a yere at the lest way it is lawful to ben houseled, for sothely ones a yere all things in the earth renovelen."
—*The Persone's Tale.*

Were further space allow'd,
Then, reader! might I sing, though but in part,
That beverage, with whose sweetness I had ne'er
Been sated.

Canto XXXIII., lines 134—137.

PARADISE.

THE VISION OF DANTE.

Paradise.

CANTO I.

ARGUMENT.

The Poet ascends with Beatrice towards the first heaven, and is by her resolved of certain doubts which arise in his mind.

HIS glory, by whose might all things are moved,
    Pierces the universe,[1] and in one part
Sheds more resplendence, elsewhere less. In heaven,
That largeliest of his light partakes, was I,
Witness of things, which, to relate again,
Surpasseth power of him who comes from thence ;
For that, so near approaching its desire,
Our intellect is to such depth absorb'd,
That memory cannot follow. Nathless all,
That in my thoughts I of that sacred realm
Could store, shall now[2] be matter of my song.

    Benign Apollo ![3] this last labour aid ;
And make me such a vessel of thy worth,
As thy own laurel claims, of me beloved.
Thus far[4] hath one of steep Parnassus' brows
Sufficed me ; henceforth, there is need of both
For my remaining enterprise. Do thou[5]
Enter into my bosom, and there breathe
So, as when Marsyas[6] by thy hand was dragg'd

---

[1] *Pierces the universe.*—"Per l'universo penetra," &c.

    "His magnetic beam, that gently warms
The universe, and to each inward part
With gentle penetration, though unseen,
Shoots invisible virtue ev'n to the deep."
        Milton, Paradise Lost, b. iii. 586.

[2] *Shall now.*—
"Sarà ora materia del mio canto."
"Shall be the copious matter of my song."
        Ibid., b. iii. 413.

[3] *Benign Apollo.*—Chaucer has imitated this invocation very closely, at the beginning of the "Third Booke of Fame :"

    "If, divine vertue, thou
Wilt helpe me to shewe now
That in my head ymarked is,
    *   *   *   *
Thou shalt see me go as blive
Unto the next laurer I see,
And kisse it, for it is thy tree.
Now entre thou my breast anone."

[4] *Thus far.*—He appears to mean nothing more than that this part of his poem will require a greater exertion of his powers than the former.

[5] *Do thou.*—Make me thine instrument ; and, through me, utter such sound as when thou didst contend with Marsyas.

[6] *Marsyas.*—Ovid, "Metamorphoses," lib. vi., fab. 7. Compare Boccaccio, "Il Filocopo," lib. v., p. 25,

Forth from his limbs, unsheathed. O power divine!
If thou to me of thine impart so much,
That of that happy realm the shadow'd form
Traced in my thoughts I may set forth to view;
Thou shalt behold me of thy favour'd tree
Come to the foot, and crown myself with leaves:
For to that honour thou, and my high theme
Will fit me. If but seldom, mighty Sire!
To grace his triumph, gathers thence a wreath
Cæsar, or bard[1] (more shame for human wills
Depraved), joy to the Delphic god must spring
From the Peneian foliage, when one breast
Is with such thirst inspired. From a small spark[2]
Great flame hath risen: after me, perchance,
Others with better voice may pray, and gain,
From the Cyrrhæan city, answer kind.

Through divers passages, the world's bright lamp
Rises to mortals; but through that[3] which joins
Four circles with the threefold cross, in best
Course, and in happiest constellation[4] set
He comes; and, to the worldly wax, best gives
Its temper and impression. Morning there,[5]
Here eve was well nigh by such passage made;
And whiteness had o'erspread that hemisphere,
Blackness the other part; when to the left[6]
I saw Beatrice turn'd, and on the sun
Gazing, as never eagle fix'd his ken.
As from the first a second beam[7] is wont

---

v. ii., ediz. Firenze, 1723: "Egli nel mio petto entri," &c.—"May he enter my bosom, and let my voice sound like his own, when he made that daring mortal deserve to come forth unsheathed from his limbs."

[1] *Cæsar, or bard.*—So Petrarch, "Son.," Par Prima: "Arbor vittoriosa trionfale,
　　Onor d' imperadori e di poeti."
And Frezzi, "Il Quadriregio," lib. iii., cap. 14:
　　"Alloro,
Che imperatori e poeti corona."
And Spenser, "Faery Queene," b. i., c. 1, st. 9:
　　"The laurel, meed of mighty conquerours,
　　And poets sage."

[2] *From a small spark.*—
　Πολλὰν τ' ὄρει πῦρ ἐξ ἑνὸς
　Σπέρματος ἐνθορὸν ἀΐστωσεν ὕλαν.
"Upon the mountain from one spark hath leapt
The fire, that hath a mighty forest burn'd."
　　　　　Pindar, Pyth., iii. 67.

[3] *Through that.*—"Where the four circles, the horizon, the zodiac, the equator, and the equinoctial colure join; the last three intersecting each other so as to form three crosses, as may be seen in the armillary sphere."

[4] *In happiest constellation.*—Aries. Some understand the planet Venus by the "miglior stella."

[5] *Morning there.*—It was morning where he then was, and about eventide on the earth.

[6] *To the left.*—Being in the opposite hemisphere to ours, Beatrice, that she may behold the rising sun, turns herself to the left.

[7] *As from the first a second beam.*—"Like a reflected sunbeam," which he compares to a pilgrim hastening homewards.

　　"Nè simil tanto mai raggio secondo
　　　Dal primo usci."
　　　　　Filicaja, canz. xv., st. 4.
"Sicut vir in peregrinatione constitutus, omni studio,

To issue, and reflected upwards rise,
Even as a pilgrim bent on his return;
So of her act, that through the eyesight pass'd
Into my fancy, mine was form'd: and straight,
Beyond our mortal wont, I fix'd mine eyes
Upon the sun. Much is allow'd us there,
That here exceeds our power; thanks to the place
Made[1] for the dwelling of the human kind.

I suffer'd it not long; and yet so long,
That I beheld it bickering sparks around,
As iron that comes boiling from the fire.[2]
And suddenly upon the day appear'd[3]
A day new-risen; as he, who hath the power,
Had with another sun bedeck'd the sky.

Her eyes fast fix'd on the eternal wheels,[4]
Beatrice stood unmoved; and I with ken
Fix'd upon her, from upward gaze removed,
At her aspect, such inwardly became
As Glaucus,[5] when he tasted of the herb
That made him peer among the ocean gods:
Words may not tell of that transhuman change;
And therefore let the example serve, though weak,
For those whom grace hath better proof in store.

If[6] I were only what thou didst create,
Then newly, Love! by whom the heaven is ruled;
Thou know'st, who by thy light didst bear me up.
Whenas the wheel which thou dost ever guide,

---

omnique conatu domum redire festinat, ac retrorsum non respicit sed ad domum, quam reliquerat, reverti desiderat."—*Alberici Visio,* § 25.

[1] *Made.*—And therefore best adapted, says Venturi, to the good temperament and vigour of the human body and its faculties. The poet speaks of the terrestrial paradise where he then was.

[2] *As iron that comes boiling from the fire.*—"Ardentem, et scintillas emittentem, ac si ferrum cum de fornace trahitur."—*Alberici Visio,* § 5. This simile is repeated, § 16. So Milton, "Paradise Lost," b. iii., 594:

"As glowing iron with fire."

[3] *Upon the day appear'd.*—

"If the heaven had ywonne
All new of God another sunne."
Chaucer, First Booke of Fame.

"E par ch' aggiunga un altro sole al cielo."
Ariosto, Orlando Furioso, c. x., st. 109.

"Ed ecco un lustro lampeggiar d' intorno
Che sole a sole aggiunse e giorno a giorno."
Marino, Adone, c. xl., st. 27.

"Quando a paro col sol ma più lucente
L'angelo gli appari sull' oriente."
Tasso, Gierusalemme Liberata, c. i.

"Seems another morn
Risen on mid-noon."
Milton, Paradise Lost, b. v. 311.

Compare Euripides, " Ion.," 1550. Ἀνθήλιον πρόσωπον.

[4] *Eternal wheels.*—The heavens, eternal, and always circling.

[5] *As Glaucus.*—Ovid, "Metamorphoses," lib. xiii., fab. 9. Plato, in the tenth book of the "Republic," makes a very noble comparison from Glaucus, but applies it differently. Edit. Bipont, vol. vii., p. 317. Berkeley appears not to have been aware of the passage, when he says that "Proclus compares the soul, in her descent, invested with growing prejudices, to Glaucus diving to the bottom of the sea, and there contracting divers coats of sea-weed, coral, and shells, which stick close to him, and conceal his true shape."
—*Siris,* ed. 1744, p. 151.

[6] *If.*—"Thou, O divine Spirit, knowest whether I had not risen above my human nature, and were not merely such as thou hadst then formed me."

Desired Spirit ! with its harmony,[1]
Temper'd of thee and measured, charm'd mine ear
Then seem'd to me so much of heaven[2] to blaze
With the sun's flame, that rain or flood ne'er made
A lake so broad. The newness of the sound,
And that great light, inflamed me with desire,
Keener than e'er was felt, to know their cause.

Whence she, who saw me, clearly as myself,
To calm my troubled mind, before I ask'd,
Open'd her lips, and gracious thus began:
"With false imagination thou thyself
Makest dull; so that thou seest not the thing,
Which thou hadst seen, had that been shaken off.
Thou art not on the earth as thou believest;
For lightning, scaped from its own proper place,
Ne'er ran, as thou hast hither now return'd."

Although divested of my first-raised doubt
By those brief words accompanied with smiles,
Yet in new doubt was I entangled more,
And said: "Already satisfied, I rest
From admiration deep; but now admire
How I above those lighter bodies rise."

Whence, after utterance of a piteous sigh,
She towards me bent her eyes, with such a look,
As on her frenzied child a mother casts;
Then thus began: "Among themselves all things
Have order; and from hence the form,[3] which makes
The universe resemble God. In this
The higher creatures see the printed steps
Of that eternal worth, which is the end
Whither the line is drawn.[4] All natures lean,
In this their order, diversly; some more,
Some less approaching to their primal source.
Thus they to different havens are moved on

---

[1] *Harmony.*—The harmony of the spheres.
"And after that the melodie herd he
That cometh of thilke speris thryis three,
That welles of musike ben and melodie
In this world here, and cause of harmonie."
　　　Chaucer, *The Assemble of Foules.*
"In their motion harmony divine
So smooths her charming tones, that God's own ear
Listens delighted."—*Milton, Paradise Lost,* b. v. 627.

[2] *So much of heaven.*—The sphere of fire, as Lombardi well explains it.

[3] *From hence the form.*—This order it is that gives to the universe the form of unity, and therefore of resemblance to God.

[4] *Of that eternal worth, which is the end whither the line is drawn.*—All things, as they have their beginning from the Supreme Being, so are they referred to Him again.

Through the vast sea of being, and each one
With instinct given, that bears it in its course :
This to the lunar sphere directs the fire ;
This moves the hearts of mortal animals ;
This the brute earth together knits, and binds.
Nor only creatures, void of intellect,
Are aim'd at by this bow ; but even those,
That have intelligence and love, are pierced.
That Providence, who so well orders all,
With her own light makes ever calm the heaven,[1]
In which the substance,[2] that hath greatest speed,
Is turn'd : and thither now, as to our seat
Predestined, we are carried by the force
Of that strong cord, that never looses dart
But at fair aim and glad. Yet it is true,
That as, oft-times, but ill accords the form
To the design of art, through sluggishness[3]
Of unreplying matter ; so this course[4]
Is sometimes quitted by the creature, who
Hath power, directed thus, to bend elsewhere ;
As from a cloud the fire is seen to fall,
From its original impulse warp'd to earth,
By vitious fondness. Thou no more admire
Thy soaring (if I rightly deem), than lapse
Of torrent downwards from a mountain's height.
There would[5] in thee for wonder be more cause,
If, free of hindrance, thou hadst stay'd below,
As living fire unmoved upon the earth."
So said, she turn'd toward the heaven her face.

---

[1] *Heaven.*—The empyrean, which is always motionless.
[2] *The substance.*—The primum mobile.
[3] *Through sluggishness.*—

"Perch' a risponder la materia è sorda."
So Filicaja, canz. vi., st. 9 :
"Perche a risponder la discordia è sorda.'

"The workman hath in his heart a purpose, he carrieth in mind the whole form which his work should have ; there wanteth not in him skill and desire to bring his labour to the best effect ; only the matter, which he hath to work on, is unframable."—*Hooker's Ecclesiastical Polity*, b. v., § 9. Our poet, in his "De Monarchiâ," has expressed the same thought more fully : "Sciendum," &c., lib. ii., p. 115. "We must know, that as art is found in a triple degree, in the mind that is of the artist, in the instrument, and in the matter formed by art, so we may contemplate nature also in a triple degree. For nature is in the mind of the first mover, who is God ; then in heaven, as in an instrument, by means of which the similitude of the eternal goodness is unfolded in variable matter ; and, as the artist being perfect, and the instrument in the best order, if there is any fault in the form of art, it is to be imputed only to the matter ; so, since God reaches to the end of perfection, and His instrument, which is heaven, is not in any wise deficient of due perfection (as appears from what we know by philosophy concerning heaven), it remaineth that whatever fault is in inferior things, is a fault of the matter worked on, and clean beside the intention of God and of heaven."

[4] *Course.*—Some beings, abusing the liberty given them by God, are repugnant to the order established by Him.

[5] *There would.*—Hence, perhaps, Milton :
"In our proper motion we ascend
Up to our native seat : descent and fall
To us were adverse."—*Paradise Lost*, b. ii., v. 77

CANTO II.

ARGUMENT.

Dante and his celestial guide enter the moon. The cause of the spots or shadows which appear in that body is explained to him.

ALL ye, who in small bark[1] have following sail'd,
    Eager to listen, on the adventurous track
Of my proud keel, that singing cuts her way,
Backward return with speed, and your own shores
Revisit; nor put out to open sea,
Where losing me, perchance ye may remain
Bewilder'd in deep maze. The way I pass,
Ne'er yet was run: Minerva breathes the gale;
Apollo guides me; and another Nine,
To my rapt sight, the arctic beams reveal.
Ye other few who have outstretch'd the neck
Timely for food of angels, on which here
They live, yet never know satiety;
Through the deep brine ye fearless may put out
Your vessel; marking well the furrow broad
Before you in the wave, that on both sides
Equal returns. Those, glorious, who pass'd o'er
To Colchos, wonder'd not as ye will do,
When they saw Jason following the plough.
    The increate perpetual thirst,[2] that draws
Toward the realm of God's own form, bore us
Swift almost as the heaven ye behold.
    Beatrice upward gazed, and I on her;
And in such space as on the notch a dart
Is placed, then loosen'd flies, I saw myself
Arrived, where wondrous thing engaged my sight.
Whence she, to whom no care of mine was hid,
Turning to me, with aspect glad as fair,

---

[1] *Bark.*—"Con la barchetta mia cantando in rima."
    Pulci, Morgante Maggiore, c. xxviii.
"Io me n'andrò con la barchetta mia.
Quanto l'acqua comporta un picciol legno."—*Ibid.*

"Say, shall my little bark attendant sail?"
    Pope, Essay on Man, Ep. iv.
[2] *The increate perpetual thirst.*—The desire of celestial beatitude natural to the soul.

Bespake me: "Gratefully direct thy mind
To God, through whom to this first star[1] we come."
Meseem'd as if a cloud had cover'd us,
Translucent, solid, firm, and polish'd bright,
Like adamant, which the sun's beam had smit.
Within itself the ever-during pearl
Received us; as the wave a ray of light
Receives, and rests unbroken. If I then
Was of corporeal frame, and it transcend
Our weaker thought, how one dimension thus
Another could endure, which needs must be
If body enter body; how much more
Must the desire inflame us to behold
That essence, which discovers by what means
God and our nature join'd! There will be seen
That, which we hold through faith; not shown by proof,
But in itself intelligibly plain,
E'en as the truth[2] that man at first believes.

   I answer'd: "Lady! I with thoughts devout,
Such as I best can frame, give thanks to him,
Who hath removed me from the mortal world.
But tell, I pray thee, whence the gloomy spots
Upon this body, which below on earth
Give rise to talk of Cain[3] in fabling quaint?"

   She somewhat smiled, then spake: "If mortals err
In their opinion, when the key of sense
Unlocks not, surely wonder's weapon keen
Ought not to pierce thee: since thou find'st, the wings
Of reason to pursue the senses' flight
Are short. But what thy own thought is, declare."

   Then I: "What various here above appears,
Is caused, I deem, by bodies dense or rare."[4]

---

[1] *This first star.*—The moon.

[2] *E'en as the truth.*—"Like a truth, that does not need demonstration, but is self-evident." Thus Plato, at the conclusion of the sixth book of the "Republic," lays down four principles of information in the human mind: "1st, intuition of self-evident truth, νόησις; 2nd, demonstration by reasoning, διάνοια; 3rd, belief on testimony, πίστις; 4th, probability, or conjecture, εἰκασία." I cannot resist adding a passage to the like effect from Hooker's "Ecclesiastical Polity," b. ii., § 7: "The truth is, that the mind of man desireth evermore to know the truth, according to the most infallible certainty which the nature of things can yield. The greatest assurance generally with all men, is that which we have by plain aspect and intuitive beholding. Where we cannot attain unto this, there what appeareth to be true, by strong and invincible demonstration, such as wherein it is not by any way possible to be deceived, thereunto the mind doth necessarily assent, neither is it in the choice thereof to do otherwise. And in case these both do fail, then which way greatest probability leadeth, thither the mind doth evermore incline."

[3] *Cain.*—Compare "Hell," canto xx. 123, and note.

[4] *By bodies dense or rare.*—Lombardi observes, that the opinion respecting the spots in the moon, which

She then resumed: "Thou certainly wilt see
In falsehood thy belief o'erwhelm'd, if well
Thou listen to the arguments which I
Shall bring to face it. The eighth sphere displays
Numberless lights,[1] the which, in kind and size,
May be remark'd of different aspects:
If rare or dense of that were cause alone,
One single virtue then would be in all;
Alike distributed, or more, or less.
Different virtues needs must be the fruits
Of formal principles; and these, save one,[2]
Will by thy reasoning be destroy'd. Beside,
If rarity were of that dusk the cause,
Which thou inquirest, either in some part
That planet must throughout be void, nor fed
With its own matter; or, as bodies share
Their fat and leanness, in like manner this
Must in its volume change the leaves.[3] The first,
If it were true, had through the sun's eclipse
Been manifested, by transparency
Of light, as through aught rare beside effused.
But this is not. Therefore remains to see
The other cause: and, if the other fall,
Erroneous so must prove what seem'd to thee.
If not from side to side this rarity
Pass through, there needs must be a limit, whence
Its contrary no further lets it pass.
And hence the beam, that from without proceeds,
Must be pour'd back; as colour comes, through glass
Reflected, which behind it lead conceals.
Now wilt thou say, that there of murkier hue,
Than, in the other part, the ray is shown,

Dante represents himself as here yielding to the arguments of Beatrice, is professed by our author in the "Convito," so that we may conclude that work to have been composed before this portion of the "Divina Commedia." "The shadow in the moon is nothing else but the rarity of its body, which hinders the rays of the sun from terminating and being reflected, as in other parts of it."—Page 70.

[1] *Numberless lights.*—The fixed stars, which differ both in bulk and splendour.

[2] *Save one.*—"Except that principle of rarity and denseness which thou hast assigned." By "formal principles," *principii formali*, are meant "constituent or essential causes." Milton, in imitation of this passage, introduces the angel arguing with Adam respecting the causes of the spots on the moon. But, as a late French translator of the "Paradise," M. Artaud, well remarks, his reasoning is physical: that of Dante partly metaphysical and partly theologic.

"Whence in her visage round those spots, unpurged
Vapours not yet into her substance turn'd."
   Milton, *Paradise Lost*, b. v. 420.

[3] *Must in its volume change the leaves.*—Would, like leaves of parchment, be darker in some part than others.

By being thence refracted further back.
From this perplexity will free thee soon
Experience, if thereof thou trial make,
The fountain whence your arts derive their streams.
Three mirrors shalt thou take, and two remove
From thee alike; and more remote the third,
Betwixt the former pair, shall meet thine eyes:
Then turn'd toward them, cause behind thy back
A light to stand, that on the three shall shine,
And thus reflected come to thee from all.
Though that, beheld most distant, do not stretch
A space so ample, yet in brightness thou
Wilt own it equaling the rest. But now
As under snow the ground, if the warm ray
Smites it, remains dismantled of the hue
And cold, that cover'd it before; so thee,
Dismantled in thy mind, I will inform
With light so lively, that the tremulous beam
Shall quiver where it falls. Within the heaven,
Where peace divine inhabits,[1] circles round
A body, in whose virtue lies the being
Of all that it contains. The following heaven,
That hath so many lights, this being divides,
Through different essences, from it distinct,
And yet contain'd within it. The other orbs
Their separate distinctions variously
Dispose, for their own seed and produce apt.
Thus do these organs of the world proceed,
As thou beholdest now, from step to step;
Their influences from above deriving,
And thence transmitting downwards. Mark me well;
How through this passage to the truth I ford,
The truth thou lovest; that thou henceforth, alone,
Mayst know to keep the shallows, safe, untold.

"The virtue and motion of the sacred orbs,

---

[1] *Within the heaven, where peace divine inhabits.*—According to our poet's system, there are ten heavens. The heaven, "where peace divine inhabits," is the empyrean; the body within it, that "circles round," is the primum mobile; "the following heaven," that of the fixed stars; and "the other orbs," the seven lower heavens, are Saturn, Jupiter, Mars, the Sun, Venus, Mercury, and the Moon. Thus Milton, "Paradise Lost," b. iii. 481:
"They pass the planets seven, and pass the fix'd,
And that crystalline sphere whose balance weighs
The trepidation talk'd, and that first moved."

As mallet by the workman's hand, must needs
By blessed movers[1] be inspired. This heaven,[2]
Made beauteous by so many luminaries,
From the deep spirit,[3] that moves its circling sphere,
Its image takes and impress as a seal:
And as the soul, that dwells within your dust,
Through members different, yet together form'd,
In different powers resolves itself; e'en so
The intellectual efficacy unfolds
Its goodness multiplied throughout the stars;
On its own unity revolving still.
Different virtue[4] compact different
Makes with the precious body it enlivens,
With which it knits, as life in you is knit.
From its original nature full of joy,
The virtue mingled[5] through the body shines,
As joy through pupil of the living eye.
From hence proceeds that which from light to light
Seems different, and not from dense or rare.
This is the formal cause, that generates,
Proportion'd to its power, the dusk or clear."

---

[1] *By blessed movers.*—By angels.
[2] *This heaven.*—The heaven of fixed stars.
[3] *Many luminaries, from the deep spirit.*—The moving angel.
[4] *Different virtue.*—"There is one glory of the sun, and another glory of the moon, and another glory of the stars: for one star differeth from another star in glory."—1 Cor. xv. 41. The words are nearly Plato's, whom St. Paul seems to have had in view throughout this part of his argument. Μία μὲν [δυνάμις] ἡλίου· μία δὲ, σελήνης· μία δὲ, τῶν πάντων ἄστρων, κ. τ. λ.—"Epinomis," ed. Bip., v. ix., p. 262.
[5] *The virtue mingled.*—Virgil, "Æneid," lib. vi. 724: "Principio cælum," &c.

Such saw I many a face,
All stretch'd to speak.
Canto III., lines 14, 15.

CANTO III.

ARGUMENT.

In the moon Dante meets with Piccarda, the sister of Forese, who tells him that this planet is allotted to those who, after having made profession of chastity and a religious life, had been compelled to violate their vows; and she then points out to him the spirit of the Empress Costanza.

  THAT sun,[1] which erst with love my bosom warm'd,
  Had of fair truth unveil'd the sweet aspect,
By proof of right, and of the false reproof;
And I, to own myself convinced and free
Of doubt, as much as needed, raised my head
Erect for speech. But soon a sight appear'd,
Which, so intent to mark it, held me fix'd,
That of confession I no longer thought.

  As through translucent and smooth glass, or wave
Clear and unmoved, and flowing not so deep
As that its bed is dark, the shape returns
So faint of our impictured lineaments,
That, on white forehead set, a pearl as strong
Comes to the eye; such saw I many a face,
All stretch'd to speak; from whence I straight conceived,
Delusion[2] opposite to that, which raised,
Between the man and fountain, amorous flame.

  Sudden, as I perceived them, deeming these
Reflected semblances, to see of whom
They were, I turn'd mine eyes, and nothing saw;
Then turn'd them back, directed on the light
Of my sweet guide, who, smiling, shot forth beams
From her celestial eyes. "Wonder not thou,"
She cried, "at this my smiling, when I see
Thy childish judgment; since not yet on truth
It rests the foot, but, as it still is wont,
Makes thee fall back in unsound vacancy.
True substances are these, which thou behold'st,
Hither through failure of their vow exiled.
But speak thou with them; listen, and believe,

---

[1] *That sun.*—Beatrice.
[2] *Delusion.*—"An error the contrary to that of Narcissus; because he mistook a shadow for a substance; I, a substance for a shadow."

That the true light, which fills them with desire,
Permits not from its beams their feet to stray."
    Straight to the shadow, which for converse seem'd
Most earnest, I address'd me: and began
As one by over-eagerness perplex'd:
"O spirit, born for joy! who in the rays
Of life eternal, of that sweetness know'st
The flavour, which, not tasted, passes far
All apprehension; me it well would please,
If thou wouldst tell me of thy name, and this
Your station here." Whence she with kindness prompt,
And eyes glistering with smiles: " Our charity,
To any wish by justice introduced,
Bars not the door; no more than she above,
Who would have all her court be like herself.
I was a virgin sister in the earth:
And if thy mind observe me well, this form,
With such addition graced of loveliness
Will not conceal me long; but thou wilt know
Piccarda,[1] in the tardiest sphere thus placed,
Here 'mid these other blessed also blest.
Our hearts, whose high affections burn alone
With pleasure from the Holy Spirit conceived,
Admitted to his order, dwell in joy.
And this condition, which appears so low,
Is for this cause assign'd us, that our vows
Were, in some part, neglected and made void."
    Whence I to her replied: "Something divine
Beams in your countenances wonderous fair;
From former knowledge quite transmuting you.
Therefore to recollect was I so slow.
But what thou say'st hath to my memory
Given now such aid, that to retrace your forms
Is easier. Yet inform me, ye, who here
Are happy; long ye for a higher place,
More to behold, and more in love to dwell?"
    She with those other spirits gently smiled;
Then answer'd with such gladness, that she seem'd

---

[1] *Piccarda.*—The sister of Corso Donati, and of Forese, whom we have seen in the "Purgatory," canto xxiii. Petrarch has been supposed to allude to this lady in his "Triumph of Chastity," v. 160, &c.

With love's first flame to glow: "Brother! our will
Is, in composure, settled by the power
Of charity, who makes us will alone
What we possess, and nought beyond desire:
If we should wish to be exalted more,
Then must our wishes jar with the high will
Of him who sets us here; which in these orbs
Thou wilt confess not possible, if here
To be in charity must needs befall,
And if her nature well thou contemplate.
Rather it is inherent in this state
Of blessedness, to keep ourselves within
The divine will, by which our wills with his
Are one. So that, as we, from step to step,
Are placed throughout this kingdom, pleases all,
Even as our King, who in us plants his will;
And in his will is our tranquillity:
It is the mighty ocean, whither tends
Whatever it creates and nature makes."

Then saw I clearly how each spot in heaven
Is Paradise, though with like gracious dew
The supreme virtue shower not over all.

But as it chances, if one sort of food
Hath satiated, and of another still
The appetite remains, that this is ask'd,
And thanks for that return'd; even so did I,
In word and motion, bent from her to learn
What web it was,[1] through which she had not drawn
The shuttle to its point. She thus began:
"Exalted worth and perfectness of life
The Lady[2] higher up inshrine in heaven,
By whose pure laws upon your nether earth
The robe and veil they wear; to that intent,
That e'en till death they may keep watch, or sleep,
With their great bridegroom, who accepts each vow,
Which to his gracious pleasure love conforms.
I from the world, to follow her, when young

---

[1] *In word and motion, bent from her to learn what web it was.*—"What vow of religious life it was that she had been hindered from completing, had been compelled to break."

[2] *The Lady.*—St. Clare, the foundress of the order called after her. She was born of opulent and noble parents at Assisi, in 1193, and died in 1253. See "Biogr. Univ.," t. i., p. 598, 8vo, Paris, 1813.

Escaped; and, in her vesture mantling me,
Made promise of the way her sect enjoins.
Thereafter men, for ill than good more apt,
Forth snatch'd me from the pleasant cloister's pale.
God knows[1] how, after that, my life was framed.
This other splendid shape, which thou behold'st
At my right side, burning with all the light
Of this our orb, what of myself I tell
May to herself apply. From her, like me
A sister, with like violence were torn
The saintly folds, that shaded her fair brows.
E'en when she to the world again was brought
In spite of her own will and better wont,
Yet not for that the bosom's inward veil
Did she renounce. This is the luminary
Of mighty Constance,[2] who from that loud blast,
Which blew the second[3] over Suabia's realm,
That power produced, which was the third and last."

    She ceased from further talk, and then began
"Ave Maria" singing; and with that song
Vanish'd, as heavy substance through deep wave.

    Mine eye, that, far as it was capable,
Pursued her, when in dimness she was lost,
Turn'd to the mark where greater want impell'd
And bent on Beatrice all its gaze.
But she, as lightning, beam'd upon my looks;
So that the sight sustain'd it not at first.
Whence I to question her became less prompt.

---

[1] *God knows.*—Rodolfo da Tossignano, "Hist. Seraph. Relig.," P. i., p. 138, as cited by Lombardi, relates the following legend of Piccarda:—"Her brother Corso, inflamed with rage against his virgin sister, having joined with him Farinata, an infamous assassin, and twelve other abandoned ruffians, entered the monastery by a ladder, and carried away his sister forcibly to his own house; and then, tearing off her religious habit, compelled her to go in a secular garment to her nuptials. Before the spouse of Christ came together with her new husband, she knelt down before a crucifix and recommended her virginity to Christ. Soon after her whole body was smitten with leprosy, so as to strike grief and horror into the beholders; and thus in a few days, through the divine disposal, she passed with a palm of virginity to the Lord." Perhaps, adds the worthy Franciscan, our poet, not being able to certify himself entirely of this occurrence, has chosen to pass it over discreetly, by making Piccarda say—
"God knows how, after that, my life was framed."

[2] *Constance.*—Daughter of Ruggieri, King of Sicily, who being taken by force out of a monastery where she had professed, was married to the Emperor Henry VI., and by him was mother to Frederick II. She was fifty years old or more at the time, and "because it was not credited that she could have a child at that age, she was delivered in a pavilion, and it was given out that any lady who pleased was at liberty to see her. Many came, and saw her; and the suspicion ceased."—*Ricordano Malaspina, in Muratori, Rerum Italicarum Scriptores,* t. viii., p. 939; and G. Villani, in the same words, "Hist.," lib. v., c. xvi. The French translator above mentioned speaks of her having poisoned her husband. The death of Henry VI. is recorded in the "Chronicon Siciliæ," by an anonymous writer (Muratori, t. x.), but not a word of his having been poisoned by Constance; and Ricordano Malaspina even mentions her decease as happening before that of her husband, Henry V., for so this author, with some others, terms him.

[3] *The second.*—Henry VI., son of Frederick I., was the second emperor of the house of Suabia; and his son, Frederick II., "the third and last."

CANTO IV.

ARGUMENT.

While they still continue in the moon, Beatrice removes certain doubts which Dante had conceived respecting the place assigned to the blessed, and respecting the will absolute or conditional. He inquires whether it is possible to make satisfaction for a vow broken.

BETWEEN two kinds of food,[1] both equally
Remote and tempting, first a man might die
Of hunger, ere he one could freely chuse.
E'en so would stand a lamb between the maw
Of two fierce wolves, in dread of both alike:
E'en so between two deer[2] a dog would stand.
Wherefore, if I was silent, fault nor praise
I to myself impute; by equal doubts
Held in suspense; since of necessity
It happen'd. Silent was I, yet desire
Was painted in my looks; and thus I spake
My wish more earnestly than language could.
    As Daniel, when the haughty king he freed[3]
From ire, that spurr'd him on to deeds unjust
And violent; so did Beatrice then.
    "Well I discern," she thus her words address'd,
"How thou art drawn by each of these desires;[4]
So that thy anxious thought is in itself
Bound up and stifled, nor breathes freely forth.
Thou arguest: if the good intent remain,
What reason that another's violence
Should stint the measure of my fair desert?
    "Cause too thou find'st for doubt, in that it seems

---

[1] *Between two kinds of food.*—" Si aliqua dico sunt penitus æqualia, non magis movetur homo ad unum quam ad aliud; sicut famelicus, si habet cibum æqualiter appetibilem in diversis partibus, et secundum a:qualem distantiam, non magis movetur ad unum quam ad alterum."—*Thomas Aquinas, Summ. Theolog.*

[2] *Between two deer.*—
" Tigris ut, auditis, diversâ valle duorum,
    Exstimulata fame, mugitibus armentorum,
Nescit utrò potius ruat, et ruere ardet utroque."
        Ovid, Metamorphoses, lib. v. 166.

[3] *As Daniel, when the haughty king he freed.*—See Daniel ii. Beatrice did for Dante what Daniel did for Nebuchadnezzar, when he freed the king from the uncertainty respecting his dream, which had enraged him against the Chaldeans. Lombardi conjectures that " Fe si Beatrice " should be read, instead of " Fessi Beatrice;" and his conjecture has since been confirmed by the Monte Casino MS.

[4] *How thou art drawn by each of these desires.*—His desire to have each of the doubts which Beatrice mentions resolved.

That spirits to the stars, as Plato[1] deem'd,
Return. These are the questions which thy will
Urge equally; and therefore I, the first,
Of that[2] will treat which hath the more of gall.[3]
Of seraphim[4] he who is most enskied,
Moses and Samuel, and either John,
Chuse which thou wilt, nor even Mary's self,
Have not in any other heaven their seats,
Than have those spirits which so late thou saw'st;
Nor more or fewer years exist; but all
Make the first circle[5] beauteous, diversly
Partaking of sweet life, as more or less
Afflation of eternal bliss pervades them.
Here were they shown thee, not that fate assigns
This for their sphere, but for a sign to thee
Of that celestial furthest from the height.
Thus needs, that ye may apprehend, we speak:
Since from things sensible alone ye learn
That, which, digested rightly, after turns
To intellectual. For no other cause
The Scripture, condescending graciously
To your perception, hands and feet[6] to God
Attributes, nor so means; and holy church
Doth represent with human countenance
Gabriel, and Michäel, and him who made
Tobias whole.[7] Unlike what here thou seest,
The judgment of Timæus,[8] who affirms

---

[1] *Plato.*—Ξυστήσας δὲ, κ. τ. λ., Plato, "Timæus," v. ix., p. 326, edit. Bip. "The Creator, when He had framed the universe, distributed to the stars an equal number of souls, appointing to each soul its several star."

[2] *Of that.*—Plato's opinion.

[3] *Which hath the more of gall.*—Which is the more dangerous.

[4] *Of seraphim.*—"He amongst the seraphim who is most nearly united with God, Moses, Samuel, and both the Johns, the Baptist and the Evangelist, dwell not in any other heaven than do those spirits whom thou hast just beheld; nor does even the blessed Virgin herself dwell in any other: nor is their existence either longer or shorter than that of these spirits." She first resolves his doubt whether souls do not return to their own stars, as he had read in the "Timæus" of Plato. Angels, then, and beatified spirits, she declares, dwell all and eternally together, only partaking more or less of the divine glory, in the empyrean; although, in condescension to human understanding, they appear to have different spheres allotted to them.

[5] *The first circle.*—The empyrean.

[6] *Hands and feet.*—Thus Milton:
"What surmounts the reach
Of human sense, I shall delineate so,
By likening spiritual to corporeal forms,
As shall express them best."
Paradise Lost, b. v. 575.

These passages, rightly considered, may tend to remove the scruples of some who are offended by any attempts at representing the Deity in pictures.

[7] *Him who made Tobias whole.*—
"Raphael, the sociable spirit, that deign'd
To travel with Tobias, and secured
His marriage with the seven times wedded maid."
Ibid, 223.

[8] *Timæus.*—In the "Convito," p. 92, our author again refers to the "Timæus" of Plato, on the subject of the mundane system; but it is in order to give the preference to the opinion respecting it held by Aristotle.

Each soul restored to its particular star;
Believing it to have been taken thence,
When nature gave it to inform her mold:
Yet to appearance his intention is
Not what his words declare: and so to shun
Derision, haply thus he hath disguised
His true opinion.¹ If his meaning be,
That to the influencing of these orbs revert
The honour and the blame in human acts,
Perchance he doth not wholly miss the truth.
This principle, not understood aright,
Erewhile perverted well nigh all the world;
So that it fell to fabled names of Jove,
And Mercury, and Mars. That other doubt,
Which moves thee, is less harmful; for it brings
No peril of removing thee from me.

"That, to the eye of man,² our justice seems
Unjust, is argument for faith, and not
For heretic declension. But, to the end
This truth³ may stand more clearly in your view,
I will content thee even to thy wish.

"If violence be, when that which suffers, nought
Consents to that which forceth, not for this
These spirits stood exculpate. For the will,
That wills not, still survives unquench'd, and doth,
As nature doth in fire, though violence
Wrest it a thousand times; for, if it yield
Or more or less, so far it follows force.
And thus did these, when they had power to seek
The hallow'd place again. In them, had will
Been perfect, such as once upon the bars
Held Laurence⁴ firm, or wrought in Scævola⁵
To his own hand remorseless; to the path,

---

¹ *His true opinion.*—In like manner, our learned Stillingfleet has professed himself "somewhat inclinable to think that Plato knew more of the lapse of mankind than he would openly discover, and for that end disguised it after his usual manner in that hypothesis of pre-existence."—*Origines Sacræ*, b. iii., c. iii., § 15.
² *That, to the eye of man.*—"That the ways of divine justice are often inscrutable to man, ought rather to be a motive to faith than an inducement to heresy." Such appears to me the most satisfactory explanation of the passage.

³ *This truth.*—That it is no impeachment of God's justice, if merit be lessened through compulsion of others, without any failure of good intention on the part of the meritorious. After all, Beatrice ends by admitting that there was a defect in the will, which hindered Constance and the others from seizing the first opportunity that offered itself to them of returning to the monastic life.
⁴ *Laurence.*—Who suffered martyrdom in the third century.
⁵ *Scævola.*—See Livy, "Hist.," Dec. 1, lib. ii. 12.

S

Whence they were drawn, their steps had hasten'd back,
When liberty return'd: but in too few,
Resolve, so stedfast, dwells. And by these words,
If duly weigh'd, that argument is void,
Which oft might have perplex'd thee still. But now
Another question thwarts thee, which, to solve,
Might try thy patience without better aid.
I have, no doubt, instill'd into thy mind,
That blessed spirit may not lie; since near
The source of primal truth it dwells for aye:
And thou mightst after of Piccarda learn
That Constance held affection to the veil;
So that she seems to contradict me here.
Not seldom, brother, it hath chanced for men
To do what they had gladly left undone;
Yet, to shun peril, they have done amiss:
E'en as Alcmæon,[1] at his father's[2] suit
Slew his own mother;[3] so made pitiless,
Not to lose pity. On this point bethink thee,
That force and will are blended in such wise
As not to make the offence excusable.
Absolute will agrees not to the wrong;
But inasmuch as there is fear of woe
From non-compliance, it agrees. Of will[4]
Thus absolute, Piccarda spake, and I
Of the other; so that both have truly said."

Such was the flow of that pure rill, that well'd
From forth the fountain of all truth; and such
The rest, that to my wandering thoughts I found.

"O thou, of primal love the prime delight,
Goddess!" I straight replied, "whose lively words
Still shed new heat and vigour through my soul;
Affection fails me to requite thy grace
With equal sum of gratitude: be his
To recompense, who sees and can reward thee.

---

[1] *Alcmæon.*—Ovid, "Metamorphoses," lib. ix., f. 10:
"Ultusque parente parentem
Natus, erit facto pius et sceleratus eodem."

[2] *His father's.*—Amphiaräus.

[3] *His own mother.*—Eriphyle.

[4] *Of will.*—"What Piccarda asserts of Constance, that she retained her affection to the monastic life, is said absolutely and without relation to circumstances; and that which I affirm is spoken of the will conditionally and respectively: so that our apparent difference is without any disagreement."

Well I discern, that by that truth[1] alone
Enlighten'd, beyond which no truth may roam,
Our mind can satisfy her thirst to know:
Therein she resteth, e'en as in his lair
The wild beast, soon as she hath reach'd that bound.
And she hath power to reach it; else desire
Were given to no end. And thence doth doubt
Spring, like a shoot, around the stock of truth;
And it is nature which, from height to height,
On to the summit prompts us. This invites,
This doth assure me, Lady! reverently
To ask thee of another truth, that yet
Is dark to me. I fain would know, if man
By other works well done may so supply
The failure of his vows, that in your scale
They lack not weight." I spake; and on me straight
Beatrice look'd, with eyes that shot forth sparks
Of love celestial, in such copious stream,
That, virtue sinking in me overpower'd,
I turn'd; and downward bent, confused, my sight.

---

[1] *Well I discern, that by that truth.*—The light of divine truth.

CANTO V.

ARGUMENT.

The question proposed in the last canto is answered. Dante ascends with Beatrice to the planet Mercury, which is the second heaven; and here he finds a multitude of spirits, one of whom offers to satisfy him of anything he may desire to know from them.

"IF beyond earthly wont,[1] the flame of love
    Illume me, so that I o'ercome thy power
Of vision, marvel not: but learn the cause
In that perfection of the sight, which, soon
As apprehending, hasteneth on to reach
The good it apprehends. I well discern,
How in thine intellect already shines
The light eternal, which to view alone
Ne'er fails to kindle love; and if aught else
Your love seduces, 'tis but that it shows
Some ill-mark'd vestige of that primal beam.

"This wouldst thou know: if failure of the vow
By other service may be so supplied,
As from self-question to assure the soul."

Thus she her words, not heedless of my wish,
Began; and thus, as one who breaks not off
Discourse, continued in her saintly strain.
"Supreme of gifts,[2] which God, creating, gave
Of his free bounty, sign most evident
Of goodness, and in his account most prized,
Was liberty of will; the boon, wherewith
All intellectual creatures, and them sole,
He hath endow'd. Hence now thou mayst infer
Of what high worth the vow, which so is framed,
That when man offers, God well-pleased accepts:

---

[1] *If beyond earthly wont.*—Dante having been unable to sustain the splendour of Beatrice, as we have seen at the end of the last canto, she tells him to attribute her increase of brightness to the place in which they were.

[2] *Supreme of gifts.*—So in the "De Monarchiâ," lib. i., pp. 107 and 108, "Si ergo judicium moveat," &c.: "If, then, the judgment altogether move the appetite, and is in no wise prevented by it, it is free. But if the judgment be moved by the appetite in any way preventing it, it cannot be free: because it acts not of itself, but is led captive by another. And hence it is that brutes cannot have free judgment, because their judgments are always prevented by appetite. And hence it may also appear manifest, that intellectual substances, whose wills are immutable, and likewise souls separated from the body, and departing from it well and holily, lose not the liberty of choice on account of the immutability of the will, but retain it most perfectly and powerfully. This being discerned, it is again plain that this liberty, or principle of all our liberty, is the greatest good conferred on human nature by God; because by this very thing we are here made happy, as men; by this we are elsewhere happy, as divine beings."

For in the compact between God and him,
This treasure, such as I describe it to thee,
He makes the victim; and of his own act.
What compensation therefore may he find?
If that, whereof thou hast oblation made,
By using well thou think'st to consecrate,
Thou wouldst of theft do charitable deed.[1]
Thus I resolve thee of the greater point.

"But forasmuch as holy church, herein
Dispensing, seems to contradict the truth
I have discover'd to thee, yet behoves
Thou rest a little longer at the board,
Ere the crude aliment which thou hast ta'en,
Digested fitly, to nutrition turn.
Open thy mind to what I now unfold;
And give it inward keeping. Knowledge comes
Of learning well retain'd, unfruitful else.

"This sacrifice, in essence, of two things[2]
Consisteth; one is that, whereof 'tis made;
The covenant, the other. For the last,
It ne'er is cancel'd, if not kept: and hence
I spake, erewhile, so strictly of its force.
For this it was enjoin'd the Israelites,[3]
Though leave were given them, as thou know'st, to change
The offering, still to offer. The other part,
The matter and the substance of the vow,
May well be such, as that, without offence,
It may for other substance be exchanged.
But, at his own discretion, none may shift
The burden on his shoulders; unreleased
By either key,[4] the yellow and the white.
Nor deem of any change, as less than vain,
If the last bond[5] be not within the new
Included, as the quatre in the six.
No satisfaction therefore can be paid

---

[1] *Thou wouldst of theft do charitable deed.*—"Licet fur de furto," &c.—*De Monarchiâ*, lib. ii., p. 123. "Although a thief should out of that which he has stolen give help to a poor man, yet is that not to be called almsgiving."

[2] *Two things.*—The one, the substance of the vow, as of a single life for instance, or of keeping fast; the other, the compact, or form of it.

[3] *It was enjoin'd the Israelites.*—See Lev. xii. and xxvii.

[4] *Either key.*—"Purgatory," canto ix. 108.

[5] *If the last bond.*—If the thing substituted be not far more precious than that which is released.

For what so precious in the balance weighs,
That all in counterpoise must kick the beam.
Take then no vow at random: ta'en, with faith
Preserve it; yet not bent, as Jephthah once,
Blindly to execute a rash resolve,
Whom better it had suited to exclaim,
'I have done ill,' than to redeem his pledge
By doing worse: or, not unlike to him
In folly, that great leader of the Greeks;
Whence, on the altar, Iphigenia mourn'd
Her virgin beauty, and hath since made mourn
Both wise and simple, even all, who hear
Of so fell sacrifice. Be ye more staid,
O Christians! not, like feather, by each wind
Removable; nor think to cleanse yourselves
In every water. Either testament,
The old and new, is yours: and for your guide,
The shepherd of the church. Let this suffice
To save you. When by evil lust enticed,
Remember ye be men, not senseless beasts;
Nor let the Jew, who dwelleth in your streets,
Hold you in mockery. Be not as the lamb,
That, fickle wanton, leaves its mother's milk,
To dally with itself in idle play."

Such were the words that Beatrice spake:
These ended, to that region,[1] where the world
Is liveliest, full of fond desire she turn'd.

Though mainly prompt new question to propose,
Her silence and changed look did keep me dumb.
And as the arrow, ere the cord is still,
Leapeth unto its mark; so on we sped
Into the second realm. There I beheld
The dame, so joyous, enter, that the orb
Grew brighter at her smiles; and, if the star
Were moved to gladness, what then was my cheer,
Whom nature hath made apt for every change!

---

[1] *That region.*—As some explain it, the east; according to others, the equinoctial line. Lombardi supposes it to mean that she looked upwards. Monti, in his "Proposta" (vol. iii., pte. 2, p. lxxix., Milan, 1826), has adduced a passage from our author's "Convito," which fixes the sense: "Dico ancora, che quanto il Cielo è più presso al cerchio equatore, tanto è più mobile per comparazione alli suoi; perocchè ha più movimento, e più attualità, e più vita, e più forma, e più tocca di quello, che è sopra se, e per conseguente più virtuoso."—Page 48.

So drew
Full more than thousand splendours towards us.
Canto V., lines 99, 100.

As in a quiet and clear lake the fish,
If aught approach them from without, do draw
Towards it, deeming it their food; so drew
Full more than thousand splendours towards us,
And in each one was heard: "Lo! one arrived
To multiply our loves!" and as each came,
The shadow, streaming forth effulgence new,
Witness'd augmented joy. Here, Reader! think,
If thou didst miss the sequel of my tale,
To know the rest how sorely thou wouldst crave;
And thou shalt see what vehement desire
Possess'd me, soon as these had met my view,
To know their state. "O born in happy hour!
Thou, to whom grace vouchsafes, or e'er thy close
Of fleshly warfare, to behold the thrones
Of that eternal triumph; know, to us
The light communicated, which through heaven
Expatiates without bound. Therefore, if aught
Thou of our beams wouldst borrow for thine aid,
Spare not; and, of our radiance, take thy fill."

    Thus of those piteous spirits one bespake me;
And Beatrice next: "Say on; and trust
As unto gods."—"How in the light supreme
Thou harbour'st, and from thence the virtue bring'st,
That, sparkling in thine eyes, denotes thy joy,
I mark; but who thou art, am still to seek;
Or wherefore, worthy spirit! for thy lot
This sphere[1] assign'd, that oft from mortal ken
Is veil'd by other's beams." I said; and turn'd
Toward the lustre, that with greeting kind
Erewhile had hail'd me. Forthwith, brighter far
Than erst, it wax'd: and, as himself the sun
Hides through excess of light, when his warm gaze[2]
Hath on the mantle of thick vapours prey'd;
Within its proper ray the saintly shape
Was, through increase of gladness, thus conceal'd;
And, shrouded so in splendour, answer'd me,
E'en as the tenour of my song declares.

---

[1] *This sphere.*—The planet Mercury, which, being nearest to the sun, is oftenest hidden by that luminary.

[2] *When his warm gaze.*—When the sun has dried up the vapours that shaded his brightness.

CANTO VI.

ARGUMENT.

The spirit, who had offered to satisfy the inquiries of Dante, declares himself to be the Emperor Justinian; and after speaking of his own actions, recounts the victories, before him, obtained under the Roman Eagle. He then informs our Poet that the soul of Romeo the pilgrim is in the same star.

"AFTER that Constantine the eagle turn'd[1]
Against the motions of the heaven, that roll'd
Consenting with its course, when he of yore,
Lavinia's spouse, was leader of the flight;
A hundred years twice told and more,[2] his seat
At Europe's extreme point,[3] the bird of Jove
Held, near the mountains, whence he issued first;
There under shadow of his sacred plumes
Swaying the world, till through successive hands
To mine he came devolved. Cæsar I was;
And am Justinian; destined by the will
Of that prime love, whose influence I feel,
From vain excess to clear the incumber'd laws.[4]
Or e'er that work engaged me, I did hold
In Christ one nature only;[5] with such faith
Contented. But the blessed Agapete,[6]
Who was chief shepherd, he with warning voice
To the true faith recall'd me. I believed
His words: and what he taught, now plainly see,
As thou in every contradiction seest
The true and false opposed. Soon as my feet

---

[1] *After that Constantine the eagle turn'd.*—Constantine, in transferring the seat of empire from Rome to Byzantium, carried the eagle, the Imperial ensign, from the west to the east. Æneas, on the contrary, had, with better augury, moved along with the sun's course, when he passed from Troy to Italy.

[2] *A hundred years twice told and more.*—The Emperor Constantine entered Byzantium in 324; and Justinian began his reign in 527.

[3] *At Europe's extreme point.*—Constantinople being situated at the extreme of Europe, and on the borders of Asia, near those mountains in the neighbourhood of Troy from whence the first founders of Rome had emigrated.

[4] *To clear the incumber'd laws.*—The code of laws was abridged and reformed by Justinian.

"Giustiniano son io, disse il primajo,
Che 'l troppo e 'l van secai for delle leggi,
Ora soggette all' arme e al denajo."
Frezzi, Il Quadriregio, lib. iv., cap. 13.

[5] *In Christ one nature only.*—Justinian is said to have been a follower of the heretical opinions held by Eutyches, "who taught that in Christ there was but one nature, viz., that of the incarnate word."—*Maclaine's Mosheim*, tom. ii., cent. v., p. ii., cap. v., § 13.

[6] *Agapete.*—"Agapetus, Bishop of Rome, whose 'Scheda Regia,' addressed to the Emperor Justinian, procured him a place among the wisest and most judicious writers of this century."—*Ibid.*, cent. vi., p. ii., cap. ii., § 8. Compare Fazio degli Uberti, "Dittamondo," l. ii., cap. xvi.

Were to the church reclaim'd, to my great task,
By inspiration of God's grace impell'd,
I gave me wholly ; and consign'd mine arms
To Belisarius, with whom heaven's right hand
Was link'd in such conjointment, 'twas a sign
That I should rest. To thy first question thus
I shape mine answer, which were ended here,
But that its tendency doth prompt perforce
To some addition ; that thou well mayst mark,
What reason on each side they have to plead,
By whom that holiest banner is withstood,
Both who pretend its power[1] and who oppose.[2]

"Beginning from that hour, when Pallas died[3]
To give it rule, behold the valorous deeds
Have made it worthy reverence. Not unknown[4]
To thee, how for three hundred years and more
It dwelt in Alba, up to those fell lists
Where, for its sake, were met the rival three ;[5]
Nor aught unknown to thee, which it achieved
Down[6] from the Sabines' wrong to Lucrece' woe ;
With its seven kings conquering the nations round ;
Nor all it wrought, by Roman worthies borne
'Gainst Brennus and the Epirot prince,[7] and hosts
Of single chiefs, or states in league combined
Of social warfare : hence, Torquatus stern,
And Quintius[8] named of his neglected locks,
The Decii, and the Fabii hence acquired
Their fame, which I with duteous zeal embalm.[9]
By it the pride of Arab hordes[10] was quell'd,
When they, led on by Hannibal, o'erpass'd

---

[1] *Who pretend its power.*—The Ghibellines.
[2] *And who oppose.*—The Guelphs.
[3] *Pallas died.*—See Virgil, "Æneid," lib x.
[4] *Not unknown.*—In the second book of his treatise "De Monarchiâ," where Dante endeavours to prove that the Roman people had a right to govern the world, he refers to their conquests and successes in nearly the same order as in this passage. "The Roman," he affirms, "might truly say, as the Apostle did to Timothy, There is laid up for me a crown of righteousness ; laid up, that is, in the eternal providence of God."—Page 131. And again : "Now it is manifest, that by *duel* (per duellum) the Roman people acquired the Empire ; therefore they acquired it by right, to prove which is the main purpose of the present book."—Page 132.

[5] *The rival three.*—The Horatii and Curiatii.
[6] *Down.*—" From the rape of the Sabine women to the violation of Lucretia."
[7] *The Epirot prince.*—King Pyrrhus.
[8] *Quintius.*—Quintius Cincinnatus.
"E Cincinnato dall' inculta chioma."
Petrarca.
Compare " De Monarchiâ," lib. ii., p. 121, &c. "Itaque, inquit, et majores nostri," &c.
[9] *Embalm.*—The word in the original is " mirro," which some think is put for " miro," " I behold or regard ;" and others understand as I have rendered it.
[10] *Arab hordes.*—The Arabians seem to be put for the barbarians in general. Lombardi's comment is, that as the Arabs are an Asiatic people, and it is not

The Alpine rocks, whence glide thy currents, Po!
Beneath its guidance, in their prime of days
Scipio and Pompey triumph'd; and that hill[1]
Under whose summit[2] thou didst see the light,
Rued its stern bearing. After, near the hour,[3]
When heaven was minded that o'er all the world
His own deep calm should brood, to Cæsar's hand
Did Rome consign it; and what then it wrought[4]
From Var unto the Rhine, saw Isere's flood,
Saw Loire and Seine, and every vale, that fills
The torrent Rhone. What after that it wrought,
When from Ravenna it came forth, and leap'd
The Rubicon, was of so bold a flight,
That tongue nor pen may follow it. Towards Spain
It wheel'd its bands, then towards Dyrrachium smote,
And on Pharsalia, with so fierce a plunge,
E'en the warm Nile was conscious to the pang;
Its native shores Antandros, and the streams
Of Simois revisited, and there
Where Hector lies; then ill for Ptolemy
His pennons shook again; lightening thence fell
On Juba; and the next, upon your west,
At sound of the Pompeian trump, return'd.

"What following, and in its next bearer's gripe,[5]
It wrought, is now by Cassius and Brutus
Bark'd of[6] in hell; and by Perugia's sons,
And Modena's, was mourn'd. Hence weepeth still
Sad Cleopatra, who, pursued by it,
Took from the adder black and sudden death.

---

recorded that Hannibal had any other troops except his own countrymen the Carthaginians, who were Africans, we must understand that Dante denominates that people Arabs on account of their origin. "Ab Africo Arabiæ Felicis rege, qui omnium primus hanc terram (Africam) incoluisse fertur," &c.—*Leo Africanus, Africæ Descriptio,* lib. i., cap. i.

[1] *That hill.*—The city of Fesulæ, which was sacked by the Romans after the defeat of Catiline.

[2] *Under whose summit.*—"At the foot of which is situated Florence, thy birth-place."

[3] *Near the hour.*—Near the time of our Saviour's birth. "The immeasurable goodness of the Deity being willing again to conform to itself the human creature, which by transgression of the first man had from God departed, and fallen from His likeness, it was determined in that most high and closest consistory of the Godhead, the Trinity, that the Son of God should descend upon earth to make this agreement. And because it was behoveful that at His coming, the world, not only the heaven but the earth, should be in the best possible disposition—and the best disposition of the earth is when it is a monarchy, that is, all under one prince, as hath been said above—therefore through the divine forecast was ordained that people and that city for the accomplishment, namely, the glorious Rome."—*Convito,* p. 138. The same argument is repeated at the conclusion of the first book of our author's treatise "De Monarchiâ."

[4] *What then it wrought.*—In the following fifteen lines the poet has comprised the exploits of Julius Cæsar, for which, and for the allusions in the greater part of this speech of Justinian's, I must refer my reader to the history of Rome.

[5] *In its next bearer's gripe.*—With Augustus Cæsar.

[6] *Bark'd of.*—

τοιαῦθ᾽ ὑλακτεῖ.

Sophocles, Electra, 299.

With him it ran e'en to the Red Sea coast;
With him composed the world to such a peace,
That of his temple Janus barr'd the door.

"But all the mighty standard yet had wrought,
And was appointed to perform thereafter,
Throughout the mortal kingdom which it sway'd,
Falls in appearance dwindled and obscured,
If one with steady eye and perfect thought
On the third Cæsar[1] look; for to his hands,
The living Justice, in whose breath I move,
Committed glory, e'en into his hands,
To execute the vengeance of its wrath.

"Hear now, and wonder at, what next I tell.
After with Titus it was sent to wreak
Vengeance for vengeance[2] of the ancient sin.
And, when the Lombard tooth, with fang impure,
Did gore the bosom of the holy church,
Under its wings, victorious Charlemain[3]
Sped to her rescue. Judge then for thyself
Of those, whom I erewhile accused to thee,
What they are, and how grievous their offending,
Who are the cause of all your ills. The one[4]
Against the universal ensign rears
The yellow lilies;[5] and with partial aim,
That, to himself, the other[6] arrogates:
So that 'tis hard to see who most offends.
Be yours, ye Ghibellines,[7] to veil your arts

---

[1] *The third Cæsar.*—The eagle in the hand of Tiberius, the third of the Cæsars, outdid all its achievements, both past and future, by becoming the instrument of that mighty and mysterious act of satisfaction made to the divine justice in the crucifixion of our Lord. This is Lombardi's explanation; and he deserves much credit for being right, where all the other commentators, as far as I know, are wrong. See note to "Purgatory," canto xxxii. 50.

[2] *Vengeance for vengeance.*—This will be afterwards explained by the poet himself. See next canto vii., 47, and note.

[3] *Charlemain.*—Dante could not be ignorant that the reign of Justinian was long prior to that of Charlemain; but the spirit of the former emperor is represented, both in this instance and in what follows, as conscious of the events that had taken place after his own time.

[4] *The one.*—The Guelph party.
[5] *The yellow lilies.*—The French ensign.
[6] *The other.*—The Ghibelline party.
[7] *Ye Ghibellines.*—"Authors differ much as to the beginning of these factions, and the origin of the names by which they were distinguished. Some say that they began in Italy as early as the time of the Emperor Frederick I. in his well-known disputes with Pope Alexander III. about the year 1160. Others make them more ancient, dating them from the reign of the Emperor Henry IV., who died in 1125. But the most common opinion is that they arose in the contests between the Emperor Frederick II. and Pope Gregory IX., and that this Emperor, wishing to ascertain who were his own adherents, and who those of the Pope, caused the former to be marked by the appellation of Ghibellines, and the latter by that of Guelphs. It is more probable, however, that the factions were at this time either renewed or diffused more widely, and that their origin was of an earlier date, since it is certain that G. Villani, b. v., c. xxxvii., Ricordano Malaspina, c. civ., and Pietro Buoninsegni, b. i., of their histories of Florence, are agreed, that even from 1215—that is, long before Frederick had succeeded to the Empire, and Gregory to the Pontificate, by the death of Buondelmonte Buondelmonti,

Beneath another standard: ill is this
Follow'd of him, who severs it and justice:
And let not with his Guelphs the new-crown'd Charles[1]
Assail it; but those talons hold in dread,
Which from a lion of more lofty port
Have rent the casing. Many a time ere now
The sons have for the sire's transgression wail'd:
Nor let him trust the fond belief, that heaven
Will truck its armour for his lilied shield.

"This little star is furnish'd with good spirits,
Whose mortal lives were busied to that end,
That honour and renown might wait on them:
And, when desires[2] thus err in their intention,
True love must needs ascend with slacker beam.
But it is part of our delight, to measure
Our wages with the merit; and admire
The close proportion. Hence doth heavenly justice
Temper so evenly affection in us,
It ne'er can warp to any wrongfulness.
Of diverse voices is sweet music made:
So in our life the different degrees
Render sweet harmony among these wheels.

"Within the pearl, that now encloseth us,
Shines Romeo's light,[3] whose goodly deed and fair

---

one of the chief gentlemen in Florence (see 'Paradise,' canto xvi., v. 139)—the factions of the Guelfi and Ghibellini were introduced into that city."—*A. G. Artegiani*, Annot. on the "Quadriregio," p. 180. "The same variety of opinion prevails with regard to the origin of the names. Some deduce them from two brothers, who were Germans, the one called Guelph and the other Gibel, who, being the partisans of two powerful families in Pistoia, the Panciatichi and the Cancellieri, then at enmity with each other, were the first occasion of these titles having been given to the two discordant factions. Others, with more probability, derive them from Guelph or Guelfone, Duke of Bavaria, and Gibello, a castle where his antagonist, the Emperor Conrad III., was born; in consequence of a battle between Guelph and Henry the son of Conrad, which was fought (according to Mini, in his 'Defence of Florence,' p. 48) A.D. 1138. Others assign to them an origin yet more ancient; asserting that at the election of Frederick I. to the Empire, the Electors concurred in choosing him, in order to extinguish the inveterate discords between the Guelphs and the Ghibellines, that prince being descended by the paternal line from the Ghibellines, and by the maternal from the Guelphs. Bartolo, however, in his tractate 'De Guelphis et Gibellinis,' gives an intrinsic meaning to these names from certain passages in Scripture: 'Sicut Gibellus interpretatur locus fortitu- dinis, ita Gibellini appellantur confidentes in fortitudine militum et armorum, et sicut Guelpha interpretatur os loquens, ita Guelphi interpretantur confidentes in orationibus et in divinis.' What value is to be put on this interpretation, which well accords with the genius of those times, when it was perhaps esteemed a marvellous mystery, we leave it to others to decide."—*Ibid*.

[1] *Charles*.—The commentators explain this to mean Charles II., King of Naples and Sicily. Is it not more likely to allude to Charles of Valois, son of Philip III. of France, who was sent for, about this time, into Italy by Pope Boniface, with the promise of being made emperor? See G. Villani, lib. viii., cap. xlii.

[2] *When desires*.—When honour and fame are the chief motives to action, that love, which has heaven for its object, must necessarily become less fervent.

[3] *Romeo's light*.—The story of Romeo is involved in some uncertainty. The name of Romeo signified, as we have seen in the note "Purgatory," canto xxxiii., v. 78, one who went on a pilgrimage to Rome. The French writers assert the continuance of his ministerial office even after the decease of his sovereign, Raymond Berenger, Count of Provence; and they rest this assertion chiefly on the fact of a certain Romieu de Villeneuve, who was the contemporary of that prince, having left large possessions behind him, as appears by his will preserved in the archives of the bishopric

Met ill acceptance. But the Provençals,
That were his foes, have little cause for mirth.
Ill shapes that man his course, who makes his wrong
Of other's worth. Four daughters[1] were there born
To Raymond Berenger;[2] and every one
Became a queen: and this for him did Romeo,
Though of mean state and from a foreign land.
Yet envious tongues incited him to ask
A reckoning of that just one, who return'd
Twelve fold to him for ten. Aged and poor
He parted thence: and if the world did know
The heart he had, begging his life by morsels,
'Twould deem the praise it yields him scantly dealt."

---

of Vence. That they are right as to the name at least would appear from the following marginal note on the Monte Casino MS.: " Romeo de Villanova districtus civitatis Ventiæ de Provincia olim ministratoris Ramundi Belingerj Comitis Provinciæ—ivit peregrinando contemplativus ad Deum." Yet it is improbable, on the other hand, that the Italians, who lived so near the time, should be misinformed in an occurrence of such notoriety. According to them, after he had long been a faithful steward to Raymond, when an account was required from him of the revenues which he had carefully husbanded, and his master as lavishly disbursed, " he demanded the little mule, the staff, and the scrip, with which he had first entered into the Count's service, a stranger pilgrim from the shrine of St. James, in Galicia, and parted as he came ; nor was it ever known whence he was, or whither he went."—*G. Villani*, lib. vi., c. xcii. The same incidents are told of him at the conclusion of cap. xxviii., lib. ii., of Fazio degli Uberti's " Dittamondo."

[1] *Four daughters*.—Of the four daughters of Raymond Berenger, Margaret, the eldest, was married to Louis IX. of France; Eleanor, the next, to Henry III. of England; Sancha, the third, to Richard, Henry's brother, and King of the Romans; and the youngest, Beatrix, to Charles I., King of Naples and Sicily, and brother to Louis.

[2] *Raymond Berenger*.—This prince, the last of the house of Barcelona, who was Count of Provence, died in 1245. He is in the list of Provençal poets. See Millot, " Hist. Littéraire des Troubadours," tom. ii., p. 212. But M. Raynouard could find no manuscript of his works. See " Choix des Poésies des Troubadours," tom. v., p. vii.

CANTO VII.

ARGUMENT.

In consequence of what had been said by Justinian, who together with the other spirits have now disappeared, some doubts arise in the mind of Dante respecting the human redemption. These difficulties are fully explained by Beatrice.

"HOSANNA[1] Sanctus Deus Sabaoth,
    Superillustrans claritate tuâ
Felices ignes horum malahoth."
Thus chanting saw I turn that substance bright,[2]
With fourfold lustre to its orb again,
Revolving; and the rest, unto their dance,
With it, moved also; and, like swiftest sparks,
In sudden distance from my sight were veil'd.
    Me doubt possess'd; and "Speak," it whisper'd me,
"Speak, speak unto thy lady; that she quench
Thy thirst with drops of sweetness." Yet blank awe,
Which lords it o'er me, even at the sound
Of Beatrice's name, did bow me down
As one in slumber held. Not long that mood
Beatrice suffer'd: she, with such a smile,
As might have made one blest amid the flames,[3]
Beaming upon me, thus her words began:
"Thou in thy thought art pondering (as I deem,
And what I deem is truth) how just revenge
Could be with justice punish'd: from which doubt
I soon will free thee; so thou mark my words;
For they of weighty matter shall possess thee.
    Through suffering not a curb upon the power
That will'd in him, to his own profiting,
That man, who was unborn,[4] condemn'd himself;
And, in himself, all who since him have lived,
His offspring: whence, below, the human kind

---

[1] *Hosanna.*—"Hosanna holy God of Sabaoth, abundantly illumining with Thy brightness the blessed fires of these kingdoms."
[2] *That substance bright.*—Justinian.
[3] *As might have made one blest amid the flames.*—So Giusto de' Conti, "Bella Mano," "Qual salamandra:"
   "Che puommi nelle fiamme far beato."
[4] *That man, who was unborn.*—Adam.

Lay sick in grievous error many an age;
Until it pleased the Word of God to come
Amongst them down, to his own person joining
The nature from its Maker far estranged,
By the mere act of his eternal love.
Contemplate here the wonder I unfold.
The nature with its Maker thus conjoin'd,
Created first was blameless, pure and good;
But, through itself alone, was driven forth
From Paradise, because it had eschew'd
The way of truth and life, to evil turn'd.
Ne'er then was penalty so just as that
Inflicted by the cross, if thou regard
The nature in assumption doom'd; ne'er wrong
So great, in reference to him, who took
Such nature on him, and endured the doom.
So different effects flow'd from one act:[1]
For by one death God and the Jews were pleased;
And heaven was open'd, though the earth did quake.
Count it not hard henceforth, when thou dost hear
That a just vengeance[2] was, by righteous court,
Justly revenged. But yet I see thy mind,
By thought on thought arising, sore perplex'd;
And, with how vehement desire, it asks
Solution of the maze. What I have heard,
Is plain, thou sayst: but wherefore God this way
For our redemption chose, eludes my search.

"Brother! no eye of man not perfected,
Nor fully ripen'd in the flame of love,
May fathom this decree. It is a mark,
In sooth, much aim'd at, and but little kenn'd:
And I will therefore show thee why such way
Was worthiest. The celestial love,[3] that spurns

---

[1] *Different effects flow'd from one act.*—The death of Christ was pleasing to God, inasmuch as it satisfied the divine justice; and to the Jews, because it gratified their malignity; and while heaven opened for joy at the ransom of man, the earth trembled through compassion for its Maker.

[2] *A just vengeance.*—The punishment of Christ by the Jews, although just, as far as regarded the human nature assumed by Him, and so a righteous vengeance of sin, yet, being unjust as it regarded the divine nature, was itself justly revenged on the Jews by the destruction of Jerusalem.

[3] *The celestial love.*—From Boëtius, "De Consol. Philosoph.," lib. iii., Metr. 9:

"Quem non externæ pepulerunt fingere causæ
Materiæ fluitantis opus, verum insita summi
Forma boni livore carens; tu cuncta superno
Ducis ab exemplo, pulchrum pulcherrimus ipse
Mundum mente gerens, similique in imagine formans,
Perfectasque jubens perfectum absolvere partes."

All envying in its bounty, in itself
With such effulgence blazeth, as sends forth
All beauteous things eternal. What distils[1]
Immediate thence, no end of being knows;
Bearing its seal immutably imprest.
Whatever thence immediate falls, is free,
Free wholly, uncontrollable by power
Of each thing new: by such conformity
More grateful to its author, whose bright beams,
Though all partake their shining, yet in those
Are liveliest, which resemble him the most.
These tokens of pre-eminence[2] on man
Largely bestow'd, if any of them fail,
He needs must forfeit his nobility,
No longer stainless. Sin alone is that,
Which doth disfranchise him, and make unlike
To the chief good; for that its light in him
Is darken'd. And to dignity thus lost
Is no return; unless, where guilt makes void,
He for ill pleasure pay with equal pain.
Your nature, which entirely in its seed
Transgress'd, from these distinctions fell, no less
Than from its state in Paradise; nor means
Found of recovery (search all methods out
As strictly as thou may) save one of these,
The only fords were left through which to wade:
Either, that God had of his courtesy
Released him merely; or else, man himself
For his own folly by himself atoned.

" Fix now thine eye, intently as thou canst,
On the everlasting counsel; and explore,
Instructed by my words, the dread abyss.

" Man in himself had ever lack'd the means
Of satisfaction, for he could not stoop
Obeying, in humility so low,
As high, he, disobeying, thought to soar:

---

[1] *What distils.*—" That which proceeds immediately from God, and without the intervention of secondary causes, is immortal."

[2] *These tokens of pre-eminence.*—The before-mentioned gifts of immediate creation by God, independence on secondary causes, and consequent similitude and agreeableness to the divine Being, all at first conferred on man.

And, for this reason, he had vainly tried,
Out of his own sufficiency, to pay
The rigid satisfaction. Then behoved
That God should by his own ways lead him back
Unto the life, from whence he fell, restored:
By both his ways I mean, or one alone.[1]
But since the deed is ever prized the more,
The more the doer's good intent appears;
Goodness celestial, whose broad signature
Is on the universe, of all its ways
To raise ye up, was fain to leave out none.
Nor aught so vast or so magnificent,
Either for him who gave or who received,
Between the last night and the primal day,
Was or can be. For God more bounty show'd,
Giving himself to make man capable
Of his return to life, than had the terms
Been mere and unconditional release.
And for his justice, every method else
Were all too scant, had not the Son of God
Humbled himself to put on mortal flesh.

"Now, to content thee fully, I revert;
And further in some part[2] unfold my speech,
That thou mayst see it clearly as myself.

"I see, thou sayst, the air, the fire I see,
The earth and water, and all things of them
Compounded, to corruption turn, and soon
Dissolve. Yet these were also things create.
Because, if what were told me had been true,
They from corruption had been therefore free.

"The angels, O my brother! and this clime
Wherein thou art, impassible and pure,
I call created, even as they are
In their whole being. But the elements,

---

[1] *By both his ways, I mean, or one alone.*—Either by mercy and justice united, or by mercy alone.

[2] *In some part.*—She reverts to that part of her discourse where she had said that what proceeds immediately from God "no end of being knows." She then proceeds to tell him that the elements, which, though he knew them to be created, he yet saw dissolved, received their form not immediately from God, but from a virtue or power created by God; that the soul of brutes and plants is in like manner drawn forth by the stars with a combination of those elements meetly tempered, "di complession potenziata;" but that the angels and the heavens may be said to be created in that very manner in which they exist, without any intervention of agency.

Which thou hast named, and what of them is made,
Are by created virtue inform'd : create,
Their substance ; and create, the informing virtue
In these bright stars, that round them circling move.
The soul of every brute and of each plant,
The ray and motion of the sacred lights,
Draw[1] from complexion with meet power endued.
But this our life the eternal good inspires
Immediate, and enamours of itself ;
So that our wishes rest for ever here.
  " And hence thou mayst by inference conclude
Our resurrection certain,[2] if thy mind
Consider how the human flesh was framed,
When both our parents at the first were made."

---

[1] *Draw.*—I had before rendered this differently, and I now think erroneously :
  " With complex potency attract and turn."

[2] *Our resurrection certain.*—Venturi appears to mistake the poet's reasoning when he observes, " Wretched for us, if we had not arguments more convincing, and of a higher kind, to assure us of the truth of our resurrection." It is, perhaps, here intended that the whole of God's dispensation should be taken into the account. The conclusion may be, that as before sin man was immortal, and even in flesh proceeded immediately from God, so being restored to the favour of heaven by the expiation made for sin, he necessarily recovers his claim to immortality even in the body. There is much in this poem to justify the encomium which the learned Salvini has passed on it, when, in an epistle to Redi, imitating what Horace had said of Homer, that the duties of life might be better learnt from the Grecian bard than from the teachers of the porch or the academy, he says :

" And dost thou ask, what themes my mind engage ?
  The lonely hours I give to Dante's page ;
  And meet more sacred learning in his lines,
  Than I had gain'd from all the school divines."

" Se volete saper la vita mia,
  Studiando io sto lungi da tutti gli uomini ;
Ed ho imparato più teologia
  In questi giorni, che ho riletto Dante,
  Che nelle scuole fatto io non avria."

CANTO VIII.

ARGUMENT.

The Poet ascends with Beatrice to the third heaven, which is the planet Venus; and here finds the soul of Charles Martel, King of Hungary, who had been Dante's friend on earth, and who now, after speaking of the realms to which he was heir, unfolds the cause why children differ in disposition from their parents.

THE world[1] was, in its day of peril dark,
    Wont to believe the dotage of fond love,
From the fair Cyprian deity, who rolls
In her third epicycle,[2] shed on men
By stream of potent radiance : therefore they
Of elder time, in their old error blind,
Not her alone with sacrifice adored
And invocation, but like honours paid
To Cupid and Dione, deem'd of them
Her mother, and her son, him whom they feign'd
To sit in Dido's bosom :[3] and from her,
Whom I have sung preluding, borrow'd they
The appellation of that star, which views
Now obvious,[4] and now averse, the sun.
    I was not ware that I was wafted up
Into its orb ; but the new loveliness,
That graced my lady, gave me ample proof
That we had enter'd there. And as in flame
A sparkle is distinct, or voice in voice
Discern'd, when one its even tenour keeps,
The other comes and goes ; so in that light
I other luminaries saw, that coursed
In circling motion, rapid more or less.

---

[1] *The world.*—The poet, on his arrival at the third heaven, tells us that the world, in its days of heathen darkness, believed the influence of sensual love to proceed from the star to which, under the name of Venus, they paid divine honours ; as they worshipped the supposed mother and son of Venus, under the names of Dione and Cupid.

[2] *Epicycle.*—
          "The sphere
With centric and eccentric scribbled o'er,
Cycle and epicycle."
        Milton, Paradise Lost, b. viii. 84.

[3] "In sul dosso di questo cerchio," &c.—*Convito di Dante*, p. 48. "Upon the back of this circle, in the heaven of Venus, whereof we are now treating, is a little sphere, which has in that heaven a revolution of its own ; whose circle the astronomers term epicycle."

[3] *To sit in Dido's bosom.*—Virgil, "Æneid," lib. i. 718.

[4] *Now obvious.*—Being at one part of the year a morning, and at another an evening star. So Frezzi :
    "Il raggio della stella
Che 'l sol vagheggia or drieto or davanti."
        Il Quadriregio, lib. i., c. i.
    "Whose ray,
Being page and usher to the day,
Does mourn behind the sun, before him play."
        John Hall.

As their[1] eternal vision each impels.
　　Never was blast from vapour charged with cold,
Whether invisible to eye or no,[2]
Descended with such speed, it had not seem'd
To linger in dull tardiness, compared
To those celestial lights, that towards us came,
Leaving the circuit of their joyous ring,
Conducted by the lofty seraphim.
And after them, who in the van appear'd,
Such an Hosanna sounded as hath left
Desire, ne'er since extinct in me, to hear
Renew'd the strain.　Then, parting from the rest,
One near us drew, and sole began: "We all
Are ready at thy pleasure, well disposed
To do thee gentle service.　We are they
To whom thou in the world erewhile didst sing;
'O ye! whose intellectual ministry[3]
Moves the third heaven:' and in one orb we roll,
One motion, one impulse, with those who rule
Princedoms in heaven;[4] yet are of love so full,
That to please thee 'twill be as sweet to rest."
　　After mine eyes had with meek reverence
Sought the celestial guide, and were by her
Assured, they turn'd again unto the light,
Who had so largely promised; and with voice
That bare the lively pressure of my zeal,
"Tell who ye are," I cried.　Forthwith it grew
In size and splendour, through augmented joy;
And thus it answer'd: "A short date, below,
The world possess'd me.　Had the time been more,[5]
Much evil, that will come, had never chanced.
My gladness hides thee from me, which doth shine
Around, and shroud me, as an animal

---

[1] *As their.*—As each, according to their several deserts, partakes more or less of the beatific vision.

[2] *Whether invisible to eye or no.*—He calls the blast invisible, if unattended by gross vapour; otherwise, visible.

[3] *O ye! whose intellectual ministry.*—
"Voi ch' intendendo il terzo ciel movete."
The first line in our poet's first Canzone. See his 'Convito,' p. 40.

[4] *Princedoms in heaven.*—See canto xxviii. 112, where the princedoms are, as here, made co-ordinate with this third sphere.　In his "Convito," p. 54, he has ranked them differently, making the thrones the moving intelligences of Venus.

[5] *Had the time been more.*—The spirit now speaking is Charles Martel, crowned King of Hungary, and son of Charles II., King of Naples and Sicily, to which dominions, dying in his father's lifetime, he did not succeed.　The evil, that would have been prevented by the longer life of Charles Martel, was that resistance which his brother Robert, King of Sicily, who succeeded him, made to the Emperor Henry VII.　See G. Villani, lib. ix., cap. xxxviii.

The left bank,
That Rhone, when he hath mix'd with Sorga, laves
In me its lord expected.
Canto VIII., lines 60—62.

In its own silk enswathed. Thou lovedst me well,[1]
And hadst good cause; for had my sojourning
Been longer on the earth, the love I bare thee
Had put forth more than blossoms. The left bank,[2]
That Rhone, when he hath mix'd with Sorga, laves,
In me its lord expected, and that horn
Of fair Ausonia,[3] with its boroughs old,
Bari, and Croton, and Gaeta piled,
From where the Trento disembogues his waves,
With Verde mingled, to the salt-sea flood.
Already on my temples beam'd the crown,
Which gave me sovereignty over the land[4]
By Danube wash'd, whenas he strays beyond
The limits of his German shores. The realm,
Where, on the gulf by stormy Eurus lash'd,
Betwixt Pelorus and Pachynian heights,
The beautiful Trinacria[5] lies in gloom
(Not through Typhœus,[6] but the vapoury cloud
Bituminous upsteam'd), *that* too did look
To have its sceptre wielded by a race
Of monarchs, sprung through me from Charles and Rodolph;[7]
Had not ill-lording,[8] which doth desperate make[9]
The people ever, in Palermo raised
The shout of 'death,' re-echoed loud and long.
Had but my brother's foresight[10] kenn'd as much,

---

[1] *Thou lovedst me well.*—Charles Martel might have been known to our poet at Florence, whither he came to meet his father in 1295, the year of his death. The retinue and the habiliments of the young monarch are minutely described by G. Villani, who adds, that "he remained more than twenty days in Florence, waiting for his father King Charles and his brothers; during which time great honour was done him by the Florentines, and he showed no less love towards them, and he was much in favour with all."—Lib. viii., cap. xiii. His brother Robert, King of Naples, was the friend of Petrarch.

[2] *The left bank.*—Provence

[3] *That horn of fair Ausonia.*—The kingdom of Naples.

[4] *The land.*—Hungary.

[5] *The beautiful Trinacria.*—Sicily; so called from its three promontories, of which Pachynus and Pelorus, here mentioned, are two.

[6] *Typhæus.*—The giant whom Jupiter is fabled to have overwhelmed under the mountain Ætna, from whence he vomited forth smoke and flame.

[7] *Sprung through me from Charles and Rodolph.*—"Sicily would be still ruled by a race of monarchs, descended through me from Charles I. and Rodolph I., the former my grandfather, King of Naples and Sicily; the latter, Emperor of Germany, my father-in-law;" both celebrated in the "Purgatory," canto vii.

[8] *Had not ill-lording.*—"If the ill conduct of our governors in Sicily had not excited the resentment and hatred of the people, and stimulated them to that dreadful massacre at the Sicilian Vespers;" in consequence of which the kingdom fell into the hands of Peter III. of Arragon, in 1282.

"Miracol parve ad ogni persona
Che ad una voce tutta la Cicilia
Si rubellò dall' una all' altra nona,
Gridando, mora mora la famiglia
Di Carlo, mora mora gli franceschi,
E così ne tagliò ben otto miglia.
O quanto i forestier che giungon freschi
Nell' altrui terre, denno esser cortesi,
Fuggir lussuria e non esser maneschi."
Fazio degli Uberti, Dittamondo, lib. ii., cap. 39.

[9] *Desperate make.*—"Accuora." Monti, in his "Proposta," construes this "afflicts." Vellutello's interpretation of it, which is "makes desperate," appears to be nearer the mark.

[10] *My brother's foresight.*—He seems to tax his brother Robert with employing necessitous and greedy Catalonians to administer the affairs of his kingdom.

He had been warier, that the greedy want
Of Catalonia might not work his bale.
And truly need there is that he forecast,
Or other for him, lest more freight be laid
On his already over-laden bark.
Nature in him, from bounty fallen to thrift,
Would ask the guard of braver arms, than such
As only care to have their coffers fill'd."

"My liege! it doth enhance the joy thy words
Infuse into me, mighty as it is,
To think my gladness manifest to thee,
As to myself, who own it, when thou look'st
Into the source and limit of all good,
There, where thou markest that which thou dost speak,
Thence prized of me the more. Glad thou hast made me:
Now make intelligent, clearing the doubt
Thy speech hath raised in me; for much I muse,
How bitter can spring up,[1] when sweet is sown."

I thus inquiring; he forthwith replied:
"If I have power to show one truth, soon that
Shall face thee, which thy questioning declares
Behind thee now conceal'd. The Good,[2] that guides
And blessed makes this realm which thou dost mount,
Ordains its providence to be the virtue
In these great bodies: nor the natures only
The all-perfect mind provides for, but with them
That which preserves them too; for nought, that lies
Within the range of that unerring bow,
But is as level with the destined aim,
As ever mark to arrow's point opposed.
Were it not thus, these heavens thou dost visit,
Would their effect so work, it would not be

---

[1] *How bitter can spring up.*—"How a covetous son can spring from a liberal father." Yet that father has himself been accused of avarice in the "Purgatory," canto xx. 78; though his general character was that of a bounteous prince.

[2] *The Good.*—The Supreme Being uses these spheres as the intelligent instruments of His providence in the conduct of terrestrial natures; so that these natures cannot but be conducted aright, unless these heavenly bodies should themselves fail from not having been made perfect at first, or the Creator of them should fail. To this Dante replies, that nature, he is satisfied, thus directed must do her part. Charles Martel then reminds him that he had learned from Aristotle, that human society requires a variety of conditions, and consequently a variety of qualifications in its members. Accordingly, men, he concludes, are born with different powers and capacities, caused by the influence of the heavenly bodies at the time of their nativity; on which influence, and not on their parents, those powers and capacities depend. Having thus resolved the question proposed, Charles Martel adds, by way of corollary, that the want of observing their natural bent in the destination of men to their several offices in life, is the occasion of much of the disorder that prevails in the world.

Art, but destruction; and this may not chance,
If the intellectual powers, that move these stars,
Fail not, and who, first faulty made them, fail.
Wilt thou this truth more clearly evidenced?"

To whom I thus: "It is enough: no fear,
I see, lest nature in her part should tire."

He straight rejoin'd: "Say, were it worse for man,
If he lived not in fellowship on earth?"

"Yea," answer'd I; "nor here a reason needs."

"And may that be, if different estates
Grow not of different duties in your life?
Consult your teacher,[1] and he tells you 'no.'"

Thus did he come, deducing to this point,
And then concluded: "For this cause behoves,
The roots, from whence your operations come,
Must differ. Therefore one is Solon born;
Another, Xerxes; and Melchisedec
A third; and he a fourth, whose airy voyage
Cost him his son.[2] In her circuitous course,
Nature, that is the seal to mortal wax,
Doth well her art, but no distinction owns
'Twixt one or other household. Hence befalls
That Esau is so wide of Jacob:[3] hence
Quirinus[4] of so base a father springs,
He dates from Mars his lineage. Were it not
That Providence celestial overruled,
Nature, in generation, must the path
Traced by the generator still pursue
Unswervingly. Thus place I in thy sight
That, which was late behind thee. But, in sign

---

[1] *Consult your teacher.*—Aristotle, ἐπεὶ ἐξ ἀνομοίων ἡ πόλις, κ. τ. λ., "De Rep.," lib. iii., cap. 4. "Since a state is made up of members differing from one another (for even as an animal, in the first instance, consists of soul and body; and the soul, of reason and desire; and a family, of man and woman; and property, of master and slave; in like manner a state consists both of all these, and besides these of other dissimilar kinds), it necessarily follows, that the excellence of all the members of the state cannot be one and the same."

[2] *Whose airy voyage cost him his son.*—Dædalus.

[3] *Esau is so wide of Jacob.*—Gen. xxv. 22. Venturi blames our poet for selecting an instance, which, as that commentator says, proves the direct contrary of that which he intended, as they were born under the same ascendant; and, therefore, if the stars had any influence, the two brothers should have been born with the same temperament and disposition. This objection is well answered by Lombardi, who quotes a passage from Roger Bacon, to show that the smallest diversity of place was held to make a diversity in the influence of the heavenly bodies, so as to occasion an entire discrepancy even between children in the same womb. It must be recollected, that whatever power may be attributed to the stars by our poet, he does not suppose it to put any constraint on the freedom of the human will; so that, chimerical as his opinion appears to us, it was, in a moral point of view at least, harmless.

[4] *Quirinus.*—Romulus, born of so obscure a father, that his parentage was attributed to Mars.

Of more affection for thee, 'tis my will
Thou wear this corollary. Nature ever,
Finding discordant fortune, like all seed
Out of its proper climate, thrives but ill.
And were the world below content to mark
And work on the foundation nature lays,
It would not lack supply of excellence.
But ye perversely to religion strain
Him, who was born to gird on him the sword,
And of the fluent phraseman make your king:
Therefore[1] your steps have wander'd from the path."

---

[1] *Therefore.*—" The wisdom of God hath divided the genius of men according to the different affairs of the world; and varied their inclinations according to the variety of actions to be performed therein. Which they who consider not, rudely rushing upon professions and ways of life unequal to their natures, dishonour not only themselves and their functions, but pervert the harmony of the whole world."—*Brown, on Vulgar Errors,* b. i., ch. 5.

CANTO IX.

ARGUMENT.

The next spirit, who converses with our Poet in the planet Venus, is the amorous Cunizza. To her succeeds Folco, or Folques, the Provençal bard, who declares that the soul of Rahab the harlot is there also; and then, blaming the Pope for his neglect of the Holy Land, prognosticates some reverse to the Papal power.

AFTER solution of my doubt, thy Charles,
O fair Clemenza,[1] of the treachery[2] spake,
That must befall his seed: but, "Tell it not,"
Said he, "and let the destined years come round."
Nor may I tell thee more, save that the meed
Of sorrow well-deserved shall quit your wrongs.
 And now the visage of that saintly light[3]
Was to the sun, that fills it, turn'd again,
As to the good, whose plenitude of bliss
Sufficeth all. O ye misguided souls!
Infatuate, who from such a good estrange
Your hearts, and bend your gaze on vanity,
Alas for you!—And lo! toward me, next
Another of those splendent forms approach'd,
That, by its outward brightening, testified
The will it had to pleasure me. The eyes
Of Beatrice, resting, as before,
Firmly upon me, manifested forth
Approval of my wish. "And O," I cried,
"Blest spirit! quickly be my will perform'd;
And prove thou to me,[4] that my inmost thoughts
I can reflect on thee." Thereat the light,
That yet was new to me, from the recess,
Where it before was singing, thus began,
As one who joys in kindness; "In that part[5]

---

[1] *O fair Clemenza.*—Daughter of Charles Martel, and second wife of Louis X. of France.
[2] *The treachery.*—He alludes to the occupation of the kingdom of Sicily by Robert, in exclusion of his brother's son Carobert, or Charles Robert, the rightful heir. See G. Villani, lib. viii., c. cxii.
[3] *That saintly light.*—Charles Martel.
[4] *Prove thou to me.*—The thoughts of all created minds being seen by the Deity, and all that is in the Deity being the object of vision to beatified spirits, such spirits must consequently see the thoughts of all created minds. Dante therefore requests of the spirit, who now approaches him, a proof of this truth with regard to his own thoughts. See v. 70.
[5] *In that part.*—Between Rialto in the Venetian territory, and the sources of the rivers Brenta and Piave, is situated a castle called Romano, the birthplace of the famous tyrant Ezzolino or Azzolino, the brother of Cunizza, who is now speaking. The tyrant we have seen in "the river of blood," "Hell," canto xii., v. 110.

Of the depraved Italian land, which lies
Between Rialto and the fountain-springs
Of Brenta and of Piava, there doth rise,
But to no lofty eminence, a hill,
From whence erewhile a firebrand did descend,
That sorely shent the region. From one root
I and it sprang: my name on earth Cunizza:[1]
And here I glitter, for that by its light
This star o'ercame me. Yet I nought repine,[2]
Nor grude myself the cause of this my lot:
Which haply vulgar hearts can scarce conceive.

"This[3] jewel, that is next me in our heaven,
Lustrous and costly, great renown hath left,
And not to perish, ere these hundred years
Five times[4] absolve their round. Consider thou,
If to excel be worthy man's endeavour,
When such life may attend the first.[5] Yet they
Care not for this, the crowd[6] that now are girt
By Adice and Tagliamento, still
Impenitent, though scourged. The hour is near[7]
When for their stubbornness, at Padua's marsh
The water shall be changed, that laves Vicenza.
And where Cagnano meets with Sile, one[8]

---

[1] *Cunizza.*—The adventures of Cunizza, overcome by the influence of her star, are related by the chronicler Rolandino of Padua, lib. i., c. 3, in Muratori, "Rerum Italicarum Scriptores," tom. viii., p. 173. She eloped from her first husband, Richard of St. Boniface, in the company of Sordello (see "Purgatory," canto vi. and vii.), with whom she is supposed to have cohabited before her marriage: then lived with a soldier of Trevigi, whose wife was living at the same time in the same city; and on his being murdered by her brother the tyrant, was by her brother married to a nobleman of Braganzo: lastly, when he also had fallen by the same hand, she, after her brother's death, was again wedded in Verona.

[2] *Yet I nought repine.*—"I am not dissatisfied that I am not allotted a higher place."

[3] *This.*—Folco of Genoa, a celebrated Provençal poet, commonly termed Folques of Marseilles, of which place he was perhaps bishop. Many errors of Nostradamus concerning him, which have been followed by Crescimbeni, Quadrio, and Millot, are detected by the diligence of Tiraboschi, Mr. Mathias's edit., v. i., p. 18. All that appears certain is what we are told in this canto, that he was of Genoa; and by Petrarch, in the "Triumph of Love," c. iv., that he was better known by the appellation he derived from Marseilles, and at last assumed the religious habit. One of his verses is cited by Dante, "De Vulgari Eloquentia," lib. iii., c. 6.

[4] *Ere these hundred years five times.*—The five hundred years are elapsed; and unless the Provençal MSS. should be brought to light, the poetical reputation of Folco must rest on the mention made of him by the more fortunate Italians. What I scarcely ventured to hope at the time this note was written, has been accomplished by the great learning and diligence of M. Raynouard. See his "Choix des Poésies des Troubadours" and "Lexique Roman," in which Folques and his Provençal brethren are awakened into the second life augured to them by our poet.

[5] *When such life may attend the first.*—When the mortal life of man may be attended by so lasting and glorious a memory, which is a kind of second life.

[6] *The crowd.*—The people who inhabited the tract of country bounded by the river Tagliamento to the east and Adice to the west.

[7] *The hour is near.*—Cunizza foretells the defeat of Giacopo da Carrara and the Paduans, by Can Grande, at Vicenza, on the 18th September, 1314. See G. Villani, lib. ix., cap. lxii.

[8] *One.*—She predicts also the fate of Riccardo da Camino, who is said to have been murdered at Trevigi (where the rivers Sile and Cagnano meet), while he was engaged in playing at chess.

Lords it, and bears his head aloft, for whom
The web¹ is now a-warping. Feltro² too
Shall sorrow for its godless shepherd's fault,
Of so deep stain, that never, for the like,
Was Malta's³ bar unclosed. Too large should be
The skillet⁴ that would hold Ferrara's blood,
And wearied he, who ounce by ounce would weigh it,
To which this priest,⁵ in show of party-zeal,
Courteous will give; nor will the gift ill suit
The country's custom. We descry⁶ above
Mirrors, ye call them thrones, from which to us
Reflected shine the judgments of our God:
Whence these our sayings we avouch for good."

She ended; and appear'd on other thoughts
Intent, re-entering on the wheel she late
Had left. That other joyance⁷ meanwhile wax'd
A thing to marvel at,⁸ in splendour glowing,
Like choicest ruby⁹ stricken by the sun.
For, in that upper clime, effulgence¹⁰ comes
Of gladness, as here laughter: and below,
As the mind saddens, murkier grows the shade

"God seeth all: and in him is thy sight,"
Said I, "blest spirit! Therefore will of his
Cannot to thee be dark. Why then delays
Thy voice to satisfy my wish untold:
That voice, which joins the inexpressive song,

---

¹ *The web.*—The net, or snare, into which he is destined to fall.

² *Feltro.*—The Bishop of Feltro having received a number of fugitives from Ferrara, who were in opposition to the Pope, under a promise of protection, afterwards gave them up; so that they were re-conducted to that city, and the greater part of them there put to death.

³ *Malta's.*—A tower, either in the citadel of Padua, which, under the tyranny of Ezzolino, had been "with many a foul and midnight murder fed," or (as some say) near a river of the same name, that falls into the lake of Bolsena, in which the Pope was accustomed to imprison such as had been guilty of an irremissible sin.

⁴ *The skillet.*—The blood shed could not be contained in such a vessel if it were of the usual size.

⁵ *This priest.*—The bishop who, to show himself a zealous partisan of the Pope, had committed the abovementioned act of treachery. The commentators are not agreed as to the name of this faithless prelate. Troya calls him Alessandra Novello, and relates the circumstances at full. "Veltro Allegorico," p. 139.

⁶ *We descry.*—"We behold the things that we predict, in the mirrors of eternal truth."

⁷ *That other joyance.*—Folco.

⁸ *A thing to marvel at.*—"Preclara cosa." A Latinism, according to Venturi; but the word "preclara" had been already naturalised by Guido Guinicelli—

"Oro ed argento e ricche gioje preclare."

See the sonnet, of which a version has been given in a note to "Purgatory," canto xi, v. 96.

⁹ *Choicest ruby.*—"Balascio."

"No saphire in Inde no rube rich of grace
There lacked then, nor emeraude so green,
Bales."

Chaucer, The Court of Love.

Mr. Tyrwhitt—I should suppose erroneously, as to the sense at least intended by Chaucer—calls it "a sort of bastard ruby."

¹⁰ *Effulgence.*—As joy is expressed by laughter on earth, so is it by an increase of splendour in Paradise; and, on the contrary, grief is betokened in Hell by augmented darkness.

Pastime of heaven, the which those ardours sing,
That cowl them with six shadowing wings[1] outspread?
I would not wait thy asking, wert thou known
To me, as thoroughly I to thee am known

He, forthwith answering, thus his words began:
" The valley of waters,[2] widest next to that[3]
Which doth the earth engarland, shapes its course,
Between discordant shores,[4] against the sun
Inward so far, it makes meridian[5] there,
Where was before the horizon. Of that vale
Dwelt I upon the shore, 'twixt Ebro's stream
And Macra's,[6] that divides with passage brief
Genoan bounds from Tuscan. East and west
Are nearly one to Begga[7] and my land
Whose haven[8] erst was with its own blood warm.
Who knew my name, were wont to call me Folco;
And I did bear impression of this heaven,[9]
That now bears mine: for not with fiercer flame
Glow'd Belus' daughter,[10] injuring alike
Sichæus and Creusa, than did I,
Long as it suited the unripen'd down
That fledged my cheek; nor she of Rhodope,[11]
That was beguiled of Demophoon;
Nor Jove's son,[12] when the charms of Iole
Were shrined within his heart. And yet there bides
No sorrowful repentance here, but mirth,
Not for the fault (that doth not come to mind),

---

[1] *Six shadowing wings.*—" Above it stood the seraphims: each one had six wings."—Isa. vi. 2. " Ante majestatis ejus gloriam cherubim senas habentes alas semper adstantes non cessant clamare, sanctus, sanctus, sanctus."—*Alberici Visio*, § 39.

" Six wings he wore to shade
His lineaments divine."
Milton, *Paradise Lost*, b. v. 278.

[2] *The valley of waters.*—The Mediterranean Sea.

[3] *That.*—The great ocean.

[4] *Discordant shores.*—Europe and Africa.

[5] *Meridian.*—Extending to the east, the Mediterranean at last reaches the coast of Palestine, which is on its horizon when it enters the Straits of Gibraltar. " Wherever a man is," says Vellutello, " there he has, above his head, his own particular meridian circle."

[6] *'Twixt Ebro's stream and Macra's.*—Ebro, a river to the west, and Macra, to the east of Genoa, where Folco was born. Others think that Marseilles and not Genoa is here described; and then Ebro must be understood of the river in Spain.

[7] *Begga.*—A place in Africa.

[8] *Whose haven.*—Alluding to the terrible slaughter of the Genoese made by the Saracens in 936; for which event Vellutello refers to the history of Augustino Giustiniani. Those who conceive that our poet speaks of Marseilles, suppose the slaughter of its inhabitants made in the time of Julius Cæsar to be alluded to. It must, however, have been Genoa, as that place, and not Marseilles, lies opposite to Buggea, or Begga, on the African coast. Fazio degli Uberti describes Buggea as looking towards Majorca:

" Vidi Buggea che vè di grande loda;
Questa nel mare Maiorica guata."
Dittamondo, l. v., c. 6.

[9] *This heaven.*—The planet Venus, by which Folco declares himself to have been formerly influenced.

[10] *Belus' daughter.*—Dido.

[11] *She of Rhodope.*—Phyllis.

[12] *Jove's son.*—Hercules.

But for the virtue, whose o'erruling sway
And providence have wrought thus quaintly. Here
The skill is look'd into, that fashioneth
With such effectual working,[1] and the good
Discern'd, accruing to the lower world[2]
From this above. But fully to content
Thy wishes all that in this sphere have birth,
Demands my further parle. Inquire thou wouldst,
Who of this light is denizen, that here
Beside me sparkles, as the sunbeam doth
On the clear wave. Know then, the soul of Rahab[3]
Is in that gladsome harbour; to our tribe
United, and the foremost rank assign'd.
She to this heaven,[4] at which the shadow ends
Of your sublunar world, was taken up,
First, in Christ's triumph, of all souls redeem'd:
For well behoved, that, in some part of heaven,
She should remain a trophy, to declare
The mighty conquest won with either palm;[5]
For that she favour'd first the high exploit
Of Joshua on the Holy Land, whereof
The Pope[6] recks little now. Thy city, plant
Of him,[7] that on his Maker turn'd the back,
And of whose envying so much woe hath sprung,
Engenders and expands the cursed flower,[8]
That hath made wander both the sheep and lambs,
Turning the shepherd to a wolf. For this;
The gospel and great teachers laid aside,
The decretals,[9] as their stuft margins show,

---

[1] *With such effectual working.*—All the editions, except the Nidobeatina, do not, as Lombardi affirms, read " contanto ; " for Vellutello's of 1544 is certainly one exception.

[2] *To the lower world.*—I have altered my former translation here, in compliance with a reading adopted by Lombardi from the Nidobeatina: "Perche 'l mondo" instead of "Perche al mondo." But the passage is still obscure.

[3] *Rahab.*—Heb. xi. 31.

[4] *This heaven.*—"This planet of Venus, at which the shadow of the earth ends, as Ptolemy writes in his 'Almagest.'"—*Vellutello.*

[5] *With either palm.*—By both his hands nailed to the cross.

[6] *The Pope.*—" Who cares not that the Holy Land is in the possession of the Saracens." See also canto xv. 136.

" Ite superbi, O miseri Christiani
Consumando l'un l'altro ; e non vi caglia
Che 'l sepolcro di Cristo è in man di cani."
Petrarca, *Trionfo della Fama,* cap. ii.

[7] *Of him.*—Of Satan.

[8] *The cursed flower.*—The coin of Florence, called the floren ; the covetous desire of which has excited the Pope to so much evil.

[9] *The decretals.*—The canon law. So in the " De Monarchiâ," lib. iii., p. 137 ' " There are also a third set, whom they call Decretalists. These, alike ignorant of theology and philosophy, relying wholly on their decretals (which I indeed esteem not unworthy of reverence), in the hope, I suppose, of obtaining for

Are the sole study. Pope and Cardinals,
Intent on these, ne'er journey but in thought
To Nazareth, where Gabriel oped his wings.
Yet it may chance, ere long, the Vatican,[1]
And other most selected parts of Rome,
That were the grave of Peter's soldiery,
Shall be deliver'd from the adulterous bond."

---

them a paramount influence, derogate from the authority of the empire. Nor is this to be wondered at, when I have heard one of them saying, and impudently maintaining, that traditions are the foundation of the faith of the church." He proceeds to confute this opinion, and concludes " that the church does not derive its authority from traditions, but traditions from the church:" " necesse est, ut non ecclesiæ a traditionibus, sed ab ecclesiâ traditionibus accedat authoritas." In accordance with the sentiments of Dante on this point, the Church of England has framed that article, so well worthy of being duly considered and carried into practice, which begins: " It is not necessary that traditions and ceremonies be in all places one, or utterly alike ; for at all times they have been divers, and may be changed according to the diversity of countries, times, and men's manners, so that nothing be ordained against God's word."—Article xxxiv.

[1] *The Vatican.*—He alludes either to the death of Pope Boniface VIII., or, as Venturi supposes, to the coming of the Emperor Henry VII. into Italy ; or else, according to the yet more probable conjecture of Lombardi, to the transfer of the Holy See from Rome to Avignon, which took place in the pontificate of Clement V.

CANTO X.

ARGUMENT.

Their next ascent carries them into the sun, which is the fourth heaven. Here they are encompassed with a wreath of blessed spirits, twelve in number. Thomas Aquinas, who is one of these, declares the names and endowments of the rest.

LOOKING into his first-born with the love
Which breathes from both eternal, the first Might
Ineffable, wherever eye or mind
Can roam, hath in such order all disposed,
As none may see and fail to enjoy. Raise, then,
O reader! to the lofty wheels, with me,
Thy ken directed to the point,[1] whereat
One motion strikes on the other. There begin
Thy wonder of the mighty Architect,
Who loves his work so inwardly, his eye
Doth ever watch it. See, how thence oblique[2]
Brancheth the circle, where the planets roll
To pour their wished influence on the world;
Whose path not bending thus, in heaven above[3]
Much virtue would be lost, and here on earth
All power well nigh extinct; or, from direct
Were its departure distant more or less,
I' the universal order, great defect
Must, both in heaven and here beneath, ensue.

Now rest thee, reader! on thy bench, and muse
Anticipative of the feast to come;
So shall delight make thee not feel thy toil.
Lo! I have set before thee; for thyself
Feed now: the matter I indite, henceforth
Demands entire my thought. Join'd with the part,[4]
Which late we told of, the great minister[5]
Of nature, that upon the world imprints

---

[1] *The point.*—"To that part of heaven," as Venturi explains it, "in which the equinoctial circle and the zodiac intersect each other, where the common motion of the heavens from east to west may be said to strike with greatest force against the motion proper to the planets; and this repercussion, as it were, is here the strongest, because the velocity of each is increased to the utmost by their respective distance from the poles. Such at least is the system of Dante."

[2] *Oblique.*—The zodiac.

[3] *In heaven above.*—If the planets did not preserve that order in which they move, they would not receive nor transmit their due influences; and if the zodiac were not thus oblique—if towards the north it either passed or went short of the tropic of Cancer, or else towards the south it passed or went short of the tropic of Capricorn—it would not divide the seasons as it now does.

[4] *The part.*—The above-mentioned intersection of the equinoctial circle and the zodiac.

[5] *Minister.*—The sun.

The virtue of the heaven, and doles out
Time for us with his beam, went circling on
Along the spires,[1] where[2] each hour sooner comes;
And I was with him, weetless of ascent,
But as a man,[3] that weets him come, ere thinking.

For Beatrice, she who passeth on
So suddenly from good to better, time
Counts not the act, oh then how great must needs
Have been her brightness! What there was i' th' sun
(Where I had entered), not through change of hue,
But light transparent—did I summon up
Genius, art, practice—I might not so speak,
It should be e'er imagined: yet believed
It may be, and the sight be justly craved.
And if our fantasy fail of such height,
What marvel, since no eye above the sun
Hath ever travel'd? Such are they dwell here,
Fourth family of the Omnipotent Sire,[4]
Who of his spirit and of his offspring[5] shows;
And holds them still enraptured with the view.
And thus to me Beatrice: "Thank, oh thank
The Sun of angels, him, who by his grace
To this perceptible hath lifted thee."

Never was heart in such devotion bound,
And with complacency so absolute
Disposed to render up itself to God,
As mine was at those words: and so entire
The love for Him, that held me, it eclipsed
Beatrice in oblivion. Nought displeased
Was she, but smiled thereat so joyously,
That of her laughing eyes the radiance brake
And scattered my collected mind abroad.

Then saw I a bright band, in liveliness
Surpassing, who themselves did make the crown,
And us their centre: yet more sweet in voice,

---

[1] *Along the spires.*—According to our poet's system, as the earth is motionless, the sun passes, by a spiral motion, from one tropic to the other.

[2] *Where.*—In which the sun rises every day earlier after the vernal equinox.

[3] *But as a man.*—That is, he was quite insensible of it.

[4] *Such are they dwell here, fourth family of the Omnipotent Sire.*—The inhabitants of the sun, the fourth planet.

[5] *Of his spirit and of his offspring.*—The procession of the third, and the generation of the second person in the Trinity.

Than, in their visage, beaming. Cinctured thus,
Sometime Latona's daughter we behold,
When the impregnate air retains the thread
That weaves her zone. In the celestial court,
Whence I return, are many jewels found,
So dear and beautiful, they cannot brook
Transporting from that realm: and of these lights
Such was the song.[1] Who doth not prune his wing
To soar up thither, let him[2] look from thence
For tidings from the dumb. When, singing thus,
Those burning suns had circled round us thrice,
As nearest stars around the fixed pole;
Then seem'd they like to ladies, from the dance
Not ceasing, but suspense, in silent pause,
Listening, till they have caught the strain anew:
Suspended so they stood: and, from within,
Thus heard I one, who spake: "Since with its beam
The grace, whence true love lighteth first his flame
That after doth increase by loving, shines
So multiplied in thee, it leads thee up
Along this ladder, down whose hallow'd steps
None e'er descend, and mount them not again;
Who from his phial should refuse thee wine
To slake thy thirst, no less constrained[3] were,
Than water flowing not unto the sea.
Thou fain wouldst hear, what plants are these, that bloom
In the bright garland, which, admiring, girds
This fair dame round, who strengthens thee for heaven.
I, then,[4] was of the lambs, that Dominic
Leads, for his saintly flock, along the way
Where well they thrive, not swoln with vanity.
He, nearest on my right hand, brother was,
And master to me: Albert of Cologne.[5]

---

[1] *Such was the song.*—The song of these spirits was ineffable. It was like a jewel so highly prized, that the exportation of it to another country is prohibited by law.

[2] *Let him.*—Let him not expect any intelligence at all of that place, for it surpasses description.

[3] *No less constrained.*—"The rivers might as easily cease to flow towards the sea, as we could deny thee thy request."

[4] *I, then.*—"I was of the Dominican order."

[5] *Albert of Cologne.*—Albertus Magnus was born at Lauingen, in Thuringia, in 1193, and studied at Paris and at Padua; at the latter of which places he entered into the Dominican order. He then taught theology in various parts of Germany, and particularly at Cologne. Thomas Aquinas was his favourite pupil. In 1260, he reluctantly accepted the bishopric of Ratisbon, and in two years after resigned it, and returned to his cell in Cologne, where the remainder of his life was passed in superintending the school, and in composing his voluminous works on divinity and natural science. He died in 1280. The absurd imputation of his having dealt in the magical art is well known; and his biographers take some pains to

Is this; and, of Aquinum, Thomas[1] I.
If thou of all the rest wouldst be assured,
Let thine eye, waiting on the words I speak,
In circuit journey round the blessed wreath.
That next resplendence issues from the smile
Of Gratian,[2] who to either forum[3] lent
Such help, as favour wins in Paradise.
The other, nearest, who adorns our quire,
Was Peter,[4] he that with the widow gave[5]
To holy church his treasure. The fifth light,[6]
Goodliest of all, is by such love inspired,
That all your world craves tidings of his doom :[7]
Within, there is the lofty light, endow'd
With sapience so profound, if truth be truth,
That with a ken of such wide amplitude
No second hath arisen. Next behold
That taper's radiance,[8] to whose view was shown,
Clearliest, the nature and the ministry
Angelical, while yet in flesh it dwelt.
In the other little light serenely smiles
That pleader[9] for the Christian temples, he,

---

clear him of it. "Scriptores Ordinis Prædicatorum," by Quetif and Echard, Lut., Par., 1719, fol., tom. i., p. 162. Frezzi places Albertus Magnus next in rank to Aristotle:
"Alberto Magno è dopo lui 'l secondo:
Egli supplì li membri, e 'l vestimento
Alla Filosofia in questo mondo."
     Il Quadriregio, lib. iv., cap. 9.
[1] *Of Aquinum, Thomas.*—Thomas Aquinas, of whom Bucer is reported to have said, "Take but Thomas away, and I will overturn the Church of Rome ; " and whom Hooker terms "the greatest among the school divines" ("Ecclesiastical Polity," b. iii., § 9), was born of noble parents, who anxiously but vainly endeavoured to divert him from a life of celibacy and study. He died in 1274, at the age of forty-seven. Echard and Quetif, ibid., p. 271. See also "Purgatory," canto xx., v. 67. A modern French writer has collected some particulars relating to the influence which the writings of Thomas Aquinas and Buonaventura had on the opinions of Dante. See the third part of Ozanam's "Dante et la Philosophie Catholique au treizième siècle," 8vo, Par., 1839.
[2] *Gratian.*—"Gratian, a Benedictine monk belonging to the Convent of St. Felix and Nabor, at Bologna, and by birth a Tuscan, composed, about the year 1130, for the use of the schools, an abridgment or epitome of canon law, drawn from the letters of the pontiffs, the decrees of councils, and the writings of the ancient doctors."—*Maclaine's Mosheim*, v. iii., cent. xii., part ii., cap. i., § 6.
[3] *To either forum.*—"By reconciling," as Venturi explains it, "the civil with the canon law."
[4] *Peter.*—" Pietro Lombardo was of obscure origin, nor is the place of his birth in Lombardy ascertained. With a recommendation from the Bishop of Lucca to St. Bernard, he went into France to continue his studies ; and for that purpose remained some time at Rheims, whence he afterwards proceeded to Paris. Here his reputation was so great, that Philip, brother of Louis VII., being chosen Bishop of Paris, resigned that dignity to Pietro, whose pupil he had been. He held his bishopric only one year, and died 1160. His 'Liber Sententiarum' is highly esteemed. It contains a system of scholastic theology, so much more complete than any which had been yet seen, that it may be deemed an original work."—*Tiraboschi, Storia della Lett. Ital.*, tom. iii., lib. iv., cap. ii.
[5] *That with the widow gave.*—This alludes to the beginning of the " Liber Sententiarum," where Peter says: " Cupiens aliquid de penuriâ ac tenuitate nostrâ cum pauperculâ in gazophylacium domini mittere," &c.
[6] *The fifth light.*—Solomon.
[7] *His doom.*—It was a common question, it seems, whether Solomon were saved or no.
[8] *That taper's radiance.*—St. Dionysius, the Areopagite. "The famous Grecian fanatic, who gave himself out for Dionysius the Areopagite, disciple of St. Paul, and who, under the protection of this venerable name, gave laws and instructions to those that were desirous of raising their souls above all human things, in order to unite them to their great source by sublime contemplation, lived most probably in this century (the fourth) ; though some place him before, others after, the present period."—*Maclaine's Mosheim*, v. i., cent. iv., p. ii., c. iii., § 12.
[9] *That pleader.*—In the fifth century, Paulus Orosius "acquired a considerable degree of reputation by the

Who did provide Augustin of his lore.
Now, if thy mind's eye pass from light to light,
Upon my praises following, of the eighth[1]
Thy thirst is next. The saintly soul, that shows
The world's deceitfulness, to all who hear him,
Is, with the sight of all the good that is,
Blest there. The limbs, whence it was driven, lie
Down in Cieldauro;[2] and from martyrdom
And exile came it here. Lo! further on,
Where flames the arduous spirit of Isidore;[3]
Of Bede;[4] and Richard,[5] more than man, erewhile,
In deep discernment. Lastly this, from whom
Thy look on me reverteth, was the beam
Of one, whose spirit, on high musings bent,
Rebuked the lingering tardiness of death.
It is the eternal light of Sigebert,[6]
Who escaped not envy, when of truth he argued,
Reading in the straw-litter'd street."[7] Forthwith,
As clock, that calleth up the spouse of God[8]
To win her bridegroom's love at matin's hour,
Each part of other fitly drawn and urged,
Sends out a tinkling sound, of note so sweet,
Affection springs in well-disposed breast;
Thus saw I move the glorious wheel; thus heard
Voice answering voice, so musical and soft,
It can be known but where day endless shines.

History he wrote to refute the cavils of the Pagans against Christianity, and by his books against the Pelagians and Priscillianists."—*Ibid.*, v. ii., cent. v., p. ii., c. ii., § 11. A similar train of argument was pursued by Augustine, in his book "De Civitate Dei." Orosius is classed by Dante, in his treatise "De Vulgari Eloquentia," lib. ii., cap. vi., as one of his favourite authors, among those "qui usi sunt altissimas prosas"—"who have written prose with the greatest loftiness of style." The others are Cicero, Livy, Pliny, and Frontinus. Some commentators, with less probability, suppose that this seventh spirit is St. Ambrose, and not Orosius.

[1] *The eighth.*—"Boëtius, whose book "De Consolatione Philosophiæ" excited so much attention during the middle ages, was born, as Tiraboschi conjectures, about 470. "In 524 he was cruelly put to death by command of Theodoric, either on real or pretended suspicion of his being engaged in a conspiracy."—*Della Lett. Ital.*, tom. iii., lib. i., cap. iv.

[2] *Cieldauro.*—Boëtius was buried at Pavia, in the monastery of St. Pietro in Ciel d'oro.

[3] *Isidore.*—He was Archbishop of Seville during forty years, and died in 635. See Mariana, "Hist.," lib. vi., cap. vii. Mosheim, whose critical opinions in general must be taken with some allowance, observes, that "his grammatical, theological, and historical productions discover more learning and pedantry than judgment and taste."

[4] *Bede.*—Bede, whose virtues obtained him the appellation of the Venerable, was born in 672, at Wearmouth and Jarrow, in the bishopric of Durham, and died in 735. Invited to Rome by Pope Sergius I., he preferred passing almost the whole of his life in the seclusion of a monastery. A catalogue of his numerous writings may be seen in Kippis's "Biographia Britannica," v. ii.

[5] *Richard.*—Richard of St. Victor, a native either of Scotland or Ireland, was canon and prior of the monastery of that name at Paris, and died in 1173. "He was at the head of the Mystics in this century; and his treatise, entitled the 'Mystical Ark,' which contains as it were the marrow of this kind of theology, was received with the greatest avidity."—*Maclaine's Mosheim*, v. iii., cent. xii., p. ii., c. ii., § 23.

[6] *Sigebert.*—"A monk of the abbey of Gemblours, who was in high repute at the end of the eleventh, and beginning of the twelfth century."—*Dict. de Moreri.*

[7] *The straw-litter'd street.*—The name of a street in Paris, the "Rue de Fouarre."

[8] *The spouse of God.*—The church.

CANTO XI.

ARGUMENT.

Thomas Aquinas enters at large into the life and character of St. Francis; and then solves one of two difficulties which he perceived to have risen in Dante's mind from what he had heard in the last canto.

O FOND anxiety of mortal men![1]
How vain and inconclusive arguments
Are those, which make thee beat thy wings below.
For statutes one, and one for aphorisms[2]
Was hunting; this the priesthood follow'd; that,
By force or sophistry, aspired to rule;
To rob, another; and another sought,
By civil business, wealth; one, moiling, lay
Tangled in net of sensual delight;
And one to wistless indolence resign'd;
What time from all these empty things escaped,
With Beatrice, I thus gloriously
Was raised aloft, and made the guest of heaven.
    They of the circle to that point, each one,
Where erst it was, had turn'd; and steady glow'd,
As candle in his socket. Then within
The lustre,[3] that erewhile bespake me, smiling
With merer gladness, heard I thus begin:
    "E'en as his beam illumes me, so I look
Into the eternal light, and clearly mark
Thy thoughts from whence they rise. Thou art in doubt,
And wouldst that I should bolt my words afresh
In such plain open phrase, as may be smooth
To thy perception, where I told thee late
That 'well they thrive;'[4] and that 'no second such[5]
Hath risen,' which no small distinction needs.
    "The Providence, that governeth the world,
In depth of counsel by created ken

---

[1] *O fond anxiety of mortal men.*—Lucretius, lib. ii. 14:
"O miseras hominum mentes! O pectora cæca!
Qualibus in tenebris vitæ, quantisque periclis
Degitur hoc ævi quodcunque est!"

[2] *Aphorisms.*—The study of medicine.
[3] *The lustre.*—The spirit of Thomas Aquinas.
[4] *That 'well they thrive.'*—See the last canto, v. 93.
[5] *'No second such.'*—See the last canto, v. 111.

Unfathomable, to the end that she,[1]
Who with loud cries was 'spoused in precious blood,
Might keep her footing towards her well-beloved,[2]
Safe in herself and constant unto him,
Hath two ordain'd, who should on either hand
In chief escort her : one,[3] seraphic all
In fervency ; for wisdom upon earth,
The other,[4] splendour of cherubic light.
I but of one will tell : he tells of both,
Who one commendeth, which of them soe'er
Be taken : for their deeds were to one end.

"Between Tupino,[5] and the wave that falls
From blest Ubaldo's chosen hill, there hangs
Rich slope of mountain high, whence heat and cold[6]
Are wafted through Perugia's eastern gate :
And Nocera with Gualdo, in its rear,
Mourn for their heavy yoke.[7] Upon that side,
Where it doth break its steepness most, arose
A sun upon the world, as duly this
From Ganges doth : therefore let none, who speak
Of that place, say Ascesi ; for its name
Were lamely so deliver'd : but the East,[8]
To call things rightly, be it henceforth styled.
He was not yet much distant from his rising,
When his good influence 'gan to bless the earth.
A dame,[9] to whom none openeth pleasure's gate
More than to death, was, 'gainst his father's will,[10]
His stripling choice : and he did make her his,
Before the spiritual court,[11] by nuptial bonds,
And in his father's sight : from day to day,
Then loved her more devoutly. She, bereaved

---

[1] *She.*—The church.
[2] *Her well-beloved.*—Jesus Christ.
[3] *One.*—St. Francis.
[4] *The other.*—St. Dominic.
[5] *Tupino.*—Thomas Aquinas proceeds to describe the birthplace of St. Francis, between Tupino, a rivulet near Assisi, or Ascesi, where the saint was born in 1182, and Chiasciò, a stream that rises in the mountain near Agobbio, chosen by St. Ubaldo for the place of his retirement.
[6] *Heat and cold.*—Cold from the snow, and heat from the reflection of the sun.
[7] *Yoke.*—Vellutello understands this of the vicinity of the *mountain* to Nocera and Gualdo ; and Venturi (as I have taken it) of the heavy impositions laid on those places by the Perugians ; for *giogo*, like the Latin *jugum*, will admit of either sense.
[8] *The East.*—"This is the east, and Juliet is the sun."—*Shakespeare*.
[9] *A dame.*—There is in the under church of St. Francis, at Assisi, a picture painted by Giotto from this subject. It is considered one of the artist's best works. See Kugler's "Hand-book of the History of Painting," translated by a lady, Lond., 1842, p. 48.
[10] *'Gainst his father's will.*—In opposition to the wishes of his natural father.
[11] *Before the spiritual court.*—He made a vow of poverty in the presence of the bishop and of his natural father.

Of her first husband,[1] slighted and obscure,
Thousand and hundred years and more, remain'd
Without a single suitor, till he came.
Nor aught avail'd, that, with Amyclas,[2] she
Was found unmoved at rumour of his voice,
Who shook the world: nor aught her constant boldness
Whereby with Christ she mounted on the cross,
When Mary stay'd beneath. But not to deal
Thus closely with thee longer, take at large
The lovers' titles—Poverty and Francis.
Their concord and glad looks, wonder and love,
And sweet regard gave birth to holy thoughts,
So much, that venerable Bernard[3] first
Did bare his feet, and, in pursuit of peace
So heavenly, ran, yet deem'd his footing slow.
O hidden riches! O prolific good!
Egidius[4] bares him next, and next Sylvester,[5]
And follow, both, the bridegroom: so the bride
Can please them. Thenceforth goes he on his way
The father and the master, with his spouse,
And with that family, whom now the cord[6]
Girt humbly: nor did abjectness of heart
Weigh down his eyelids, for that he was son
Of Pietro Bernardone,[7] and by men
In wondrous sort despised. But royally
His hard intention he to Innocent[8]
Set forth: and, from him, first received the seal
On his religion. Then, when numerous flock'd
The tribe of lowly ones, that traced *his* steps,
Whose marvellous life deservedly were sung
In heights empyreal; though Honorius'[9] hand

---

[1] *Her first husband.*—Christ.
[2] *Amyclas.*—Lucan makes Cæsar exclaim, on witnessing the secure poverty of the fisherman Amyclas:
"O vitæ tuta facultas
Pauperis, angustique lares! O munera nondum
Intellecta deûm! quibus hoc contingere templis,
Aut potuit muris, nullo trepidare tumultu,
Cæsareâ pulsante manu?"—*Pharsalia*, lib. v. 531.
"O happy poverty! thou greatest good
Bestow'd by heaven, but seldom understood!
Here nor the cruel spoiler seeks his prey,
Nor ruthless armies take their dreadful way."—*Rowe*.
A translation in prose of these lines is introduced by our poet in his "Convito," p. 170.

[3] *Bernard.*—Of Quintavalle, one of the lowers of the saint.
[4] *Egidius.*—The third of his disciples, w1 1262. His work, entitled "Verba Aur published in 1534, at Antwerp. See Luc dingus, "Annales Ordinis Minoris," p. 5.
[5] *Sylvester.*—Another of his earliest associ
[6] *Whom now the cord.*—St. Francis bound with a cord, in sign that he considered it ,as and that it required, like a beast, to be led by
[7] *Pietro Bernardone.*—A man in an humb of life at Assisi.
[8] *Innocent.*—Pope Innocent III.
[9] *Honorius.*—His successor Honorius I granted certain privileges to the Franciscans.

A second crown, to deck their Guardian's virtues,
Was by the eternal Spirit inwreathed : and when
He had, through thirst of martyrdom, stood up
In the proud Soldan's presence,[1] and there preach'd
Christ and his followers, but found the race
Unripen'd for conversion; back once more
He hasted (not to intermit his toil),
And reap'd Ausonian lands. On the hard rock,[2]
'Twixt Arno and the Tiber, he from Christ
Took the last signet,[3] which his limbs two years
Did carry. Then, the season come that he,
Who to such good had destined him, was pleased
To advance him to the meed, which he had earn'd
By his self-humbling ; to his brotherhood,
As their just heritage, he gave in charge
His dearest lady :[4] and enjoin'd their love
And faith to her ; and, from her bosom, will'd
His goodly spirit should move forth, returning
To its appointed kingdom ; nor would have
His body[5] laid upon another bier.

"Think now of one, who were a fit colleague
To keep the bark of Peter, in deep sea,
Helm'd to right point ; and such our Patriarch[6] was.
Therefore who follow him as he enjoins,
Thou mayst be certain, take good lading in.
But hunger of new viands tempts his flock ;[7]
So that they needs into strange pastures wide
Must spread them : and the more remote from him
The stragglers wander, so much more they come
Home, to the sheep-fold, destitute of milk.
There are of them, in truth, who fear their harm,
And to the shepherd cleave ; but these so few,
A little stuff may furnish out their cloaks.

"Now, if my words be clear ; if thou have ta'en
Good heed ; if that, which I have told, recall

---

[1] *In the proud Soldan's presence.*—The Soldan of Egypt, before whom St. Francis is said to have preached.
[2] *On the hard rock.*—The mountain Alverna in the Apennine.
[3] *The last signet.*—Alluding to the stigmata, or marks resembling the wounds of Christ, said to have been found on the saint's body.
[4] *His dearest lady.*—Poverty.
[5] *His body.*—He forbad any funeral pomp to be observed at his burial ; and, as it is said, ordered that his remains should be deposited in a place where criminals were executed and interred.
[6] *Our Patriarch.*—St. Dominic, to whose order Thomas Aquinas belonged.
[7] *His flock.*—The Dominicans.

To mind; thy wish may be in part fulfill'd:
For thou wilt see the plant from whence they split;[1]
And he shall see, who girds him, what that means,[2]
'That well they thrive, not swoln with vanity.'"

---

[1] *The plant from whence they split.*—"The rule of their order, which the Dominicans neglect to observe."

[2] *And he shall see, who girds him, what that means.*—Lombardi, after the Nidobeatina edition, together with four MSS., reads "il correggiar," or "il coregièr," which gives the sense that now stands in the text of this version. The Dominicans might be called "coreggieri," from their wearing a leathern girdle, as the Franciscans were called "cordiglieri," from their being girt with a cord. I had before followed the common reading, "il corregger;" and translated the line according to Venturi's interpretation of it: "Nor miss of the reproof which that implies."

CANTO XII.

ARGUMENT.

A second circle of glorified souls encompasses the first. Buonaventura, who is one of them, celebrates the praises of Saint Dominic, and informs Dante who the other eleven are that are in this second circle or garland.

SOON as its final word the blessed flame[1]
   Had raised for utterance, straight the holy mill[2]
Began to wheel; nor yet had once revolved,
Or e'er another, circling, compass'd it,
Motion to motion, song to song, conjoining;
Song, that as much our muses doth excel,
Our Syrens with their tuneful pipes, as ray
Of primal splendour doth its faint reflex.

   As when, if Juno bid her handmaid forth,
Two arches parallel, and trick'd alike,
Span the thin cloud, the outer taking birth
From that within (in manner of that voice[3]
Whom love did melt away, as sun the mist)
And they who gaze, presageful call to mind
The compact, made with Noah, of the world
No more to be o'erflow'd; about us thus,
Of sempiternal roses, bending, wreathed
Those garlands twain; and to the innermost
E'en thus the external answer'd. When the footing,
And other great festivity, of song,
And radiance, light with light accordant, each
Jocund and blythe, had at their pleasure still'd
(E'en as the eyes, by quick volition moved,
Are shut and raised together), from the heart

---

[1] *The blessed flame.*—Thomas Aquinas.
[2] *The holy mill.*—The circle of spirits.
[3] *In manner of that voice.*—One rainbow giving back the image of the other, as sound is reflected by Echo, that nymph, who was melted away by her fondness for Narcissus, as vapour is melted by the sun. The reader will observe in the text not only a second and third simile within the first, but two mythological and one sacred allusion bound up together with the whole. Even after this accumulation of imagery, the two circles of spirits, by whom Beatrice and Dante were encompassed, are by a bold figure termed two garlands of never-fading roses. Indeed, there is a fulness of splendour, even to prodigality, throughout the beginning of this canto.

Of one[1] amongst the new lights[2] moved a voice,
That made me seem[3] like needle to the star,
In turning to its whereabout;[4] and thus
Began: "The love,[5] that makes me beautiful,
Prompts me to tell of the other guide, for whom
Such good of mine is spoken. Where one is,
The other worthily should also be;
That as their warfare was alike, alike
Should be their glory. Slow, and full of doubt,
And with thin ranks, after its banner moved
The army of Christ (which it so dearly cost
To reappoint), when its imperial Head,
Who reigneth ever, for the drooping host
Did make provision, through grace alone,
And not through its deserving. As thou heard'st,[6]
Two champions to the succour of his spouse
He sent, who by their deeds and words might join
Again his scatter'd people. In that clime[7]
Where springs the pleasant west-wind to unfold
The fresh leaves, with which Europe sees herself
New-garmented; nor from those billows[8] far
Beyond whose chiding, after weary course,
The sun doth sometimes[9] hide him; safe abides
The happy Callaroga,[10] under guard
Of the great shield, wherein the lion lies
Subjected and supreme. And there was born
The loving minion of the Christian faith,[11]

---

[1] *One.*—St. Buonaventura, general of the Franciscan order, in which he effected some reformation; and one of the most profound divines of his age. "He refused the archbishopric of York, which was offered him by Clement IV., but afterwards was prevailed on to accept the bishopric of Albano and a cardinal's hat. He was born at Bagnoregio, or Bagnorea, in Tuscany, A.D. 1221, and died in 1274."—*Dict. Histor. par Chaudon et Delandine*, ed. Lyon, 1804.

[2] *Amongst the new lights.*—In the circle that had newly surrounded the first.

[3] *That made me seem.*—"That made me turn to it, as the magnetic needle does to the pole."

[4] *To its whereabout.*—"Al suo dove."

"The very stones prate of my whereabout."
  Shakespeare, Macbeth, act ii., sc. 1.

[5] *The love.*—By an act of mutual courtesy, Buonaventura, a Franciscan, is made to proclaim the praises of St. Dominic, as Thomas Aquinas, a Dominican, has celebrated those of St. Francis; and in like manner each blames the irregularities, not of the other's order, but of that to which himself belonged. Even Macchiavelli, no great friend to the church, attributes the revival of Christianity to the influence of these two saints. "Quanto alle Sette, si vede ancora queste rinovazioni esser necessarie, per l' essempio della nostra Religione, la quale, se non fusse stata ritirata verso il suo principio da San Francesco e da San Domenico, sarebbe al tutto spenta."—*Discorsi sopra la prima Deca di T. Livio*, lib. iii., c. 1. "As to sects, it is seen that these renovations are necessary, by the example of our religion, which, if it had not been drawn back to its principle by St. Francis and St. Dominic, would be entirely extinguished."

[6] *As thou heard'st.*—See the last canto, v. 33.

[7] *In that clime.*—Spain.

[8] *Those billows.*—The Atlantic.

[9] *Sometimes.*—During the summer solstice.

[10] *Callaroga.*—Between Osma and Aranda, in Old Castile designated by the royal coat of arms.

[11] *The loving minion of the Christian faith.*—Dominic was born April 5, 1170, and died August 6, 1221. His birthplace Callaroga; his father and mother's names, Felix and Joanna; his mother's dream; his name of Dominic, given him in consequence of a vision by a noble matron who stood sponsor to

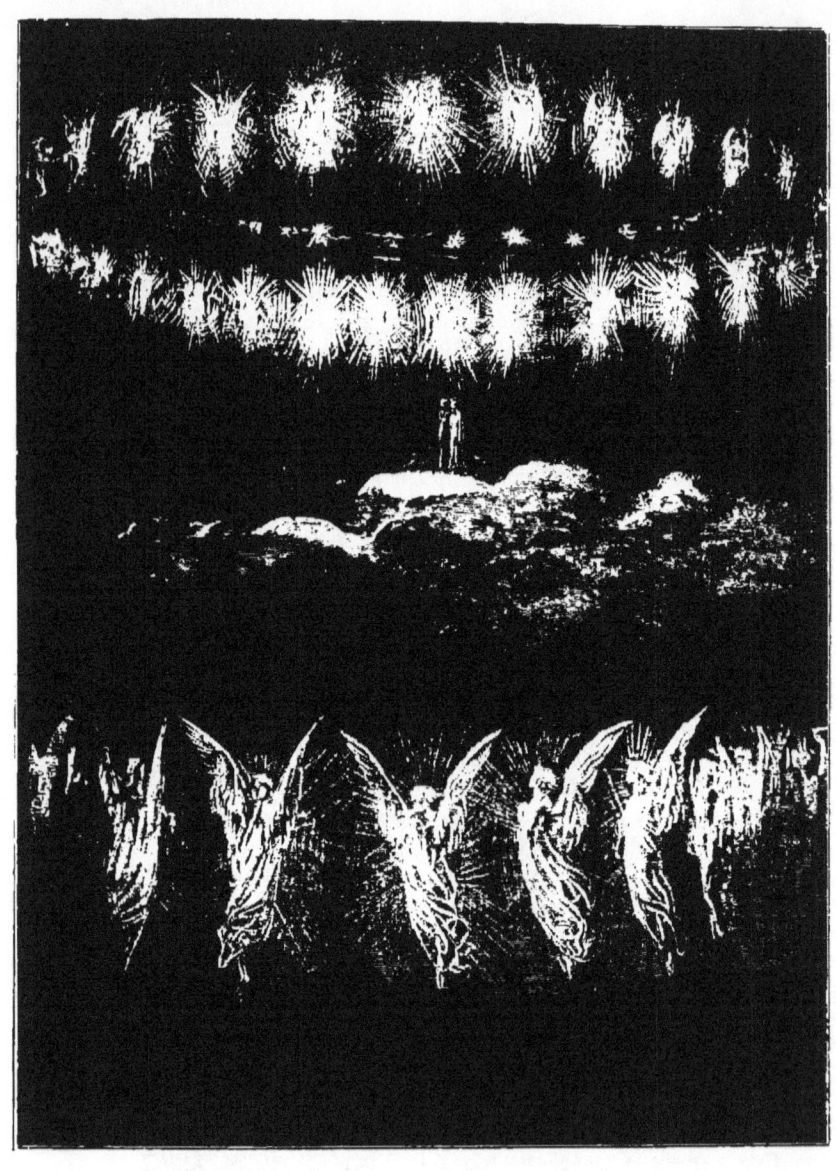

About us thus,
Of sempiternal roses, bending, wreathed
Those garlands twain; and to the innermost
E'en thus the external answer'd.
Canto XII., lines 16—19.

The hallow'd wrestler, gentle[1] to his own,
And to his enemies terrible. So replete
His soul with lively virtue, that when first
Created, even in the mother's womb,[2]
It prophesied. When, at the sacred font,
The spousals were complete 'twixt faith and him,
Where pledge of mutual safety was exchanged,
The dame,[3] who was his surety, in her sleep
Beheld the wondrous fruit, that was from him
And from his heirs to issue. And that such
He might be construed, as indeed he was,
She was inspired to name him of his owner
Whose he was wholly; and so call'd him Dominic.
And I speak of him, as the labourer,
Whom Christ in his own garden chose to be
His help-mate. Messenger he seem'd, and friend
Fast-knit to Christ; and the first love he show'd,
Was after the first counsel[4] that Christ gave.
Many a time[5] his nurse, at entering, found
That he had risen in silence, and was prostrate,
As who should say, 'My errand was for this.'
O happy father! Felix[6] rightly named.
O favoured mother! rightly named Joanna;
If that do mean, as men interpret it.[7]
Not for the world's sake, for which now they toil
Upon Ostiense[8] and Taddeo's[9] lore,

him—are all told in an anonymous life of the saint, said to be written in the thirteenth century, and published by Quetif and Echard, "Scriptores Ordinis Prædicatorum," Par., 1719, fol., tom. i., p. 25. These writers deny his having been an inquisitor, and, indeed, the establishment of the inquisition itself before the fourth Lateran Council."—*Ibid.*, p. 88.

[1] *Gentle.*—Βαρεῖαν ἐχθροῖς, καὶ φίλοισιν εὐμενῆ.
Euripides, Medea, v. 805.
"Lofty and sour to those, that loved him not,
But to those men, that sought him, sweet as summer,"
Shakespeare, Henry VIII., act iv., sc. 2.

[2] *In the mother's womb.*—His mother, when pregnant with him, is said to have dreamt that she should bring forth a white and black dog with a lighted torch in his mouth, which were signs of the habit to be worn by his order, and of his fervent zeal.

[3] *The dame.*—His godmother's dream was, that he had one star in his forehead and another in the nape of his neck, from which he communicated light to the east and the west.

[4] *After the first counsel.*—"Jesus said unto him, If thou wilt be perfect, go and sell that thou hast, and give to the poor, and thou shalt have treasure in heaven; and come and follow me."—*Matt. xix. 21.* Dominic is said to have followed this advice.

[5] *Many a time.*—His nurse, when she returned to him, often found that he had left his bed, and was prostrate, and in prayer.

[6] *Felix.*—Felix Gusman.

[7] *As men interpret it.*—Grace or gift of the Lord.

[8] *Ostiense.*—Arrigo, a native of Susa, formerly a considerable city in Piedmont, and cardinal of Ostia and Velletri, whence he acquired the name of Ostiense, was celebrated for his lectures on the five books of the "Decretals." He flourished about the year 1250. He is classed by Frezzi with Accorso the Florentine:

"Poi Ostiense, e'l Fiorentino Accorso,
Che fè le chiose, e dichiarò 'l mio testo,
E alle leggi diede gran soccorso."
Il Quadriregio, lib. iv., cap. 13.

[9] *Taddeo.*—It is uncertain whether he speaks of the physician or the lawyer of that name. The former, Taddeo d' Alderotto, a Florentine, called the Hippocratean, translated the ethics of Aristotle into Latin,

But for the real manna, soon he grew
Mighty in learning; and did set himself
To go about the vineyard, that soon turns
To wan and wither'd, if not tended well:
And from the see[1] (whose bounty to the just
And needy is gone by, not through its fault,
But his who fills it basely) he besought,
No dispensation[2] for commuted wrong,
Nor the first vacant fortune,[3] nor the tenths
That to God's paupers rightly appertain,
But, 'gainst an erring and degenerate world,
Licence to fight, in favour of that seed[4]
From which the twice twelve cions gird thee round.
Then, with sage doctrine and good will to help,
Forth on his great apostleship he fared,
Like torrent bursting from a lofty vein;
And, dashing 'gainst the stocks of heresy,
Smote fiercest, where resistance was most stout.
Thence many rivulets have since been turn'd
Over the garden catholic to lead
Their living waters, and have fed its plants.

"If such, one wheel[5] of that two-yoked car,
Wherein the holy church defended her,
And rode triumphant through the civil broil;
Thou canst not doubt its fellow's excellence,
Which Thomas,[6] ere my coming, hath declared
So courteously unto thee. But the track,[7]
Which its smooth fellies made, is now deserted:
That, mouldy mother is, where late were lees.
His family, that wont to trace his path,

---

and died at an advanced age towards the end of the thirteenth century. The other, who was of Bologna, and celebrated for his legal knowledge, left no writings behind him. He is also spoken of by Frezzi:

"Azzo e Taddeo già funno li maggiori;
E ora ognun' è oscuro, e tal appare
Qual' è la luna alli febei splendori."
Il Quadriregio, lib. iv., cap. 13.

[1] *The see.*—"The apostolic see, which no longer continues its wonted liberality towards the indigent and deserving; not, indeed, through its own fault, as its doctrines are still the same, but through the fault of the pontiff who is seated in it."

[2] *No dispensation.*—Dominic did not ask licence to compound for the use of unjust acquisitions by dedicating a part of them to pious purposes.

[3] *Nor the first vacant fortune.*—Not the first benefice that fell vacant.

[4] *In favour of that seed.*—"For that seed of the divine word, from which have sprung up these four-and-twenty plants, these holy spirits that now environ thee."

[5] *One wheel.*—Dominic; as the other wheel is Francis.

[6] *Thomas.*—Thomas Aquinas.

[7] *But the track.*—"But the rule of St. Francis is already deserted, and the lees of the wine are turned into mouldiness."

Turn backward, and invert their steps; erelong
To rue the gathering in of their ill crop,
When the rejected tares[1] in vain shall ask
Admittance to the barn. I question not[2]
But he, who search'd our volume, leaf by leaf,
Might still find page with this inscription on't,
'I am as I was wont.' Yet such were not
From Acquasparta nor Casale, whence,
Of those who come to meddle with the text,
One stretches and another cramps its rule.
Bonaventura's life in me behold,
From Bagnoregio; one, who, in discharge
Of my great offices, still laid aside
All sinister aim. Illuminato here,
And Agostino[3] join me: two they were,
Among the first of those barefooted meek ones,
Who sought God's friendship in the cord: with them
Hugues of Saint Victor;[4] Pietro Mangiadore;[5]
And he of Spain[6] in his twelve volumes shining;
Nathan the prophet; Metropolitan
Chrysostom;[7] and Anselmo;[8] and, who deign'd

---

[1] *Tares.*—He adverts to the parable of the tares and the wheat.

[2] *I question not.*—"Some indeed might be found who still observe the rule of the order, but such would come neither from Casale nor Acquasparta." At Casale, in Monferrat, the discipline had been enforced by Uberto with unnecessary rigour; and at Acquasparta, in the territory of Todi, it had been equally relaxed by the Cardinal Matteo, general of the order. Lucas Waddingus, as cited by Lombardi, corrects the errors of the commentators who had confounded these two.

[3] *Illuminato here, and Agostino.*—Two among the earliest followers of St. Francis.

[4] *Hugues of Saint Victor.*—Landino makes him of Pavia; Venturi calls him a Saxon; and Lombardi, following Alexander Natalis, "Hist. Eccl.," Sæc. xi., cap. 6, art. 9, says that he was from Ypres. He was of the monastery of St. Victor at Paris, and died in 1142, at the age of forty-four. His ten books, illustrative of the celestial hierarchy of Dionysius the Areopagite, according to the translation of Joannes Scotus, are inscribed to King Louis, son of Louis le Gros, by whom the monastery had been founded. "Opera Hug. de S. Vict.," fol., Paris, 1526, tom. i. 329. "A man distinguished by the fecundity of his genius, who treated, in his writings, of all the branches of sacred and profane erudition that were known in his time, and who composed several dissertations that are not destitute of merit."—*Maclaine's Mosheim, Eccl. Hist.*, v. ii., cent. xii., p. ii., c. ii., § 23. I have looked into his writings, and found some reason for this high eulogium.

[5] *Pietro Mangiadore.*—"Petrus Comestor, or the Eater, born at Troyes, was canon and dean of that church, and afterwards chancellor of the church of Paris. He relinquished these benefices to become a regular canon of St. Victor at Paris, where he died in 1198."—*Chaudon et Delandine, Dict. Hist.*, ed. Lyon, 1804. The work by which he is best known is his "Historia Scolastica," which I shall have occasion to cite in the notes to canto xxvi.

[6] *He of Spain.*—"To Pope Adrian V. succeeded John XXI., a native of Lisbon; a man of great genius and extraordinary acquirements, especially in logic and in medicine, as his books written in the name of Peter of Spain (by which he was known before he became Pope) may testify. His life was not much longer than that of his predecessors, for he was killed at Viterbo, by the falling of the roof of his chamber after he had been pontiff only eight months and as many days," A.D. 1277.—*Mariana, Hist. de Esp.*, l. xiv., c. 2. His "Thesaurus Pauperum" is referred to in Brown's "Vulgar Errors," b. vii., ch. 7.

[7] *Chrysostom.*—The eloquent patriarch of Constantinople.

[8] *Anselmo.*—"Anselm, Archbishop of Canterbury, was born at Aosta, about 1034, and studied under Lanfranc, at the monastery of Bec in Normandy, where he afterwards devoted himself to a religious life, in his twenty-seventh year. In three years he was made prior, and then abbot of that monastery; from whence he was taken, in 1093, to succeed to the archbishopric, vacant by the death of Lanfranc. He enjoyed this dignity till his death, in 1109, though it was disturbed by many dissensions with William II. and Henry I.

To put his hand to the first art, Donatus.[1]
Raban[2] is here; and at my side there shines
Calabria's abbot, Joachim,[3] endow'd
With soul prophetic. The bright courtesy
Of friar Thomas and his goodly lore,
Have moved me to the blazon of a peer[4]
So worthy; and with me have moved this throng."

---

respecting immunities and investitures. There is much depth and precision in his theological works."—*Tiraboschi, Stor. della Lett. Ital.*, tom. iii., lib. iv., cap. 2. *Ibid.*, c. v. "It is an observation made by many modern writers, that the demonstration of the existence of God, taken from the idea of a Supreme Being, of which Des Cartes is thought to be the author, was so many ages back discovered and brought to light by Anselm. Leibnitz himself makes the remark, vol. v., 'Oper.,' p. 570, edit. Genev., 1768."

[1] *Donatus.*—Ælius Donatus, the grammarian, in the fourth century, one of the preceptors of St. Jerome. So Fazio degli Uberti, "Dittamondo," lib. ii., cap. 13:

" In questo tempo Donato vivea,
    Che delle arti in si breve volume
    L'uscio n'aperse e la prima scalea."

[2] *Raban.*—" He was made Archbishop of Mentz in 847. His Latino-Theotische Glossary of the Bible is still preserved in the imperial library at Vienna. See Lambesius, 'Comment. de Bibl.,' lib. ii., pp. 416 and 932."—*Gray's Works*, 4to, Lond., 1814, vol. ii., p. 33. "Rabanus Maurus, Archbishop of Mentz, is deservedly placed at the head of the Latin writers of this age."—*Mosheim*, v. ii., cent. ix., p. ii., c. ii., § 14.

[3] *Joachim.*—Abbot of Flora in Calabria; "whom the multitude revered as a person divinely inspired, and equal to the most illustrious prophets of ancient times."—*Mosheim*, v. iii., cent. xiii., p. ii., c. ii., § 33.

[4] *A peer.*—St. Dominic.

CANTO XIII.

ARGUMENT.

Thomas Aquinas resumes his speech. He solves the other of those doubts which he discerned in the mind of Dante, and warns him earnestly against assenting to any proposition without having duly examined it.

LET him,[1] who would conceive what now I saw,
    Imagine (and retain the image firm
As mountain rock, the whilst he hears me speak),
Of stars, fifteen, from midst the ethereal host
Selected, that, with lively ray serene,
O'ercome the massiest air: thereto imagine
The wain, that, in the bosom of our sky,
Spins ever on its axle night and day,
With the bright summit of that horn, which swells
Due from the pole, round which the first wheel rolls,
To have ranged themselves in fashion of two signs
In heaven, such as Ariadne made,
When death's chill seized her; and that one of them
Did compass in the other's beam; and both
In such sort whirl around, that each should tend
With opposite motion: and conceiving thus,
Of that true constellation, and the dance
Twofold, that circled me, he shall attain
As 'twere the shadow; for things there as much
Surpass our usage, as the swiftest heaven
Is swifter than the Chiana.[2] There was sung
No Bacchus, and no Io Pæan, but
Three persons in the Godhead, and in one
Person that nature and the human join'd.

    The song and round were measured: and to us
Those saintly lights attended, happier made
At each new ministering. Then silence brake
Amid the accordant sons of Deity,

---

[1] *Let him.*—"Whoever would conceive the sight that now presented itself to me, must imagine to himself fifteen of the brightest stars in heaven, together with seven stars of Arcturus Major and two of Arcturus Minor, ranged in two circles, one within the other, each resembling the crown of Ariadne, and moving round in opposite directions."

[2] *The Chiana.*—See "Hell," canto xxix 45.

That luminary,[1] in which the wondrous life
Of the meek man of God[2] was told to me;
And thus it spake: "One ear[3] o' the harvest thresh'd
And its grain safely stored, sweet charity
Invites me with the other to like toil.

"Thou know'st that in the bosom,[4] whence the rib
Was ta'en to fashion that fair cheek, whose taste
All the world pays for; and in that, which pierced
By the keen lance, both after and before
Such satisfaction offer'd as outweighs
Each evil in the scale; whate'er of light
To human nature is allow'd, must all
Have by his virtue been infused, who form'd
Both one and other: and thou thence admirest
In that I told thee, of beatitudes,
A second there is none to him enclosed
In the fifth radiance. Open now thine eyes
To what I answer thee; and thou shalt see
Thy deeming and my saying meet in truth,
As centre in the round. That[5] which dies not,
And that which can die, are but each the beam
Of that idea, which our Sovereign Sire
Engendereth loving; for that lively light,[6]
Which passeth from his splendour, not disjoin'd
From him, nor from his love triune with them,[7]
Doth, through his bounty, congregate itself,
Mirror'd, as 'twere, in new existences;[8]
Itself unalterable, and ever one.

"Descending hence unto the lowest powers,[9]

---

[1] *That luminary.*—Thomas Aquinas.
[2] *The meek man of God.*—St. Francis. See canto xi. 25.
[3] *One ear.*—" Having solved one of thy questions, I proceed to answer the other. Thou thinkest then that Adam and Christ were both endued with all the perfection of which the human nature is capable; and therefore wonderest at what has been said concerning Solomon."
[4] *In the bosom.*—" Thou knowest that in the breast of Adam, whence the rib was taken to make that fair cheek of Eve, which, by tasting the apple, brought death into the world; and also in the breast of Christ, which, being pierced by the lance, made satisfaction for the sins of the whole world; as much wisdom resided as human nature was capable of: and thou dost therefore wonder that I should have spoken of Solomon as the wisest." See canto x. 105.

[5] *That.*—" Things corruptible and incorruptible are only emanations from the archetypal idea residing in the Divine Mind."
[6] *Light.*—The Word: the Son of God.
[7] *His love triune with them.*—The Holy Ghost.
[8] *New existences.*—Angels and human souls. If we read, with some editions and many MSS., " nove," instead of " nuove," it should be rendered " nine existences," and then means " the nine heavens;" and this reading is approved by Lombardi, Biagioli, and Monti. In the terms " sussistenze " and " contingenze," " existences and contingencies," Dante follows the language of the scholastic writers, which I have endeavoured to preserve.
[9] *The lowest powers.*—Irrational life and brute matter.

Its energy so sinks, at last it makes
But brief contingencies; for so I name
Things generated, which the heavenly orbs
Moving, with seed or without seed, produce.
Their wax, and that which molds it,[1] differ much:
And thence with lustre, more or less, it shows
The ideal stamp imprest: so that one tree,
According to his kind, hath better fruit,
And worse: and, at your birth, ye, mortal men,
Are in your talents various. Were the wax
Molded with nice exactness, and the heaven[2]
In its disposing influence supreme,
The brightness of the seal[3] should be complete:
But nature renders it imperfect ever;
Resembling thus the artist, in her work,
Whose faltering hand is faithless to his skill.
Therefore,[4] if fervent love dispose, and mark
The lustrous image of the primal virtue,
There all perfection is vouchsafed; and such
The clay[5] was made, accomplish'd with each gift,
That life can teem with; such the burden fill'd
The virgin's bosom: so that I commend
Thy judgment, that the human nature ne'er
Was, or can be, such as in them it was.

"Did I advance no further than this point;
'How then had he no peer?' thou mightst reply.
But, that what now appears not, may appear
Right plainly, ponder, who he was, and what
(When he was bidden 'Ask') the motive, sway'd
To his requesting. I have spoken thus,
That thou mayst see, he was a king, who ask'd[6]
For wisdom, to the end he might be king
Sufficient: not, the number[7] to search out

---

[1] *Their wax, and that which molds it.*—Matter, and the virtue or energy that acts on it.

[2] *The heaven.*—The influence of the planetary bodies.

[3] *The brightness of the seal.*—The brightness of the Divine idea before spoken of.

[4] *Therefore.*—Daniello, says Lombardi, has shown his sagacity in remarking that our poet intends this for a brief description of the Trinity: the primal virtue signifying the Father; the lustrous image, the Son; the fervent love, the Holy Ghost.

[5] *The clay.*—Adam.

[6] *Who ask'd.*—"He did not desire to know the number of the celestial intelligences, or to pry into the subtleties of logical, metaphysical, or mathematical science: but asked for that wisdom which might fit him for his kingly office."

[7] *The number.*—This question is discussed by our poet himself in the "Convito," p. 49

Of the celestial movers; or to know,
If necessary[1] with contingent e'er
Have made necessity; or whether that
Be granted, that first motion[2] is; or if,
Of the mid circle,[3] can by art be made
Triangle, with its corner blunt or sharp.

"Whence, noting that, which I have said, and this,
Thou kingly prudence and that ken[4] mayst learn,
At which the dart of my intention aims.
And, marking clearly, that I told thee, 'Risen,
Thou shalt discern it only hath respect
To kings, of whom are many, and the good
Are rare. With this distinction take my words,
And they may well consist with that which thou
Of the first human father dost believe,
And of our well-beloved. And let this
Henceforth be lead unto thy feet, to make
Thee slow in motion, as a weary man,
Both to the 'yea' and to the 'nay' thou seest not.
For he among the fools is down full low,
Whose affirmation, or denial,[5] is
Without distinction, in each case alike.
Since it befalls, that in most instances
Current opinion leans to false: and then
Affection bends the judgment to her ply.

"Much more than vainly doth he loose from shore,
Since he returns not such as he set forth,
Who fishes for the truth and wanteth skill.
And open proofs of this unto the world
Have been afforded in Parmenides,
Melissus, Bryso,[6] and the crowd beside,

---

[1] *If necessary.*—"If a premise necessarily true, with one not necessarily true, ever produced a necessary consequence: a question resolved in the negative by the art of logic, with that general rule, conclusio sequitur debiliorem partem."—*Lombardi.*

[2] *That first motion.*—"If we must allow one first motion, which is not caused by other motion: a question resolved affirmatively by metaphysics, according to that principle, repugnat in causis processus in infinitum."—*Lombardi.*

[3] *Of the mid circle.*—"If in the half of the circle a rectilinear triangle can be described, one side of which shall be the diameter of the same circle, without its forming a right angle with the other two sides; which geometry shows to be impossible."—*Lombardi.*

[4] *That ken.*—See canto x. 110.

[5] *Whose affirmation, or denial.*—Τῶν γὰρ ἄρτι δεινότερα ἄν τις ὁμολογήσειε, μὴ προσχῶν τοῖς ῥήμασι τὸν νοῦν, ᾗ τοπολὺ εἰθίσμεθα φάναι τε καὶ ἀπαρνεῖσθαι.—*Plato, Theætetus,* ed. Bip., v. ii., p. 97. "For any one might make yet absurder concessions than these, not paying strict attention to terms, according to the way in which we are for the most part accustomed both to affirm and to deny."

[6] *Parmenides, Melissus, Bryso.*—For the singular opinions entertained by the two former of these heathen

Who journey'd on, and knew not whither: so did
Sabellius, Arius,[1] and the other fools,
Who, like to scymitars,[2] reflected back
The scripture-image by distortion marr'd.
  " Let not the people be too swift to judge;
As one who reckons on the blades in field,
Or e'er the crop be ripe. For I have seen
The thorn frown rudely all the winter long,
And after bear the rose upon its top;
And bark, that all her way across the sea
Ran straight and speedy, perish at the last
E'en in the haven's mouth. Seeing one steal,
Another bring his offering to the priest,
Let not[3] Dame Birtha and Sir Martin[4] thence
Into heaven's counsels deem that they can pry:
For one of these may rise, the other fall."

---

philosophers, see Diogenes Laertius, lib. ix., and Aristotle, " De Cælo," lib. iii., cap. i., and " Phys.," lib. i., cap. ii. The last is also twice adduced by Aristotle (" Anal. Post.," lib. i., cap. ix., and " Rhet.," lib. iii., cap. ii.) as affording instances of false reasoning. Our poet refers to the philosopher's refutation of them in the " De Monarchiâ," lib. iii., p. 138. See also Plato in the " Theætetus," the " Sophist," and the " Parmenides."

  [1] *Sabellius, Arius.*—Well-known heretics.

  [2] *Scymitars.*—A passage in the travels of Bertradon de la Brocquière, translated by Mr. Johnes, will explain this allusion, which has given some trouble to the commentators. That traveller, who wrote before Dante, informs us, p. 138, that the wandering Arabs used their scymitars as mirrors.

  [3] *Let not.*—" Let not short-sighted mortals presume to decide on the future doom of any man, from a consideration of his present character and actions." This is meant as an answer to the doubts entertained respecting the salvation of Solomon. See canto x. 107.

  [4] *Dame Birtha and Sir Martin.*—Names put generally for any persons who have more curiosity than discretion.

CANTO XIV

ARGUMENT.

Solomon, who is one of the spirits in the inner circle, declares what the appearance of the blest will be after the resurrection of the body. Beatrice and Dante are translated into the fifth heaven, which is that of Mars, and here behold the souls of those who had died fighting for the true faith ranged in the sign of a cross, athwart which the spirits move to the sound of a melodious hymn.

FROM centre to the circle, and so back
From circle to the centre, water moves
In the round chalice, even as the blow
Impels it, inwardly, or from without.
Such was the image[1] glanced into my mind,
As the great spirit of Aquinum ceased;
And Beatrice, after him, her words
Resumed alternate: "Need there is (though yet
He tells it to you not in words, nor e'en
In thought) that he should fathom to its depth
Another mystery. Tell him, if the light,
Wherewith your substance blooms, shall stay with you
Eternally, as now; and, if it doth,
How, when[2] ye shall regain your visible forms,
The sight may without harm endure the change,
That also tell." As those, who in a ring
Tread the light measure, in their fitful mirth
Raise loud the voice, and spring with gladder bound;
Thus, at the hearing of that pious suit,
The saintly circles, in their tourneying
And wondrous note, attested new delight.

Whoso laments, that we must doff this garb
Of frail mortality, thenceforth to live
Immortally above; he hath not seen
The sweet refreshing of that heavenly shower.[3]
Him,[4] who lives ever, and for ever reigns
In mystic union of the Three in One,
Unbounded, bounding all, each spirit thrice
Sang, with such melody, as, but to hear,

---

[1] *Such was the image.*—The voice of Thomas Aquinas proceeding from the circle to the centre, and that of Beatrice from the centre to the circle.
[2] *When.*—When ye shall be again clothed with your bodies at the resurrection.
[3] *That heavenly shower.*—That effusion of beatific light.

[4] *Him.*—Literally translated by Chaucer, "Troilus and Cresseide," book v.:

"Thou one, two, and three eterne on live,
That raignest aie in three, two, and one,
Uncircumscript, and all maist circonscrive."

And I beheld myself,
Sole with my lady, to more lofty bliss
Translated.
                    Canto XIV., lines 77—79.

For highest merit were an ample meed.
And from the lesser orb the goodliest light,[1]
With gentle voice and mild, such as perhaps
The angel's once to Mary, thus replied:
"Long as the joy of Paradise shall last,
Our love shall shine around that raiment, bright
As fervent; fervent as, in vision, blest;
And that as far, in blessedness, exceeding,
As it hath grace, beyond its virtue, great.
Our shape, regarmented with glorious weeds
Of saintly flesh, must, being thus entire,
Show yet more gracious. Therefore shall increase
Whate'er, of light, gratuitous imparts
The Supreme Good; light, ministering aid,
The better to disclose his glory: whence,
The vision needs increasing, must increase
The fervour which it kindles; and that too
The ray, that comes from it. But as the gleed
Which gives out flame, yet in its whiteness shines
More livelily than that, and so preserves
Its proper semblance; thus this circling sphere
Of splendour shall to view less radiant seem,
Than shall our fleshly robe, which yonder earth
Now covers. Nor will such excess of light
O'erpower us, in corporeal organs made
Firm, and susceptible of all delight."

So ready and so cordial an "Amen"
Follow'd from either choir, as plainly spoke
Desire of their dead bodies; yet perchance
Not for themselves, but for their kindred dear,
Mothers and sires, and those whom best they loved,
Ere they were made imperishable flame.

And lo! forthwith there rose up round about
A lustre, over that already there;
Of equal clearness, like the brightening up
Of the horizon. As at evening hour
Of twilight, new appearances through heaven
Peer with faint glimmer, doubtfully descried;
So, there, new substances, methought, began

---

[1] *The goodliest light.*—Solomon.

To rise in view beyond the other twain,
And wheeling, sweep their ampler circuit wide.
  O genuine glitter of eternal Beam!
With what a sudden whiteness did it flow,
O'erpowering vision in me. But so fair,
So passing lovely, Beatrice show'd,
Mind cannot follow it, nor words express
Her infinite sweetness. Thence mine eyes regain'd
Power to look up; and I beheld myself,
Sole with my lady, to more lofty bliss[1]
Translated: for the star, with warmer smile
Impurpled, well denoted our ascent.
  With all the heart, and with that tongue which speaks
The same in all, an holocaust I made
To God, befitting the new grace vouchsafed.
And from my bosom had not yet upsteam'd
The fuming of that incense, when I knew
The rite accepted. With such mighty sheen
And mantling crimson, in two listed rays
The splendours shot before me, that I cried,
"God of Sabaoth! that dost prank them thus!"
  As leads the galaxy from pole to pole,
Distinguish'd into greater lights and less,
Its pathway,[2] which the wisest fail to spell;
So thickly studded in the depth of Mars,
Those rays described the venerable sign,[3]
That quadrants in the round conjoining frame.
  Here memory mocks the toil of genius. Christ
Beam'd on that cross; and pattern fails me now.

---

[1] *Sole with my lady, to more lofty bliss.*—To the planet Mars.

[2] *Its pathway.*—See the "Convito," p. 74, "E da sapere," &c. "It must be known, that, concerning the galaxy, philosophers have entertained different opinions. The Pythagoreans say that the sun once wandered out of his way, and passing through other parts not suited to his heat, scorched the place through which he passed; and that there was left that appearance of the scorching. I think they grounded their opinion on the fable of Phaëton, which Ovid relates at the beginning of his 'Metamorphoses.' Others (as Anaxagoras and Democritus) said that it proceeded from a partial repercussion of the solar light, which they proved by such reasons as they could bring to demonstrate it. What Aristotle has said cannot well be known, because his meaning is not made the same in one translation as in another; and I think it must have been an error in the translators; for, in the new, he seems to say that it is a collection of vapours under the stars, which they always attract in that part; and this appears devoid of any true reason. In the old he says that the galaxy is nothing else than a multitude of fixed stars in that part, so small, that here below we cannot distinguish them, but that they form the appearance of that whiteness which we call the galaxy. And it may be that the heaven in that part is dense, and therefore retains and represents that light; and in this opinion Avicen and Ptolemy seem to agree with Aristotle." M. Letronne's remarks on this passage of the "Convito," inserted in M. Artaud's "Histoire de Dante" (8vo, Par., 1841, p. 157), are worth consulting.

[3] *The venerable sign.*—The cross, which is placed in the planet of Mars, to denote the glory of those who fought in the crusades.

Christ
Beam'd on that cross; and pattern fails me now.
Canto XIV., lines 96—97.

But whoso takes his cross, and follows Christ,
Will pardon me for that I leave untold,
When in the flecker'd dawning he shall spy
The glitterance of Christ. From horn to horn,
And 'tween the summit and the base, did move
Lights, scintillating, as they met and pass'd.
Thus oft are seen with ever-changeful glance,
Straight or athwart, now rapid and now slow,
The atomies of bodies,[1] long or short,
To move along the sunbeam, whose slant line
Checkers the shadow interposed by art
Against the noontide heat. And as the chime
Of minstrel music, dulcimer, and harp
With many strings, a pleasant dinning makes
To him, who heareth not the distinct note;
So from the lights, which there appear'd to me,
Gather'd along the cross a melody,
That, indistinctly heard, with ravishment
Possess'd me. Yet I mark'd it was a hymn
Of lofty praises; for there came to me
"Arise," and "Conquer," as to one who hears
And comprehends not. Me such ecstasy
O'ercame, that never, till that hour, was thing
That held me in so sweet imprisonment.

Perhaps my saying overbold appears,
Accounting less the pleasure of those eyes,
Whereon to look fulfilleth all desire.
But he,[2] who is aware those living seals
Of every beauty work with quicker force,
The higher they are risen; and that there
I had not turn'd me to them; he may well
Excuse me that, whereof in my excuse
I do accuse me, and may own my truth;
That holy pleasure here not yet reveal'd,[3]
Which grows in transport as we mount aloof.

---

[1] *The atomies of bodies.*—
"As thick as motes in the sun-beame."
       Chaucer, edit. 1603, fol. 35.
"As thick and numberless,
As the gay motes that people the sunbeam."
       Milton, Il Penseroso.

[2] *He.*—"He who considers that the eyes of Beatrice became more radiant the higher we ascended, must not wonder that I do not except even them, as I had not yet beheld them since our entrance into this planet." Lombardi understands by "living seals," "vivi suggelli," "the stars;" and this explanation derives some authority from the Latin notes on the Monte Casino MS., "id est cæli imprimentes ut sigilla."

[3] *Reveal'd.*—"Dischiuso." Lombardi explains this word "excluded," as indeed Vellutello had done before him; and as it is also used in the seventh canto. If this interpretation were adopted, the line should stand thus:

"That holy pleasure not excluded here."

But the word is capable of either meaning; and it would not be easy to determine which is the right in this passage.

W

CANTO XV.

ARGUMENT.

The spirit of Cacciaguida, our Poet's ancestor, glides rapidly to the foot of the cross, tells who he is, and speaks of the simplicity of the Florentines in his days, since then much corrupted.

TRUE love, that ever shows itself as clear
　　In kindness, as loose appetite in wrong,
Silenced that lyre harmonious, and still'd
The sacred chords, that are by heaven's right hand
Unwound and tighten'd. How to righteous prayers
Should they not hearken, who, to give me will
For praying, in accordance thus were mute?
He hath in sooth good cause for endless grief,
Who, for the love of thing that lasteth not,
Despoils himself for ever of that love.
　　As oft along the still and pure serene,
At nightfall, glides a sudden trail of fire,
Attracting with involuntary heed
The eye to follow it, erewhile at rest;
And seems some star[1] that shifted place in heaven,
Only that, whence it kindles, none is lost,
And it is soon extinct: thus from the horn,
That on the dexter of the cross extends,
Down to its foot, one luminary ran
From mid the cluster shone there; yet no gem
Dropp'd from its foil: and through the beamy list,
Like flame in alabaster, glow'd its course.
　　So forward stretch'd him (if of credence aught
Our greater muse[2] may claim) the pious ghost
Of old Anchises, in the Elysian bower,
When he perceived his son. "O thou, my blood!

---

[1] *Some star.*—"Pare una stella che tramuti loco."
　　Frezzi, Il Quadriregio, lib. i., cap. 13.
"Sæpe etiam stellas, vento impendente, videbis,
Præcipites cœlo labi, noctisque per umbram
Flammarum longos a tergo albescere tractus."
　　　　Virgil, Georgics, lib. i. 367.
Compare Arat., Διοσημ., 194.

[2] *If of credence aught our greater muse.*—Virgil,
"Æneid," lib. vi. 684:
　"Isque ubi tendentem adversum per gramina
　　vidit
　Ænean, alacris palmas utrasque tetendit.
　Venisti tandem, tuaque spectata parenti
　Vicit iter durum pietas?"

O most exceeding grace divine! to whom,
As now to thee, hath twice the heavenly gate
Been e'er unclosed?" So spake the light: whence I
Turn'd me toward him; then unto my dame
My sight directed: and on either side
Amazement waited me; for in her eyes
Was lighted such a smile, I thought that mine
Had dived unto the bottom of my grace
And of my bliss in Paradise. Forthwith,
To hearing and to sight grateful alike,
The spirit to his proem added things
I understood not, so profound he spake:
Yet not of choice, but through necessity,
Mysterious; for his high conception soar'd
Beyond the mark of mortals. When the flight
Of holy transport had so spent its rage,
That nearer to the level of our thought
The speech descended; the first sounds I heard
Were, "Blest be thou, Triunal Deity!
That hast such favour in my seed vouchsafed."
Then follow'd: "No unpleasant thirst, though long,[1]
Which took me reading in the sacred book,
Whose leaves or white or dusky never change,
Thou hast allay'd, my son! within this light,
From whence my voice thou hear'st: more thanks to her
Who, for such lofty mounting, has with plumes
Begirt thee. Thou dost deem thy thoughts to me
From Him transmitted, who is first of all,
E'en as all numbers ray from unity;[2]
And therefore dost not ask me who I am,
Or why to thee more joyous I appear,
Than any other in this gladsome throng.
The truth is as thou deem'st; for in this life
Both less and greater in that mirror look,
In which thy thoughts, or e'er thou think'st, are shown.

---

[1] *No unpleasant thirst, though long.*—"Thou hast satisfied the long yet pleasing desire which I have felt to see thee, through my knowledge of thee, obtained in the immutable decrees of the divine Providence."

[2] *Unity.*—Πάντων ἄρα τὸ ἓν πρῶτον γέγονε τῶν ἀριθμῶν ἐχόντων.—Plato, "Parmenides," ed. Bip., vol. x., p. 130. Perhaps the mention of Parmenides in the last canto but one suggested this thought to Dante, which he has expressed by specifying two particular numbers intended to stand for all. There is something similar to it in his treatise "De Vulgari Eloquio," lib. i., c. xvi.: "Sicut in numero cuncta mensurantur uno, et plura vel pauciora dicuntur, secundum quod distant ab uno, vel ei propinquant."

But, that the love, which keeps me wakeful ever,
Urging with sacred thirst of sweet desire,
May be contented fully; let thy voice,
Fearless, and frank, and jocund, utter forth
Thy will distinctly, utter forth the wish,
Whereto my ready answer stands decreed."

I turn'd me to Beatrice; and she heard
Ere I had spoken, smiling an assent,
That to my will gave wings; and I began:
"To each among your tribe,[1] what time ye kenn'd
The nature, in whom nought unequal dwells,
Wisdom and love were in one measure dealt;
For that they are so equal in the sun,
From whence ye drew your radiance and your heat,
As makes all likeness scant. But will and means,
In mortals, for the cause ye well discern,
With unlike wings are fledge. A mortal, I
Experience inequality like this;
And therefore give no thanks, but in the heart,
For thy paternal greeting. This howe'er
I pray thee, living topaz! that ingemm'st
This precious jewel; let me hear thy name."

"I am thy root,[2] O leaf! whom to expect
Even, hath pleased me." Thus the prompt reply
Prefacing, next it added: "He, of whom[3]
Thy kindred appellation comes, and who,
These hundred years and more, on its first ledge
Hath circuited the mountain, was my son,
And thy great-grandsire. Well befits, his long
Endurance should be shorten'd by thy deeds.

"Florence,[4] within her ancient limit-mark,
Which calls her still[5] to matin prayers and noon,
Was chaste and sober, and abode in peace.

---

[1] *To each among your tribe.*—"In you, glorified spirits, love and knowledge are made equal, because they are equal in God. But with us mortals it is otherwise, for we have often the will without the means of expressing our affections; and I can therefore thank thee only in my heart."

[2] *I am thy root.*—Cacciaguida, father to Alighieri, of whom our poet was the great-grandson.

[3] *He, of whom.*—"Thy great grandfather, Alighieri, has been in the first round of Purgatory more than a hundred years; and it is fit that thou by thy good deserts shouldst endeavour to shorten the time of his remaining there." For what is known of Alighieri, see Pelli, "Memor. Opere di Dante," ediz. Zatta, 1758, tom. iv., P. 2da, p. 21. His son Bellincione was living in 1266; and of him was born the father of our poet, whom Benvenuto da Imola calls a lawyer by profession.—*Pelli, ibid.*

[4] *Florence.*—See G. Villani, lib. iii., cap. ii.

[5] *Which calls her still.*—The public clock being still within the circuit of the ancient walls.

She had no armlets and no head-tires then;
No purfled dames; no zone, that caught the eye
More than the person did. Time was not yet,
When[1] at his daughter's birth the sire grew pale,
For fear the age and dowry should exceed,
On each side, just proportion. House was none
Void[2] of its family: nor yet had come
Sardanapalus,[3] to exhibit feats
Of chamber prowess. Montemalo[4] yet
O'er our suburban turret[5] rose; as much
To be surpass'd in fall, as in its rising.
I saw Bellincion Berti[6] walk abroad
In leathern girdle, and a clasp of bone;
And, with no artful colouring on her cheeks,
His lady leave the glass. The sons I saw
Of Nerli, and of Vecchio,[7] well content
With unrobed jerkin; and their good dames handling
The spindle and the flax: O happy they!
Each[8] sure of burial in her native land,
And none left desolate a-bed in France.
One waked to tend the cradle, hushing it
With sounds that lull'd the parent's infancy:
Another, with her maidens, drawing off
The tresses from the distaff, lectured them

---

[1] *When.*—When the women were not married at too early an age, and did not expect too large a portion.

[2] *Void.*—Through the civil wars and banishments. Or he may mean that houses were not formerly built merely for pomp and show, nor of greater size than was necessary for containing the families that inhabited them. For it has been understood in both these ways.

[3] *Sardanapalus.*—The luxurious monarch of Assyria. Juvenal is here imitated, who uses his name for an instance of effeminacy, Sat. x. 362.

[4] *Montemalo.*—Either an elevated spot between Rome and Viterbo, or Monte Mario, the site of the villa Mellini, commanding a view of Rome.

[5] *Our suburban turret.*—Uccellatojo, near Florence, from whence that city was discovered. Florence had not yet vied with Rome in the grandeur of her public buildings.

[6] *Bellincion Berti.*—" Hell," canto xvi. 38, and notes. There is a curious description of the simple manner in which the earlier Florentines dressed themselves, in G. Villani, lib. vi., c. lxxi.: "And observe that in the time of the said people (A.D. 1259), and before and for a long time after, the citizens of Florence lived soberly, on coarse viands, and at little cost, and in many customs and courtesies of life were rude and unpolished; and dressed themselves and their women in coarse cloths: many wore plain leather, without cloth over it; bonnets on their heads; and all boots on the feet: and the Florentine women were without ornament; the better sort content with a close gown of scarlet cloth of Ypres or of camlet, bound with a girdle in the ancient mode, and a mantle lined with fur, and a hood to it, which was worn on the head; the common sort of women were clad in a coarse gown of Cambral in like manner. One hundred pounds (libre) was the common portion for a wife; and two or three hundred was accounted a magnificent one; and the young women were for the most part twenty years old or more before they were given in marriage. Such was the dress, and thus coarse were the manners of the Florentines: but they were of good faith and loyal both among themselves and to the state, and with their coarse way of living and poverty did greater and more virtuous deeds than have been done in our times with greater refinement and wealth."

[7] *Of Nerli, and of Vecchio.*—Two of the most opulent families in Florence.

[8] *Each.*—" None fearful either of dying in banish-

Old tales of Troy, and Fesole, and Rome.
A Salterello and Cianghella[1] we
Had held as strange a marvel, as ye would
A Cincinnatus or Cornelia now.

"In such composed and seemly fellowship,
Such faithful and such fair equality,
In so sweet household, Mary[2] at my birth
Bestow'd me, call'd on with loud cries: and there,
In your old baptistery, I was made
Christian at once and Cacciaguida; as were
My brethren Eliseo and Moronto.

"From Valdipado[3] came to me my spouse;
And hence thy surname grew. I follow'd then
The Emperor Conrad:[4] and his knighthood he
Did gird on me; in such good part he took
My valiant service. After him I went
To testify against that evil law,
Whose people,[5] by the shepherd's fault, possess
Your right usurp'd. There I by that foul crew
Was disentangled from the treacherous world
Whose base affection many a spirit soils;
And from the martyrdom came to this peace."

---

ment, or of being deserted by her husband on a scheme of traffic in France."

[1] *A Salterello and Cianghella.*—The latter a shameless woman of the family of Tosa, married to Lito degli Alidosi of Imola; the former Lapo Salterello, a lawyer, with whom Dante was at variance. "We should have held an abandoned character, like these, as great a wonder, as ye would the contrary now." There is a sonnet by Lapo Salterello in Corbinelli's collection printed with the "Bella Mano," ed. Firenze, 1715, p. 150.

[2] *Mary.*—The Virgin was invoked in the pains of child-birth. "Purgatory," canto xx. 21.

[3] *Valdipado.*—Cacciaguida's wife, whose family name was Alighieri, came from Ferrara, called Val di Pado, from its being watered by the Po.

[4] *Conrad.*—The Emperor Conrad III., who died in 1152. See G. Villani, lib. iv. xxxiv.

[5] *Whose people.*—The Mahometans, who were left in possession of the Holy Land, through the supineness of the Pope. See canto ix. 123.

CANTO XVI.

ARGUMENT.

Cacciaguida relates the time of his birth, and, describing the extent of Florence when he lived there, recounts the names of the chief families who then inhabited it. Its degeneracy, and subsequent disgrace, he attributes to the introduction of families from the neighbouring country and villages, and to their mixture with the primitive citizens.

O SLIGHT respect of man's nobility!
   I never shall account it marvellous,
That our infirm affection here below
Thou movest to boasting; when I could not chuse,
E'en in that region of unwarp'd desire,
In heaven itself, but make my vaunt in thee.
Yet cloak thou art soon shorten'd; for that Time,
Unless thou be eked out from day to day,
Goes round thee with his shears. Resuming then,
With greeting[1] such as Rome was first to bear,
But since hath disaccustom'd, I began:
And Beatrice,[2] that a little space
Was sever'd, smiled; reminding me of her,
Whose cough embolden'd (as the story holds)
To first offence the doubting Guenever.[3]
   "You are my sire," said I: "you give me heart
Freely to speak my thought: above myself
You raise me. Through so many streams with joy
My soul is fill'd, that gladness wells from it;
So that it bears the mighty tide, and bursts not.
Say then, my honour'd stem! what ancestors
Were those you sprang from, and what years were mark'd
In your first childhood? Tell me of the fold,[4]
That hath Saint John for guardian, what was then

---

[1] *With greeting.*—The poet, who had addressed the spirit, not knowing him to be his ancestor, with a plain "Thou," now uses more ceremony, and calls him "You," according to a custom introduced among the Romans in the latter times of the empire.

[2] *Beatrice.*—Lombardi observes, that in order to show us that his conversation with Cacciaguida had no connection with sacred subjects, Beatrice is described as standing at a little distance; and her smiling at his formal address to his ancestor makes him fall into a greater freedom of manner. See the next canto, v. 15.

[3] *Guenever.*—Beatrice's smile reminded him of the female servant who, by her coughing, emboldened Queen Guenever to admit the freedoms of Lancelot. See "Hell," canto v. 124.

[4] *The fold.*—Florence, of which John the Baptist was the patron saint.

Its state, and who in it were highest seated!"
As embers, at the breathing of the wind,
Their flame enliven; so that light I saw
Shine at my blandishments; and, as it grew
More fair to look on, so with voice more sweet,
Yet not in this our modern phrase, forthwith
It answer'd: "From the day,[1] when it was said
'Hail Virgin!' to the throes by which my mother,
Who now is sainted, lighten'd her of me
Whom she was heavy with, this fire had come
Five hundred times and fourscore, to relume
Its radiance underneath the burning foot
Of its own lion. They, of whom I sprang,
And I, had there our birthplace, where the last[2]
Partition of our city first is reach'd
By him that runs her annual game. Thus much
Suffice of my forefathers: who they were,
And whence they hither came, more honourable
It is to pass in silence than to tell.
All those, who at that time were there, betwixt
Mars[3] and the Baptist, fit to carry arms,
Were but the fifth, of them this day alive.
But then the citizen's blood, that now is mix'd
From Campi and Certaldo and Fighine,[4]

---

[1] *From the day.*—From the incarnation of our Lord to the birth of Cacciaguida, the planet Mars had returned five hundred and eighty times to the constellation of Leo, with which it is supposed to have a congenial influence. As Mars, then, completes his revolution in a period forty-three days short of two years, Cacciaguida was born about 1090. This is Lombardi's computation, and it squares well both with the old reading—

"Cinquecento cinquanta
E trenta fiate,"

and with the time when Cacciaguida might have fallen fighting under Conrad III., who died in 1152. Not so the computation made by the old commentators in general, who, reckoning two years for the revolution of Mars, placed the birth of Cacciaguida in 1106; the impossibility of which being perceived by the Academicians della Crusca (as it had before been by Pietro, the son of our poet, or by the author of the commentary which passes for his), they altered the word "trenta" into "tre," "thirty" into "three;" and so, still reckoning the revolution of Mars at two years, brought Cacciaguida's birth to 1106. The way in which Lombardi has got over the difficulty appears preferable, as it retains the old reading; and I have accordingly altered the translation, which before stood thus:

"This fire had come,
Five hundred fifty times and thrice, its beams

To re-illumine underneath the foot
Of its own lion."

Since this note was written, Monti has given his assent to Lombardi's opinion. See his "Proposta," under the word "Rinfiammare," t. iii., pte. ii. 210.

[2] *The last.*—The city was divided into four compartments. The Elisei, the ancestors of Dante, resided near the entrance of that, named from the Porta S. Piero, which was the last reached by the competitor in the annual race at Florence. See G. Villani, lib. iv., cap. x.

[3] *Mars.*—The Padre d'Aquino understands this to refer to the population of Florence in Guido's time; for, according to him, "tra Marte e'l Batista" means the space between the statue of Mars placed on the Ponte Vecchio and the Baptistery; and Lombardi assents to this interpretation. Venturi supposes that the portion of land so described would have been insufficient to hold the population which Florence contained at the supposed date of this poem, that is, in the year 1300; and agrees with the elder commentators, who consider the description as relating to time and not to place, and as indicating the two periods of heathenism and Christianity. See canto xiii. 144. It would not be easy to determine the real sense of a passage thus equivocal.

[4] *Campi and Certaldo and Fighine.*—Country places near Florence.

Ran purely through the last mechanic's veins.
O how much better were it, that these people[1]
Were neighbours to you; and that at Galluzzo.
And at Trespiano ye should have your boundary;
Than to have them within, and bear the stench
Of Aguglione's hind, and Signa's,[2] him,
That hath his eye already keen for bartering.[3]
Had not the people,[4] which of all the world
Degenerates most, been stepdame unto Cæsar,
But, as a mother to her son been kind,
Such one, as hath become a Florentine,
And trades and traffics, had been turn'd adrift
To Simifonte,[5] where his grandsire plied
The beggar's craft: the Conti were possess'd
Of Montemurlo[6] still: the Cerchi still
Were in Acone's parish: nor had haply
From Valdigrieve past the Buondelmonti.
The city's malady hath ever source
In the confusion of its persons, as
The body's, in variety of food:
And the blind bull[7] falls with a steeper plunge,
Than the blind lamb: and oftentimes one sword
Doth more and better execution,
Than five. Mark Luni; Urbisaglia[8] mark;
How they are gone; and after them how go
Chiusi and Sinigaglia:[9] and 'twill seem
No longer new, or strange to thee, to hear
That families fail, when cities have their end.
All things that appertain to ye, like yourselves,
Are mortal: but mortality in some
Ye mark not; they endure so long, and you

---

[1] *That these people.*—"That the inhabitants of the above-mentioned places had not been mixed with the citizens; nor the limits of Florence extended beyond Galluzzo and Trespiano."

[2] *Aguglione's hind, and Signa's.*—Baldo of Aguglione, and Bonifazio of Signa.

[3] *His eye already keen for bartering.*—See "Hell," canto xxi. 40, and note.

[4] *Had not the people.*—If Rome had continued in her allegiance to the emperor, and the Guelph and Ghibelline factions had thus been prevented, Florence would not have been polluted by a race of upstarts, nor lost the most respectable of her ancient families.

[5] *Simifonte.*—A castle dismantled by the Florentines. G. Villani, lib. v., cap. xxx. The person here alluded to is no longer known.

[6] *Montemurlo.*—G. Villani, lib. v., cap. xxxi., relates that the Conti Guidi, not being able to defend their castle from the Pistoians, sold it to the state of Florence.

[7] *The blind bull.*—So Chaucer, "Troilus and Cresseide," b. ii.:

"For swifter course cometh thing that is of wight
When it descendeth than done things light."

Compare Aristotle, "Ethic. Nic.," lib. vi., cap. xiii.: σώματι ἰσχυρῷ, κ. τ. λ.

[8] *Luni; Urbisaglia.*—Cities formerly of importance, but then fallen to decay.

[9] *Chiusi and Sinigaglia.*—The same.

Pass by so suddenly. And as the moon[1]
Doth, by the rolling of her heavenly sphere,
Hide and reveal the strand unceasingly;
So fortune deals with Florence. Hence admire not
At what of them I tell thee, whose renown
Time covers, the first Florentines. I saw
The Ughi,[2] Catilini, and Filippi,
The Alberichi, Greci, and Ormanni,
Now in their wane illustrious citizens
And great as ancient, of Sannella him,
With him of Arca saw, and Soldanieri,
And Ardinghi, and Bostichi. At the poop[3]
That now is laden with new felony
So cumbrous it may speedily sink the bark,
The Ravignani sat, of whom is sprung
The County Guido, and whoso hath since
His title from the famed Bellincion ta'en.
Fair governance was yet an art well prized
By him of Pressa: Galigaio show'd
The gilded hilt and pommel,[4] in his house:
The column, clothed with verrey,[5] still was seen
Unshaken; the Sacchetti still were great,
Giuochi, Sifanti, Galli, and Barucci,
With them[6] who blush to hear the bushel named.
Of the Calfucci still the branchy trunk
Was in its strength: and, to the curule chairs,
Sizii and Arrigucci[7] yet were drawn.
How mighty them[8] I saw, whom, since, their pride
Hath undone! And in all their goodly deeds
Florence was, by the bullets of bright gold,[9]

---

[1] *As the moon.*—"The fortune of us, that are the moon's men, doth ebb and flow like the sea."—*Shakespeare*, 1 *Henry IV.*, act i., sc. 2.

[2] *The Ughi.*—Whoever is curious to know the habitations of these and the other ancient Florentines, may consult G. Villani, lib. iv.

[3] *At the poop.*—The Cerchi, Dante's enemies, had succeeded to the houses over the gate of St. Peter, formerly inhabited by the Ravignani and the Count Guido. G. Villani, lib. iv., cap. x. Many editions read *porta*, "gate."—The same metaphor is found in Æschylus, "Supplices," 356, and is there also scarce understood by the critics:

Αἰδοῦ σὺ πρύμναν πόλεος ὧδ' ἐστεμμένην.

"Respect these wreaths, that crown your city's poop."

[4] *The gilded hilt and pommel.*—The symbols of knighthood.

[5] *The column, clothed with verrey.*—The arms of the Pigli, or, as some write it, the Billi.

[6] *With them.*—Either the Chiaramontesi, or the Tosinghi; one of which had committed a fraud in measuring out the wheat from the public granary. See "Purgatory," canto xii. 99.

[7] *Sizii and Arrigucci.*—"These families still obtained the magistracies."

[8] *Them.*—The Uberti; according to the Latin note on the Monte Casino MS., with which the editor of the extracts from those notes says that Benvenuto agrees.

[9] *The bullets of bright gold.*—The arms of the Abbati, as it is conjectured; or of the Lamberti, according to the authorities referred to in the last note.

O'erflourish'd. Such the sires of those,[1] who now,
As surely as your church is vacant, flock
Into her consistory, and at leisure
There stall them and grow fat. The o'erweening brood,[2]
That plays the dragon after him that flees,
But unto such as turn and show the tooth,
Ay or the purse, is gentle as a lamb,
Was on its rise, but yet so slight esteem'd,
That Ubertino of Donati grudged
His father-in-law should yoke him to its tribe.
Already Caponsacco[3] had descended
Into the mart from Fesole: and Giuda
And Infangato[4] were good citizens.
A thing incredible I tell, though true:[5]
The gateway[6] named from those of Pera, led
Into the narrow circuit of your walls.
Each one, who bears the sightly quarterings
Of the great Baron[7] (he whose name and worth
The festival of Thomas still revives),
His knighthood and his privilege retain'd;
Albeit one,[8] who borders them with gold,
This day is mingled with the common herd.
In Borgo yet the Gualterotti dwelt,
And Importuni:[9] well for its repose,
Had it still lack'd of newer neighbourhood.[10]

---

[1] *The sires of those.*—"Of the Visdomini, the Tosinghi, and the Cortigiani, who, being sprung from the founders of the bishopric of Florence, are the curators of its revenues, which they do not spare, whenever it becomes vacant."

[2] *The o'erweening brood.*—The Adimari. This family was so little esteemed, that Ubertino Donato, who had married a daughter of Bellincion Berti, himself indeed derived from the same stock (see note to "Hell," canto xvi. 38), was offended with his father-in-law for giving another of his daughters in marriage to one of them.

[3] *Caponsacco.*—The family of Caponsacchi, who had removed from Fesole, lived at Florence in the Mercato Vecchio.

[4] *Giuda, and Infangato.*—Giuda Giudi and the family of Infangati.

[5] *A thing incredible I tell, though true.*—"Io dirò cosa incredibile e vera." Ἐγὼ σοι ἐρῶ, ἔφη, ὦ Σώκρατες, ἄπιστον μὲν νὴ τοὺς θεοὺς, ἀληθὲς δε.—*Plato, Theages*, Bipont. edit., tom. ii., p. 23.

[6] *The gateway.*—Landino refers this to the smallness of the city; Vellutello, with less probability, to the simplicity of the people in naming one of the gates after a private family.

[7] *The great Baron.*—The Marchese Ugo, who resided at Florence as lieutenant of the Emperor Otho III., gave many of the chief families licence to bear his arms. See G. Villani, lib. iv., cap. ii., where the vision is related, in consequence of which he sold all his possessions in Germany, and founded seven abbeys; in one whereof his memory was celebrated at Florence on St. Thomas's day. "The marquis, when hunting, strayed away from his people, and wandering through a forest, came to a smithy, where he saw black and deformed men tormenting others with fire and hammers; and, asking the meaning of this, he was told that they were condemned souls, who suffered this punishment, and that the soul of the Marquis Ugo was doomed to suffer the same if he did not repent. Struck with horror, he commended himself to the Virgin Mary; and soon after founded the seven religious houses."

[8] *One.*—Giano della Bella, belonging to one of the families thus distinguished, who no longer retained his place among the nobility, and had yet added to his arms a bordure or. See Macchiavelli, "Ist. Fior.," lib. ii., p. 86, ediz. Giolito.

[9] *Gualterotti dwelt, and Importuni.*—Two families in the compartment of the city called Borgo.

[10] *Newer neighbourhood.*—Some understand this of the Bardi, and others of the Buondelmonti.

The house,[1] from whence your tears have had their spring,
Through the just anger, that hath murder'd ye,
And put a period to your gladsome days,
Was honour'd; it, and those consorted with it.
O Buondelmonti! what ill counselling
Prevail'd on thee to break the plighted bond?
Many, who now are weeping, would rejoice,
Had God to Ema[2] given thee, the first time
Thou near our city camest. But so was doom'd:
Florence! on that maim'd stone[3] which guards the bridge,
The victim, when thy peace departed, fell.

"With these and others like to them, I saw
Florence in such assured tranquillity,
She had no cause at which to grieve: with these
Saw her so glorious and so just, that ne'er
The lily[4] from the lance had hung reverse,
Or through division been with vermeil dyed."

---

[1] *The house.*—Of Amidei. See notes to canto xxviii. of "Hell," 102.

[2] *To Ema.*—"It had been well for the city if thy ancestor had been drowned in the Ema, when he crossed that stream on his way from Montebuono to Florence."

[3] *On that maim'd stone.*— See "Hell," canto xiii. 144. Near the remains of the statue of Mars, Buondelmonti was slain, as if he had been a victim to the god; and Florence had not since known the blessing of peace.

[4] *The lily.*—"The arms of Florence had never hung reversed on the spear of her enemies, in token of her defeat, nor been changed from argent to gules;" as they afterwards were when the Guelfi gained the predominance.

But so was doom'd:
Florence! on that maim'd stone which guards the bridge,
The victim, when thy peace departed, fell.
Canto XVI., lines 143—145.

CANTO XVII.

ARGUMENT.

Cacciaguida predicts to our Poet his exile and the calamities he had to suffer; and, lastly, exhorts him to write the present poem.

SUCH as the youth,[1] who came to Clymene,
To certify himself of that reproach
Which had been fasten'd on him (he whose end
Still makes the fathers chary to their sons),
E'en such was I; nor unobserved was such
Of Beatrice, and that saintly lamp,[2]
Who had erewhile for me his station moved;
When thus my lady: "Give thy wish free vent,
That it may issue, bearing true report
Of the mind's impress: not that aught thy words
May to our knowledge add, but to the end
That thou mayst use thyself to own thy thirst,[3]
And men may mingle for thee when they hear."
   "O plant, from whence I spring! revered and loved!
Who soar'st so high a pitch, that thou as clear,[4]
As earthly thought determines two obtuse
In one triangle not contain'd, so clear
Dost see contingencies, ere in themselves
Existent, looking at the point[5] whereto
All times are present; I, the whilst I scaled
With Virgil the soul-purifying mount[6]
And visited the nether world[7] of woe,
Touching my future destiny have heard
Words grievous, though I feel me on all sides

---

[1] *The youth.*—Phaëton, who came to his mother Clymene, to inquire of her if he were indeed the son of Apollo. See Ovid, "Metamorphoses," lib. i. ad finem.
[2] *That saintly lamp.*—Cacciaguida.
[3] *To own thy thirst.*—"That thou mayst obtain from others a solution of any doubt that may occur to thee."

[4] *That thou as clear.*—"Thou beholdest future events with the same clearness of evidence that we discern the simplest mathematical demonstrations."
[5] *The point.*—The divine nature.
[6] *The soul-purifying mount.*—See "Purgatory," canto viii. 133, and canto xi. 140.
[7] *The nether world.*—See "Hell," canto x. 77, and canto xv. 61.

Well squared[1] to fortune's blows. Therefore my will
Were satisfied to know the lot awaits me.
The arrow,[2] seen beforehand, slacks his flight."

So said I to the brightness, which erewhile
To me had spoken; and my will declared,
As Beatrice will'd, explicitly.
Nor with oracular response obscure,
Such as, or e'er the Lamb of God was slain,
Beguiled the credulous nations: but, in terms
Precise, and unambiguous lore, replied
The spirit of paternal love, enshrined,
Yet in his smile apparent; and thus spake:
"Contingency,[3] whose verge extendeth not
Beyond the tablet of your mortal mold,
Is all depictured in the eternal sight;
But hence deriveth not necessity,[4]
More than the tall ship, hurried down the flood,
Is driven by the eye that looks on it.
From thence,[5] as to the ear sweet harmony
From organ comes, so comes before mine eye
The time prepared for thee. Such as driven out
From Athens, by his cruel stepdame's[6] wiles,
Hippolytus departed; such must thou
Depart from Florence. This they wish, and this
Contrive, and will ere long effectuate, there,[7]
Where gainful merchandise is made of Christ
Throughout the live-long day. The common cry,[8]
Will, as 'tis ever wont, affix the blame

---

[1] *Well squared.*—See Plato, "Protagoras," ed. Bipont., vol. iii., p. 145, and Aristotle, "Rhetor.," lib. iii., where Pietro Vettori, in his Commentary, p. 656, remarks: "Quis nescit Dantem etiam suo in poemate tetragonum vocasse apposite hominem, qui adversis casibus non frangitur sed resistit fortiter ipsis?"

[2] *The arrow.*—A line repeated by Ruccellai in his "Oreste:"
"Nam prævisa minus lædere tela solent."
Ovid.
"Che piaga antiveduta assai men duole."
Petrarca, Trionfo del Tempo.

[3] *Contingency.*—
"La contingenza, che fuor del quaderno
Della vostra materia non si stende."
I had before understood this, "Contingency, which is not exposed to view on the tablet of your nature," "which is not discoverable by your human understanding," and had translated it accordingly; but have now adopted Lombardi's explanation: "Contingency, which has no place beyond the limits of the material world."

[4] *Necessity.*—"The evidence with which we see casual events portrayed in the source of all truth no more necessitates those events, than does the image reflected in the sight by a ship sailing down a stream necessitate the motion of the vessel."

[5] *From thence.*—"From the eternal sight; the view of the Deity himself."

[6] *His cruel stepdame.*—Phædra.

[7] *There.*—At Rome, where the expulsion of Dante's party from Florence was then plotting, in 1300.

[8] *The common cry.*—The multitude will, as usual, be ready to blame those who are sufferers, whose cause will at last be vindicated by the overthrow of their enemies.

Unto the party injured : but the truth
Shall, in the vengeance it dispenseth, find
A faithful witness. Thou shalt leave each thing[1]
Beloved most dearly : this is the first shaft
Shot from the bow of exile. Thou shalt prove
How salt the savour is of other's bread ;
How hard the passage, to descend and climb
By other's stairs. But that shall gall thee most,
Will be the worthless and vile company,
With whom thou must be thrown into these straits.
For all ungrateful, impious all, and mad,
Shall turn 'gainst thee : but in a little while,
Theirs,[2] and not thine, shall be the crimson'd brow,
Their course shall so evince their brutishness,
To have ta'en thy stand apart shall well become thee.

"First refuge thou must find, first place of rest,
In the great Lombard's[3] courtesy, who bears,
Upon the ladder perch'd, the sacred bird.
He shall behold thee with such kind regard,
That 'twixt ye two, the contrary to that
Which 'falls 'twixt other men, the granting shall
Forerun the asking. With him shalt thou see
That mortal,[4] who was at his birth imprest
So strongly from this star, that of his deeds
The nations shall take note. His unripe age
Yet holds him from observance ; for these wheels
Only nine years have compast him about.
But, ere the Gascon[5] practise on great Harry,[6]
Sparkles of virtue shall shoot forth in him,
In equal scorn[7] of labours and of gold.
His bounty shall be spread abroad so widely
As not to let the tongues, e'en of his foes,

---

[1] *Thou shalt leave each thing.*—Compare Euripides, "Phœnissæ," 399, &c.

[2] *Theirs.*—"They shall be ashamed of the part they have taken against thee." Lombardi, I think, is very unhappy in his conjecture, that "rotta la tempia," a reading of the Nidobeatina edition, should be adopted, and that it may mean "the broken heads of his companions."

[3] *The great Lombard.*—Either Bartolommeo della Scala, or Alboino his brother ; although our poet has spoken ambiguously of him in his "Convito," p. 179. Their coat of arms was a ladder and an eagle. For an account of the rise of this family from a very mean condition, see G. Villani, lib. xi., cap. xciv.

[4] *That mortal.*—Can Grande della Scala, born under the influence of Mars, but at this time only nine years old. He was, as the other two, a son of Alberto della Scala.

[5] *The Gascon.*—Pope Clement V. See "Hell," canto xix. 86, and note, and "Paradise," canto xxvii. 53, and canto xxx. 141.

[6] *Great Harry.*—The Emperor Henry VII. See canto xxx. 135.

[7] *In equal scorn.*—See "Hell," canto i. 98.

Be idle in its praise. Look thou to him,
And his beneficence : for he shall cause
Reversal of their lot to many people ;
Rich men and beggars interchanging fortunes.
And thou shalt bear this written in thy soul,
Of him, but tell it not :" and things he told
Incredible to those who witness them ;
Then added : "So interpret thou, my son,
What hath been told thee.—Lo ! the ambushment
That a few circling seasons hide for thee.
Yet envy not thy neighbours : time extends
Thy span beyond their treason's chastisement."

    Soon as the saintly spirit, by silence, mark'd
Completion of that web, which I had stretch'd
Before it, warped for weaving ; I began,
As one, who in perplexity desires
Counsel of other, wise, benign, and friendly :
" My father ! well I mark how time spurs on
Toward me, ready to inflict the blow,
Which falls most heavily on him who most
Abandoneth himself. Therefore 'tis good
I should forecast, that, driven from the place[1]
Most dear to me, I may not lose myself[2]
All other by my song. Down through the world
Of infinite mourning ; and along the mount,
From whose fair height my lady's eyes did lift me ;
And, after, through this heaven, from light to light ;
Have I learnt that, which if I tell again,
It may with many wofully disrelish :
And, if I am a timid friend to truth,
I fear my life may perish among those,
To whom these days shall be of ancient date."

    The brightness, where enclosed the treasure[3] smiled,
Which I had found there, first shone glisteringly,
Like to a golden mirror in the sun ;
Next answered : " Conscience, dimm'd or by its own

---

[1] *Driven from the place.*—Our poet here discovers both that Florence, much as he inveighs against it, was still the dearest object of his affections, and that it was not without some scruple he indulged his satirical line.

[2] *I may not lose myself.*—" That being driven out of my country, I may not deprive myself of every other place by the boldness with which I expose in my writings the vices of mankind."

[3] *The treasure.*—Cacciaguida.

Or other's shame, will feel thy saying sharp.
Thou, notwithstanding, all deceit removed,
See the whole vision be made manifest.
And let them wince, who have their withers wrung.
What though, when tasted first, thy voice shall prove
Unwelcome: on digestion, it will turn
To vital nourishment. The cry thou raisest,[1]
Shall, as the wind doth, smite the proudest summits;
Which is of honour no light argument.
For this, there only have been shown to thee,
Throughout these orbs, the mountain, and the deep,
Spirits, whom fame hath note of. For the mind
Of him, who hears, is loth to acquiesce
And fix its faith, unless the instance brought
Be palpable, and proof apparent urge."

---

[1] *The cry thou raisest.*—"Thou shalt stigmatise the faults of those who are most eminent and powerful; for men are naturally less moved by instances adduced from among those who are in the lower classes of life."

CANTO XVIII.

ARGUMENT.

Dante sees the souls of many renowned warriors and crusaders in the planet Mars, and then ascends with Beatrice to Jupiter, the sixth heaven, in which he finds the souls of those who had administered justice rightly in the world, so disposed, as to form the figure of an eagle. The canto concludes with an invective against the avarice of the clergy, and especially of the Pope.

NOW[1] in his word, sole, ruminating, joy'd
    That blessed spirit: and I fed on mine,
Tempering the sweet with bitter.[2] She meanwhile,
Who led me unto God, admonish'd: "Muse
On other thoughts: bethink thee, that near Him
I dwell, who recompenseth every wrong."
    At the sweet sounds of comfort straight I turn'd;
And, in the saintly eyes what love was seen,
I leave in silence here, nor through distrust
Of my words only, but that to such bliss
The mind remounts not without aid. Thus much
Yet may I speak; that, as I gazed on her,
Affection found no room for other wish.
While the everlasting pleasure, that did full
On Beatrice shine, with second view
From her fair countenance my gladden'd soul
Contented; vanquishing me with a beam
Of her soft smile, she spake: "Turn thee, and list.
These eyes are not thy only Paradise."
    As here, we sometimes in the looks may see
The affection mark'd, when that its sway hath ta'en
The spirit wholly; thus the hallow'd light,
To whom I turn'd, flashing,[3] bewray'd its will
To talk yet further with me, and began:
"On this fifth lodgment of the tree,[4] whose life

---

[1] *Now.*—The spirit of Cacciaguida enjoyed its own thoughts in silence.

[2] *Tempering the sweet with bitter.*—
  "Chewing the cud of sweet and bitter fancy."
    Shakespeare, As You Like It, act. iii., sc. 3.

[3] *Thus the hallow'd light, to whom I turn'd, flashing.*—In which the spirit of Cacciaguida was enclosed.

[4] *On this fifth lodgment of the tree.*—Mars, the fifth of the heavens.

Is from its top, whose fruit is ever fair
And leaf unwithering, blessed spirits abide,
That were below ere they arrived in heaven,
So mighty in renown, as every muse
Might grace her triumph with them. On the horns
Look, therefore, of the cross: he whom I name,
Shall there enact, as doth in summer cloud
Its nimble fire." Along the cross I saw,
At the repeated name of Joshua,
A splendour gliding; nor, the word was said,
Ere it was done: then, at the naming, saw,
Of the great Maccabee,[1] another move
With whirling speed; and gladness was the scourge
Unto that top. The next for Charlemain[2]
And for the peer Orlando, two my gaze
Pursued, intently, as the eye pursues
A falcon flying. Last, along the cross,
William, and Renard,[3] and Duke Godfrey[4] drew
My ken, and Robert Guiscard.[5] And the soul
Who spake with me, among the other lights
Did move away, and mix; and with the quire
Of heavenly songsters proved his tuneful skill.

To Beatrice on my right I bent,
Looking for intimation, or by word
Or act, what next behoved; and did descry
Such mere effulgence in her eyes, such joy,
It passed all former wont. And, as by sense
Of new delight, the man, who perseveres
In good deeds, doth perceive, from day to day,

---

[1] *The great Maccabee.*—Judas Maccabeus.

[2] *Charlemain.*—L. Pulci commends Dante for placing Charlemain and Orlando here:
  "Io mio confido ancor molto qui a Dante,
  Che non sanza cagion nel ciel su misse
  Carlo ed Orlando in quelle croci sante,
  Che come diligente intese e scrisse."
        Morgante Maggiore, c. xxviii.

[3] *William and Renard.*—Probably not, as the commentators have imagined, William II. of Orange, and his kinsman Raimbaud, two of the crusaders under Godfrey of Bouillon (Maimbourg, "Hist. des Croisades," ed. Par., 1682, 12mo, tom. i., p. 96), but rather the two more celebrated heroes in the age of Charlemain. The former, William I. of Orange, supposed to have been the founder of the present illustrious family of that name, died about 808, according to Joseph de la Pise, "Tableau de l'Hist. des Princes et Principauté d'Orange." Our countryman, Ordericus Vitalis, professes to give his true life, which had been misrepresented in the songs of the itinerant bards. "Vulgo canitur a joculatoribus de illo cantilena; sed jure præferenda est relatio autentica."—*Eccl. Hist. in Duchesne, Hist. Normann. Script.* p. 598. The latter is better known by having been celebrated by Ariosto, under the name of Rinaldo.

[4] *Duke Godfrey.*—Godfrey of Bouillon.
  "Poi venia solo il buon duce Goffrido,
  Che fè l'impresa santa e i passi giusti;
  Questo, di ch' io mi sdegno e'ndarno grido,
  Fece in Hierusalem con le sue mani
  Il mal guardato e già negletto nido."
        Petrarca, *Trionfo della Fama*, cap. ii.

[5] *Robert Guiscard.*—See "Hell," canto xxviii. 12.

His virtue growing; I e'en thus perceived,
Of my ascent, together with the heaven,
The circuit widen'd; noting the increase
Of beauty in that wonder. Like the change
In a brief moment on some maiden's cheek,
Which, from its fairness, doth discharge the weight
Of pudency, that stain'd it; such in her
And to mine eyes so sudden was the change,
Through[1] silvery whiteness of that temperate star,
Whose sixth orb now enfolded us. I saw,
Within that Jovial cresset, the clear sparks
Of love, that reign'd there, fashion to my view
Our language. And as birds, from river banks
Arisen, now in round, now lengthen'd troop,
Array them in their flight, greeting, as seems,
Their new-found pastures; so, within the lights,
The saintly creatures flying, sang; and made
Now D, now I, now L, figured i' the air.
First singing to their notes they moved; then, one
Becoming of these signs, a little while
Did rest them, and were mute. O nymph divine,[2]
Of Pegasean race! who souls, which thou
Inspirest, makest glorious and long-lived, as they
Cities and realms by thee; thou with thyself
Inform me; that I may set forth the shapes,
As fancy doth present them: be thy power
Display'd in this brief song. The characters,[3]
Vocal and consonant, were five-fold seven.
In order, each, as they appear'd, I mark'd
Diligite Justitiam, the first,
Both verb and noun all blazon'd; and the extreme,
Qui judicatis terram. In the M
Of the fifth word they held their station;

---

[1] *Through silvery.*—So in the "Convito," "E'l ciel di Giove," &c., p. 74: "The heaven of Jupiter may be compared to geometry, for two properties: the one is, that it moves between two heavens repugnant to its temperature, as that of Mars and that of Saturn; whence Ptolemy, in the above-cited book, says that Jupiter is a star of temperate complexion, between the coldness of Saturn and the heat of Mars: the other is, that, among all the stars, it shows itself white, as it were silvered."

[2] *O nymph divine, of Pegasean race.*—"O muse thou that makest thy votaries glorious and long-lived, as they, assisted by thee, make glorious and long-lived the cities and realms which they celebrate, now enlighten me," &c.

[3] *The characters, vocal and consonant, were five-fold seven.*—"Diligite justitiam qui judicatis terram." "Love righteousness, ye that be judges of the earth." —*Wisdom of Solomon*, i. 1.

So, within the lights,
The saintly creatures flying, sang; and made
Now D, now I, now L, figured i' the air.
Canto XVIII., lines 70—72.

Making the star seem silver streak'd with gold.
And on the summit of the M, I saw
Descending other lights, that rested there,
Singing, methinks, their bliss and primal good.
Then, as at shaking of a lighted brand,
Sparkles innumerable on all sides
Rise scatter'd, source of augury to the unwise;[1]
Thus more than thousand twinkling lustres hence
Seem'd reascending; and a higher pitch
Some mounting, and some less, e'en as the sun,
Which kindleth them, decreed. And when each one
Had settled in his place; the head and neck
Then saw I of an eagle, livelily
Graved in that streaky fire. Who painteth there,[2]
Hath none to guide Him: of Himself He guides:
And every line and texture of the nest
Doth own from Him the virtue fashions it.
The other bright beatitude,[3] that seem'd
Erewhile, with lilied crowning, well content
To over-canopy the M, moved forth,
Following gently the impress of the bird.

  Sweet star! what glorious and thick-studded gems
Declared to me our justice on the earth
To be the effluence of that heaven, which thou,
Thyself a costly jewel, dost inlay.
Therefore I pray the Sovran Mind, from whom
Thy motion and thy virtue are begun,
That He would look from whence the fog doth rise,
To vitiate thy beam; so that once more[4]
He may put forth His hand 'gainst such, as drive
Their traffic in that sanctuary, whose walls
With miracles and martyrdoms were built.

  Ye host of heaven, whose glory I survey!
O beg ye grace for those, that are, on earth,
All after ill example gone astray.
War once had for his instrument the sword:

---

[1] *Source of augury to the unwise.*—Who augur future riches to themselves in proportion to the quantity of sparks that fly from the lighted brand when it is shaken.
[2] *Who painteth there.*—The Deity Himself.
[3] *Beatitude.*—The band of spirits; for "beatitudo" is here a noun of multitude.
[4] *That once more He may put forth His hand against them.*—"That He may again drive out those who buy and sell in the temple."

But now 'tis made, taking the bread away,[1]
Which the good Father locks from none.—And thou,
That writest but to cancel,[2] think, that they,
Who for the vineyard, which thou wastest, died,
Peter and Paul, live yet, and mark thy doings.
Thou hast good cause to cry, "My heart so cleaves
To him,[3] that lived in solitude remote,
And for a dance was dragg'd to martyrdom,[4]
I wist not of the fisherman nor Paul."

---

[1] *Taking the bread away.*—" Excommunication, or interdiction of the eucharist, is now employed as a weapon of warfare."

[2] *That writest but to cancel.*—" And thou, Pope Boniface, who writest thy ecclesiastical censures for no other purpose than to be paid for revoking them."

[3] *To him.*—The coin of Florence was stamped with the impression of John the Baptist, and for this the avaricious Pope is made to declare that he felt more devotion than either for Peter or Paul. Lombardi, I knew not why, would apply this to Clement V. rather than to Boniface VIII.

[4] *And for a dance was dragg'd to martyrdom*—I am indebted to an intelligent critic in the *Monthly Review*, 1823, for pointing out my former erroneous translation of the words "per salti," "From the wilds."

Ye host of heaven, whose glory I survey!
O beg ye grace for those, that are, on earth,
All after ill example gone astray.
Canto XVIII., lines 120—122.

CANTO XIX.

ARGUMENT.

The eagle speaks as with one voice proceeding from a multitude of spirits that compose it, and declares the cause for which it is exalted to that state of glory. It then solves a doubt which our Poet had entertained respecting the possibility of salvation without belief in Christ; exposes the inefficacy of a mere profession of such belief; and prophesies the evil appearance that many Christian potentates will make at the day of judgment.

BEFORE my sight appear'd, with open wings,
The beauteous image; in fruition sweet,
Gladdening the thronged spirits. Each did seem
A little ruby, whereon so intense
The sunbeam glow'd, that to mine eyes it came
In clear refraction. And that, which next
Befalls me to pourtray, voice hath not utter'd,
Nor hath ink written,[1] nor in fantasy
Was e'er conceived. For I beheld and heard
The beak discourse; and, what intention form'd
Of many, singly as of one express,
Beginning: "For that I was just and piteous,
I am exalted to this height of glory,
The which no wish exceeds: and there on earth
Have I my memory left, e'en by the bad
Commended, while they leave its course untrod."
   Thus is one heat from many embers felt;
As in that image many were the loves,
And one the voice, that issued from them all:
Whence I address'd them: "O perennial flowers
Of gladness everlasting! that exhale
In single breath your odours manifold;
Breathe now: and let the hunger be appeased,
That with great craving long hath held my soul,
Finding no food on earth. This well I know;
That if there be in heaven a realm, that shows
In faithful mirror the celestial Justice,

---

[1] *Nor hath ink written.*—"This joie ne maie not written be with inke."—*Chaucer, Troilus and Cresseide,* b. iii.

Yours without veil reflects it. Ye discern
The heed, wherewith I do prepare myself
To hearken; ye, the doubt, that urges me
With such inveterate craving." Straight I saw,
Like to a falcon[1] issuing from the hood,
That rears his head, and claps him with his wings,
His beauty and his eagerness bewraying;
So saw I move that stately sign, with praise
Of grace divine inwoven, and high song
Of inexpressive joy. "He," it began,
"Who turn'd his compass[2] on the worlds extreme,
And in that space so variously hath wrought,
Both openly and in secret; in such wise
Could not, through all the universe, display
Impression of his glory, that the Word[3]
Of his omniscience should not still remain
In infinite excess. In proof whereof,
He first through pride supplanted, who was sum
Of each created being, waited not
For light celestial; and abortive fell.
Whence needs each lesser nature is but scant
Receptacle unto that Good, which knows
No limit, measured by itself alone.
Therefore your sight, of the omnipresent Mind
A single beam, its origin must own
Surpassing far its utmost potency.
The ken, your world is gifted with, descends
In the everlasting Justice as low down,
As eye doth in the sea; which, though it mark
The bottom from the shore, in the wide main
Discerns it not; and ne'ertheless it is;

---

[1] *Like to a falcon.—*
"Come falcon ch' uscisse dal cappello."
  Boccaccio, Il Filostrato, p. iv., st. 83.

Which Chaucer translates:
"As fresh as faucon coming out of mew."
  Troilus and Cresseide, b. iii.

"Poi come fa 'l falcon, quando si move,
Così Umiltà al cielo alzò la vista."
  Frezzi, Il Quadriregio, lib. iv., cap. 5.

"Rinaldo stà come suole il falcone
Uscito del capello a la veleta."
  L. Pulci, Morgante Maggiore, c. xi.

[2] *Who turn'd his compass.—*"When he prepared the heavens, I was there: when he set a compass upon the face of the depth." Prov. viii. 27.

" In his hand
He took the golden compasses, prepared
In God's eternal store, to circumscribe
This universe, and all created things."
  Milton, Paradise Lost, b. vii., 227.

[3] *The Word.—*"The divine nature still remained incomprehensible. Of this Lucifer was a proof; for he, though the chief of all created beings, yet, through his pride, waiting not for further supplies of the divine illumination, fell without coming to maturity." Thus our author, in the "De Vulgari Eloquio," speaking of the fallen angels, says, "divinam curam perversi expectare noluerunt."—L. i., c. 2.

Before my sight appear'd, with open wings,
The beauteous image; in fruition sweet,
Gladdening the thronged spirits.

Canto XIX., lines 1—3.

But hidden through its deepness. Light is none,
Save that which cometh from the pure serene
Of ne'er disturbed ether: for the rest,
'Tis darkness all; or shadow of the flesh,
Or else its poison. Here confess reveal'd
That covert, which hath hidden from thy search
The living Justice, of the which thou madest
Such frequent question; for thou saidst—'A man
Is born on Indus' banks, and none is there
Who speaks of Christ, nor who doth read nor write:
And all his inclinations and his acts,
As far as human reason sees, are good;
And he offendeth not in word or deed:
But unbaptized he dies, and void of faith.
Where is the justice that condemns him? where
His blame, if he believeth not?'—What then,
And who art thou, that on the stool wouldst sit
To judge a distance of a thousand miles
With the short sighted vision of a span?
To him,[1] who subtilizes thus with me,
There would assuredly be room for doubt
Even to wonder, did not the safe word
Of Scripture hold supreme authority.

   "O animals of clay! O spirits gross!
The primal will,[2] that in itself is good,
Hath from itself, the chief Good, ne'er been moved.
Justice consists in consonance with it,
Derivable by no created good,
Whose very cause depends upon its beam."

   As on her nest the stork, that turns about
Unto her young, whom lately she hath fed,
Whiles they with upward eyes do look on her;
So lifted I my gaze; and, bending so,
The ever-blessed image waved its wings,
Labouring with such deep counsel. Wheeling round
It warbled, and did say: "As are my notes
To thee, who understand'st them not; such is

---

[1] *To him.*—" He who should argue, on the words I have just used, respecting the fate of those who have wanted means of knowing the Gospel, would certainly have cause enough to doubt if he did not defer to the authority of Scripture, which pronounces God to be thoroughly just."

[2] *The primal will.*—The divine will.

The eternal judgment unto mortal ken."
Then still abiding in that ensign ranged,
Wherewith the Romans overawed the world,
Those burning splendours of the Holy Spirit
Took up the strain; and thus it spake again:
"None ever hath ascended to this realm,
Who hath not a believer been in Christ,
Either before or after the blest limbs
Were nail'd upon the wood. But lo! of those
Who call 'Christ, Christ,'[1] there shall be many found,
In judgment, further off from Him by far,
Than such to whom His name was never known.
Christians like these the Æthiop[2] shall condemn:
When that the two assemblages shall part;
One rich eternally, the other poor.

"What may the Persians say unto your kings,
When they shall see that volume,[3] in the which
All their dispraise is written, spread to view?
There amidst Albert's[4] works shall that be read
Which will give speedy motion to the pen,
When Prague[5] shall mourn her desolated realm.
There shall be read the woe that he[6] doth work
With his adulterate money on the Seine,
Who by the tusk will perish: there be read
The thirsting pride, that maketh fool alike
The English and Scot,[7] impatient of their bound.
There shall be seen the Spaniard's luxury;[8]
The delicate living there of the Bohemian,[9]
Who still to worth has been a willing stranger.

---

[1] *Who call "Christ, Christ."*—"Not every one that saith unto me, Lord, Lord, shall enter into the kingdom of heaven."—Matt. vii. 21.

[2] *The Æthiop.*—"The men of Nineveh shall rise in judgment with this generation, and shall condemn it."—Matt. xii. 41.

[3] *That volume.*—"And I saw the dead, small and great, stand before God; and the books were opened: and another book was opened, which is the book of life: and the dead were judged out of those things which were written in the books, according to their works."—Rev. xx. 12.

[4] *Albert.*—"Purgatory," canto vi. 98.

[5] *Prague.*—The eagle predicts the devastation of Bohemia by Albert, which happened soon after this time, when that emperor obtained the kingdom for his eldest son Rodolph. See Coxe's "House of Austria," 4to ed., vol. i., part i., p. 87.

[6] *He.*—Philip IV. of France, after the battle of Courtrai, 1302, in which the French were defeated by the Flemings, raised the nominal value of the coin. This king died in consequence of his horse being thrown to the ground by a wild boar, in 1314. The circumstances of his death are minutely related by Fazio degli Uberti, "Dittamondo," lib. iv., cap. 19.

[7] *The English and Scot.*—He adverts to the disputes between John Baliol and Edward I., the latter of whom is commended in the "Purgatory," canto vii. 130.

[8] *The Spaniard's luxury.*—The commentators refer this to Alonzo X. of Spain. It seems probable that the allusion is to Ferdinand IV., who came to the crown in 1295, and died in 1312, at the age of twenty-four, in consequence, as it was supposed, of his extreme intemperance. See Mariana, "Hist.," lib. xv., cap. 11.

[9] *The Bohemian.*—Winceslaus II. "Purgatory," canto vii. 99.

The halter of Jerusalem[1] shall see
A unit for his virtue; for his vices,
No less a mark than million. He,[2] who guards
The isle of fire by old Anchises honour'd,
Shall find his avarice there and cowardice;
And better to denote his littleness,
The writing must be letters maim'd, that speak
Much in a narrow space. All there shall know
His uncle[3] and his brother's[4] filthy doings,
Who so renown'd a nation and two crowns
Have bastardized.[5] And they, of Portugal[6]
And Norway,[7] there shall be exposed, with him
Of Ratza,[8] who hath counterfeited ill
The coin of Venice. O blest Hungary![9]
If thou no longer patiently abidest
Thy ill-entreating: and, O blest Navarre![10]
If with thy mountainous girdle[11] thou wouldst arm thee.
In earnest of that day, e'en now are heard
Wailings and groans in Famagosta's streets
And Nicosia's,[12] grudging at their beast,
Who keepeth even footing with the rest."[13]

---

[1] *The halter of Jerusalem.*—Charles II. of Naples and Jerusalem, who was lame. See note to "Purgatory," canto vii. 122, and xx. 78.

[2] *He.*—Frederick of Sicily, son of Peter III. of Arragon. "Purgatory," canto vii. 117. The isle of fire is Sicily, where was the tomb of Anchises.

[3] *His uncle.*—James, King of Majorca and Minorca, brother to Peter III.

[4] *His brother.*—James II. of Arragon, who died in 1327. See "Purgatory," canto vii. 117.

[5] *Bastardized.*—"Bozze," according to Bembo, is a Provençal word for "bastardo e non legitimo."—*Della Volg. Lingua.*, lib. i., p. 25, ediz. 1544. Others have understood it to mean, "one dishonoured by his wife."

[6] *Of Portugal.*—In the time of Dante, Dionysius was King of Portugal. He died in 1325, after a reign of nearly forty-six years, and does not seem to have deserved the stigma here fastened on him. See Mariana, lib. xv., cap. 18. Perhaps the rebellious son of Dionysius may be alluded to.

[7] *Norway.*—Haquin, King of Norway, is probably meant; who, having given refuge to the murderers of Eric VII., King of Denmark, A.D. 1288, commenced a war against his successor, Eric VIII., "which continued nine years, almost to the utter ruin and destruction of both kingdoms."—*Modern Univ. Hist.*, vol xxxii., p. 215.

[8] *Him of Ratza.*—One of the dynasty of the house of Nemagna, which ruled the kingdom of Rassia or Ratza, in Sclavonia, from 1161 to 1371, and whose history may be found in Mauro Orbino, "Regno degli Slavi," ediz. Pesaro, 1601. Uladislaus appears to have been the sovereign in Dante's time; but the disgraceful forgery adverted to in the text is not recorded by the historian.

[9] *Hungary.*—The kingdom of Hungary was about this time disputed by Carobert, son of Charles Martel, and Winceslaus, prince of Bohemia, son of Winceslaus II. See Coxe's "House of Austria," vol. i., part i., p. 86, 4to edit.

[10] *Navarre.*—Navarre was now under the yoke of France. It soon after (in 1328) followed the advice of Dante, and had a monarch of its own. Mariana, lib. xv., cap. 19.

[11] *Mountainous girdle.*—The Pyrenees.

[12] *Famagosta's streets and Nicosia's.*—Cities in the kingdom of Cyprus, at that time ruled by Henry II., a pusillanimous prince. Vertot, "Hist. des Chev. de Malte," lib. iii. iv. The meaning appears to be, that the complaints made by those cities of their weak and worthless governor may be regarded as an earnest of his condemnation at the last doom.

[13] *The rest.*—"Wise Poet!" thus Landino concludes his commentary on this canto, "to whom the human race owes obligations for having thus severely reprehended the faults of princes; since these are not, like the errors of private persons, harmful to one or a few only, but injure all the country which they govern; and a single one frequently causes the ruin of whole nations." Much to the same effect is a memorable sentence in Xenophon's "Agesilaus," that excellent manual for princes: καὶ τὰς μὲν τῶν ἰδιωτῶν ἁμαρτίας πώςως ἔφερε, τὰς δὲ τῶν ἀρχόντων μεγάλας ἦγε, κρίνων, τοὺς μὲν ὀλίγα, τοὺς δὲ πολλὰ, κακῶς διατιθέναι.—C. xi. 6. Compare also the opening of Demosthenes' second Speech against Aristogiton.

CANTO XX.

ARGUMENT.

The eagle celebrates the praise of certain kings, whose glorified spirits form the eye of the bird. In the pupil is David, and in the circle round it, Trajan, Hezekiah, Constantine, William II. of Sicily, and Ripheus. It explains to our Poet how the souls of those whom he supposed to have had no means of believing in Christ, came to be in heaven; and concludes with an admonition against presuming to fathom the counsels of God.

WHEN, disappearing from our hemisphere,
The world's enlightener vanishes, and day
On all sides wasteth; suddenly the sky,
Erewhile irradiate only with his beam,
Is yet again unfolded, putting forth
Innumerable lights wherein one shines.[1]
Of such vicissitude in heaven I thought;
As the great sign,[2] that marshalleth the world
And the world's leaders, in the blessed beak
Was silent: for that all those living lights,
Waxing in splendour, burst forth into songs,
Such as from memory glide and fall away.
Sweet Love, that dost apparel thee in smiles!
How lustrous was thy semblance in those sparkles,
Which merely are from holy thoughts inspired.
After[3] the precious and bright beaming stones,
That did ingem the sixth light, ceased the chiming
Of their angelic bells; methought I heard
The murmuring of a river, that doth fall
From rock to rock transpicuous, making known
The richness of his spring-head: and as sound
Of cittern, at the fret-board, or of pipe,
Is, at the wind-hole, modulate and tuned;
Thus, up the neck, as it were hollow, rose

---

[1] *Wherein one shines.*—The light of the sun, whence he supposes the other celestial bodies to derive their light. Thus, in the "Convito," p. 115, "Nullo sensibile," &c. "No sensible object in the world is more worthy to be made an example of the deity than the sun, which with sensible light enlightens first itself, and then all celestial and elementary bodies."

[2] *The great sign.*—The eagle, the Imperial ensign.

[3] *After.*—"After the spirits in the sixth planet (Jupiter) had ceased their singing."

For that all those living lights,
Waxing in splendour, burst forth into songs,
Such as from memory glide and fall away.
Canto XX., lines 10—12.

That murmuring of the eagle; and forthwith
Voice there assumed; and thence along the beak
Issued in form of words, such as my heart
Did look for, on whose tables I inscribed them.

"The part[1] in me, that sees and bears the sun
In mortal eagles," it began, "must now
Be noted steadfastly: for, of the fires,
That figure me, those, glittering in mine eye,
Are chief of all the greatest. This, that shines
Midmost for pupil, was the same who[2] sang
The Holy Spirit's song, and bare about
The ark from town to town: now doth he know
The merit of his soul-impassion'd strains
By their well-fitted guerdon. Of the five,
That make the circle of the vision, he,[3]
Who to the beak is nearest, comforted
The widow for her son: now doth he know,
How dear it costeth not to follow Christ;
Both from experience of this pleasant life,
And of its opposite. He next,[4] who follows
In the circumference, for the over-arch,
By true repenting slack'd the pace of death:
Now knoweth he, that the decrees of heaven[5]
Alter not, when, through pious prayer below,
To-day is made to-morrow's destiny.
The other following,[6] with the laws and me,
To yield the shepherd room, pass'd o'er[7] to Greece;
From good intent, producing evil fruit:
Now knoweth he, how all the ill, derived
From his well doing, doth not harm him aught;
Though it have brought destruction on the world.
That, which thou seest in the under bow,
Was William,[8] whom that land bewails, which weeps

---

[1] *The part.*—Lombardi well observes, that the head of the eagle is seen in profile, so that one eye only appears.
[2] *Who.*—David.
[3] *He.*—Trajan. See "Purgatory," canto x. 68.
[4] *He next.*—Hezekiah.
[5] *The decrees of heaven.*—The eternal counsels of God are indeed immutable, though they appear to us men to be altered by the prayers of the pious.
[6] *The other following.*—Constantine. There is no passage in which Dante's opinion of the evil that had arisen from the mixture of the civil with the ecclesiastical power is more unequivocally declared.
[7] *Pass'd o'er.*—"Left the Roman state to the Pope, and transferred the seat of the empire to Constantinople."
[8] *William.*—William II., King of Sicily, at the latter part of the twelfth century. He was of the Norman line of sovereigns, and obtained the appellation of "the Good;" and, as the poet says, his loss was as much the subject of regret in his dominions, as the presence of Charles II. of Anjou and Frederick of Arragon was of sorrow and complaint.

For Charles and Frederick living: now he knows,
How well is loved in heaven the righteous king;
Which he betokens by his radiant seeming.
Who, in the erring world beneath, would deem
That Trojan Ripheus,[1] in this round, was set,
Fifth of the saintly splendours? now he knows
Enough of that, which the world cannot see;
The grace divine: albeit e'en his sight
Reach not its utmost depth." Like to the lark,
That warbling in the air expatiates long,
Then, trilling out his last sweet melody,
Drops, satiate with the sweetness; such appear'd
That image, stampt by the everlasting pleasure,
Which fashions, as they are, all things that be.

    I, though my doubting were as manifest,
As is through glass[2] the hue that mantles it,
In silence waited not; for to my lips
" What things are these?" involuntary rush'd,
And forced a passage out: whereat I mark'd
A sudden lightening and new revelry.
The eye was kindled; and the blessed sign,
No more to keep me wondering and suspense,
Replied: " I see that thou believest these things,
Because I tell them, but discern'st not how;
So that thy knowledge waits not on thy faith:
As one, who knows the name of thing by rote,
But is a stranger to its properties,
Till other's tongue reveal them. Fervent love,
And lively hope, with violence assail
The kingdom of the heavens, and overcome
The will of the Most High; not in such sort

---

[1] *Trojan Ripheus.*—

    " Ripheus justissimus unus
  Qui fuit in Teucris, et servantissimus æqui."
              Virgil, Æneid, lib. ii. 427.
  " Then Ripheus fell, the justest far of all
    The sons of Troy."   *Pitt.*

[2] *Through glass*—This is the only allusion I have remarked in our author to the art of painting glass. Tiraboschi traces that invention in Italy as far back as to the end of the eighth century. " Storia della Lett. Ital.," tom. iii., lib. iii., cap. vi., § ii. This, however, if we may trust Mr. Warton's judgment, must have been a sort of mosaic in glass. For to express figures in glass, or what we now call the art of painting in glass, that writer observes, " was a very different work; and I believe I can show it was brought from Constantinople to Rome before the tenth century, with other ornamental arts."—*History of English Poetry*, vol. iii., p. xxii. In the following passage from the " Dittamondo " of Fazio degli Uberti, lib. v., cap. 3, the allusion is to mosaic in glass:

  " E pensa s' ai veduto e posto cura,
    Quando il musaico con vetri dipinti
    Adorna e compon ben la sua pittura,
  E quei che son più riccamente tinti
    Nelle più nobil parti gli son sempre,
    Ed e converso nel men gli più stinti."

As man prevails o'er man; but conquers it,
Because 'tis willing to be conquer'd; still,
Though conquer'd, by its mercy, conquering.
    "Those, in the eye who live the first and fifth,
Cause thee to marvel, in that thou behold'st
The region of the angels deck'd with them.
They quitted not their bodies, as thou deem'st,
Gentiles, but Christians; in firm rooted faith,
This,[1] of the feet in future to be pierced,
That,[2] of feet nail'd already to the cross.
One from the barrier of the dark abyss,
Where never any with good will returns,
Came back unto his bones. Of lively hope
Such was the meed; of lively hope, that wing'd
The prayers[3] sent up to God for his release,
And put power into them to bend His will.
The glorious Spirit, of whom I speak to thee,
A little while returning to the flesh,
Believed in him, who had the means to help;
And, in believing, nourish'd such a flame
Of holy love, that at the second death
He was made sharer in our gamesome mirth.
The other, through the riches of that grace,
Which from so deep a fountain doth distil,
As never eye created saw its rising,
Placed all his love below on just and right:
Wherefore, of grace, God oped in him the eye
To the redemption of mankind to come;
Wherein believing, he endured no more
The filth of Paganism, and for their ways
Rebuked the stubborn nations. The three nymphs,[4]
Whom at the right wheel thou beheld'st advancing,
Were sponsors for him, more than thousand years
Before baptizing. O how far removed,
Predestination! is thy root from such
As see not the First Cause entire: and ye,
O mortal men! be wary how ye judge:

---

[1] *This.*—Ripheus.
[2] *That.*—Trajan.
[3] *The prayers.*—The prayers of St. Gregory.

[4] *The three nymphs, whom at the right wheel thou beheld'st advancing.*—Faith, Hope, and Charity. "Purgatory," canto xxix. 116.

For we, who see our Maker, know not yet
The number of the chosen; and esteem
Such scantiness of knowledge our delight:
For all our good is, in that primal good,
Concentrate; and God's will and ours are one."
   So, by that form divine, was given to me
Sweet medicine to clear and strengthen sight.
And, as one handling skilfully the harp,
Attendant on some skilful songster's voice
Bids the cord vibrate; and therein the song
Acquires more pleasure: so the whilst it spake,
It doth remember me, that I beheld
The pair of blessed luminaries move,[1]
Like the accordant twinkling of two eyes,
Their beamy circlets, dancing to the sounds.

---

[1] *The pair of blessed luminaries move*—Ripheus and Trajan.

Again mine eyes were fix'd on Beatrice;
And, with mine eyes, my soul that in her looks
Found all contentment.
Canto XXI., lines 1—3.

CANTO XXI.

ARGUMENT.

Dante ascends with Beatrice to the seventh heaven, which is the planet Saturn; wherein is placed a ladder so lofty, that the top of it is out of his sight. Here are the souls of those who had passed their life in holy retirement and contemplation. Piero Damiano comes near them, and answers questions put to him by Dante; then declares who he was on earth, and ends by declaiming against the luxury of pastors and prelates in those times.

AGAIN mine eyes were fix'd on Beatrice;
And, with mine eyes, my soul that in her looks
Found all contentment. Yet no smile she wore:
And, "Did I smile," quoth she, "thou wouldst be straight
Like Semele when into ashes turn'd:
For, mounting these eternal palace-stairs,
My beauty, which the loftier it climbs,
As thou hast noted, still doth kindle more,
So shines, that, were no tempering interposed,
Thy mortal puissance would from its rays
Shrink, as the leaf doth from the thunderbolt.
Into the seventh splendour[1] are we wafted,
That, underneath the burning lion's breast,[2]
Beams, in this hour, commingled with his might.
Thy mind be with thine eyes; and, in them, mirror'd[3]
The shape, which in this mirror shall be shown."
  Whoso can deem, how fondly I had fed
My sight upon her blissful countenance,
May know, when to new thoughts I changed, what joy
To do the bidding of my heavenly guide;
In equal balance,[4] poising either weight.
  Within the crystal, which records the name
(As its remoter circle girds the world)
Of that loved monarch,[5] in whose happy reign
No ill had power to harm, I saw rear'd up,

---

[1] *The seventh splendour.*—The planet Saturn.

[2] *Underneath the burning lion's breast.*—The constellation Leo.

[3] *In them, mirror'd.*—"Let the form which thou shalt now behold in this mirror," the planet, that is, of Saturn (soon after, v. 22, called the crystal), "be reflected in the mirror of thy sight."

[4] *In equal balance.*—"My pleasure was as great in complying with her will, as in beholding her countenance."

[5] *Monarch.*—Saturn. Compare "Hell," canto xiv. 91

In colour like to sun-illumined gold,
A ladder, which my ken pursued in vain,
So lofty was the summit; down whose steps
I saw the splendours in such multitude
Descending, every light in heaven, methought,
Was shed thence. As the rooks, at dawn of day,
Bestirring them to dry their feathers chill,
Some speed their way a-field; and homeward some,
Returning, cross their flight; while some abide,
And wheel around their airy lodge: so seem'd
That glitterance,[1] wafted on alternate wing,
As upon certain stair it came, and clash'd
Its shining. And one, lingering near us, wax'd
So bright, that in my thought I said: "The love,
Which this betokens me, admits no doubt."

Unwillingly from question I refrain;
To her, by whom my silence and my speech
Are order'd, looking for a sign: whence she,
Who in the sight of Him, that seeth all,
Saw wherefore I was silent, prompted me
To indulge the fervent wish; and I began:
"I am not worthy, of my own desert,
That thou shouldst answer me: but for her sake,
Who hath vouchsafed my asking, spirit blest,
That in thy joy art shrouded! say the cause,
Which bringeth thee so near: and wherefore, say,
Doth the sweet symphony of Paradise
Keep silence here, pervading with such sounds
Of rapt devotion every lower sphere?"

"Mortal art thou in hearing, as in sight;"
Was the reply: "and what forbade the smile[2]
Of Beatrice interrupts our song.
Only to yield thee gladness of my voice,
And of the light that vests me, I thus far
Descend these hallow'd steps: not that more love
Invites me; for, lo! there aloft,[3] as much

---

[1] *That glitterance.*—"Quello sfavillar." That multitude of shining spirits, who, coming to a certain point of the ladder, made those different movements, which he has described as made by the birds.

[2] *What forbade the smile.*—"Because it would have overcome thee."

[3] *For, lo! there aloft.*—Where the other souls were.

Down whose steps
I saw the splendours in such multitude
Descending, every light in heaven, methought,
Was shed thence.

Canto XXI., lines 28—31.

Or more of love is witness'd in those flames:
But such my lot by charity assign'd,
That makes us ready servants, as thou seest,
To execute the counsel of the Highest."

"That in this court," said I, "O sacred lamp!
Love no compulsion needs, but follows free
The eternal Providence, I well discern:
This harder find to deem: why, of thy peers,
Thou only, to this office wert foredoom'd."

I had not ended, when, like rapid mill,
Upon its centre whirl'd the light; and then
The love that did inhabit there, replied:
"Splendour eternal, piercing through these folds,
Its virtue to my vision knits; and thus
Supported, lifts me so above myself,
That on the sovran essence, which it wells from,
I have the power to gaze: and hence the joy,
Wherewith I sparkle, equalling with my blaze
The keenness of my sight. But not the soul,[1]
That is in heaven most lustrous, nor the seraph,
That hath his eyes most fix'd on God, shall solve
What thou hast ask'd: for in the abyss it lies
Of th' everlasting statute sunk so low,
That no created ken may fathom it.
And, to the mortal world when thou return'st,
Be this reported: that none henceforth dare
Direct his footsteps to so dread a bourn.
The mind, that here is radiant, on the earth
Is wrapt in mist. Look then if she may do
Below, what passeth her ability
When she is ta'en to heaven." By words like these
Admonish'd, I the question urged no more;
And of the spirit humbly sued alone
To instruct me of its state. 'Twixt either shore[2]
Of Italy, nor distant from thy land,
A stony ridge[3] ariseth; in such sort,

---

[1] *Not the soul.*—The particular ends of Providence being concealed from the very angels themselves.
[2] *'Twixt either shore.*—Between the Adriatic Gulf and the Mediterranean Sea.
[3] *A stony ridge.*—A part of the Apennine. "Gibbo" is literally a "hunch." Thus Archilochus calls the island of Thasus, ὄνου ῥάχις. See Gaisford's "Poetæ Minores Græci," t. i., p. 298.

The thunder doth not lift his voice so high.
They call it Catria:[1] at whose foot, a cell
Is sacred to the lonely Eremite;
For worship set apart and holy rites."
A third time thus it spake; then added: "There
So firmly to God's service I adhered,
That with no costlier viands than the juice
Of olives, easily I pass'd the heats
Of summer and the winter frosts; content
In heaven-ward musings. Rich were the returns
And fertile, which that cloister once was used
To render to these heavens: now 'tis fallen
Into a waste so empty, that ere long
Detection must lay bare its vanity.
Pietro Damiano[2] there was I y-clept:
Pietro the sinner, when before I dwelt,
Beside the Adriatic,[3] in the house
Of our blest Lady. Near upon my close
Of mortal life, through much importuning
I was constrained to wear the hat,[4] that still
From bad to worse is shifted.—Cephas[5] came;
He came, who was the Holy Spirit's vessel;[6]
Barefoot and lean; eating their bread, as chanced,
At the first table. Modern Shepherds need
Those who on either hand may prop and lead them,
So burly are they grown; and from behind,

---

[1] *Catria.*—Now the abbey of Santa Croce, in the duchy of Urbino, about half-way between Gubbio and La Pergola. Here Dante is said to have resided for some time.

[2] *Pietro Damiano.*—" S. Pietro Damiano obtained a great and well-merited reputation, by the pains he took to correct the abuses among the clergy. Ravenna is supposed to have been the place of his birth, about 1007. He was employed in several important missions, and rewarded by Stephen IX. with the dignity of cardinal and the bishopric of Ostia, to which, however, he preferred his former retreat in the monastery of Fonte Avellana, and prevailed on Alexander II. to permit him to retire thither. Yet he did not long continue in this seclusion before he was sent on other embassies. He died in Faenza in 1072. His letters throw much light on the obscure history of these times. Besides them he has left several treatises on sacred and ecclesiastical subjects. His eloquence is worthy of a better age."—*Tiraboschi, Storia della Lett. Ital.*, tom. iii., lib. iv., cap. ii. He is mentioned by Petrarch, " De Vita Solit.," lib. ii., sec. iii., cap. xvii. : " Siquidem statum illum, pompasque sæculi suis contribulibus linquens, ipse Italiæ medio, ad sinistrum Apennini latus, quietissimam solitudinem, de qua multa conscripsit, et quæ vetus adhuc fontis Avellanæ nomen servat, perituris honoribus preferendam duxit, ubi non minus gloriose postmodum latuit quam innotuerat primum Romæ, nec dedecori illi fuit alti verticis rutilum decus squalenti cilicio permutasse." —*Petrarchæ Opera, Basil.*, 1571, p. 266.

[3] *Beside the Adriatic.*—Some editions and manuscripts have " fu," instead of " ful." According to the former of these readings, S. Pietro Damiano is made to distinguish himself from S. Pietro degli Onesti, surnamed " Il Peccator," founder of the monastery of S. Maria del Porto, on the Adriatic coast, near Ravenna, who died 1119, at about eighty years of age. If it could be ascertained that there was no religious house dedicated to the blessed Virgin before that founded by Pietro degli Onesti, to which the other Pietro might have belonged, this reading would, no doubt, be preferable; but at present it seems very uncertain which is the right.

[4] *The hat.*—The cardinal's hat.

[5] *Cephas.*—St. Peter.

[6] *The Holy Spirit's vessel.*—St. Paul. See " Hell," canto ii. 30.

Others to hoist them. Down the palfrey's sides
Spread their broad mantles, so as both the beasts
Are cover'd with one skin. O patience! thou
That look'st on this, and dost endure so long."

 I at those accents saw the splendours down
From step to step alight, and wheel, and wax,
Each circuiting, more beautiful. Round this[1]
They came, and stay'd them; utter'd then a shout
So loud, it hath no likeness here: nor I
Wist what it spake, so deafening was the thunder.

---

[1] *Round this.*—Round the spirit of Pietro Damiano.

CANTO XXII.

ARGUMENT.

He beholds many other spirits of the devout and contemplative; and amongst these is addressed by St. Benedict, who, after disclosing his own name and the names of certain of his companions in bliss, replies to the request made by our Poet that he might look on the form of the saint without that covering of splendour which then invested it; and then proceeds, lastly, to inveigh against the corruption of the monks. Next Dante mounts with his heavenly conductress to the eighth heaven, or that of the fixed stars, which he enters at the constellation of the Twins; and thence looking back, reviews all the space he has passed between his present station and the earth.

ASTOUNDED, to the guardian of my steps
I turn'd me, like the child, who always runs
Thither for succour, where he trusteth most:
And she was like the mother,[1] who her son
Beholding pale and breathless, with her voice
Soothes him, and he is cheer'd; for thus she spake,
Soothing me: "Know'st thou not, thou art in heaven?
And know'st not thou, whatever is in heaven,
Is holy; and that nothing there is done,
But is done zealously and well? Deem now,
What change in thee the song, and what my smile
Had wrought, since thus the shout had power to move thee;
In which, couldst thou have understood their prayers,
The vengeance[2] were already known to thee,
Which thou must witness ere thy mortal hour.
The sword of heaven is not in haste to smite,
Nor yet doth linger; save unto his seeming,
Who, in desire or fear, doth look for it.
But elsewhere now I bid thee turn thy view;
So shalt thou many a famous spirit behold."
    Mine eyes directing, as she will'd, I saw
A hundred little spheres, that fairer grew
By interchange of splendour. I remain'd,
As one, who fearful of o'er-much presuming,

---

[1] *And she was like the mother.—*
"Come la madre, che 'l figliuol ascolta
  Dietro a se pianger, si volge, ed aspetta,
  Poi il prende per mano e da la volta."
Fazio degli Uberti, Dittamondo, lib. iii., cap. 21.

[2] *The vengeance were already known to thee.—* Beatrice, it is supposed, intimates the approaching fate of Boniface VIII. See "Purgatory," canto xx. 86.

Abates in him the keenness of desire,
Nor dares to question; when, amid those pearls,
One largest and most lustrous onward drew,
That it might yield contentment to my wish;
And, from within it, these the sounds I heard.

"If thou, like me, beheldst the charity
That burns amongst us; what thy mind conceives,
Were utter'd. But that, ere the lofty bound
Thou reach, expectance may not weary thee
I will make answer even to the thought,
Which thou hast such respect of. In old days,
That mountain, at whose side Cassino[1] rests,
Was, on its height, frequented by a race[2]
Deceived and ill-disposed: and I it was,[3]
Who thither carried first the name of Him,
Who brought the soul-subliming truth to man.
And such a speeding grace shone over me,
That from their impious worship I reclaim'd
The dwellers round about, who with the world
Were in delusion lost. These other flames,
The spirits of men contemplative, were all
Enliven'd by that warmth, whose kindly force
Gives birth to flowers and fruits of holiness.
Here is Macarius;[4] Romoaldo[5] here;
And here my brethren, who their steps refrain'd
Within the cloisters, and held firm their heart."

I answering thus: "Thy gentle words and kind,

---

[1] *Cassino.*—A castle in the Terra di Lavoro. "The learned Benedictine, D. Angelo della Noce, in his notes on the chronicle of the monastery of Cassino (Not. cxi.), corrects the error of Cluverius and Eftenus, who describe Cassino as situated in the same place where the monastery now is; at the same time commending the veracity of our author in this passage, which places Cassino on the side of the mountain, and points out the monastery founded by St. Benedict on its summit."—*Lombardi.*

[2] *Frequented by a race.*—Lombardi here cites an opposite passage from the writings of Pope St. Gregory, "Mons tria millia," &c.—*Dialog.*, lib. ii., cap. 8: "The mountain, rising for the space of three miles, stretches its top towards the sky, where was a very ancient temple, in which, after the manner of the old heathens, Apollo was worshipped by the foolish rustics. On every side, groves had sprung up in honour of the false gods; and in these the mad multitude of unbelievers still tended on their unhallowed sacrifices. There then the man of God (St. Benedict) arriving, beat in pieces the idols, overturned the altar, cut down the groves, and in the very temple of Apollo built the shrine of St. Martin, placing that of St. John where the altar of Apollo had stood; and, by his continual preaching, called the multitude that dwelt round about to the true faith."

[3] *I it was.*—"A new order of monks, which in a manner absorbed all the others that were established in the west, was instituted A.D. 529, by Benedict of Nursia, a man of piety and reputation for the age he lived in."—*Maclaine's Mosheim, Eccles. Hist.*, vol. ii., cent. vi., p. ii., c. ii., § 6.

[4] *Macarius.*—There are two of this name enumerated by Mosheim among the Greek theologians of the fourth century, vol. i., cent. iv., p. xi., chap. ii., § 9. In the following chapter, § 10, it is said, "Macarius, an Egyptian monk, undoubtedly deserves the first rank among the practical writers of this time, as his works displayed, some few things excepted, the brightest and most lovely portraiture of sanctity and virtue."

[5] *Romoaldo.*—S. Romoaldo, a native of Ravenna, and the founder of the order of Camaldoli, died in 1027. He was the author of a commentary on the Psalms.

And this the cheerful semblance I behold.
Not unobservant, beaming in ye all,
Have raised assurance in me; wakening it
Full-blossom'd in my bosom, as a rose
Before the sun, when the consummate flower
Has spread to utmost amplitude. Of thee
Therefore intreat I, father, to declare
If I may gain such favour, as to gaze
Upon thine image by no covering veil'd."
 "Brother!" he thus rejoin'd, "in the last sphere[1]
Expect completion of thy lofty aim:
For there on each desire completion waits,
And there on mine; where every aim is found
Perfect, entire, and for fulfilment ripe.
There all things are as they have ever been:
For space is none to bound; nor pole divides.
Our ladder reaches even to that clime;
And so, at giddy distance, mocks thy view.
Thither the patriarch Jacob[2] saw it stretch
Its topmost round; when it appear'd to him
With angels laden. But to mount it now
None lifts his foot from earth: and hence my rule
Is left a profitless stain upon the leaves;
The walls, for abbey rear'd, turned into dens;
The cowls, to sacks choak'd up with musty meal.
Foul usury doth not more lift itself
Against God's pleasure, than that fruit, which makes
The hearts of monks so wanton: for whate'er
Is in the church's keeping, all pertains
To such, as sue for heaven's sweet sake; and not
To those, who in respect of kindred claim,
Or on more vile allowance. Mortal flesh
Is grown so dainty, good beginnings last not
From the oak's birth unto the acorn's setting.
His convent Peter founded without gold

---

[1] *In the last sphere.*—The Empyrean, where he afterwards sees St. Benedict, canto xxxii. 30. Beatified spirits, though they have different heavens allotted them, have all their seat in that higher sphere.
[2] *The patriarch Jacob.*—" And he dreamed, and behold, a ladder set up on the earth and the top of it reached to heaven: and behold the angels of God ascending and descending on it."—Gen. xxviii. 12. So Milton, " Paradise Lost," b. iii. 510:
 " The stairs were such, as whereon Jacob saw
  Angels ascending and descending, bands
  Of guardians bright."

Or silver; I, with prayers and fasting, mine;
And Francis, his in meek humility.
And if thou note the point, whence each proceeds,
Then look what it hath err'd to; thou shalt find
The white grown murky. Jordan was turn'd back:
And a less wonder, than the refluent sea,
May, at God's pleasure, work amendment here."

So saying, to his assembly back he drew:
And they together cluster'd into one;
Then all rolled upward, like an eddying wind.

The sweet dame beckon'd me to follow them:
And, by that influence only, so prevail'd
Over my nature, that no natural motion,
Ascending or descending here below,
Had, as I mounted, with my pennon vied.

So, reader, as my hope is to return
Unto the holy triumph, for the which
I oft-times wail my sins, and smite my breast;
Thou hadst been longer drawing out and thrusting
Thy finger in the fire, than I was, ere
The sign,[1] that followeth Taurus, I beheld,
And enter'd its precinct. O glorious stars!
O light impregnate with exceeding virtue!
To whom whate'er of genius lifteth me
Above the vulgar, grateful I refer;
With ye the parent[2] of all mortal life
Arose and set, when I did first inhale
The Tuscan air; and afterward, when grace
Vouchsafed me entrance to the lofty wheel[3]
That in its orb impels ye, fate decreed
My passage at your clime. To you my soul
Devoutly sighs, for virtue, even now.
To meet the hard emprize that draws me on.

"Thou art so near the sum of blessedness,"
Said Beatrice, "that behoves thy ken
Be vigilant and clear. And, to this end,
Or ever thou advance thee further, hence

---

[1] *The sign.*—The constellation of Gemini.
[2] *The parent.*—The sun was in the constellation of the Twins at the time of Dante's birth.
[3] *And afterward, when grace vouchsafed me entrance to the lofty wheel.*—The eighth heaven; that of the fixed stars.

THE VISION.

Look downward, and contemplate, what a world
Already stretch'd under our feet there lies :
So as thy heart may, in its blithest mood,
Present itself to the triumphal throng,
Which, through the ethereal concave, comes rejoicing."

    I straight obey'd; and with mine eye return'd
Through all the seven spheres; and saw this globe[1]
So pitiful of semblance, that perforce
It moved my smiles: and him in truth I hold
For wisest, who esteems it least; whose thoughts
Elsewhere are fix'd, him worthiest call and best.
I saw the daughter of Latona shine
Without the shadow,[2] whereof late I deem'd
That dense and rare were cause. Here I sustain'd
The visage, Hyperion, of thy son;[3]
And mark'd, how near him with their circles, round
Move Maia and Dione;[4] here discern'd
Jove's tempering 'twixt his sire and son;[5] and hence,
Their changes and their various aspects,
Distinctly scann'd. Nor might I not descry
Of all the seven, how bulky each, how swift;
Nor, of their several distances, not learn.
This petty area (o'er the which we stride
So fiercely), as along the eternal Twins
I wound my way, appear'd before me all,
Forth from the havens stretch'd unto the hills.
Then, to the beauteous eyes, mine eyes return'd.

---

[1] *This globe.*—So Chaucer, "Troilus and Cresseide," b. v. :
  "And down from thence fast he gan avise
  This little spot of earth, that with the sea
  Embraced is, and fully gan despise
  This wretched world."

  " All the world as to mine eye
  No more seemed than a prikc."
      Temple of Fame, b. ii.
Compare Cicero, "Somn. Scip.," "Jam ipsa terra ita mihi parva visa est," &c. Lucan, "Pharsalia," lib. ix. 11, and Tasso, "Gierusalemme Liberata," c. xiv., st. 9, 10, 11.

[2] *Without the shadow.*—See canto ii. 71.

[3] *Of thy son.*—The sun.

[4] *Maia and Dione.*—The planets Mercury and Venus: Dione being the mother of the latter, and Maia of the former deity.

[5] *'Twixt his sire and son.*—Betwixt Saturn and Mars.

CANTO XXIII.

ARGUMENT.

He sees Christ triumphing with His church. The Saviour ascends, followed by His virgin Mother. The others remain with St. Peter.

E'EN as the bird, who midst the leafy bower
Has, in her nest, sat darkling through the night,
With her sweet brood; impatient to descry
Their wished looks, and to bring home their food,
In the fond quest unconscious of her toil:
She, of the time prevenient, on the spray,
That overhangs their couch, with wakeful gaze
Expects the sun; nor ever, till the dawn,
Removeth from the east her eager ken:
So stood the dame erect, and bent her glance
Wistfully on that region,[1] where the sun
Abateth most his speed; that, seeing her
Suspense and wondering, I became as one,
In whom desire is waken'd, and the hope
Of somewhat new to come fills with delight.

Short space ensued; I was not held, I say,
Long in expectance, when I saw the heaven
Wax more and more resplendent; and, "Behold,"
Cried Beatrice, "the triumphal hosts
Of Christ, and all the harvest gather'd in,
Made ripe by these revolving spheres." Meseem'd,
That, while she spake, her image all did burn;
And in her eyes such fulness was of joy,
As I am fain to pass unconstrued by.

As in the calm full moon, when Trivia[2] smiles,
In peerless beauty, 'mid the eternal nymphs,[3]
That paint through all its gulfs the blue profound;
In bright pre-eminence so saw I there
O'er million lamps a sun, from whom all drew
Their radiance, as from ours the starry train:
And, through the living light, so lustrous glow'd
The substance, that my ken endured it not.

---

[1] *That region.*—Towards the south, where the course of the sun appears less rapid than when he is in the east or the west.
[2] *Trivia.*—A name of Diana.
[3] *The eternal nymphs.*—The stars.
"Σελάνα τε κατ' αἰθερ

Λαμπάδ', ἴν' ὠκυθόαι νύμφαι
'Ἱππεύουσι δι' ὀρφναίας."
Euripides, Supp., 995, edit. Barnes.

"Those starry nymphs, which dance about the pole."
Drummond, Sonnet.

O Beatrice! sweet and precious guide,
Who cheer'd me with her comfortable words:
"Against the virtue, that o'erpowereth thee,
Avails not to resist. Here is the Might,[1]
And here the Wisdom, which did open lay
The path, that had been yearned for so long,
Betwixt the heaven and earth." Like to the fire,
That, in a cloud imprison'd, doth break out
Expansive, so that from its womb enlarged,
It falleth against nature to the ground;
Thus, in that heavenly banqueting, my soul
Outgrew herself; and, in the transport lost,
Holds now remembrance none of what she was.

"Ope thou thine eyes, and mark me: thou hast seen
Things, that empower thee to sustain my smile.

I was as one, when a forgotten dream[2]
Doth come across him, and he strives in vain
To shape it in his fantasy again:
Whenas that gracious boon was proffer'd me,
Which never may be cancel'd from the book
Wherein the past is written. Now were all
Those tongues to sound, that have, on sweetest milk
Of Polyhymnia and her sisters, fed
And fatten'd; not with all their help to boot,
Unto the thousandth parcel of the truth.
My song might shadow forth that saintly smile,
How merely, in her saintly looks, it wrought.
And, with such figuring of Paradise,
The sacred strain must leap, like one that meets
A sudden interruption to his road.
But he, who thinks how ponderous the theme,
And that 'tis laid upon a mortal shoulder,
May pardon, if it tremble with the burden.
The track, our venturous keel must furrow, brooks

Musgrave and Herman would dismiss the word νύμφαι, "nymphs," from this passage in Euripides; but the use of it by our author in the text, tends to prove that it is the genuine reading: and it is thus that poets of the most distant ages, and without any knowledge of each other's writings (for we can scarcely imagine Dante to have read the plays of Euripides), may often protect one another against the verbal critics. Drummond, I believe, had learning enough to be indebted to either of his predecessors. Expressions somewhat similar in Theocritus and Tibullus are observed by Markland.

[1] *The Might.*—Our Saviour.

[2] *A forgotten dream.*—
"You might as well
Hunt half a day for a forgotten dream."
Wordsworth, Hart-Leap Well.

No unribb'd pinnace, no self-sparing pilot.
"Why doth my face," said Beatrice, "thus
Enamour thee, as that thou dost not turn
Unto the beautiful garden, blossoming
Beneath the rays of Christ? Here is the rose,[1]
Wherein the Word Divine was made incarnate;
And here the lilies,[2] by whose odour known
The way of life was follow'd." Prompt I heard
Her bidding, and encounter'd once again
The strife of aching vision. As, erewhile,
Through glance of sun-light, stream'd through broken cloud,
Mine eyes a flower-besprinkled mead have seen;
Though veil'd themselves in shade: so saw I there
Legions of splendours, on whom burning rays
Shed lightnings from above; yet saw I not
The fountain whence they flow'd. O gracious virtue!
Thou, whose broad stamp is on them, higher up
Thou didst exalt thy glory,[3] to give room
To my o'erlabour'd sight; when at the name
Of that fair flower,[4] whom duly I invoke
Both morn and eve, my soul with all her might
Collected, on the goodliest ardour fix'd.
And, as the bright dimensions of the star
In heaven excelling, as once here on earth,
Were, in my eye-balls livelily pourtray'd;
Lo! from within the sky a cresset[5] fell,
Circling in fashion of a diadem;
And girt the star; and, hovering, round it wheel'd.

Whatever melody sounds sweetest here,
And draws the spirit most unto itself,
Might seem a rent cloud, when it grates the thunder;
Compared unto the sounding of that lyre,[6]
Wherewith the goodliest sapphire,[7] that inlays
The floor of heaven, was crown'd. "Angelic Love

---

[1] *The rose.*—The Virgin Mary, who, says Lombardi, is termed by the church, Rosa Mystica. "I was exalted like a palm-tree in Engaddi, and as a rose-plant in Jericho."—Ecclesiasticus xxiv. 14.

[2] *The lilies.*—The Apostles. "And give ye a sweet savour as frankincense, and flourish as a lily."—Ecclesiasticus xxxix. 14.

[3] *Thou didst exalt thy glory.*—The divine light retired upwards, to render the eyes of Dante more capable of enduring the spectacle which now presented itself.

[4] *The name of that fair flower.*—The name of the Virgin.

[5] *A cresset.*—The angel Gabriel.

[6] *That lyre.*—By synecdoche, the lyre is put for the angel.

[7] *The goodliest sapphire.*—The Virgin.

I am, who thus with hovering flight enwheel
The lofty rapture from that womb inspired,
Where our desire did dwell : and round thee so,
Lady of Heaven ! will hover ; long as thou
Thy Son shalt follow, and diviner joy
Shall from thy presence gild the highest sphere."

Such close was to the circling melody :
And, as it ended, all the other lights
Took up the strain, and echoed Mary's name.

The robe,[1] that with its regal folds enwraps
The world, and with the nearer breath of God
Doth burn and quiver, held so far retired
Its inner hem, and skirting over us,
That yet no glimmer of its majesty
Had stream'd unto me : therefore were mine eyes
Unequal to pursue the crowned flame,[2]
That towering rose, and sought the seed[3] it bore.
And like to babe, that stretches forth its arms
For very eagerness toward the breast,
After the milk is taken ; so outstretch'd
Their wavy summits all the fervent band,
Through zealous love to Mary : then, in view,
There halted ; and "Regina Cœli"[4] sang
So sweetly, the delight hath left me never.

Oh ! what o'erflowing plenty is up-piled
In those rich-laden coffers,[5] which below
Sow'd the good seed, whose harvest now they keep.
Here are the treasures tasted, that with tears
Were in the Babylonian exile[6] won,
When gold had fail'd them. Here, in synod high
Of ancient council with the new convened,
Under the Son of Mary and of God,
Victorious he[7] his mighty triumphs holds,
To whom the keys of glory were assign'd."

---

[1] *The robe.*—The ninth heaven, the primum mobile, that enfolds and moves the eight lower heavens.
[2] *The crowned flame.*—The Virgin, with the angel hovering over her.
[3] *The seed.*—Our Saviour.
[4] *Regina Cœli.*—" The beginning of an anthem, sung by the church at Easter, in honour of our Lady." —*Volpi.*

[5] *What o'erflowing plenty is up-piled in those rich-laden coffers.*—Those spirits, who, having sown the seed of good works on earth, now contain the fruit of their pious endeavours.
[6] *In the Babylonian exile.*—During their abode in this world.
[7] *He.*—St. Peter, with the other holy men of the Old and New Testament.

CANTO XXIV.

ARGUMENT.

St. Peter examines Dante touching Faith, and is contented with his answers.

"O YE ! in chosen fellowship advanced
    To the great supper of the blessed Lamb,
Whereon who feeds hath every wish fulfill'd ;
If to this man through God's grace be vouchsafed
Foretaste of that, which from your table falls,
Or ever death his fated term prescribe ;
Be ye not heedless of his urgent will :
But may some influence of your sacred dews
Sprinkle him. Of the fount ye alway drink,
Whence flows what most he craves." Beatrice spake ;
And the rejoicing spirits, like to spheres
On firm-set poles revolving, trail'd a blaze
Of comet splendour : and as wheels, that wind
Their circles in the horologe, so work
The stated rounds, that to the observant eye
The first seems still, and as it flew, the last ;
E'en thus their carols[1] weaving variously,
They, by the measure paced, or swift, or slow,
Made me to rate the riches[2] of their joy.
    From that,[3] which I did note in beauty most
Excelling, saw I issue forth a flame

---

[1] *Their carols.*—" Carole." The annotator on the Monte Casino MS. observes, " carolæ dicuntur tripudium quoddam quod fit saliendo, ut Napolitani faciunt et dicunt." The word had also that signification, which is now the only one that common use attaches to it. " Au tiers jour il s'en partit" (the King of Cyprus coming from Canterbury to Edward III.), " et chevaucha le chemin de Londres ; et fit tant qu'il vint a Altem ; ou le roi se tenoit, et grand foison de Seigneurs appareillés pour le recevoir. Ce fut un dimenche a heure de relevee qu'il vint là. Si eut entre celle heure et le souper grans danses et grans karolles. Là etoit le jeune Seigneur de Coucy qui s'efforcoit de bien danser et de bien chanter quand son tour venoit," &c.—*Froissart*, vol. i., cap. 219, fol. edit. 1559.
    " These folke, of which I tell you so,
Upon a karole wenten tho :
A ladie karoled hem, that hight
Gladnesse, blissfull, and light,
Well could she sing, and lustely."
Chaucer, *Romaunt of the Rose*, edit. 1602, fol. 112.
    " I saw her daunce so comely,
Carol and sing so sweetly."
Chaucer, *The Dreame, or Booke of the Duchesse*, fol. 231.

[2] *The riches.*—Lombardi here reads with the Nidobeatina edition, " dalla richezza," instead of " della ricchezza," and construes it of the *amplitude* of the circles, according to which the poet estimated their greater or less degree of velocity. I have followed the other commentators.

[3] *From that.*—St. Peter.

So bright, as none was left more goodly there.
Round Beatrice thrice it wheel'd about,
With so divine a song, that fancy's ear
Records it not; and the pen passeth on,
And leaves a blank: for that our mortal speech,
Nor e'en the inward shaping of the brain,
Hath colours fine enough to trace such folds.[1]

"O saintly sister mine! thy prayer devout
Is with so vehement affection urged,
Thou dost unbind me from thy beauteous sphere."

Such were the accents towards my lady breathed
From that blest ardour, soon as it was stay'd;
To whom she thus: "O everlasting light
Of him, within whose mighty grasp our Lord
Did leave the keys, which of this wondrous bliss
He bare below! tent[2] this man as thou wilt,
With lighter probe or deep, touching the faith,
By the which thou didst on the billows walk.
If he in love, in hope, and in belief,
Be stedfast, is not hid from thee: for thou
Hast there thy ken, where all things are beheld
In liveliest portraiture. But since true faith
Has peopled this fair realm with citizens;
Meet is, that to exalt its glory more,
Thou, in his audience, shouldst thereof discourse."

Like to the bachelor, who arms himself,
And speaks not, till the master have proposed
The question, to approve,[3] and not to end it;
So I, in silence, arm'd me, while she spake,
Summoning up each argument to aid;
As was behoveful for such questioner,

---

[1] *Such folds.*—Pindar has the same bold image:

ὕμνων πτυχαῖς. Ode l. 170,

which both the Scholiast and Heyne, I think erroneously, understand of the return of the strophes. Since this note was written, I have found the same interpretation of Pindar's expression as that I had adopted, in the manuscript notes on that poet collected by Mr. St. Amand, and preserved in the Bodleian Library, No. 42: "Notandum: maximum decus vestimenti antiquitus *sinus* existimabantur, ita ut vix unquam a poetis tam Græcis quam Latinis vestis pulchra describatur sine hoc adjuncto."

[2] *Tent.*—Tenta. The word "tent," *try*, is used by our old writers, who, I think, usually spell it "taint;" as Massinger, "Parliament of Love," act. iv., sc. 3: "Do not fear, I have a staff to taint, and bravely."

[3] *To approve.*—"Per approbarla." Landino has "aiutarla." "The bachelor, or disputant in the school, arms or prepares himself to discuss the question proposed by the master, whose business it is to terminate it." Such is Vellutello's interpretation; and it has the merit of being, at least, more intelligible than Lombardi's, who, without reason, accuses the other commentators, except Venturi (whose explanation he rejects), of passing over the difficulty.

And such profession: "As good Christian ought,
Declare thee, what is faith?" Whereat I raised
My forehead to the light, whence this had breathed;
Then turn'd to Beatrice; and in her looks
Approval met, that from their inmost fount
I should unlock the waters. "May the grace,
That giveth me the captain of the church
For confessor," said I, "vouchsafe to me
Apt utterance for my thoughts:" then added: "Sire!
E'en as set down by the unerring style
Of thy dear brother, who with thee conspired
To bring Rome in unto the way of life,
Faith[1] of things hoped is substance, and the proof
Of things not seen; and herein doth consist
Methinks its essence."—"Rightly hast thou deem'd,"
Was answer'd; "if thou well discern, why first
He hath defined it substance, and then proof."

"The deep things," I replied, which here I scan
Distinctly, are below from mortal eye
So hidden, they have in belief alone
Their being; on which credence, hope sublime
Is built: and, therefore substance, it intends.
And inasmuch as we must needs infer
From such belief our reasoning, all respect
To other view excluded; hence of proof
The intention is derived." Forthwith I heard:
"If thus, whate'er by learning men attain,
Were understood; the sophist would want room
To exercise his wit." So breathed the flame
Of love; then added: "Current[2] is the coin
Thou utter'st, both in weight and in alloy.
But tell me, if thou hast it in thy purse."

"Even so glittering and so round," said I,
"I not a whit misdoubt of its assay."
    Next issued[3] from the deep-imbosom'd splendour:

---

[1] *Faith.*—Heb. xi. 1. So Marino, in one of his sonnets, which he calls "Divozioni:"

"Fede è sustanza di sperate cose,
E delle non visibili argomento."

[2] *Current.*—"The answer thou hast made, is right: but let me know if thy inward persuasion be conformable to thy profession."

[3] *Next issued.*—"We find that the more men have been acquainted with the practice of Christianity, the greater evidence they have had of the truth of it, and been more fully and rationally persuaded of it. To such I grant there are such powerful evidences of the truth of the doctrine of Christ by the effectual workings of the Spirit of God upon their souls, that all other arguments, as to their own satisfaction, may fall short of

"Say, whence the costly jewel, on the which
Is founded every virtue, came to thee."
    "The flood," I answer'd, "from the Spirit of God
Rain'd down upon the ancient bond and new,[1]—
Here is the reasoning, that convinceth me
So feelingly, each argument beside
Seems blunt, and forceless, in comparison."
    Then heard I: "Wherefore holdest thou that each,
The elder proposition and the new,
Which so persuade thee, are the voice of heaven?"
    "The works, that follow'd, evidence their truth,"
I answer'd: "Nature did not make for these
The iron hot, or on her anvil mold them."
    "Who voucheth to thee of the works themselves,"
Was the reply, "that they in very deed
Are that they purport? None hath sworn so to thee."
    "That all the world,"[2] said I, "should have been turn'd
To Christian, and no miracle been wrought,
Would in itself be such a miracle,

---

these. As to which, those verses of the poet Dantes, rendered into Latin by F. S., are very pertinent and significant; for when he had introduced the Apostle Peter, asking him what it was which his faith was founded on, he answers,

'Deinde exivit ex luce profunda
Quæ illic splendebat pretiosa gemma,
Super quam omnis virtus fundatur;'

i.e., that God was so pleased, by immediate revelation of Himself, to discover that divine truth to the world whereon our faith doth stand as on its sure foundation; but when the Apostle goes on to inquire how he knew this at first came from God, his answer to that is,

'Larga pluvia
Spiritus Sancti, quæ est diffusa
Super veteres et super novas membranas
Est syllogismus ille qui eam mihi conclusit
Adeo acute, ut præ illa demonstratione
Omnis demonstratio alia mihi videatur obtusa;'

i.e., that the Spirit of God doth so fully discover itself both in the Old and New Testament, that all other arguments are but dull and heavy if compared with this."—*Stillingfleet, Origines Sacræ*, b. ii., chap. ix., sect. xix., § 4. The reader will perceive that our learned divine has made an error in his quotation of this passage.

[1] *The ancient bond and new.*—The Old and New Testament.

[2] *That all the world.*—"We cannot conceive how the world should be at first induced to believe without manifest and uncontrouled miracles. For as Chrysostom speaks, εἰ σημεῖων χωρὶς ἐπείσαν, πολλῷ μεῖζον τὸ θαῦμα φαίνεται. It was the greatest miracle of all, if the world should believe without miracles. Which the poet Dantes hath well expressed in the twenty-fourth canto of Paradise. For when the Apostle is there brought in, asking the poet upon what account he took the Scriptures of the Old and New Testament to be the word of God, his answer is,

'Probatio quæ verum hoc mihi recludit,
Sunt opera, quæ secuta sunt, ad quæ Natura
Non candefecit ferrum unquam aut percussit incudem;'

i.e., the evidence of that is the divine power of miracles which was in those who deliver'd these things to the world. And when the Apostle catechiseth him further, how he knew those miracles were such as they pretended to be, viz., that they were true and divine, his answer is,

'Si orbis terræ sese convertit ad Christianismum
Inquiebam ego, sine miraculis; hoc unum
Est tale, ut reliqua non sint ejus centesima pars;'

i.e., if the world shou'd be converted to the Christian faith without miracles, this would be so great a miracle, that others were not to be compared with it. I conclude this, then, with that known saying of St. Austin, 'Quisquis adhuc prodigia, ut credat, inquiret, magnum est ipse prodigium qui mundo credente non credit:' 'He that seeks for miracles still to induce him to faith, when the world is converted to the Christian faith, he needs not seek for prodigies abroad; he wants only a looking-glass to discover one.' For, as he goes on, 'Unde temporibus eruditis, et omne quod fieri non potest respuentibus, sine ullis miraculis nimium mirabiliter incredibilia credidit mundus?' 'Whence came it to pass that in so learned and wary an age as that was which the Apostles preach'd in, the world should be brought to believe things, so strangely incredible as those were which Christ and His Apostles preach'd?'"—*Stillingfleet, Origines Sacræ*, b. ii., chap. x., sect. v., § 1. Donne, in his Sermons (vol. ii., p. 215, fol. edit.), quotes a similar passage from Augustine, and applies it to the demand for miracles made by Roman Catholics on Protestants.

The rest were not an hundredth part so great.
E'en thou went'st forth in poverty and hunger
To set the goodly plant, that, from the vine
It once was, now is grown unsightly bramble."
    That ended, through the high celestial court
Resounded all the spheres, "Praise we one God!"
In song of most unearthly melody.
And when that Worthy[1] thus, from branch to branch,
Examining, had led me, that we now
Approach'd the topmost bough; he straight resumed:
"The grace, that holds sweet dalliance with thy soul,
So far discreetly hath thy lips unclosed;
That, whatso'er has past them, I commend.
Behoves thee to express, what thou believest,
The next; and, whereon, thy belief hath grown."
    "O saintly sire and spirit!" I began,
"Who seest that, which thou didst so believe,
As to outstrip[2] feet younger than thine own,
Toward the sepulchre; thy will is here,
That I the tenour of my creed unfold;
And thou, the cause of it, hast likewise ask'd.
And I reply: I in one God believe;
One sole eternal Godhead, of whose love
All heaven is moved, Himself unmoved the while.
Nor demonstration physical alone,
Or more intelligential and abstruse,
Persuades me to this faith: but from that truth
It cometh to me rather, which is shed
Through Moses; the rapt Prophets; and the Psalms;
The Gospel; and what ye yourselves did write,
When ye were gifted of the Holy Ghost.
In three eternal Persons I believe;
Essence threefold and one; mysterious league
Of union absolute, which, many a time,
The word of gospel lore upon my mind

---

[1] *And when that Worthy.*—"Quel Barone." In the next canto, St. James is called "Barone." So in Boccaccio, Giorn., vi., Nov. 10, we find "Baron Messer Santo Antonio."

[2] *As to outstrip.*—Venturi insists that the poet has here "made a slip;" for that John came first to the sepulchre, though Peter was the first to enter it. But let Dante have leave to explain his own meaning, in a passage from his third book "De Monarchiâ;" "Dicit etiam Johannes ipsum (scilicet Petrum) introiisse *subito*, cum venit in monumentum, videns alium discipulum cunctantem ad ostium."—Page 146.

A A

Imprints : and from this germ, this firstling spark
The lively flame dilates; and, like heaven's star,
Doth glitter in me." As the master hears,
Well pleased, and then enfoldeth in his arms
The servant, who hath joyful tidings brought,
And having told the errand keeps his peace ;
Thus benediction uttering with song,
Soon as my peace I held, compass'd me thrice
The apostolic radiance, whose behest
Had oped my lips : so well their answer pleased.

CANTO XXV.

ARGUMENT.

St. James questions our Poet concerning Hope. Next St. John appears; and, on perceiving that Dante looks intently on him, informs him that he (St. John) had left his body resolved into earth, upon the earth; and that Christ and the Virgin alone had come with their bodies into heaven.

IF e'er the sacred poem, that hath made
   Both heaven and earth copartners in its toil,
And with lean abstinence, through many a year,
Faded my brow, be destined to prevail
Over the cruelty, which bars me forth
Of the fair sheep-fold,[1] where, a sleeping lamb,
The wolves set on and fain had worried me;
With other voice, and fleece of other grain,
I shall forthwith return; and, standing up
At my baptismal font, shall claim the wreath
Due to the poet's temples: for I there
First enter'd on the faith, which maketh souls
Acceptable to God: and, for its sake,[2]
Peter had then circled my forehead thus.

Next from the squadron, whence had issued forth
The first fruit of Christ's vicars on the earth,
Toward us moved a light, at view whereof
My Lady, full of gladness, spake to me:
Lo! lo! behold the peer of mickle might,
That makes Galicia throng'd with visitants."[3]

---

[1] *The fair sheep-fold.*—Florence, whence he was banished.
[2] *For its sake.*—For the sake of that faith.
[3] *Galicia throng'd with visitants.*—See Mariana, "Hist.," lib. xi., cap. xiii., "En el tiempo," &c. "At the time that the sepulchre of the Apostle St. James was discovered, the devotion for that place extended itself not only over all Spain, but even round about to foreign nations. Multitudes from all parts of the world came to visit it. Many others were deterred by the difficulty of the journey, by the roughness and barrenness of those parts, and by the incursions of the Moors, who made captives many of the pilgrims. The canons of St. Eloy, afterwards (the precise time is not known), with a desire of remedying these evils, built, in many places, along the whole road, which reached as far as to France, hospitals for the reception of the pilgrims." In the "Convito," p. 74, we find "la galassia," &c.: the galaxy, that is, the white circle which the common people call the way of St. James;" on which Biscioni remarks: "The common people formerly considered the Milky Way as a sign by night to pilgrims, who were going to St. James of Galicia; and this perhaps arose from the resemblance of the word galaxy to Galicia. I have often," he adds, "heard women and peasants call it the Roman road," "la strada di Roma."

" Lo there (quod he) cast up thine eye,
Se yondir, lo! the Galaxie,
The whiche men clepe the milky way,
For it is white, and some perfay,
Ycallin it han Watlynge Strete."
   Chaucer, *the House of Fame*, b. ii.

As when the ring-dove by his mate alights;
In circles, each about the other wheels,
And, murmuring, cooes his fondness: thus saw I
One, of the other[1] great and glorious prince,
With kindly greeting, hail'd; extolling, both,
Their heavenly banqueting: but when an end
Was to their gratulation, silent, each,
Before me sat they down, so burning bright,
I could not look upon them. Smiling then,
Beatrice spake: "O life in glory shrined!
Who[2] didst the largess[3] of our kingly court
Set down with faithful pen; let now thy voice,
Of hope the praises, in this height resound.
For well thou know'st, who figurest it as oft,[4]
As Jesus, to ye three, more brightly shone."

"Lift up thy head; and be thou strong in trust:
For that, which hither from the mortal world
Arriveth, must be ripen'd in our beam."
Such cheering accents from the second flame[5]
Assured me; and mine eyes I lifted up[6]
Unto the mountains, that had bow'd them late
With over-heavy burden. "Sith our Liege
Wills of his grace, that thou, or e'er thy death,
In the most secret council with his lords
Shouldst be confronted, so that having view'd
The glories of our court, thou mayst therewith
Thyself, and all who hear, invigorate

---

[1] *One, of the other.*—St. Peter and St. James.

[2] *Who.*—The Epistle of St. James is here attributed to the elder apostle of that name, whose shrine was at Compostella, in Galicia. Which of the two was the author of it, is yet doubtful. The learned and candid Michaelis contends very forcibly for its having been written by James the Elder. Lardner rejects that opinion as absurd: while Benson argues against it, but is well answered by Michaelis, who, after all, is obliged to leave the question undecided. See his Introduction to the New Testament, translated by Dr. Marsh, ed. Cambridge, 1793, vol. iv., cap. xxvi. §§ 1, 2, 3. Mr. Horne supposes, that as the elder James "was put to death by Herod Agrippa A.D. 44 (Acts xii.), it is evident that he was not the author of the epistle which bears the name of James, because it contains passages which refer to a later period, viz., v. 1—8, which intimates the then immediately approaching destruction of Jerusalem, and the subversion of the Jewish polity."—*Introduction to the Critical Study and Knowledge of the Holy Scriptures*, ed. 1818, vol. ii., p. 600.

[3] *Largess.*—He appears to allude to the Epistle of James, i. 5: "If any of you lack wisdom, let him ask of God, that giveth to all men liberally, and upbraideth not; and it shall be given him." Or, to v. 17: "Every good gift and every perfect gift is from above, and cometh down from the Father of lights." Some editions, however, read "l'allegrezza," "joy," instead of "la larghezza."

[4] *As oft.*—Landino and Venturi, who read "Quanto," explain this, that the frequency with which James had commended the virtue of hope, was in proportion to the brightness in which Jesus had appeared at his transfiguration. Vellutello, who reads "Quante," supposes that James three times recommends patient hope in the last chapter of his Epistle; and that Jesus, as many times, showed His brightness to the three disciples; once when He cleansed the lepers (Luke v.); again when He raised the daughter of Jaïrus (Mark v.); and a third time when He was transfigured. As to Lombardi, who also reads "Quante," his construction of the passage seems to me scarcely intelligible.

[5] *The second flame.*—St. James.

[6] *I lifted up.*—"I looked up to the Apostles." "I will lift up mine eyes unto the hills, from whence cometh my help."—Ps. cxxi. 1.

With hope, that leads to blissful end; declare,
What is that hope? how it doth flourish in thee?
And whence thou hadst it?" Thus, proceeding still,
The second light: and she, whose gentle love
My soaring pennons in that lofty flight
Escorted, thus preventing me, rejoin'd:
"Among her sons, not one more full of hope,
Hath the church militant: so 'tis of him
Recorded in the sun, whose liberal orb
Enlighteneth all our tribe: and ere his term
Of warfare, hence permitted he is come,
From Egypt to Jerusalem,[1] to see.
The other points, both which[2] thou hast inquired,
Not for more knowledge, but that he may tell
How dear thou hold'st the virtue; these to him
Leave I: for he may answer thee with ease,
And without boasting, so God give him grace."
 Like to the scholar, practised in his task,
Who, willing to give proof of diligence,
Seconds his teacher gladly; "Hope,"[3] said I,
"Is of the joy to come a sure expectance,
The effect of grace divine and merit preceding.
This light from many a star, visits my heart;
But flow'd to me, the first, from him who sang
The songs of the Supreme; himself supreme
Among his tuneful brethren. 'Let all hope
In thee,' so spake his anthem,[4] 'who have known
Thy name;' and, with my faith, who know not that?
From thee, the next, distilling from his spring,
In thine epistle, fell on me the drops
So plenteously, that I on others shower
The influence of their dew." Whileas I spake,
A lamping, as of quick and volley'd lightning,
Within the bosom of that mighty sheen[5]

---

[1] *From Egypt to Jerusalem.*—From the lower world to heaven.
[2] *Both which.*—One point Beatrice has herself answered; "how that hope flourishes in him." The other two remain for Dante to resolve.
[3] *Hope.*—This is from the "Sentences" of Petrus Lombardus: "Est autem spes virtus quâ spiritualia et æterna bona sperantur, id est cum fiduciâ expectantur. Est enim spes certa expectatio futuræ beatitudinis, veniens ex Dei gratiâ et ex meritis præcedentibus vel ipsam spem, quam naturâ præit charitas ut rem speratam, id est beatitudinem æternam. Sine meritis enim aliquid sperare non spes, sed præsumptio dici potest."
—*Pet. Lomb., Sent.*, lib. iii., dist. 26, ed. Bas., 1486, fol.
[4] *His anthem.*—"They that know thy name will put their trust in thee."—Ps. ix. 10.
[5] *Within the bosom of that mighty sheen.*—The spirit of St. James.

Play'd tremulous ; then forth these accents breathed :
"Love for the virtue, which attended me
E'en to the palm, and issuing from the field,
Glows vigorous yet within me ; and inspires
To ask of thee, whom also it delights,
What promise thou from hope, in chief, dost win."

"Both scriptures, new and ancient," I replied,
"Propose the mark (which even now I view)
For souls beloved of God. Isaias[1] saith,
'That, in their own land, each one must be clad
In twofold vesture ;' and their proper land
Is this delicious life. In terms more full,
And clearer far, thy brother hath set forth[2]
This revelation to us, where he tells
Of the white raiment destined to the saints."
And, as the words were ending, from above,
"They hope in thee !" first heard we cried : whereto
Answer'd the carols all. Amidst them next,
A light of so clear amplitude emerged,
That winter's month[3] were but a single day,
Were such a crystal in the Cancer's sign.

Like as a virgin[4] riseth up, and goes,
And enters on the mazes of the dance ;
Though gay, yet innocent of worse intent,
Than to do fitting honour to the bride :
So I beheld the new effulgence come
Unto the other two, who in a ring
Wheel'd, as became their rapture. In the dance,
And in the song, it mingled. And the dame
Held on them fix'd her looks ; e'en as the spouse,
Silent, and moveless. "This[5] is he, who lay

---

[1] *Isaias.*—"He hath clothed me with the garments of salvation, he hath covered me with the robe of righteousness."—Chap. lxi. 10.
[2] *Thy brother hath set forth.*—St. John in the Revelation, vii. 9.
[3] *Winter's month.*—"If a luminary, like that which now appeared, were to shine throughout the month following the winter solstice, during which the constellation Cancer appears in the east at the setting of the sun, there would be no interruption to the light, but the whole month would be as a single day."
[4] *Like as a virgin.*—There is a pretty counterpart to this simile in the "Quadriregio" of Frezzi :

" Poi come donna, che fa reverenza
   Lassando il ballo, tal' atto fè ella."—Lib. iv., cap. v.
" Then as a lady, when she leaves the dance,
   Maketh obeisance, even so did she."
The same writer has another more like that in the text:
" Come donzella, c'ha a guidar la danza,
   Che a chi l'invita reverenzia face,
   E po' incomincia vergognosa e manza,
Così colei," &c.   Lib. iv., cap. ii.

[5] *This.*—St. John, who reclined on the bosom of our Saviour, and to whose charge Jesus recommended His mother.

Upon the bosom of our pelican:
This he, into whose keeping, from the cross,
The mighty charge was given." Thus she spake:
Yet therefore nought the more removed her sight
From marking them: or e'er her words began,
Or when they closed. As he, who looks intent,
And strives with searching ken, how he may see
The sun in his eclipse, and, through desire
Of seeing, loseth power of sight; so I[1]
Peer'd on that last resplendence, while I heard:
" Why dazzlest thou thine eyes in seeking that,
Which here abides not? Earth my body is,
In earth; and shall be, with the rest, so long,
As till our number equal the decree
Of the Most High. The two that have ascended,
In this our blessed cloister, shine alone[2]
With the two garments. So report below."

As when, for ease of labour, or to shun
Suspected peril, at a whistle's breath,
The oars, erewhile dash'd frequent in the wave,
All rest: the flamy circle at that voice
So rested; and the mingling sound was still,
Which from the trinal band, soft-breathing, rose.
I turn'd, but ah! how trembled in my thought,
When, looking at my side again to see
Beatrice, I descried her not; although,
Not distant, on the happy coast she stood.

---

[1] *So I.*—He looked so earnestly, to descry whether St. John were present there in body, or in spirit only; having had his doubts raised by that saying of our Saviour's: "If I will that he tarry till I come, what is that to thee?"

[2] *The two that have ascended, in this our blessed cloister, shine alone.*—Christ and Mary, whom he has described in the last canto but one as rising above his sight.

CANTO XXVI.

ARGUMENT.

St. John examines our poet touching Charity. Afterwards Adam tells when he was created, and placed in the terrestrial Paradise; how long he remained in that state; what was the occasion of his fall; when he was admitted into heaven; and what language he spake.

WITH dazzled eyes, whilst wondering I remain'd;
Forth of the beamy flame,[1] which dazzled me,
Issued a breath, that in attention mute
Detain'd me; and these words it spake: " 'Twere well,
That, long as till thy vision, on my form
O'erspent, regain its virtue, with discourse
Thou compensate the brief delay. Say then,
Beginning, to what point thy soul aspires:
And meanwhile rest assured, that sight in thee
Is but o'erpower'd a space, not wholly quench d;
Since thy fair guide and lovely, in her look
Hath potency, the like to that, which dwelt
In Ananias' hand."[2]—I answering thus:
" Be to mine eyes the remedy, or late
Or early, at her pleasure; for they were
The gates, at which she enter'd, and did light
Her never-dying fire. My wishes here
Are centred: in this palace is the weal,
That Alpha and Omega is, to all
The lessons love can read me." Yet again
The voice, which had dispersed my fear when dazed
With that excess, to converse urged, and spake:
" Behoves thee sift more narrowly thy terms;
And say, who levell'd at this scope thy bow."
 " Philosophy," said I, " hath arguments,
And this place hath authority enough,
To imprint in me such love: for, of constraint,

---

[1] *Whilst wondering I remain'd; forth of the beamy flame.*—St. John.

[2] *Ananias' hand.*—Who, by putting his hand on St. Paul, restored his sight.—Acts ix. 17.

Say then,
Beginning, to what point thy soul aspires:
And meanwhile rest assured, that sight in thee
Is but o'erpower'd a space, not wholly quench'd.
Canto XXVI., lines 7—10.

Good, inasmuch as we perceive the good,
Kindles our love; and in degree the more,
As it comprises more of goodness in 't.
The essence then, where such advantage is,
That each good, found without it, is nought else
But of his light the beam, must needs attract
The soul of each one, loving, who the truth
Discerns, on which this proof is built. Such truth
Learn I from him,[1] who shows me the first love
Of all intelligential substances
Eternal: from his voice I learn, whose word
Is truth; that of Himself to Moses saith,
'I will make[2] all My good before thee pass:'
Lastly, from thee I learn, who chief proclaim'st
E'en at the outset[3] of thy heralding,
In mortal ears the mystery of heaven."

"Through human wisdom, and the authority
Therewith agreeing," heard I answer'd, "keep
The choicest of thy love for God. But say,
If thou yet other cords within thee feel'st,
That draw thee towards Him; so that thou report
How many are the fangs, with which this love
Is grappled to thy soul." I did not miss,
To what intent the eagle of our Lord[4]
Had pointed his demand; yea, noted well
The avowal which he led to; and resumed:
"All grappling bonds, that knit the heart to God,
Confederate to make fast our charity.
The being of the world; and mine own being;
The death which He endured, that I should live;
And that, which all the faithful hope, as I do;
To the foremention'd lively knowledge join'd;
Have from the sea of ill love saved my bark,
And on the coast secured it of the right.
As for the leaves,[5] that in the garden bloom,

---

[1] *From him.*—Some suppose that Plato is here meant, who, in his "Banquet," makes Phædrus say: ὁμολογεῖται ὁ Ἔρως ἐν τοῖς πρεσβυτάτοις εἶναι, πρεσβύτατος δὲ ὤν, μεγίστων ἀγαθῶν ἡμῖν αἴτιός ἐστιν. "Love is confessedly amongst the eldest of beings; and being the eldest, is the cause to us of the greatest goods."—Plat., *Op.*, tom. x., p. 177, Bip. ed. Others have understood it of Aristotle; and others, of the writer who goes by the name of Dionysius the Areopagite, referred to in the twenty-eighth canto.
[2] *I will make.*—Exod. xxxiii. 19.
[3] *At the outset.*—John i. 1, &c.
[4] *The eagle of our Lord.*—St. John.
[5] *The leaves.*—Created beings.

My love for them is great, as is the good
Dealt by the eternal hand, that tends them all."
    I ended: and therewith a song most sweet
Rang through the spheres; and "Holy, holy, holy,"
Accordant with the rest, my Lady sang.
And as a sleep is broken and dispersed
Through sharp encounter of the nimble light,
With the eye's spirit running forth to meet
The ray, from membrane on to membrane urged;
And the upstartled wight loathes that he sees;
So, at his sudden waking, he misdeems
Of all around him, till assurance waits
On better judgment: thus the saintly dame
Drove from before mine eyes the motes away,
With the resplendence of her own, that cast
Their brightness downward, thousand miles below.
Whence I my vision, clearer than before,
Recover'd; and well nigh astounded, ask'd
Of a fourth light, that now with us I saw.
    And Beatrice: "The first living soul,
That ever the first virtue framed,[1] admires
Within these rays his Maker." Like the leaf,
That bows its lithe top till the blast is blown;
By its own virtue rear'd, then stands aloof:
So I, the whilst she said, awe-stricken bow'd.
Then eagerness to speak embolden'd me;
And I began: "O fruit! that wast alone
Mature, when first engender'd; ancient father!
That doubly seest in every wedded bride
Thy daughter, by affinity and blood;
Devoutly as I may, I pray thee hold
Converse with me: my will thou seest: and I,
More speedily to hear thee, tell it not."
    It chanceth oft some animal bewrays,
Through the sleek covering[2] of his furry coat,

---

[1] *The first living soul, that ever the first virtue framed.*—Adam.

[2] *Through the sleek covering.*—Lombardi's explanation of this passage is somewhat ludicrous. By "un animal coverto," he understands, not an animal in its natural covering of fur or hair, but one drest up with clothes, as a dog, for instance, "so clad for sport;" "un cane per trastullo coperto." Chaucer describes, as one of the tokens of pleasure in a dog, "the smoothing down of his hairs."

"It came and crept to me as low,
Right as it had me yknow,
Held down his head, and joyned his eares
And laid all smooth downe his heares."
The Dreame of Chaucer, or the Book of the Duchesse.
ed. 1602, fol. 229.

The fondness, that stirs in him, and conforms
His outside seeming to the cheer within:
And in like guise was Adam's spirit moved
To joyous mood, that through the covering shone,
Transparent, when to pleasure me it spake:
"No need thy will be told, which I untold
Better discern, than thou whatever thing
Thou hold'st most certain: for that will I see
In Him, who is truth's mirror; and Himself,
Parhelion[1] unto all things, and nought else,
To Him. This wouldst thou hear: how long since, God
Placed me in that high garden, from whose bounds
She led me up this ladder, steep and long;
What space endured my season of delight;
Whence truly sprang the wrath that banish'd me;
And what the language, which I spake and framed.
Not that I tasted[2] of the tree, my son,
Was in itself the cause of that exile,
But only my transgressing of the mark
Assign'd me. There, whence[3] at thy lady's hest
The Mantuan moved him, still was I debarr'd
This council, till the sun had made complete,
Four thousand and three hundred rounds and twice,
His annual journey; and, through every light
In his broad pathway, saw I him return,
Thousand save seventy times, the whilst I dwelt
Upon the earth. The language[4] I did use
Was worn away, or ever Nimrod's race
Their unaccomplishable work began.
For nought,[5] that man inclines to, e'er was lasting;

---

[1] *Parhelion.*—Who enlightens and comprehends all things; but is himself enlightened and comprehended by none.

[2] *Not that I tasted.*—So Frezzi:
"Per colpa fù l' uom messo in bando,
Non solamente per gustar del pomo;
Ma perch' e' trapassò di Dio il comando."
Il Quadriregio, lib. iv., cap. I.

[3] *Whence.*—That is, from Limbo. See "Hell," canto ii. 53. Adam says that 5,232 years elapsed from his creation to the time of his deliverance, which followed the death of Christ.

[4] *The language.*—"Hac forma locutionis, locutus est Adam, hac forma locuti sunt omnes posteri ejus usque ad ædificationem turris Babel."—*De Vulgari Eloquentia*, lib. i., cap. vi. "This form of speech Adam used; this, all his posterity until the building of the tower of Babel."

[5] *For nought.*—There is a similar passage in the "De Vulgari Eloquentia," lib. i., cap. ix. "Since, therefore, all our language, except that which was created together with the first man by God, has been repaired according to our own will and pleasure, after that confusion, which was nothing else than a forgetfulness of the former; and since man is a being most unstable and variable, our language can neither be lasting nor continuous; but, like other things which belong to us, as customs and dress, must be varied by distances of places and times."

Left by his reason free, and variable
As is the sky that sways him. That he speaks,
Is nature's prompting : whether thus, or thus,
She leaves to you, as ye do most affect it.
Ere I descended into hell's abyss,
El[1] was the name on earth of the Chief Good,
Whose joy enfolds me : Eli then 'twas call'd.
And so beseemeth : for, in mortals, use[2]
Is as the leaf upon the bough : that goes,
And other comes instead. Upon the mount
Most high above the waters, all my life,[3]
Both innocent and guilty, did but reach
From the first hour, to that which cometh next
(As the sun changes quarter) to the sixth."

---

[1] *El.*—Some read *Un,* "One," instead of *El :* but the latter of these readings is confirmed by a passage from Dante's treatise "De Vulgari Eloquentia," lib. i. cap. iv.: "Quod prius vox primi loquentis sonaverit, viro sanæ mentis in promptu esse non dubito ipsum fuisse quod Deus est, videlicet El." St. Isidore, in the "Origines," lib. vii., cap. i, had said, " Primum apud Hebræos Dei nomen El dicitur."

[2] *For, in mortals, use.*—From Horace, "Ars. Poet.," 62.

[3] *Most high above the waters, all my life.*—"I remained in the terrestial Paradise only to the seventh hour." In the "Historia Scolastica" of Petrus Comestor, it is said of our first parents : "Quidam tradunt eos fuisse in Paradiso septem horas."—f. 9, ed. Par., 1513, 4to.

CANTO XXVII.

ARGUMENT.

St. Peter bitterly rebukes the covetousness of his successors in the apostolic see, while all the heavenly host sympathise in his indignation: they then vanish upwards. Beatrice bids Dante again cast his view below. Afterwards they are borne into the ninth heaven, of which she shows him the nature and properties; blaming the perverseness of man, who places his will on low and perishable things.

THEN "Glory to the Father, to the Son,
And to the Holy Spirit," rang aloud
Throughout all Paradise; that with the song
My spirit reel'd, so passing sweet the strain.
And what I saw was equal ecstasy:
One universal smile[1] it seem'd of all things;
Joy past compare; gladness unutterable;
Imperishable life of peace and love;
Exhaustless riches, and unmeasured bliss.
 Before mine eyes stood the four torches[2] lit:
And that,[3] which first had come, began to wax
In brightness; and, in semblance, such became,
As Jove might be, if he and Mars were birds,
And interchanged their plumes. Silence ensued,
Through the blest quire; by Him, who here appoints
Vicissitude of ministry, enjoin'd;
When thus I heard: "Wonder not, if my hue
Be changed; for, while I speak, these shalt thou see
All in like manner change with me. My place
He[4] who usurps on earth (my place, ay, mine,
Which in the presence of the Son of God
Is void), the same hath made my cemetery
A common sewer of puddle and of blood:
The more below his triumph, who from hence

---

[1] *One universal smile.—*
 "Ivi ogni cosa intorno m'assembrava
 Un' allegrezza di giocondo riso."
  Frezzi, Il Quadriregio, lib. iv., cap. ii.
 "All things smiled."
  Milton, Paradise Lost, b. viii. 265.

[2] *Four torches.*—St. Peter, St. James, St. John, and Adam.

[3] *And that.*—St. Peter, who looked as the planet Jupiter would, if it assumed the sanguine appearance of Mars.

[4] *He.*—Boniface VIII.

Malignant fell." Such colour,[1] as the sun,
At eve or morning, paints an adverse cloud,
Then saw I sprinkled over all the sky.
And as the unblemish'd dame, who, in herself
Secure from censure, yet at bare report
Of other's failing, shrinks with maiden fear;
So Beatrice, in her semblance, changed:
And such eclipse in heaven, methinks, was seen,
When the Most Holy suffer'd. Then the words
Proceeded, with voice, alter'd from itself
So clean, the semblance did not alter more.
"Not to this end was Christ's spouse with my blood,
With that of Linus, and of Cletus,[2] fed;
That she might serve for purpose of base gold:
But for the purchase of this happy life,
Did Sextus, Pius, and Callixtus bleed,
And Urban;[3] they, whose doom was not without
Much weeping seal'd. No purpose was of ours,[4]
That on the right hand of our successors,
Part of the Christian people should be set,
And part upon their left; nor that the keys,
Which were vouchsafed me, should for ensign serve
Unto the banners, that do levy war
On the baptized: nor I, for sigil-mark,
Set upon sold and lying privileges:
Which makes me oft to bicker and turn red.
In shepherd's clothing, greedy wolves[5] below
Range wide o'er all the pastures. Arm of God!
Why longer sleep'st thou? Cahorsines and Gascons[6]
Prepare to quaff our blood. O good beginning!
To what a vile conclusion must thou stoop.
But the high providence, which did defend,

---

[1] *Such colour.*—
"Qui color infectis adversi solis ab ictu
Nubibus esse solet aut purpureæ Auroræ."
   Ovid, Metamorphoses, lib. iii. 184.

[2] *Of Linus, and of Cletus.*—Bishops of Rome in the first century.

[3] *Did Sextus, Pius, and Calixtus bleed, and Urban.*—The former two, bishops of the same see, in the second, and the others in the fourth century.

[4] *No purpose was of ours.*—"We did not intend that our successors should take any part in the political divisions among Christians; or that my figure (the seal of St. Peter) should serve as a mark to authorise iniquitous grants and privileges."

[5] *Wolves.*—
" Wolves shall succeed to teachers, grievous wolves."
   Milton, Paradise Lost, b. xii. 508.

[6] *Cahorsines and Gascons.*—He alludes to Jacques d'Ossa, a native of Cahors, who filled the papal chair in 1316, after it had been two years vacant, and assumed the name of John XXII., and to Clement V., a Gascon, of whom see "Hell," canto xix., 86, and note.

Then "Glory to the Father, to the Son,
And to the Holy Spirit," rang aloud
Throughout all Paradise; that with the song
My spirit reel'd, so passing sweet the strain.
Canto XXVII., lines 1—4.

Through Scipio, the world's empery for Rome,
Will not delay its succour: and thou, son,[1]
Who through thy mortal weight shalt yet again
Return below, open thy lips, nor hide
What is by me not hidden." As a flood
Of frozen vapours streams adown the air,
What time the she-goat[2] with her skiey horn
Touches the sun; so saw I there stream wide
The vapours, who with us had linger'd late,
And with glad triumph deck the ethereal cope.
Onward my sight their semblances pursued;
So far pursued, as till the space between
From its reach sever'd them: whereat the guide
Celestial, marking me no more intent
On upward gazing, said, "Look down, and see
What circuit thou hast compass'd." From the hour[3]
When I before had cast my view beneath,
All the first region overpast I saw,
Which from the midmost to the boundary winds;
That onward, thence, from Gades,[4] I beheld
The unwise passage of Laertes' son;
And hitherward the shore,[5] where thou, Europa,
Madest thee a joyful burden; and yet more
Of this dim spot had seen, but that the sun,[6]
A constellation off and more, had ta'en
His progress in the zodiac underneath.

Then by the spirit, that doth never leave
Its amorous dalliance with my lady's looks,
Back with redoubled ardour were mine eyes
Led unto her: and from her radiant smiles,
Whenas I turn'd me, pleasure so divine
Did lighten on me, that whatever bait
Or art or nature in the human flesh,

---

[1] *Thou, son.*—"Beatrus Petrus—multaque locutus est, et docuit me de veteri testamento, *de hominibus tiam adhuc in seculo adhuc viventibus plura peccata ntonuit mihi*, precepitque, ut ea quæ de illis audieram eis referrem."—*Alberici Visio*, § 45.

[2] *What time the she-goat.*—When the sun is in Capricorn.

[3] *From the hour.*—Since he had last looked (see canto xxii.) he perceived that he had passed from the meridian circle to the eastern horizon; the half of our hemisphere, and a quarter of the heaven.

[4] *From Gades.*—See "Hell," canto xxvi. 106.

[5] *The shore.*—Phœnicia, where Europa, the daughter of Agenor, mounted on the back of Jupiter, in his shape of a bull.

[6] *The sun.*—Dante was in the constellation of Gemini, and the sun in Aries. There was, therefore, part of those two constellations, and the whole of Taurus, between them.

Or in its limn'd resemblance, can combine
Through greedy eyes to take the soul withal,
Were, to her beauty, nothing. Its boon influence
From the fair nest of Leda[1] rapt me forth,
And wafted on into the swiftest heaven.

What place for entrance Beatrice chose,
I may not say; so uniform was all,
Liveliest and loftiest. She my secret wish
Divined; and, with such gladness, that God's love
Seem'd from her visage shining, thus began:
"Here is the goal, whence motion on his race
Starts: motionless the centre, and the rest
All moved around. Except the soul divine,
Place in this heaven is none; the soul divine,
Wherein the love, which ruleth o'er its orb,
Is kindled, and the virtue, that it sheds:
One circle, light and love, enclasping it,
As this doth clasp the others; and to Him,
Who draws the bound, its limit only known.
Measured itself by none, it doth divide
Motion to all, counted unto them forth,
As by the fifth or half ye count forth ten.
The vase, wherein time's roots[2] are plunged, thou seest:
Look elsewhere for the leaves. O mortal lust!
That canst not lift thy head above the waves
Which whelm and sink thee down. The will in man
Bears goodly blossoms; but its ruddy promise
Is, by the dripping of perpetual rain,
Made mere abortion: faith and innocence
Are met with but in babes; each taking leave,
Ere cheeks with down are sprinkled: he, that fasts
While yet a stammerer, with his tongue let loose
Gluts every food alike in every moon:
One, yet a babbler, loves and listens to

---

[1] *The fair nest of Leda.*—"From the Gemini;" thus called because Leda was the mother of the twins Castor and Pollux.

[2] *Time's roots.*—"Here," says Beatrice, "are the roots, from whence time springs: for the parts, into which it is divided, the other heavens must be considered." And she then breaks out into an exclamation on the degeneracy of human nature, which does not lift itself to the contemplation of divine things. Thus in the "Quadriregio," lib. ii., cap. vi.:

"Il tempo, e'l ciel, che sopra noi e volto,
E una cosa, e non voltando il cielo,
Ciò che da tempo pende saria tolto."

"Time, and the heaven that turneth o'er our heads,
Are but as one; and if the heaven turn'd not,
That, which depends on time, were done away."

His mother; but no sooner hath free use
Of speech, than he doth wish her in her grave.
So suddenly doth the fair child of him,[1]
Whose welcome is the morn and eve his parting,
To negro blackness change her virgin white.

"Thou, to abate thy wonder, note, that none[2]
Bears rule in earth; and its frail family
Are therefore wanderers. Yet before the date,[3]
When, through the hundredth in his reckoning dropt,
Pale January must be shoved aside
From winter's calendar, these heavenly spheres
Shall roar so loud, that fortune shall be fain[4]
To turn the poop, where she hath now the prow;
So that the fleet run onward: and true fruit,
Expected long, shall crown at last the bloom."

---

[1] *The fair child of him.*—There is something very similar in our author's treatise "De Monarchiâ," lib. i., p. 104: "Humanum genus filius est cœli quod est perfectissimum in omni opere suo. Generat enim homo hominem et sol juxta secundum in Naturali Auditu." This, therefore, is intended for a philosophical truth, and not for a figure, as when Pindar calls "the day" "child of the sun:"

    'Ἀμέραν
. . . παῖδ' Ἀλίου.   *Ol.*, ii. 59.

[2] *None.*—Because, as has been before said, the shepherds are become wolves.

[3] *Before the date.*—"Before many ages are past; before those fractions, which are dropt in the reckoning of every year, shall amount to so large a portion of time, that January shall be no more a winter month."

By this periphrasis is meant "in a short time;" as we say familiarly, such a thing will happen before a thousand years are over, when we mean it will happen soon. Thus Petrarch:

"Ben sa ch' il prova, e fiati cosa piana
 Anzi mill' anni." *Trionfo d' Amore*, cap. i.

[4] *Fortune shall be fain.*—The commentators, in general, suppose that our poet here augurs that great reform, which he vainly hoped would follow on the arrival of the Emperor Henry VII. in Italy. Lombardi refers the prognostication to Can Grande della Scala: and when we consider that this canto was not finished till after the death of Henry, as appears from the mention that is made of John XXII., it cannot be denied but the conjecture is probable. Troya ("Veltro Allegorico," p. 186) suggests Matteo Visconti, or Castruccio Castracani, as the expected reformer.

CANTO XXVIII.

ARGUMENT.

Still in the ninth heaven, our Poet is permitted to behold the divine essence; and then sees, in three hierarchies, the nine choirs of angels. Beatrice clears some difficulties which occur to him on this occasion.

So she, who doth imparadise my soul,
    Had drawn the veil from off our present life,
And bared the truth of poor mortality:
When lo! as one who, in a mirror, spies
The shining of a flambeau at his back,
Lit sudden ere he deem of its approach,
And turneth to resolve him, if the glass
Have told him true, and sees the record faithful
As note is to its metre; even thus,
I well remember, did befall to me,
Looking upon the beauteous eyes, whence love
Had made the leash to take me. As I turn'd:
And that which none, who in that volume[1] looks,
Can miss of, in itself apparent, struck
My view; a point I saw, that darted light
So sharp, no lid, unclosing, may bear up
Against its keenness. The least star we ken
From hence, had seem'd a moon; set by its side,
As star by side of star. And so far off,
Perchance, as is the halo from the light
Which paints it, when most dense the vapour spreads:
There wheel'd about the point a circle of fire,
More rapid than the motion which surrounds,
Speediest, the world. Another this enring'd;
And that a third; the third a fourth, and that
A fifth encompass'd; which a sixth next bound;
And over this, a seventh, following, reach'd
Circumference so ample, that its bow,
Within the span of Juno's messenger,
Had scarce been held entire. Beyond the seventh,
Ensued yet other two. And every one,
As more in number distant from the first,

---

[1] *That volume.*—The ninth heaven, as Vellutello, I think, rightly interprets it.

Not unlike
To iron in the furnace, every cirque,
Ebullient, shot forth scintillating fires.
Canto XXVIII., lines 80—82.

Was tardier in motion: and that glow'd
With flame most pure, that to the sparkle of truth,
Was nearest; as partaking most, methinks,
Of its reality. The guide beloved
Saw me in anxious thought suspense, and spake:
"Heaven, and all nature, hangs upon that point.[1]
The circle thereto most conjoin'd observe;
And know, that by intenser love its course
Is, to this swiftness, wing'd." To whom I thus:
"It were enough; nor should I further seek,
Had I but witness'd order, in the world
Appointed, such as in these wheels is seen.
But in the sensible world such difference[2] is,
That in each round shows more divinity,
As each is wider from the centre. Hence
If in this wondrous and angelic temple,
That hath, for confine, only light and love,
My wish may have completion, I must know
Wherefore such disagreement is between
The exemplar and its copy: for myself,
Contemplating, I fail to pierce the cause."

"It is no marvel, if thy fingers foil'd
Do leave the knot untied: so hard 'tis grown
For want of tenting." Thus she said: "But take,"
She added, "if thou wish thy cure, my words,
And entertain them subtly. Every orb,
Corporeal, doth proportion its extent
Unto the virtue through its parts diffused.
The greater blessedness preserves the more.
The greater is the body (if all parts
Share equally) the more is to preserve.
Therefore the circle, whose swift course enwheels

---

[1] *Heaven, and all nature, hangs upon that point.*— ἐκ τοιαύτης ἄρα ἀρχῆς ἤρτηται ὁ οὐρανὸς καὶ ἡ φύσις.—*Aristotle, Metaph.*, lib. xii., c. 7. "From that beginning depend heaven and nature."

[2] *Such difference.*—The material world and the intelligential (the copy and the pattern) appear to Dante to differ in this respect, that the orbits of the latter are more swift, the nearer they are to the centre, whereas the contrary is the case with the orbits of the former. The seeming contradiction is thus accounted for by Beatrice. In the material world, the more ample the body is, the greater is the good of which it is capable, supposing all the parts to be equally perfect. But in the intelligential world, the circles are more excellent and powerful, the more they approximate to the central point, which is God. Thus the first circle, that of the seraphim, corresponds to the ninth sphere, or primum mobile; the second, that of the cherubim, to the eighth sphere, or heaven of fixed stars; the third, or circle of thrones, to the seventh sphere, or planet of Saturn: and in like manner throughout the two other trines of circles and spheres.

"In orbs
Of circuit inexpressible they stood,
Orb within orb."
Milton, Paradise Lost, b. v. 596.

The universal frame, answers to that
Which is supreme in knowledge and in love.
Thus by the virtue, not the seeming breadth
Of substance, measuring, thou shalt see the heavens,
Each to the intelligence that ruleth it,
Greater to more, and smaller unto less,
Suited in strict and wondrous harmony."

As when the north blows from his milder cheek[1]
A blast, that scours the sky, forthwith our air,
Clear'd of the rack that hung on it before,
Glitters; and, with his beauties all unveil'd,
The firmament looks forth serene, and smiles:
Such was my cheer, when Beatrice drove
With clear reply the shadows back, and truth
Was manifested as a star in heaven.
And when the words were ended, not unlike
To iron in the furnace, every cirque,
Ebullient, shot forth scintillating fires:
And every sparkle shivering to new blaze,
In number[2] did outmillion the account
Reduplicate upon the chequer'd board.
Then heard I echoing on, from choir to choir,
"Hosanna," to the fixed point, that holds,
And shall for ever hold them to their place,
From everlasting, irremovable.

Musing awhile I stood: and she, who saw
My inward meditations, thus began:
"In the first circles, they, whom thou beheld'st,
Are seraphim and cherubim. Thus swift
Follow their hoops, in likeness to the point,
Near as they can, approaching; and they can
The more, the loftier their vision. Those
That round them fleet, gazing the Godhead next,
Are thrones; in whom the first trine ends. And all
Are blessed, even as their sight descends
Deeper into the truth, wherein rest is

---

[1] *As when the north blows from his milder cheek.*—By "ond' è più leno," some understand that point from whence "the wind is *mildest;*" others, that "in which there is most *force.*" The former interpretation is probably right.

[2] *In number.*—The sparkles exceeded the number which would be produced by the sixty-four squares of a chess-board, if for the first we reckoned one; for the next, two; for the third, four; and so went on doubling to the end of the account.

For every mind. Thus happiness hath root
In seeing, not in loving, which of sight
Is aftergrowth. And of the seeing such
The meed, as unto each, in due degree,
Grace and good-will their measure have assign'd.
The other trine, that with still opening buds
In this eternal springtide blossom fair,
Fearless of bruising from the nightly ram,[1]
Breathe up in warbled melodies threefold
Hosannas, blending ever; from the three,
Transmitted, hierarchy of gods, for aye
Rejoicing; dominations[2] first; next them,
Virtues; and powers the third; the next to whom
Are princedoms and archangels, with glad round
To tread their festal ring; and last, the band
Angelical, disporting in their sphere.
All, as they circle in their orders, look
Aloft; and, downward, with such sway prevail,
That all with mutual impulse tend to God.
These once a mortal view beheld. Desire,
In Dionysius,[3] so intensely wrought,
That he, as I have done, ranged them; and named
Their orders, marshal'd in his thought. From him,
Dissentient, one refused his sacred read.
But soon as in this heaven his doubting eyes
Were open'd, Gregory[4] at his error smiled.
Nor marvel, that a denizen of earth
Should scan such secret truth; for he had learnt[5]
Both this and much beside of these our orbs,
From an eye-witness to heaven's mysteries."

---

[1] *Fearless of bruising from the nightly ram.*—Not injured, like the productions of our spring, by the influence of autumn, when the constellation Aries rises at sunset.

[2] *Dominations.*—

"Hear, all ye angels, progeny of light,
Thrones, dominations, princedoms, virtues, powers."
  Milton, Paradise Lost, b. v. 601.

[3] *Dionysius.*—The Areopagite, in his book "De Cœlesti Hierarchiâ."

[4] *Gregory.*—Gregory the Great. "Novem vero angelorum ordines diximus; quia videlicet esse, testante sacro eloquio, scimus: Angelos, archangelos, virtutes, potestates, principatus, dominationes, thronos, cherubin atque seraphin."—*Divi Gregorii, Hom.* xxxiv., f. 125, ed. Par., 1518, fol.

[5] *He had learnt.*—Dionysius, he says, had learnt from St. Paul. It is almost unnecessary to add that the book above referred to which goes under his name, was the production of a later age. In Bishop Bull's seventh sermon, which treats of the different degrees of beatitude in heaven, there is much that resembles what is said on the same subject by our poet. The learned prelate, however, appears a little inconsistent, when, after having blamed Dionysius the Areopagite, "for reckoning up exactly the several orders of the angelical hierarchy, as if he had seen a muster of the heavenly host before his eyes" (v. i., p. 313), he himself then speaks rather more particularly of the several orders in the celestial hierarchy than he is warranted in doing by Holy Scripture.

CANTO XXIX.

ARGUMENT.

Beatrice beholds, in the mirror of divine truth, some doubts which had entered the mind of Dante. These she resolves; and then digresses into a vehement reprehension of certain theologians and preachers in those days, whose ignorance or avarice induced them to substitute their own inventions for the pure word of the Gospel.

NO longer,[1] than what time Latona's twins
. Cover'd of Libra and the fleecy star,
Together both, girding the horizon hang;
In even balance, from the zenith poised;
Till from that verge, each, changing hemisphere,
Part the nice level; e'en so brief a space
Did Beatrice's silence hold. A smile
Sat painted on her cheek; and her fix'd gaze
Bent on the point, at which my vision fail'd:
When thus, her words resuming, she began:
"I speak, nor what thou wouldst inquire, demand;
For I have mark'd it, where all time and place
Are present. Not for increase to himself
Of good, which may not be increased, but forth
To manifest his glory by its beams;
Inhabiting his own eternity,
Beyond time's limit or what bound soe'er
To circumscribe his being; as he will'd,
Into new natures, like unto himself,
Eternal love unfolded: nor before,
As if in dull inaction, torpid, lay,
For, not in process of before or aft,[2]
Upon these waters moved the Spirit of God.
Simple and mix'd, both form and substance,[3] forth

---

[1] *No longer.*—As short a space as the sun and moon are in changing hemispheres, when they are opposite to one another, the one under the sign of Aries, and the other under that of Libra, and both hang, for a moment, poised as it were in the hand of the zenith.

[2] *For, not in process of before or aft.*—There was neither "before nor after," no distinction, that is, of time, till the creation of the world.

[3] *Simple and mix'd, both form and substance.*—Simple and unmixed form answers to "pure intelligence," v. 33 ("puro atto"), the highest of created being; simple and unmixed substance, to "mere

To perfect being started, like three darts
Shot from a bow three-corded. And as ray
In crystal, glass, and amber, shines entire,
E'en at the moment of its issuing; thus
Did, from the eternal Sovran, beam entire
His threefold operation,[1] at one act
Produced coeval. Yet, in order, each
Created his due station knew: those highest,
Who pure intelligence were made; mere power,
The lowest; in the midst, bound with strict league,
Intelligence and power, unsever'd bond.
Long tract of ages by the angels past,
Ere the creating of another world,
Described on Jerome's pages,[2] thou hast seen.
But that what I disclose to thee is true,
Those penmen,[3] whom the Holy Spirit moved,
In many a passage of their sacred book,
Attest; as thou by diligent search shalt find:
And reason,[4] in some sort, discerns the same,
Who scarce would grant the heavenly ministers,
Of their perfection void, so long a space.
Thus when and where these spirits of love were made,
Thou know'st, and how: and, knowing, hast allay'd

---

power," v. 33 ("pura potenzia") the lowest; and form mixed with substance, to "intelligence and power," v. 35, ("potenzia con atto"), that which holds the middle place between the other two. This, which appears sufficiently plain, Lombardi has contrived to perplex; not being aware of the high sense in which our poet here and elsewhere uses the word "forma," as the Greek writers employed the term μορφή, and particularly St. Paul, Philipp. ii. 6. The following is a remarkable instance in our language: "A man, though he have one form already, viz., the natural soul; it hinders not but he may have also another, the quickening Spirit of God."—*Henry More, Disc.* xiii.

[1] *His threefold operation.*—He means that spiritual beings, brute matter, and the intermediate part of the creation which participates both of spirit and matter, were produced at once.

"For, as there are three natures, schoolmen call
One corporal only, th' other spiritual,
Like single; so there is a third commixt
Of body and spirit together, placed betwixt
Those other two," *Ben Jonson, Eupheme.*

[2] *On Jerome's pages.*—St. Jerome had described the angels as created long before the rest of the universe; an opinion which Thomas Aquinas controverted; and the latter, as Dante thinks, had Scripture on his side. "Sex millia nondum nostri orbis implentur anni; et quantas prius æternitates, quanta tempora, quantas sæculorum origines fuisse arbitrandum est, in quibus Angeli, Throni, Dominationes, cæteræque Virtutes servierint Deo; et absque temporum vicibus atque mensuris Deo jubente substiterint."—*Hieronym., In Epist. ad Titum,* 1, Paris edit., 1706, tom. iv., part i., p. 411. "Dicendum, quod supra hoc invenitur duplex sanctorum doctorum sententia, illa tamen probabilior videtur, quod angeli simul cum creatura corporea sunt creati. Angeli enim sunt quædam pars universi. Non enim constituunt per se unum universum, sed tam ipsi quam creatura corporea in constitutionem unius universi conveniunt. Quod apparet ex ordine unius creaturæ ad aliam. Ordo enim rerum adinvicem est bonum universi. Nulla autem pars perfecta est a suo toto separata. Non est igitur probabile, ut Deus cujus perfecta sunt opera, ut dicitur Deuteron. 32, creaturam angelicam seorsum ante alias creaturas creaverit. Quamvis contrarium non sit reputandum erroneum, præcipue propter sententiam Greg. Nazian. cujus tanta est in doctrina Christiana authoritas, ut nullus unquam ejus dictis calumniam inferre præsumpserit sicut nec Athanasii Documentis, ut Hieron. dicit."— *Thomas Aquinas, Summa Theolog.,* P. 1ma, Quæst. LXI., art. iii.

[3] *Those penmen.*—As in Gen. i. 1, and Ecclesiasticus xviii. 1.

[4] *Reason.*—The heavenly ministers ("motori") would have existed to no purpose if they had been created before the corporeal world, which they were to govern.

Thy thirst, which from the triple question[1] rose.
Ere one had reckon'd twenty, e'en so soon,
Part of the angels fell: and, in their fall,
Confusion to your elements[2] ensued.
The others kept their station: and this task,
Whereon thou look'st, began, with such delight,
That they surcease not ever, day nor night,
Their circling. Of that fatal lapse the cause
Was the curst pride of him, whom thou hast seen
Pent[3] with the world's incumbrance. Those, whom here
Thou seest, were lowly to confess themselves
Of his free bounty, who had made them apt
For ministries so high: therefore their views
Were, by enlightening grace and their own merit,
Exalted; so that in their will confirm'd
They stand, nor fear to fall. For do not doubt,
But to receive the grace, which Heaven vouchsafes,
Is meritorious,[4] even as the soul
With prompt affection welcometh the guest.
Now, without further help, if with good heed
My words thy mind have treasured, thou henceforth
This consistory round about mayst scan,
And gaze thy fill. But, since thou hast on earth
Heard vain disputers, reasoners in the schools,
Canvass the angelic nature, and dispute
Its powers of apprehension, memory, choice;
Therefore, 'tis well thou take from me the truth,
Pure and without disguise; which they below,
Equivocating, darken and perplex.

"Know thou, that, from the first, these substances,
Rejoicing in the countenance of God,
Have held unceasingly their view, intent
Upon the glorious vision, from the which
Nought absent is nor hid: where then no change

---

[1] *The triple question.*—He had wished to know where, when, and how the angels had been created, and these three questions had been resolved.

[2] *Elements.*—"Alimenti" was sometimes put for "elementi" by the old Tuscan writers. See the notes to Redi's "Bacco in Toscano," vol. i., p. 125. Redi, Opere, 8vo, Milan, 1809. There is therefore no necessity for the alteration made in some editions.

[3] *Pent.*—See "Hell," canto xxxiv. 105.

[4] *Meritorious.*—The collator of the Monte Casino MS. boasts of that being the only text which has "meritorio," "concistorio," and "adjutorio." The reading is probably right, but I find it is in Landino's edition of 1484, and Vellutello's of 1544; and it may perhaps, be in many others.

Of newness, with succession, interrupts,
Remembrance, there, needs none to gather up
Divided thought and images remote.
  " So that men, thus at variance with the truth,
Dream, though their eyes be open; reckless some
Of error; others well aware they err,
To whom more guilt and shame are justly due.
Each the known track of sage philosophy
Deserts, and has a by-way of his own:
So much the restless eagerness to shine,
And love of singularity, prevail.
Yet this, offensive as it is, provokes
Heaven's anger less, than when the book of God
Is forced to yield to man's authority,
Or from its straightness warp'd: no reckoning made
What blood the sowing of it in the world
Has cost; what favour for himself he wins,
Who meekly clings to it. The aim of all
Is how to shine: e'en they, whose office is
To preach the gospel, let the gospel sleep,
And pass their own inventions off instead.
One tells, how at Christ's suffering the wan moon
Bent back her steps, and shadow'd o'er the sun
With intervenient disk, as she withdrew:
Another, how the light shrouded itself
Within its tabernacle, and left dark
The Spaniard, and the Indian, with the Jew.
Such fables Florence in her pulpit hears,
Bandied about more frequent, than the names
Of Bindi and of Lapi[1] in her streets.
The sheep,[2] meanwhile, poor witless ones, return
From pasture, fed with wind: and what avails
For their excuse, they do not see their harm?
Christ said not to His first conventicle,
' Go forth and preach impostures to the world,'
But gave them truth[3] to build on; and the sound

---

[1] *Of Bindi and of Lapi.*—Common names of men at Florence.

[2] *The sheep.*—So Milton, " Lycidas : "
" The hungry sheep look up and are not fed,
But swoln with wind and the rank mist they draw,
Rot inwardly."

[3] *But gave them truth.*—" Go ye into all the world, and preach the gospel to every creature."—Mark xvi. 15.

Was mighty on their lips: nor needed they,
Beside the gospel, other spear or shield,
To aid them in their warfare for the faith.
The preacher[1] now provides himself with store
Of jests and gibes; and, so there be no lack
Of laughter, while he vents them, his big cowl
Distends, and he has won the meed he sought:
Could but the vulgar catch a glimpse the while
Of that dark bird which nestles in his hood,
They scarce would wait to hear the blessing said,
Which now the dotards hold in such esteem,
That every counterfeit, who spreads abroad
The hands of holy promise, finds a throng
Of credulous fools beneath. Saint Anthony
Fattens with this his swine,[2] and others worse
Than swine, who diet at his lazy board,
Paying with unstampt metal[3] for their fare.

"But (for we far have wander'd) let us seek
The forward path again; so as the way
Be shorten'd with the time. No mortal tongue,
Nor thought of man, hath ever reach'd so far,
That of these natures he might count the tribes.
What Daniel[4] of their thousands hath reveal'd,
With finite number, infinite conceals.
The fountain, at whose source these drink their beams,
With light supplies them in as many modes,
As there are splendours that it shines on: each
According to the virtue it conceives,
Differing in love and sweet affection.
Look then how lofty and how huge in breadth
The eternal might, which, broken and dispersed
Over such countless mirrors, yet remains
Whole in itself and one, as at the first."

---

[1] *The preacher.*—Thus Cowper, "Task," b. ii.:

"'Tis pitiful
To court a grin when you should woo a soul," &c.

[2] *Saint Anthony fattens with this his swine.*—On the sale of these blessings, the brothers of St. Anthony supported themselves and their paramours. From behind the swine of St. Anthony, our poet levels a blow at the object of his inveterate enmity, Boniface VIII., from whom, "in 1297, they obtained the dignity and privileges of an independent congregation." See Mosheim's "Ecclesiastical History," in Dr. Maclaine's translation, v. ii., cent. xi., p. ii., c. ii., § 28.

[3] *Paying with unstampt metal.*—With false indulgences.

[4] *Daniel.*—"Thousand thousands ministered unto him, and ten thousand times ten thousand stood before him."—Dan. vii. 10.

CANTO XXX.

ARGUMENT.

Dante is taken up with Beatrice into the empyrean; and there having his sight strengthened by her aid, and by the virtue derived from looking on the river of light, he sees the triumph of the angels and of the souls of the blessed.

NOON'S fervid hour perchance six thousand miles[1]
    From hence is distant; and the shadowy cone
Almost to level on our earth declines;
When, from the midmost of this blue abyss,
By turns some star is to our vision lost.
And straightway as the handmaid of the sun
Puts forth her radiant brow, all, light by light,
Fade; and the spangled firmament shuts in,
E'en to the loveliest of the glittering throng.
Thus vanish'd gradually from my sight
The triumph, which plays ever round the point,
That overcame me, seeming (for it did)
Engirt[2] by that it girdeth. Wherefore love,
With loss of other object, forced me bend
Mine eyes on Beatrice once again.
    If all, that hitherto is told of her,
Were in one praise concluded, 'twere too weak
To furnish out this turn.[3] Mine eyes did look
On beauty, such, as I believe in sooth,
Not merely to exceed our human; but,
That save its Maker, none can to the full
Enjoy it. At this point o'erpower'd I fail;
Unequal to my theme; as never bard
Of buskin or of sock hath fail'd before.
For as the sun doth to the feeblest sight,
E'en so remembrance of that witching smile

---

[1] *Six thousand miles.*—He compares the vanishing of the vision to the fading away of the stars at dawn, when it is noon-day six thousand miles off, and the shadow formed by the earth over the part of it inhabited by the poet, is about to disappear.

[2] *Engirt.*—"Appearing to be encompassed by these angelic bands, which are in reality encompassed by it."

[3] *This turn.*—"Questa vice." Hence perhaps Milton, "Paradise Lost," b. viii. 491:
    "This turn hath made amends."

Hath dispossest my spirit of itself.
Not from that day, when on this earth I first
Beheld her charms, up to that view of them,
Have I with song applausive ever ceased
To follow; but now follow them no more;
My course here bounded, as each artist's is,
When it doth touch the limit of his skill.
    She (such as I bequeath her to the bruit
Of louder trump than mine, which hasteneth on,
Urging its arduous matter to the close)
Her words resumed, in gesture and in voice
Resembling one accustom'd to command:
"Forth[1] from the last corporeal are we come
Into the heaven, that is unbodied light;
Light intellectual, replete with love;
Love of true happiness, replete with joy;
Joy, that transcends all sweetness of delight.
Here shalt thou look on either mighty host[2]
Of Paradise; and one in that array,
Which in the final judgment thou shalt see."
    As when the lightning, in a sudden spleen
Unfolded, dashes from the blinding eyes
The visive spirits, dazzled and bedimm'd;
So, round about me, fulminating streams
Of living radiance play'd, and left me swathed
And veil'd in dense impenetrable blaze.
Such weal is in the love, that stills this heaven;
For its own flame[3] the torch thus fitting ever.
    No sooner to my listening ear had come
The brief assurance, than I understood
New virtue into me infused, and sight
Kindled afresh, with vigour to sustain
Excess of light however pure. I look'd;
And, in the likeness of a river, saw
Light flowing,[4] from whose amber-seeming waves

---

[1] *Forth.*—From the ninth sphere to the empyrean, which is mere light.
[2] *Either mighty host.*—Of angels that remained faithful, and of beatified souls; the latter in that form which they will have at the last day.
[3] *For its own flame.*—Thus disposing the spirits to receive its own beatific light.

[4] *Light flowing.*—" And he shewed me a pure river of water of life, clear as crystal, proceeding out of the throne of God and of the Lamb."—Rev. xxii. 1.

"Underneath a bright sea flow'd
Of jasper or of liquid pearl."
    Milton, Paradise Lost, b. iii., 518.

Flash'd up effulgence, as they glided on
'Twixt banks, on either side, painted with spring,
Incredible how fair: and, from the tide,
There ever and anon, outstarting, flew
Sparkles instinct with life; and in the flowers
Did set them, like to rubies chased in gold:
Then, as if drunk with odours, plunged again
Into the wondrous flood; from which, as one
Re-enter'd, still another rose. "The thirst
Of knowledge high, whereby thou art inflamed,
To search the meaning of what here thou seest,
The more it warms thee, pleases me the more.
But first behoves thee of this water drink,
Or e'er that longing be allay'd." So spake
The day-star of mine eyes: then thus subjoin'd:
"This stream; and these, forth issuing from its gulf,
And diving back, a living topaz each;
With all this laughter on its bloomy shores;
Are but a preface, shadowy of the truth[1]
They emblem: not that, in themselves, the things
Are crude; but on thy part is the defect,
For that thy views not yet aspire so high."

Never did babe that had outslept his wont,
Rush, with such eager straining, to the milk,
As I toward the water; bending me,
To make the better mirrors of mine eyes
In the refining wave: and as the eaves
Of mine eyelids[2] did drink of it, forthwith
Seem'd it unto me turned from length to round.
Then as a troop of maskers, when they put
Their vizors off, look other than before;
The counterfeited semblance thrown aside;
So into greater jubilee were changed
Those flowers and sparkles; and distinct I saw,
Before me, either court[3] of heaven display'd.
  O prime enlightener! thou who gavest me strength

---

[1] *Shadowy of the truth.*—
 "Son di lor vero ombriferi prefazii."
So Mr. Coleridge, in his " Religious Musings," v. 406:
 "Life is a vision shadowy of truth."

[2] *As the eaves of mine eyelids.*—Thus Shakespeare calls the eyelids " penthouse lids."—*Macbeth*, act i., sc. 3.

[3] *Either court.*—See note to v. 44.

On the high triumph of thy realm to gaze,
Grant virtue now to utter what I kenn'd.

There is in heaven a light, whose goodly shine
Makes the Creator visible to all
Created, that in seeing Him alone
Have peace; and in a circle spreads so far,
That the circumference were too loose a zone
To girdle in the sun. All is one beam,
Reflected from the summit of the first,
That moves, which being hence and vigour takes.
And as some cliff,[1] that from the bottom eyes
His image mirror'd in the crystal flood,
As if to admire his brave apparelling
Of verdure and of flowers; so, round about,
Eying the light, on more than million thrones,
Stood, eminent, whatever from our earth
Has to the skies return'd. How wide the leaves,
Extended to their utmost, of this rose,
Whose lowest step embosoms such a space
Of ample radiance! Yet, nor amplitude
Nor height impeded, but my view with ease[2]
Took in the full dimensions of that joy.
Near or remote, what there avails, where God
Immediate rules, and Nature, awed, suspends
Her sway? Into the yellow of the rose
Perennial, which, in bright expansiveness,
Lays forth its gradual blooming, redolent
Of praises to the never-wintering sun,
As one, who fain would speak yet holds his peace,
Beatrice led me; and, "Behold," she said,
"This fair assemblage; stoles of snowy white,
How numberless. The city, where we dwell,
Behold how vast; and these our seats so throng'd
Few now are wanting here. In that proud stall,[3]

---

[1] *As some cliff.*—
"A lake,
That to the fringed bank with myrtle crown'd
Her crystal mirror holds."
Milton, Paradise Lost, b. iv. 263.

[2] *My view with ease.*—
"Far and wide his eye commands;
For sight no obstacle found here, nor shade,
But all sun-shine."
Milton, Paradise Lost, b. iii. 616.

[3] *In that proud stall.*—"Ostenditque mihi circa Paradisum lectum claris et splendidissimis operimentis adornatum—in quo lecto quendam jacere conspexi cujus nomen ab Apostolo audivi, sed prohibuit ne cui illud dicerem."—*Alberici Visio*, § 31.

On which, the crown, already o'er its state
Suspended, holds thine eyes—or e'er thyself
Mayst at the wedding sup—shall rest the soul
Of the great Harry,[1] he who, by the world
Augustus hail'd, to Italy must come,
Before her day be ripe. But ye are sick,
And in your tetchy wantonness as blind,
As is the bantling, that of hunger dies,
And drives away the nurse. Nor may it be,
That he,[2] who in the sacred forum sways,
Openly or in secret, shall with him
Accordant walk : whom God will not endure
I' the holy office long ; but thrust him down
To Simon Magus, where Alagna's priest[3]
Will sink beneath him : such will be his meed."

---

[1] *Of the great Harry.*—The Emperor Henry VII., who died in 1313. "Henry, Count of Luxemburgh, held the imperial power three years, seven months, and eighteen days, from his first coronation to his death. He was a man wise, and just, and gracious ; brave and intrepid in arms ; a man of honour and a good Catholic ; and although by his lineage he was of no great condition, yet he was of a magnanimous heart, much feared and held in awe ; and if he had lived longer, would have done the greatest things."—G. *Villani,* lib. ix., cap. i. Compare Dino Compagni, Muratori, "Rerum Italicarum Scriptores," tom. ix., lib. iii., p. 524 ; and Fazio degli Uberti, "Dittamondo," l. ii., cap. 30.

[2] *Nor may it be, that he.*—Pope Clement V. See canto xxvii. 53.

[3] *Alagna's priest.*—Pope Boniface VIII. "Hell," canto xix. 79.

CANTO XXXI.

ARGUMENT.

The Poet expatiates further on the glorious vision described in the last Canto. On looking round for Beatrice, he finds that she has left him, and that an old man is at his side. This proves to be St. Bernard, who shows him that Beatrice has returned to her throne, and then points out to him the blessedness of the Virgin Mother.

IN fashion, as a snow white rose, lay then
   Before my view the saintly multitude,[1]
Which in His own blood Christ espoused. Meanwhile,
That other host,[2] that soar aloft to gaze
And celebrate His glory, whom they love,
Hover'd around; and, like a troop of bees,[3]
Amid the vernal sweets alighting now,
Now, clustering, where their fragrant labour glows,
Flew downward to the mighty flower, or rose
From the redundant petals, streaming back
Unto the stedfast dwelling of their joy.
Faces had they of flame, and wings of gold;[4]
The rest was whiter than the driven snow;
And, as they flitted down into the flower,
From range to range, fanning their plumy loins
Whisper'd the peace and ardour, which they won
From that soft winnowing. Shadow none, the vast
Interposition of such numerous flight
Cast, from above, upon the flower, or view
Obstructed aught. For, through the universe,
Wherever merited, celestial light
Glides freely, and no obstacle prevents.
   All there, who reign in safety and in bliss,
Ages long past or new, on one sole mark
Their love and vision fix'd. O trinal beam

---

[1] *The saintly multitude.*—Human souls, advanced to this state of glory through the mediation of Christ.
[2] *That other host.*—The angels.
[3] *Bees.*—Compare Homer, "Iliad," ii. 87; Virgil, "Æneid," i. 430; and Milton, "Paradise Lost," b. i. 768.

[4] *Wings of gold.*—
      "The middle pair
*   *   *   *   *   *
Skirted his loins and thighs with downy gold."
      Milton, Paradise Lost, b. v. 282.

In fashion, as a snow white rose, lay then
Before my view the saintly multitude,
Which in His own blood Christ espoused.
Canto XXXI., lines 1—3.

Of individual star, that charm'st them thus!
Vouchsafe one glance to gild our storm below.[1]

If the grim brood,[2] from Arctic shores that roam'd
(Where Helice[3] for ever, as she wheels,
Sparkles a mother's fondness on her son),
Stood in mute wonder 'mid the works of Rome,
When to their view the Lateran arose[4]
In greatness more than earthly; I, who then
From human to divine had past, from time
Unto eternity, and out of Florence
To justice and to truth, how might I chuse
But marvel too? 'Twixt gladness and amaze,
In sooth no will had I to utter aught,
Or hear. And, as a pilgrim, when he rests
Within the temple of his vow, looks round
In breathless awe, and hopes some time to tell
Of all its goodly state; e'en so mine eyes
Coursed up and down along the living light,
Now low, and now aloft, and now around,
Visiting every step. Looks I beheld,
Where charity in soft persuasion sat;
Smiles from within, and radiance from above;
And, in each gesture, grace and honour high.

So roved my ken, and in its general form
All Paradise survey'd: when round I turn'd
With purpose of my lady to inquire
Once more of things, that held my thought suspense,
But answer found from other than I ween'd;
For, Beatrice when I thought to see,
I saw instead a senior, at my side,
Robed, as the rest, in glory. Joy benign

---

[1] *To gild our storm below.*—To guide us through the dangers to which we are exposed in this tempestuous life.

[2] *If the grim brood.*—The northern hordes who invaded Rome. Landino justly observes that "this is a most excellent comparison to show how great his astonishment was at beholding the realms of the blest."

[3] *Helice.*—Callisto, and her son Arcas, changed into the constellations of the Greater Bear and Arctophylax, or Boötes. See Ovid, "Metamorphoses," lib. ii., fab. v. vi.

[4] *The Lateran arose.*—
"Quando Laterano
Alle cose mortali andò di sopra."

This reminds us of the celebrated passage in Akenside:

"Mark how the dread Pantheon stands,
Amid the domes of modern hands."
Ode xviii., b. i.

It is remarkable that Dante has no allusion to the magnificence of Gothic architecture, which was then in so much perfection, and which, as Tiraboschi endeavours to show, by a passage in Cassiodorus, describing its peculiar character of slender columns and lanceated arches, was introduced into Italy so early as the end of the fifth century. See "Storia della Lett. Ital.," tom. iii., lib. i.

Glow'd in his eye, and o'er his cheek diffused,
With gestures such as spake a father's love,
And, "Whither is she vanish'd?" straight I ask'd.
　"By Beatrice summon'd," he replied,
"I come to aid thy wish. Looking aloft
To the third circle from the highest, there
Behold her on the throne, wherein her merit
Hath placed her." Answering not, mine eyes I raised,
And saw her, where aloof she sat, her brow
A wreath reflecting of eternal beams.
Not from the centre of the sea so far
Unto the region of the highest thunder,
As was my ken from hers; and yet the form
Came through that medium down, unmix'd and pure.
　"O lady! thou in whom my hopes have rest;
Who, for my safety, hast not scorn'd, in hell
To leave the traces of thy footsteps mark'd;
For all mine eyes have seen, I to thy power
And goodness, virtue owe and grace. Of slave
Thou hast to freedom brought me: and no means,
For my deliverance apt, hast left untried.
Thy liberal bounty still toward me keep:
That, when my spirit, which thou madest whole,
Is loosen'd from this body, it may find
Favour with thee." So I my suit preferr'd:
And she, so distant, as appear'd, look'd down,
And smiled; then towards the eternal fountain turn'd.
　And thus the senior, holy and revered:
"That thou at length mayst happily conclude
Thy voyage (to which end I was dispatch'd,
By supplication moved and holy love),
Let thy upsoaring vision range, at large,
This garden through: for so, by ray divine
Kindled, thy ken a higher flight shall mount;
And from heaven's queen, whom fervent I adore,
All gracious aid befriend us; for that I
Am her own faithful Bernard."[1] Like a wight,

---

[1] *Bernard.*—St. Bernard, the venerable abbot of Clairvaux, and the great promoter of the second crusade, who died A.D. 1153, in his sixty-third year. His sermons are called by Henault, "chefs-d'œuvres de sentiment et de force."—*Abrégé Chron. de l'Hist. de Fr.*, 1145. They have even been preferred to all

Answering not, mine eyes I raised,
And saw her, where aloof she sat, her brow
A wreath reflecting of eternal beams.
Canto XXXI., lines 64—66.

Who haply from Croatia wends to see
Our Veronica;[1] and the while 'tis shown,
Hangs over it with never-sated gaze,
And, all that he hath heard revolving, saith
Unto himself in thought: "And did'st thou look
E'en thus, O Jesus, my true Lord and God?
And was this semblance Thine?" So gazed I then
Adoring; for the charity of him,[2]
Who musing, in this world *that* peace enjoy'd,
Stood livelily before me. "Child of grace!"
Thus he began: "thou shalt not knowledge gain
Of this glad being, if thine eyes are held
Still in this depth below. But search around
The circles, to the furthest, till thou spy
Seated in state, the queen,[3] that of this realm
Is sovran." Straight mine eyes I raised; and bright,
As, at the birth of morn, the eastern clime
Above the horizon, where the sun declines;
So to mine eyes, that upward, as from vale
To mountain sped, at the extreme bound, a part
Excell'd in lustre all the front opposed.
And as the glow burns ruddiest o'er the wave,
That waits the ascending team, which Phaëton
Ill knew to guide, and on each part the light
Diminish'd fades, intensest in the midst;
So burn'd the peaceful oriflamb,[4] and slack'd
On every side the living flame decay'd.

---

the productions of the ancients, and the author has been termed the last of the fathers of the church. It is uncertain whether they were not delivered originally in the French tongue.—*Ibid.* That the part he acts in the present poem should be assigned to him, appears somewhat remarkable, when we consider that he severely censured the new festival established in honour of the Immaculate Conception of the Virgin, and "opposed the doctrine itself with the greatest vigour, as it supposed her being honoured with a privilege which belonged to Christ alone."—*Dr. Maclaine's Mosheim,* vol. iii., cent. xii., part ii., c. iii., § 19.

[1] *Our Veronica.*—
"A vernicle had he sewed upon his cappe."
Chaucer, Prol. to the Canterbury Tales.
"Vernicle, diminutive of Veronike, Fr. A copy in miniature of the picture of Christ, which is supposed to have been miraculously imprinted upon a handkerchief preserved in the church of St. Peter at Rome.—*Du Cange in v. Veronica.* Madox, 'Form. Angl.,' I, p. 428, Testam. Joh. de Nevill, an. 1386. Item Domino Archiepiscopo Eborum fratri meo, vestimentum rubeum de velvet cum le verouike (r. Veronike) in granis rosarum de super Brondata (r. broudata). It was usual for persons returning from pilgrimages, to bring with them certain tokens of the several places which they had visited; and therefore the Pardoner, who is just arrived from Rome, is represented with a vernicle sewed upon his cappe. See Pierce Plowman, 28, b."—*Tyrwhitt's Glossary to Chaucer.* Our poet alludes to this custom in his "Vita Nuova," p. 275, "Avvenne in quel tempo," &c." It happened, at that time, that many people were going to see that blessed image, which Jesus Christ left to us for a pattern of His most beautiful form, which my lady now beholds in glory."

[2] *Him.*—St. Bernard.
[3] *The queen.*—The Virgin Mary.
[4] *Oriflamb.*—Menage, on this word, quotes the "Roman des Royaux Lignages" of Guillaume Ghyart:

"Oriflamme est une banniere
De cendal roujoyant et simple
Sans portraiture d'autre affaire,"

And in that midst their sportive pennons waved
Thousands of angels; in resplendence each
Distinct, and quaint adornment. At their glee
And carol, smiled the Lovely One of heaven,
That joy was in the eyes of all the blest.
    Had I a tongue in eloquence as rich,
As is the colouring in fancy's loom,
'Twere all too poor to utter the least part
Of that enchantment. When he saw mine eyes
Intent on her, that charm'd him; Bernard gazed
With so exceeding fondness, as infused
Ardour into my breast, unfelt before.

CANTO XXXII.

ARGUMENT.

St. Bernard shows him, on their several thrones, the other blessed souls, both of the Old and New Testament; explains to him that their places are assigned them by grace, and not according to merit; and lastly, tells him that if he would obtain power to descry what remained of the heavenly vision, he must unite with him in supplication to Mary.

FREELY the sage, though wrapt in musings high,
    Assumed the teacher's part, and mild began:
"The wound that Mary closed she[1] open'd first,
Who sits so beautiful at Mary's feet.
The third in order, underneath her, lo!
Rachel with Beatrice: Sarah next;
Judith; Rebecca; and the gleaner-maid,
Meek ancestress[2] of him, who sang the songs
Of sore repentance in his sorrowful mood.
All, as I name them, down from leaf to leaf,
Are, in gradation, throned on the rose.
And from the seventh step, successively,
Adown the breathing tresses of the flower,
Still doth the file of Hebrew dames proceed.
For these are a partition wall, whereby
The sacred stairs are sever'd, as the faith
In Christ divides them. On this part, where blooms
Each leaf in full maturity, are set
Such as in Christ, or e'er He came, believed.
On the other, where an intersected space
Yet shows the semicircle void, abide
All they, who look'd to Christ already come.
And as our Lady on her glorious stool,
And they who on their stools beneath her sit,
This way distinction make; e'en so on his,
The mighty Baptist that way marks the line
(He who endured the desert, and the pains
Of martyrdom, and, for two years,[3] of hell,
Yet still continued holy), and beneath,

---

[1] *The wound that Mary closed she.*—Eve.

[2] *Ancestress.*—Ruth, the ancestress of David.

[3] *Two years.*—The time that elapsed between the death of the Baptist and his redemption by the death of Christ.

Augustin;[1] Francis;[2] Benedict;[3] and the rest,
Thus far from round to round. So heaven's decree
Forecasts, this garden, equally to fill,
With faith in either view, past or to come.
Learn too, that downward from the step, which cleaves,
Midway, the twain compartments, none there are
Who place obtain for merit of their own,
But have through others' merit been advanced,
On set conditions; spirits all released,
Ere for themselves they had the power to chuse.
And, if thou mark and listen to them well,
Their childish looks and voice declare as much.

"Here, silent as thou art, I know thy doubt;
And gladly will I loose the knot, wherein
Thy subtil thoughts have bound thee. From this realm
Excluded, chance no entrance here may find;
No more than hunger, thirst, or sorrow can.
A law immutable hath stablish'd all;
Nor is there aught thou seest, that doth not fit,
Exactly, as the finger to the ring.
It is not, therefore, without cause, that these,
O'erspeedy comers to immortal life,
Are different in their shares of excellence.
Our Sovran Lord, that settleth this estate
In love and in delight so absolute,
That wish can dare no further, every soul,
Created in his joyous sight to dwell,
With grace, at pleasure, variously[4] endows.
And for a proof the effect may well suffice.
And 'tis moreover most expressly mark'd
In holy Scripture,[5] where the twins are said

---

[1] *Augustin.*—Bishop of Hippo, in the fourth century; the celebrated writer who has been mentioned before, canto x. 117.
[2] *Francis.*—See canto xi.
[3] *Benedict.*—See canto xxii.
[4] *Variously.*—There can be no doubt but that "Intra se," and not "Entrassi," is the right reading at v. 60 of the original. The former seems to have been found in only a few MSS.; but it appears from Landino's notes that he had intended to adopt it; although Lombardi has been, as far as I know, the first to admit it into the text.
[5] *In holy Scripture.*—"And the children struggled together within her."—Gen. xxv. 22. "When Rebekah also had conceived by one, even by our father Isaac; (for the children being not yet born, neither having done any good or evil, that the promise of God according to election might stand, not of works, but of him that calleth;) it was said unto her, The elder shall serve the younger."—Rom. ix. 10, 11, 12. Care must be taken that the doctrine of election is not pushed further than St. Paul appears to have intended by this text, which regards the preference of the Jews to the Gentiles, and not merely the choice of particular persons, without any respect to merit.

To have struggled in the womb. Therefore, as grace
Inweaves the coronet, so every brow
Weareth its proper hue of orient light.
And merely in respect to his prime gift,
Not in reward of meritorious deed,
Hath each his several degree assign'd.
In early times with their own innocence
More was not wanting, than the parents' faith.
To save them: those first ages past, behoved
That circumcision in the males should imp
The flight of innocent wings: but since the day
Of grace hath come, without baptismal rites
In Christ accomplish'd, innocence herself
Must linger yet below. Now raise thy view
Unto the visage most resembling Christ:
For, in her splendour only, shalt thou win
The power to look on Him." Forthwith I saw
Such floods of gladness on her visage shower'd,
From holy spirits, winging that profound;
That, whatsoever I had yet beheld,
Had not so much suspended me with wonder,
Or shown me such similitude of God.
And he, who had to her descended, once
On earth, now hail'd in heaven; and on poised wing,
"Ave Maria, gratia plena," sang:
To whose sweet anthem all the blissful court,
From all parts answering, rang: that holier joy
Brooded the deep serene. "Father revered!
Who deign'st, for me, to quit the pleasant place
Wherein thou sittest, by eternal lot;
Say, who that angel is, that with such glee
Beholds our queen, and so enamour'd glows
Of her high beauty, that all fire he seems."
    So I again resorted to the lore
Of my wise teacher, he, whom Mary's charms
Embellish'd, as the sun the morning star;
Who thus in answer spake: "In him are summ'd,
Whate'er of buxomness and free delight
May be in spirit, or in angel, met:
And so beseems: for that he bare the palm

Down unto Mary, when the Son of God
Vouchsafed to clothe Him in terrestrial weeds.
Now let thine eyes wait heedful on my words;
And note thou of this just and pious realm
The chiefest nobles. Those, highest in bliss,
The twain, on each hand next our empress throned,
Are as it were two roots unto this rose:
He to the left, the parent, whose rash taste
Proves bitter to his seed: and, on the right,
That ancient father of the holy church,
Into whose keeping Christ did give the keys
Of this sweet flower; near whom behold the seer,[1]
That, ere he died, saw all the grievous times
Of the fair bride, who with the lance and nails
Was won. And, near unto the other, rests
The leader, under whom, on manna, fed
The ungrateful nation, fickle, and perverse.
On the other part, facing to Peter, lo!
Where Anna sits, so well content to look
On her loved daughter, that with moveless eye
She chants the loud hosanna: while, opposed
To the first father of your mortal kind,
Is Lucia,[2] at whose hest thy lady sped,
When on the edge of ruin closed thine eye.

"But (for the vision hasteneth to an end)
Here break we off, as the good workman doth,
That shapes the cloak according to the cloth;
And to the primal love our ken shall rise;
That thou mayst penetrate the brightness, far
As sight can bear thee. Yet, alas! in sooth
Beating thy pennons, thinking to advance,
Thou backward fall'st. Grace then must first be gain'd;
Her grace, whose might can help thee. Thou in prayer
Seek her: and, with affection, whilst I sue,
Attend, and yield me all thy heart." He said;
And thus the saintly orison began.

---

[1] *Near whom behold the seer.*—St. John. | [2] *Lucia.*—See "Hell," canto ii. 97, and "Purgatory," ix. 50.

CANTO XXXIII.

ARGUMENT.

St. Bernard supplicates the Virgin Mary that Dante may have grace given him to contemplate the brightness of the Divine Majesty, which is accordingly granted; and Dante then himself prays to God for ability to show forth some part of the celestial glory in his writings. Lastly, he is admitted to a glimpse of the great mystery; the Trinity, and the union of man with God.

"O VIRGIN mother,[1] daughter of thy Son!
Created beings all in lowliness
Surpassing, as in height above them all;
Term by the eternal counsel pre-ordain'd;
Ennobler of thy nature, so advanced
In thee, that its great Maker did not scorn,
To make Himself His own creation;[2]
For in thy womb rekindling shone the love
Reveal'd, whose genial influence makes now
This flower to germin in eternal peace:
Here thou to us, of charity and love,
Art, as the noon-day torch; and art, beneath,
To mortal men, of hope a living spring.
So mighty art thou, lady, and so great,
That he, who grace desireth, and comes not
To thee for aidance, fain would have desire[3]
Fly without wings. Not only him, who asks,
Thy bounty succours; but doth freely oft

---

[1] *O virgin mother.*—
"Thou maide and mother daughter of thy son,
Thou wel of mercy, sinful soules cure,
In whom that God of bountee chees to won;
Thou humble and high over every creature,
Thou nobledest so far forth our nature,
That no disdaine the maker had of kinde
His son in blood and flesh to clothe and winde.
Within the cloistre blisful of thy sides
Toke mannes shape the eternal love and pees,
That of the trine compas Lord and guide is,
Whom erthe, and sea, and heven out of rellees
Ay herien; and thou virgin wemmeles
Bare of thy body (and dweltest maiden pure)
The Creatour of every creature.
Assembled in thee magnificence
With mercy, goodness, and with such pitee,
That thou that art the sunne of excellence
Not only helpest hem that praisen thee,
But oftentime of thy benignitee
Ful freely, or that men thin helpe beseche,
Thou goest beforne, and art hir lives leche."
Chaucer, The Second Nonnes Tale.
In the stanza preceding this, Chaucer alludes to St. Bernard's writings:
"And thou that art floure of virgins all,
Of whom that Bernard list so well to write."

[2] *To make Himself His own creation.*—
"Non si sdegnò di farsi sua fattura."
I had translated this line,
"Himself in His own work enclosed to dwell,"
and have corrected it at the suggestion of my friend, the Rev. William Digby, who points out a parallel passage in Bishop Hopkins, on the Lord's Prayer, ed. 1692, p. 190. "In Him omnipotence became weak; eternity, mortal; innocence itself, guilty; God, man; the Creator, a creature; the Maker of all, His own workmanship."

[3] *Desire.*—"Lo his desire woll flie withouten winges."
Chaucer, Troilus and Cresseide, lib. iii.

Forerun the asking. Whatsoe'er may be
Of excellence in creature, pity mild,
Relenting mercy, large munificence,
Are all combined in thee. Here kneeleth one,
Who of all spirits hath review'd the state,
From the world's lowest gap unto this height.
Suppliant to thee he kneels, imploring grace
For virtue yet more high, to lift his ken
Toward the bliss supreme. And I, who ne'er
Coveted sight, more fondly, for myself,
Than now for him, my prayers to thee prefer
(And pray they be not scant), that thou wouldst drive
Each cloud of his mortality away,
Through thine own prayers,[1] that on the sovran joy
Unveil'd he gaze. This yet, I pray thee, Queen,
Who canst do what thou wilt; that in him thou
Wouldst, after all he hath beheld, preserve
Affection sound, and human passions quell.
Lo! where, with Beatrice, many a saint
Stretch their clasp'd hands, in furtherance of my suit."

    The eyes, that heaven with love and awe regards,
Fix'd on the suitor, witness'd, how benign
She looks on pious prayers: then fasten'd they
On the everlasting light, wherein no eye
Of creature, as may well be thought, so far
Can travel inward. I, meanwhile, who drew
Near to the limit, where all wishes end,
The ardour of my wish (for so behoved)
Ended within me. Beckoning smiled the sage
That I should look aloft: but, ere he bade,
Already of myself aloft I look'd;
For visual strength, refining more and more,
Bare me into the ray authentical
Of sovran light. Thenceforward, what I saw,
Was not for words to speak, nor memory's self
To stand against such outrage on her skill.

"Che 'l desiderio sempre move l'ale
Dietro all' oggetto della mente appreso."
    Frezzi, Il Quadriregio, lib. iii., cap. 3.
[1] *Through thine own prayers.*—Here again I am indebted to Mr. Digby for noticing the omission of "co' prieghi tuoi" in my former translation of the passage, which stood thus:

"That on the sovran pleasure he may gaze.
This also I entreat of thee, O queen."

As one, who from a dream awaken'd, straight,
All he hath seen forgets; yet still retains
Impression of the feeling in his dream;
E'en such am I: for all the vision dies,
As 'twere, away; and yet the sense of sweet,
That sprang from it, still trickles in my heart.
Thus in the sun-thaw is the snow unseal'd;
Thus in the winds on flitting leaves was lost
The Sibyl's sentence.[1] O eternal beam!
(Whose height what reach of mortal thought may soar?)
Yield me again some little particle
Of what thou then appearedst; give my tongue
Power, but to leave one sparkle of thy glory,
Unto the race to come, that shall not lose
Thy triumph wholly, if thou waken aught
Of memory in me, and endure to hear
The record sound in this unequal strain.

 Such keenness[2] from the living ray I met,
That, if mine eyes had turn'd away, methinks,
I had been lost; but, so embolden'd, on
I pass'd, as I remember, till my view
Hover'd the brink of dread infinite.

 O grace, unenvying of thy boon! that gavest
Boldness to fix so earnestly my ken
On the everlasting splendour, that I look'd,
While sight was unconsumed; and, in that depth,
Saw in one volume clasp'd of love, whate'er
The universe unfolds; all properties[3]
Of substance and of accident, beheld,
Compounded, yet one individual light
The whole. And of such bond methinks I saw
The universal form; for that whene'er
I do but speak of it, my soul dilates
Beyond her proper self; and, till I speak,
One moment[4] seems a longer lethargy,

---

[1] *The Sibyl's sentence.*—Virgil, "Æneid," iii. 445.
[2] *Such keenness.*— "Th' air
 No where so clear, sharpen'd his visual ray,
 To objects distant far."
   Milton, Paradise Lost, b. iii. 621.
[3] *All properties.*—Thus in the "Parmenides" of Plato, it is argued that all conceivable quantities and qualities, however contradictory, are necessarily inherent in our idea of a universe or unity.

[4] *One moment.*—"A moment seems to me more tedious than five-and-twenty ages would have appeared to the Argonauts, when they had resolved on their expedition." Lombardi proposes a new interpretation of this difficult passage, and would understand our author

Than five-and-twenty ages had appear'd
To that emprize, that first made Neptune wonder
At Argo's shadow[1] darkening on his flood.

    With fixed heed, suspense and motionless,
Wondering I gazed; and admiration still
Was kindled as I gazed. It may not be,
That one, who looks upon that light, can turn
To other object, willingly, his view.
For all the good, that will may covet, there
Is summ'd; and all elsewhere defective found,
Complete. My tongue shall utter now, no more
E'en what remembrance keeps, than could the babe's
That yet is moisten'd at his mother's breast.
Not that the semblance of the living light
Was changed. (that ever as at first remain'd),
But that my vision quickening, in that sole
Appearance, still new miracles descried,
And toil'd me with the change. In that abyss
Of radiance, clear and lofty, seem'd, methought,
Three orbs of triple hue, clipt in one bound:[2]
And, from another, one reflected seem'd,
As rainbow is from rainbow: and the third
Seem'd fire, breathed equally from both. O speech!
How feeble and how faint art thou, to give
Conception birth. Yet this to what I saw
Is less than little.[3] O eternal light!
Sole in thyself that dwell'st; and of thyself
Sole understood, past, present, or to come;
Thou smiledst,[4] on that circling,[5] which in thee

---

to say that "one moment elapsed after the vision, occasioned a greater forgetfulness of what he had seen, than the five-and-twenty centuries, which passed between the Argonautic expedition and the time of his writing this poem, had caused oblivion of the circumstances attendant on that event."

[1] *Argo's shadow.*—
"Quæ simul ac rostro ventosum proscidit æquor,
Tortaque remigio spumis incanduit unda,
Emersere feri candenti e gurgite vultus
Æquoreæ monstrum Nereïdes admirantes."
    Catullus, De Nupt. Pel. et Thet., 15.
"The wondred Argo, which in wondrous piece
First through the Euxine seas bore all the flower
of Greece."
    Spenser, Faery Queen, b. ii., c. 12, st. 44.

[2] *Three orbs of triple hue, clipt in one bound.*—The Trinity. This passage may be compared to what Plato, in his second Epistle, enigmatically says of a first, second, and third, and of the impossibility that the human soul should attain to what it desires to know of them, by means of anything akin to itself.

[3] *Less than little.*—
"Che 'l pavon vi parrebbe men che poco."
    Fazio degli Uberti, Dittamondo, l. ii., cap. 5.

[4] *Thou smiledst.*—Some MSS. and editions, instead of "intendente te a me arridi," have "intendente te ami ed arridi," "who, understanding thyself, lovest and enjoyest thyself;" which Lombardi thinks much preferable.

[5] *That circling.*—The second of the circles, "Light of Light," in which he dimly beheld the mystery of the incarnation.

Seem'd as reflected splendour, while I mused;
For I therein, methought, in its own hue
Beheld our image painted: steadfastly
I therefore pored upon the view. As one,
Who versed in geometric lore, would fain
Measure the circle; and, though pondering long
And deeply, that beginning, which he needs,
Finds not: e'en such was I, intent to scan
The novel wonder, and trace out the form,
How to the circle fitted, and therein
How placed: but the flight was not for my wing;
Had not a flash darted athwart my mind,
And, in the spleen, unfolded what it sought.

    Here vigour fail'd the towering fantasy:
But yet the will roll'd onward, like a wheel
In even motion, by the love impell'd,
That moves the sun in heaven and all the stars.

THE END.

www.ingramcontent.com/pod-product-compliance
Lightning Source LLC
Chambersburg PA
CBHW022105300426
44117CB00007B/587